LIBERTY AGAINST THE LAW

====

CHRISTOPHER HILL

LIBERTY AGAINST THE LAW

SOME SEVENTEENTH-CENTURY CONTROVERSIES

ALLEN LANE
THE PENGUIN PRESS

ALLEN LANE
THE PENGUIN PRESS

Published by the Penguin Group
Penguin Books Ltd, 27 Wrights Lane, London w8 5tz, England
Penguin Books USA Inc., 375 Hudson Street, New York, New York 10014, USA
Penguin Books Australia Ltd, Ringwood, Victoria, Australia
Penguin Books Canada Ltd, 10 Alcorn Avenue, Toronto, Ontario, Canada m4v 3b2
Penguin Books (NZ) Ltd, 182-190 Wairau Road, Auckland 10, New Zealand

Penguin Books Ltd, Registered Offices: Harmondsworth, Middlesex, England

First published 1996
1 3 5 7 9 10 8 6 4 2
First edition

Filmset by Datix International Limited, Bungay, Suffolk
Printed in England by Clays Ltd, St Ives plc
Set in 11/13 pt Monophoto Bembo

A CIP catalogue record for this book is available from the British Library

ISBN 0-713-99119-4

For Bridget,

but for whose firm insistence
this book might never have been started,
and without whose constant encouragement and help
it would certainly never have been completed.

Contents

═══

V. SOCIETY, LAW AND LIBERTY

VI. AFTERMATH

Preface

====

I explain in my first chapter the origin of this book. It started as a contribution to a posthumous tribute to the late Margot Heinemann. All competent scholars owe a great deal to her work linking English literature and English history in the seventeenth century. If she had lived to discuss and criticize this book it would have been very much better than it is.

The expansion of an article into a book is due to Bridget, whose role I have tried to acknowledge in my dedication. She read, I think, all of it at various stages; my footnotes acknowledge some of her more specific contributions, but as usual the whole book owes much to her advice, suggestions and patience. A further debt is due to our son Andrew, who when told of my theme at once produced a long list of subjects which must necessarily be explored. I have tried to follow up his programme as far as I was able.

Those – like Lord Acton and Professor Hexter – who write histories of freedom in seventeenth-century England beg a great number of questions. They acclaim the liberties which the propertied minority in the country won for themselves – and very important liberties they were, even if we can now see their limitations. It is impossible now to know whether the landless or nearly landless classes were numerically equal to those who formed the Parliamentary electorate: I suspect they were far more numerous. But they too had lives to live, and though they did not write manifestos some of them managed during the revolutionary 1640s and 1650s to express points of view different from those of their betters. Gerrard Winstanley's *The Law of Freedom*, which I discuss in Chapter 23, is a serious project for putting an end to the rule of a propertied minority over the unpropertied majority. In the history of England the claims, the small successes and the failures of the inarticulate majority seem to me worth trying to recapture.

So this book aspires to be a contribution to the history of 'liberty' in England, offered as a possible counterblast to the histories of the liberties won by the men of property who ruled England, not ineffectively, for the two centuries after the English Revolution. Unlike Edward Thompson, whose *Making of the English Working Class* rescued 'the poor stockinger, the Luddite cropper, the "obsolete" hand-loom weaver, the "utopian" artisan, and even the deluded follower of Joanna Southcott, from the enormous condescension of posterity', my aim is – with the help of ballads and other forms of popular literature, to rescue the landless ex-peasantry from posterity's enormous silence. Charles Lamb, whether he knew it or not, came at the end of a long line of paradox-makers when he said that 'the beggar is the only free man in the universe.'

I am conscious of more debts than I can acknowledge – to articles in *Albion's Fatal Tree: Crime and Society in Eighteenth-century England* (ed. Douglas Hay, Peter Linebaugh, J. C. Rule, Edward Thompson and Cal Winslow, 1975); to Eric Hobsbawm's *Bandits* (1985) and to his article 'Scottish Reformers and Capitalist Agriculture' in *Peasants in History: Essays in Honour of Daniel Thorner* (ed. Hobsbawm and four others, Oxford U.P., 1960); and to the writings of Edward Thompson. I have benefited greatly from the writings of and discussions with Marcus Rediker and Peter Linebaugh. I have reproduced some material from three articles which I wrote several years ago without being conscious of the angle of vision suggested in this book, but which seem to me now to anticipate some of its points. They are (1) 'The Norman Yoke', originally published in a Festschrift for Dona Torr, who opened up for me and for many others new vistas on the history of freedom in England; reprinted in my *Puritanism and Revolution* (1958); (2) 'Pottage for freeborn Englishmen: Attitudes to Wage Labour', in *Change and Continuity in 17th-century England*, 1974, and (3) 'The Poor and the People', originally published in a Festschrift for George Rudé, *History from Below: Studies in Popular Protest and Popular Ideology* (ed. F. Krantz, Concordia University, Montreal, 1985), reprinted in my *People and Ideas in 17th-century England* (Brighton, 1986).

I tried out some of the ideas developed here in papers which I was invited to give in Pittsburgh, Berkeley, Oxford and Warwick universities, and gained a lot from discussions on these occasions.

I am grateful to Peter Carson of Penguin Books for initial encouragement, for patience when I failed to keep my deadline, and for very helpful suggestions for improving the book. I owe much to the skill of Judith Flanders, whom I have already described as the perfect editor. Jo Whitfield, not for the first time, earned my gratitude as a reliable and conscientious typist who has acquired a sure understanding of my handwriting, which some pretend to find difficult.

Throughout I use the words 'liberty' and 'freedom' as alternatives with identical meanings. No subtle distinction is to be detected when I use one or the other.

Sibford Ferris
18 March 1995

I. INTRODUCTION

===

1. *From* A Jovial Crew *(1641) to* The Beggar's Opera *(1728)*

In the world look out and see
Where the nation lives so free, so merry as do we.
And enjoy our easy rest . . .
Hang all officers we say, and the Magistrate too,
Nor will any go to law with the beggars for a straw.
All which happiness he hugs, he doth owe unto his rags.

Francis Beaumont and John Fletcher, *The Beggars Bush* (1622),
Act II, scene ii.

What mirth doth want when beggars meet?
  A beggar's life is for a king.
Eat, drink, and play, sleep when we list,
  Go where we will – so stocks be miss'd . . .
The world is ours, and ours alone,
  For we alone have world at will.

'Frank Davison's song, which he made 40 years ago' (Izaak
Walton, *The Compleat Angler*, ed. R. Le Gallienne, n.d., p. 135.
First published 1653).

Since I have seen that men could be serious in apprehending the
increase of rogues and robberies from the frequent representations
of the *Beggar's Opera*, I am persuaded that there really are such
wrongheads in the world as will fancy vices to be encouraged
when they see them exposed.

Bernard Mandeville, *The Fable of the Bees*, Part II (2nd edition,
1733), p. iv.

The Royal Shakespeare Company recently revived Brome's *A Jovial
Crew* (1636/1641) and Gay's *Beggar's Opera* (1728). My wife and I saw the
two plays within a week of each other. Separated by almost a century,
they have much in common: both make the paradoxical claim that beggars are more free than the propertied, and they raise questions about the

conflict between liberty and property as a theme in English literature. Similar questions were raised by the Robin Hood ballads, which reached a peak of popularity in the sixteenth and early seventeenth centuries, and later in popular accounts of highwaymen who claimed to be more honourable than speculating businessmen. As we discussed the rather unusual angle of vision in these two plays in connection with this popular literature there seemed to be a series of linked themes which might be worth exploring – both in literature and in historical reality.

A great deal has been written about the struggle for constitutional liberty in seventeenth-century England. The Parliamentary electorate comprised a small minority of the population, and it seems probable that the majority were inarticulate and remained silent; the majority have been taken as representing all their countrymen. In these days of history from below it would be nice to get at the views of those who had no share in making laws, who were legislated against. It might make a difference to our triumphalist view of English history if we could find out about them. We get a lot of information about their betters from state papers, Parliamentary speeches and the correspondence of the gentry – the traditional sources for historians. I have a certain scepticism here. We have learnt from recent experience that most state papers are works of fiction; at best they make assumptions which it is difficult for us to recover now. Government statements are usually intended to deceive. We need other sources.

Might not ballads, plays and other popular literary forms neglected by real historians provide fresh insights? And after 1640 the collapse of censorship and of ecclesiastical controls permits us some glimpses into the thinking of the lower, less articulate classes. Pamphlets written by people with no university education – by women even – could get into print, conveying hitherto unpublishable views. Such views might be expected to differ from those of their social superiors; they might not accept the eighteenth-century orthodoxy of a struggle for freedom which after 1688 was finally guaranteed by law. It is worth asking ourselves seriously what late seventeenth- and eighteenth-century society looked like when seen from below.

At first sight *A Jovial Crew* seems an escapist utopian fantasy. Two sisters persuade their lovers to join a band of beggars and run away from the responsibilities of life under their father, the melancholy Oldrents, to enjoy 'absolute freedom, such as the very beggars have'. The plot recalls *As You Like It*, in which two cousins flee to the Forest of Arden in male disguise. There they find something of a golden age restored. But the plot is not the most important thing about Brome's play, in which romance soon ends. The beggars live rough; they are liable to be flogged, their women to be seduced by their betters, for which they will be flogged again. The beggars have some freedoms: they escape from the slavery of wage labour, and within limits they organize their own lives. But they have no political liberty, only freedom of choice between equally miserable alternatives. They are powerless and rightless, and have no redress against the arbitrary brutality which is more typical of the society than Oldrents's generosity. The lovers learn the untruth of the 'proverb that says, "where love is, there's no lack"' (Act III, scene i). So ultimately they quit, disillusioned not with the beggars, for whom they retain affection, but recognizing the realities of life for outcasts exposed to the savagery of upper-class law. They return to the comforts of middle-class society, whilst the beggars depart to their hazardous liberty.

We are left with a vision of freedom from property-ownership as well as the satirical comparison between courtiers and beggars. The irony in the beggars' claim that lack of property was true freedom, coming at a time when Parliamentarians were insisting on the intimate connection between liberty and property, must be deliberate. Beggars contrast liberty both with property and with law. Oldrents, of all people, asks

> What is an estate
> Of wealth and power, balanced with their freedom,
> But a mere load of outward compliment,
> When they enjoy the fruits of rich content. (Act II, scene i)

The freedom claimed by the beggars was prepared for from the first scene of the play, when Springlove, Oldrents's devoted and faithful steward, the most attractive character in the play, announces that his 'strong desire of liberty' forces him to ask for leave of absence for an indefinite period, despite his master's objections, in order to go off with the beggars and share the freedom of the fields, woods and open roads.

The beggars' demands are pitched high. They expect freedom of speech, freedom to marry or not to marry. The political tone of the play, as Martin Butler emphasizes, stresses a strong localism, which in the 1640s was to be associated with active neutralism in the conflict between crown and Parliament. 'The country' is realistically portrayed, not sentimentalized.[1]

---

1. Martin Butler, *Theatre and Crisis, 1632–1642* (Cambridge U.P., 1984), p. 275.

Beggars regard their skill with a certain professional pride. But they also insist on traditional customary rights. Beggars are

> The only freemen of a commonwealth;
> Free above Scot-free; that observe no law,
> Obey no governor, use no religion,
> But what they draw from their own ancient custom,
> Or constitute themselves, yet are no rebels.[2]

The outlaw community of beggars sees itself as very stable. In their 'commonwealth utopia' there are

> No fears of war, or state disturbances,
> No alteration in a Common-wealth,
> Or innovation.

'Without taxation' they 'lend or give, upon command, the whole/ Strength of our wealth for public benefit' (Act IV, scene ii). When the play was acted in 1641 this must have seemed desperately topical. But when he wrote it in 1636–7 Brome was criticizing existing society rather than advocating a brave new one. Nevertheless, himself a court dramatist, his comparison of beggars with courtiers who live off the earnings of others makes its own point. 'A courtier . . . begged till wealth had laden him with cares' (Act I, scene i).

With Charles I's personal rule on the verge of breakdown, Brome asked questions without supplying answers. Escapism is not enough. Old-rents's traditional hospitality and generosity to beggars is a sham: his wealth derives from a swindling ancestor. He himself had an affair with a beggar girl who produced a son. Oldrents did absolutely nothing for either of them: he didn't even know of the child's existence. This ambiguity about the virtuous no doubt helps to explain the play's popularity when it was revived after 1660.[3] Pepys loved it. He saw *A Jovial Crew* three times between 25 July and the end of August 1661, describing it as 'as merry and the most innocent play that ever I saw'. He also saw Brome's *The Antipodes* on 26 August of the same year, but thought less well of it: 'much mirth but no great matter else'. When he saw *A Jovial Crew* for a

---

2. Act II, scene i. As Morse observes, 'Scot-free' was provocative in 1640, when Charles was being held to ransom by an invading Scottish army which had been welcomed by the opposition in Parliament (D. Morse, *England's Time of Crisis: From Shakespeare to Milton*, 1989, p. 117).

3. Nancy K. Maguire, *Regicide and Restoration: English tragicomedy, 1660–1671* (Cambridge U.P., 1992), p. 95.

fourth time in July 1669 he was disappointed: it was ill acted.[4] It was revived again in 1724, but ran for only one performance.[5] It was followed by several plays on similar themes. The public were ready for *The Beggar's Opera*.[6]

Brome's even more outspokenly critical play, *The Court Beggar*, though staged earlier (May 1640) than *A Jovial Crew*, was written later. It is an unsparing demonstration of the bankruptcy of personal rule, an attack on all that the court represented. The King is Lord of Beggars: a hierarchy of scroungers is bleeding the country white. The play also attacked the Court of Wards, which Parliament had been trying to abolish since the first decade of the century and actually did abolish in 1646, as soon as the civil war was won. In his epilogue to *The Court Beggar* Brome made a covert appeal to Parliament, 'the great assembly' then sitting. After this play the actors were imprisoned and their theatre closed – ten days before the King dissolved the Short Parliament. Butler sees *The Court Beggar* as 'the tip of an iceberg of popular political drama' which has not survived.[7]

Brome's name is not to be found in Douglas Bush's volume in *The Oxford History of English Literature*.[8] Attention was drawn to him by Martin Butler in *Theatre and Crisis, 1632–1642*. Brome was in one sense a court poet, but unlike Davenant and Suckling he is a reformist rather than a committed royalist. He was 'the Caroline dramatist most sensitive throughout the 1630s to country hostility towards the court'.[9] His *Queen and Concubine*, which Butler dates to 1636 (the year in which *A Jovial Crew* is believed to have been written) shows a court in exile in the country. 'The countrymen with whom she [the Queen] consorts are attractively painted as energetic, downright and ruthlessly egalitarian common men. They hate courtiers and anyone with pretensions to birth.' 'Not a gentleman, / Much less a Courtier dares breathe amongst us'. The countrymen's 'pettie Parliament' restores free, non-arbitrary government; but peers and bishops have been replaced by a 'hobnayl'd Common wealth'.[10]

---

4. Pepys, *Diary*, 25 July, 26 August and 1 November 1661; 11 January 1669.
5. W. H. Irving, *John Gay: Favourite of the Wits* (Duke U.P., 1940), p. 203.
6. See pp. 15–18 below.
7. Butler, op. cit., pp. 135–6, 220–33. For the Court of Wards, see pp. 41, 278, 335 below.
8. Bush, *English Literature in the Earlier Seventeenth Century*, 1600–1660 (Oxford U.P., 1962).
9. Butler, op. cit., pp. 263–5.
10. Ibid., pp. 39–40.

The idea that wealth is inimical to liberty is not confined to characters in Brome's plays. In one of his poems he wrote 'In getting wealth we lose our liberty'. Alexander Brome (no relation, apparently) wrote of his namesake, 'Poor he came into the world, and poor went out'.[11] *The Love-Sick Court* (posthumously printed 1650) parodies the conventions of courtly love, its stylized adoration of women and the precious language adopted by courtiers. The court is seen to be isolated and in danger of being held in contempt. 'We are the laughing-stock of the nation', one character says.[12] *The Sparagus Garden* (acted 1635, printed 1640), like *A Jovial Crew*, criticizes parental control of children's marriage and marriage for money. It mocks the social-climbing gentry who have to adopt commercial methods in order to survive economically. *The Queen's Exchange* (*c*.1634–6?, printed 1657) emphasizes country as against court values. In *The Antipodes*, written at almost the same time as *A Jovial Crew* (1636–7, acted 1638, printed 1640) the world is turned upside down, with agreeably comic results. A Doctor tells us

> There's no such honest men there in their world
> As are their lawyers . . .
> Being all handicrafts or labouring men
> They work (poor hearts, full hard) in the vacation
> To give their law for nothing in the term times.
> No fees are taken.

Wrangling law-suits are left to the divines. The lawyers may 'go and shake their ears, / If they have any' – as poor Prynne had none. Despite its topsy-turviness, *The Antipodes* is a play of common life, including a roaring girl and a male scold who is ducked by women.[13]

Court dramatists were like court jesters – licensed up to a point. But *A Jovial Crew* went beyond that limit when it was produced in the tense circumstances of 1641. Neither Brome nor Gay was a revolutionary. Brome was a court dramatist, Gay an aspirant to court office. But Brome was sensitive to the pre-revolutionary crisis of English society in the years before 1640, Gay to social problems and to the unpopularity of Sir Robert Walpole's Whig government. During the century that separated them there had been a revolution and significant changes in the law. But the

11. Richard Brome, *Five New Playes* (1653), Epistle by Alexander Brome, 'On the Comedies of . . . Richard Brome'.
12. Brome, *The Antipodes* (ed. A. Haaken, 1967), pp. 33, 38.
13. Ibid., pp. 6–7, 64–5, 73, 86–7.

characters in both *A Jovial Crew* and *The Beggar's Opera* seem to assume that beggars are more free than the propertied and that the law is something alien. How far is this a general attitude, or is it just a literary fantasy?

The ideas are not new. The Fox in Spenser's *Mother Hubberd's Tale* concluded that 'Sith then we are free born', he and the ape, 'like two free men', had a right to share the property

> which a few
> Now hold in hugger mugger in their hand
> And all the rest do rob of good and land.

Spenser does not seriously hold the Fox's view, any more than he approves of the communist giant who said he would

> Throw down these mountains high
> And make them level with the lowly plain ...
> Tyrants, that make men subject to their law
> I will suppress, that they no more may reign.[14]

But he must have heard such subjects discussed.

Sir John Falstaff, we recall, made a jest of highway robbery being his 'vocation'. In Shirley's *The Sisters*, played in 1642, the year of breakdown, a sub-plot contains a gang of thieves who have their own kingdom and repudiate laws. ('Hang laws / And those that make 'em'.)[15] The world had changed by the time of *The Beggar's Opera*. Late seventeenth- and early eighteenth-century governments, in the interests of trade, are busily suppressing pirates, highwaymen and robbers. 'Farewell to all my jovial crew' are dying words attributed to a condemned robber:

> The life which once I had
> By Law is now controlled.[16]

The Black Act of 1723 'turned the judicial system into a ruthless engine for crushing poachers.' It was all part of a single policy, consequent on Parliament's victory of 1688–9, of making the world safe for English merchants and landlords to increase in wealth and so to contribute to the new power of the English state.[17]

14. Spenser, *The Faerie Queene*, Book V, Canto II, stanza xxviii.
15. Op. cit., quoted by Martin Butler, *Theatre and Crisis, 1632–1642*, p. 263.
16. 'The Notorious Robbers Lamentation, or Whitings Sorrowful Ditty', in *Bagford Ballads* (ed. J. W. Ebsworth), II, 1878, pp. 556–9. Whiting was hanged in 1695.
17. Ed. A. L. Young, *Beyond the American Revolution: Explorations in the History of American Radicalism* (Northern Illinois U.P., 1993), p. 31.

There is a double irony in *A Jovial Crew* and *The Beggar's Opera*.
Brome and Gay compare or equate beggars with courtiers and politicians;
and by implication they accept the beggars' own claims to freedom and
honour. There is nothing very novel about criticisms of the court. Under
James I there were many ballads directed against Scottish court beggars.
Ben Jonson's *The Gypsies Metamorphosed* (1621) suggested parallels between them and begging courtiers, and indeed between courtiers and
thieves. John Taylor in *The Praise, Antiquity and Commodity of Beggars*
(1621) depicted a courtier as a 'gallant beggar'.[18] There had been snide
remarks about courts and courtiers in the anonymous *The Puritaine
Widdow* and *Westward Ho* (1607), in many plays by Massinger, in Beaumont and Fletcher's *Beggars' Bush* (1622)[19], Suckling's *The Goblins* (1638).
Drayton in *Polyolbion*, the Spenserian William Browne in *An Elegy on
Thomas Ayleworth* (1615) and *Britannia's Pastorals* (1625), and the politically
radical George Wither in *Philarete* (1622) and *Hallelujah* (1641) all contributed to the picture. Fulke Greville, courtier, in his closet drama *Mustapha*
uses a Turkish setting to denounce the corruption of courts and courtiers.
George Herbert gave up a possible court career to become a country
parson, telling a friend that 'I can now behold the court with an impartial
eye, and see plainly that it is made up of fraud and titles and flattery'. 'The
blessings in the holy Scriptures', he observed on another occasion, 'are
never given to the rich but to the poor.'[20]

> Perhaps great places and thy praise
> Do not so well agree,

he declared in a poem addressed to God.

> Gold and grace did never yet agree
> Religion always sides with poverty.[21]

18. B. Capp, *The World of John Taylor the Water-Poet, 1578–1653* (Oxford U.P.,
1994), p. 95.
19. See epigraph – beggars proclaim their freedom.
20. Herbert, *Works* (ed. R. A. Willmott, n.d.), pp. 94–5; Izaak Walton, *The Lives of
John Donne, Sir Henry Wotton, Richard Hooker, George Herbert and Robert Sanderson*
(World's Classics), pp. 305, 277. First published 1670.
21. Herbert, op. cit., pp. 94–5, 136, 139, 209. For Herbert's opposition to enclosure
and his love for good old customs, see Sidney Gottlieb's insightful 'The Social and
Political Backgrounds of George Herbert's Poetry', in *'The Muses Common-Weale':
Poetry and Politics in the Seventeenth Century* (ed. C. J. Summers and T.-L. Pebworth,
Missouri U.P., 1988), pp. 112–14.

'Contemporary commentators', observes Derek Hirst, 'especially in the [civil] war years, were firm in the belief that the meaner sort were hostile to the court'. He gives many examples. At Bury St Edmunds at election time in 1626 'in general they would give no voice to any Courtier, especially at this time of all others'. It was held against one M.P. that he 'had forsaken the country and was turned courtier'.[22]

Milton's *Comus* is more explicitly a critique of the values and habits of the court:

> If every just man that now pines with want
> Had but a moderate and beseeming share
> Of that which lewdly-pampered Luxury
> Now heaps upon some few with vast excess
> . . . the giver would be better thanked.
> . . . Swinish gluttony
> Ne'er looks at heaven amidst his gorgeous feast,
> But with besotted base ingratitude
> Crams, and blasphemes his feeder. (lines 767–78)

Leah Marcus suggests that 'a contemporary audience with even the slightest political awareness' would have recognized that 'Comus's palace is itself an enclosure' from the royal Forest of Dean. Charles I had granted monopoly patents to courtiers for developing mining and manufacturing in the forest, and it was to further these projects that large areas of the forest were enclosed, leading to fierce rioting in protest.[23] Milton returned to the theme in *Paradise Lost*, à propos Belial:

> In courts and palaces he also reigns
> . . . where the noise
> Of riot ascends above their loftiest towers,
> And injury and outrage . . . (I. 490–500; cf. IV. 765–70)

The Duke of Newcastle, a former patron of Brome's, in exile wrote verses to his future wife:

> Sweet heart, we are beggars; our comfort's, 'tis seen
> That we are undone for the King and the Queen.
> Then when the weather grows cold and raw

22. D. Hirst, *The Representative of the People? Voters and Voting in England under the Early Stuarts* (Cambridge U.P., 1975), pp. 132, 141–53, 161–80.
23. Leah Marcus, *The Politics of Mirth* (Chicago U.P., 1978), pp. 193–4. See Chapter 7 below.

We'll into the barn and tumble in straw;
And when the spring on our love sets an edge
We'll kiss and we'll play under every hedge.

The Duke of Newcastle, as Harbage records, 'refused to write like a courtier'.[24]

During the revolutionary decades courts and courtiers offered easy targets. But after the restoration the royalist (albeit rather a disgruntled one) Samuel Butler wrote a caustic character of 'A Court Beggar': 'He values himself and his place not upon the honour or allowances of it, but the convenient opportunity of begging'.

So those at court that do address
By low ignoble offices,
Can stoop to anything that's base
To wriggle into trust and grace,
Are like to rise to greatness sooner
Than those that go by worth and honour.[25]

In 1672 Wycherley was still denouncing court bribery.[26]

There is a great difference between Brome's jovial beggars who occasionally steal and Gay's organized group of thieves who also beg. But they have in common – or say they have – an ideology of freedom which they proclaim loudly and which looks back to Robin Hood and his outlaws. Both Brome and Gay are interested less in the truth of the myth of the beggars' greater freedom than in its use to criticize governments and courtiers. In Brome's play it is the sentimental middle-class girls who believe in the beggars' freedom. In *The Beggar's Opera* the beggars themselves proclaim their greater moral respectability and liberty. Pirates, as we shall see, also claimed, in ballads if not in real life, to be free; they organized their ships and settlements in a remarkably democratic way.[27] The word beggars had become famous through its (originally contemptuous) application to the Netherlands revolutionaries in the early days of the revolt against Spanish overlordship. 'They call us beggars',

24. 'A Songe', in *The Phanseys of William Cavendish, Marquis of Newcastle* (ed. D. Grant, 1956), pp. 75–6; A. Harbage, *Cavalier Drama* (1926), p. 117.
25. In *Character Writings of the Seventeenth Century* (ed. H. Morley, 1891), pp. 320–22; Butler, *Poetical Works* (ed. G. Gilfillan, Edinburgh, 1854), II, p. 246.
26. *Love in a Wood; or St. James's Park*, in *Plays* (ed. W. C. Ward, Mermaid Series), p. 24.
27. See Chapter 9 below.

said one of the revolt's leaders: 'let us accept the name'. *'Vivat les gueulx'* became the rebels' rallying cry.[28] There were many plays about the Dutch revolt in early seventeenth-century England.[29]

A Jovial Crew was originally staged in 1641, the last effective year of the old monarchy; by 1728 the real ruler of Britain was not King George II but the Whig magnate Sir Robert Walpole. In *The Beggar's Opera*, as in Brome's play, beggars are equated with courtiers. Peachum sang in the opening scene:

> The statesman because he's so great
> Thinks his trade as honest as mine.

Whereas in fact courtiers and officials have to be bribed if honest men are to get their due (Act II, scene v). And there is not much honour among thieves either. Well-timed treachery or desertion could be beneficial. 'Macheath's time is come, Lucy', said Lockit to his daughter, Macheath's 'wife'. 'We know our own affairs, therefore let us have no more whimpering or whining'.

> Ourselves, like the great, to secure a retreat,
> When matters require it, must give up our gang,
> And good reason why.
> > Or instead of the fry
> > Even Peachum and I
> Like poor petty rascals might hang, hang . . .
> (Act III, scene xi; cf. scene ii)

The limit is reached when Peachum's daughter, Polly, proposes to ruin her financial prospects by marrying the highwayman Macheath (who anyway already has a wife of sorts). Peachum arranges for Macheath to be betrayed and hanged.

So the relationship between the governed and their governors is the theme. Direct political satire plays a much bigger part than in *A Jovial Crew*. Money is now decisive. Macheath justified highwaymen who 'have still known enough to break through the corruptions of the world'. But his song in Act III, scene iv,

> Friendship for interest is but a loan,
> Which they let out for what they can get,

28. J. L. Motley, *The Rise of the Dutch Republic* (1892), I, pp. 481–90.
29. Butler, *Theatre and Crisis*, p. 235.

is sung to the tune of 'Lilliburlero', the Whig theme-song which drummed James II out of the country in 1688 and led to the Revolution settlement.[30] Macheath hopes for release because

> Gold from law can take out the sting;
> And if rich men like us were to swing,
> 'Twould thin the land such numbers to string
> Upon Tyburn tree! (Act III, scene xiii)

But he is not rich enough.

The points are pressed home in Gay's sequel, *Polly*. Many of the characters have fled to the West Indies, where the bawd Mrs Trapes sings

> Morals and honesty leave to the poor
> As they do at London. (Act I, scene i)

She is capped by Ducat:

> But even the rich are brave
> When money is at stake. (Act I, scene xii)

The native Indians have different standards ('How can you expect anything else from a creature who hath never seen a civilized country?' – Act II, scene viii). And Polly confirms 'You may rely upon the prince's word as if he was a poor man' (Act II, scene xii).

Like Brome's, Gay's social origins were relatively lowly. His maternal uncles were west-country dissenting ministers; he himself was apprenticed to a London silk-mercer. He moved up socially as he became secretary first to a former schoolmate, Aaron Hill, the poet and dramatist; then to the Duchess of Monmouth. Gay aimed at a place at court, often meeting 'with my usual success – a disappointment', but in 1723 he became Commissioner for State Lotteries at £150 a year. Dr Johnson quoted a lady who said that Gay's poetry was 'of a lower order' – perhaps socially as well as in a literary sense. Adina Forsgren describes Gay's *Rural Sports* (1713) as 'heroic poetry of a low kind'.[31] In *The Shepherd's Week* (1714) Gay parodies and ridicules Whig patriotism; his footnotes reject sublimity. Gay is said to have continued to prefer country girls to court ladies. He

30. When in 1711 the authorities broke up a pope-burning procession on Queen Elizabeth's Day, bag-pipers in the demonstration were playing 'Lillibulero' (D. Cressy, *Bonfires and Bells: National Memory and the Protestant Calendar in Elizabethan and Stuart England*, 1989), p. 188.
31. Adina Forsgren, *John Gay: Poet of 'a lower order'* (Stockholm, 1964), pp. 82, 119, 166, 168, 190.

seems to have had a genuine feeling for low life, and for rural as against country life. He has a friendly reference to gypsies' fortune-telling, for instance, and to the poor's need for charity.[32] Politicians and courtiers regularly come in for criticism.[33] Absolute monarchy, lawyers and the idle aristocracy are impartially attacked.[34] So is marriage for money, but Gay also suggests that Quaker rejection of outward forms of matrimony is a cover for rejecting marriage altogether. In his plays he has a predilection for women as major characters.

I am not entirely convinced by Gay's latest (and best) biographer, David Nokes, that the 'true' Gay is a man who 'spent much of his life rejecting and concealing his family background in nonconformity and trade'. Gay may indeed have fashioned himself into 'a new "polite" social identity' which allowed him to exchange flippant and snobbish witticisms with his catholicizing friends.[35] He would have liked a court post, not least because he needed the money to keep up with his literary circle. But a small-town (Barnstaple) commercial and nonconformist background and upbringing like his would drive deeper roots: it is not easily shaken off and picked up again.

Trivia, or the Art of Walking the Streets of London (1716, twelve years before *The Beggar's Opera*) advertises the fact that the author walks on foot, and does not travel in the 'gilded chariots' in which the upper class

> loll at ease,
> And lazily ensure a life's disease . . .
> Proud coaches pass, regardless of the moan
> Of infant orphans, and the widow's groan;
> While charity still moves the walker's mind,
> His lib'ral purse relieves the lame and blind.[36]

The whole point of *The Beggar's Opera* is that beggars are like courtiers

---

32. W. H. Irving, *John Gay: Favourite of the Wits* (Duke U.P., 1940), pp. 14, 24–9, 107, 119, 125, 211, 217. Gay, *Poetical Works* (ed. G. C. Faber, Oxford U.P., 1926), pp. 116, 37–8, 75.
33. Ibid., pp. 85, 124, 127, 162, 186–8, 237–8, 258–61, 279–84, 286–91, 293–6.
34. Ibid., pp. 161, 187, 277, 291–3, 296–8. For lawyers, cf. *The Beggar's Opera*, Act I, scene ix, Act II, scene v, Act III, scene xiii; see Chapter 22 below.
35. Ibid., pp. 146, 169, 245–6, 301. Cf. Ducat in *Polly*, 'Why, I married her in a reasonable way, only for her money' (*Poetical Works*, p. 542). David Nokes, *John Gay: A Profession of Friendship* (Oxford U.P., 1995), p. 28.
36. Gay, *Poetical Works*, p. 208.

and courtiers are like beggars; both are unsatisfactory when judged by bourgeois nonconformist standards.

In *The Beggar's Opera* 'honour was nothing but a trade'. The opera's popularity with rank and file London citizens – traditional foes of court power and privileges – suggests that their values too were uncontaminated by the corruption of big business in the age of the South Sea Bubble. Gay fairly consistently occupies a middle position between the thieving and beggary of the lowest and highest classes in society. Beggars are no worse than courtiers but not much better except in their lack of humbug.

Nokes draws attention to 'the citizens' language of plain dealing', which 'represented a wholesome alternative to the vain pretensions and false promises of a corrupt court'. 'The noble savages in *Polly* receive a special praise for the merit of honest industry'. But this is nothing new for Gay. His *Fables* (published 1727, though he had been working on them for some time earlier) repeatedly emphasize the virtues of industry and trade. Nokes quotes a paean to trade by Barter in *The Distressed Wife*, written though not performed before *The Beggar's Opera*: 'on what depends the glory, the credit, the power of the nation? On commerce'. In this play, Gay constantly contrasts the moral integrity of the industrious tradesmen with the corruption of the court, against whose 'affections' Gay 'stood up for Barnstaple values'.[37]

Gay's *The What-d'ye call it* (1715) opposes rural tyrants on behalf of a lower class. An anonymous critic sang 'See John Gay on porters' shoulders rise'. He was dubbed 'the prince of street corner poets'. His taste for ballads, roundelays and catches fits this picture. His *Fables* were a best-seller and his song 'Molly Mogg' was perhaps his most successful production before *The Beggar's Opera* 'made Gay rich and Rich gay'. Much earlier Gay had jeered at courtiers and politicians:

> A Courtier's promise is so slight
> 'Tis made at noon, and broke at night.[38]

Gay's prospects of court promotion suffered from his association with Pope, Swift and the Bolingbroke group. In *The Beggar's Opera* Macheath was taken for Walpole, not least by Walpole himself. Swift described the opera as 'a very severe satire upon the most pernicious villainies of mankind'. That was putting it rather strongly, but Gay was turned out of his lodgings in Whitehall. *Polly*, its successor, was described as 'this theatrical

37. Ibid., pp. 378–9, 468–9, 478, 495–8, 523.
38. 'To a Lady on her Passion for Old China', in Gay, *Poetical Works*, p. 180.

Craftsman' (with reference to Bolingbroke) and was not allowed to be put on the stage. It was not finally produced until 1777.[39]

The Beggar's Opera was popular not only because of its attack on Walpole and his government but because of the wit with which the comparison of rulers to beggars and thieves was carried through. At the end of the opera the Beggar discusses with the Player the moral: 'Do the fine gentlemen imitate the gentlemen of the road or the gentlemen of the road the fine gentlemen?' The Beggar's original intention in writing, he said, had been to show that 'the lower sort of people have their vices in a degree as well as the rich. And that *they* are punished for them.'[40]

The opera deals not only with beggars but with organized criminals preying on capitalist society – like the highwaymen and pirates we shall be considering later. They are only carrying to an extreme the logic of that society. As Macheath put it, 'Money well timed, and properly applied, will do anything' (Act II, scene xii). Money was the reason of that society, as for our present government the market is the reason of our society.

Beggars stood outside society and its politics. As a song said to have been sung in *A Jovial Crew* put it:

> Of all occupations
> > A beggar's life's the best.
> > For whenever he's weary
> > He'll lay him down and rest.[41]

The relationship of *A Jovial Crew* to the political crisis of the years between 1636 (when it was written) and 1641, when it was staged, is obvious. *The Beggar's Opera* also came at a time of crisis, though one whose consequences were less dramatic. The 1720s saw the South Sea Bubble, a time of wild speculation which ended in disaster for many smaller investors, and wealth for a few speculators. The years from 1723 onwards saw much alarm about hunting and poaching gangs in royal forests: men were hanged for hunting deer in royal parks, including

39. Irving, op. cit., pp. 67, 107, 209, 211, 216, 221, 226, 237, 248, 252, 277, 272–3.
40. Ibid., p. 531. My italics.
41. See 'The Poor and the People' in my *People and Ideas in 17th-century England* (Brighton, 1986), pp. 253–4, 257–8; 'The Beggar's Choice' (ed. R. Bell, *Ballads and Songs of the Peasantry of England*, n.d., pp. 251–2). This does not appear in the printed text of *A Jovial Crew* and was probably an interpolation – perhaps from the ballad opera version of *A Jovial Crew* produced in 1732.

Richmond Park where Gay's friend Pope lived. The Black Act was passed in 1723; its fierce penalties were the culmination of a series of legislative measures against 'brotherhoods and fraternities' of deer-stealers. *A Jovial Crew* was revived in 1724, after a long interval; it was followed by a succession of plays on similar themes. Forest gangs were connected with London by the trade in venison, run by a London gang one of whose members was known as 'Wild's man', Fielding's Jonathan Wild the Great being a familiar figure to characters in *The Beggar's Opera*.[42] In 1726 there was an outbreak of crime following a run of books on pirates and other criminals, including Defoe's *Life of Captain Singleton* and *The King of Pirates* (both 1720), and *The History of the Pyrates* (1724).

With his unique eye for illuminating literary evidence Edward Thompson drew attention to these facts, and to the links between Gay and Pope, whose *Windsor Forest* was published in 1713 and later revised. At one time the two poets rode together in Windsor Forest three or four days a week. They could not but have discussed the Black Act in the years before *The Beggar's Opera* was staged in 1728. Pope's brother-in-law was accused of being a Berkshire Black.[43]

Were there other 'fraternities' like the Waltham Blacks? Thompson had to do a great deal of research in order to find out about the one which he records.[44]

42. Thompson, *Whigs and Hunters: The Origin of the Black Act* (1975), esp. pp. 21–4, 58, 64, 114. See Irving, op. cit., p. 203, and pp. 47–66 below. For venison see Chapter 7 below.
43. Thompson, op. cit., pp. 216–18, 278–94.
44. See Chapter 7 below.

2. Customary Liberties and Legal Rights

====

> Woe to the worldly men, whose covetous
> Ambition labours to join house to house,
> Lay field to field, till their enclosures edge
> The plain, girdling a country [i.e. county] with one hedge;
> That leave no place unbought, no piece of earth
> Which they will not engross, making a dearth
> Of all inhabitants, until they stand
> Unneighbour'd, as unblest, within their land.

Henry King, 'The Woes of Esay', in *Minor Poets of the Caroline Period* (ed. G. Saintsbury, Oxford U.P., 1921), III, p. 230

> They said they were an-hungry, sighed forth proverbs –
> That hunger broke stone walls, that dogs must eat,
> That meat was made for mouths, that the gods sent not
> Corn for the rich men only.

Martius, speaking of the 'mutinous citizens', Shakespeare, *Coriolanus*, Act I, scene i

> The wealth around them makes them doubly poor.

Crabbe, 'The Village' (1783), in *Works* (ed. A. J. Carlyle and R. M. Carlyle, Oxford U.P., 1914), p. 36

I

When I was young, sixty-odd years ago, we used to be told that in the seventeenth century there was a great struggle for liberty in England. Professor Hexter still goes on telling us. What has always worried me (and not only me) was that the question 'liberty for whom?' was never asked. 'Liberty and property' were always associated in the minds of Parliamentarian propagandists during the civil war, and the propertied did indeed get liberty. But one man's liberty can be another man's slavery. A quite different English tradition, whose popularity is supported by its presence in so many ballads, held that the law was the enemy of freedom.

It is this alternative tradition – or these alternative traditions, for there is no single tradition – which I intend to look at.

For the Parliamentary electorate – gentry and merchants – the most important liberty to be defended was the sanctity of private property; and the institution on which they relied to safeguard property was Parliament, the representative body of the propertied class. For most of the population, owning no property or very little, the sanctity of private property was not a major issue. The abolition of tithes, security of tenure for copyholders, freedom from church courts and perhaps freedom of worship were the issues that mattered to the lower orders. Regular meetings of Parliament and the independence of the judiciary (which interpreted the laws protecting property) had little or no significance for the mass of the population. Parliament refused to abolish tithes; big landowners voted security of tenure for themselves by abolishing feudal tenures and the Court of Wards but specifically refused to grant similar security to copyholders. Such changes in the law as occurred between 1641 and the early eighteenth century increased popular hostility towards it.[1] Why should the lower classes respect laws which asserted property rights *against* traditional popular customs in the villages? Victims of enclosure had to look for employment as wage-labourers – in industry, if they were lucky; others who found no labour in their villages took to the road. For those of the beneficiaries of enclosure who were both improving and efficient, profits were secure.[2]

As early as Edward VI's reign, Robert Crowley repeatedly insisted that greedy landlords were the cause of sedition, rather than the peasants who reacted and who always bore the blame.[3] Bishop Cooper and Archbishop Bancroft both noted the popularity of what John Cleveland was to call 'that levelling lewd text', 'When Adam delved and Eve span / Who was then the gentleman?' – which dated from the late fourteenth century and was never forgotten.[4]

1. See pp. 34–43 below.
2. R. H. Tawney, *The Agrarian Problem in the Sixteenth Century* (1912), pp. 131–9, 160, 194, 244–7, 301; M. Campbell, *The English Yeoman* (Yale U.P., 1942), pp. 133–4, 139–42; L. A. Parker, 'The Agrarian Revolution at Cotesbach, 1501–1612', in *Studies in Leicestershire Agrarian History* (ed. W. G. Hoskins, Leicestershire Archaeological Society, 1949), pp. 57–76; C. G. A. Clay, *Economic Expansion and Social Change in England, 1500–1700* (Cambridge U.P., 1984), I, pp. 107, 126, 140–42.
3. Crowley, *Select Works* (Early English Text Soc., 1872), pp. 87–90, 108, 132–3, 142–7, 164–9.
4. A. Patterson, *Shakespeare and the Popular Voice* (Oxford, 1989), pp. 39–42; Cleveland, *Works* (1687), p. 402.

Settlement Acts, Canute-like, tried to reverse the tide of social mobility by having vagabonds flogged back to their villages. In Edward VI's reign legislation had helped landless agricultural labourers to find a place in which to squat or build a cottage,[5] but in the 1570s it was declared that 'common of pasture' maintains 'the idlers and beggary of the cottagers'; failure to prevent consumption of wood from common lands 'is the only occasion of resort of so many naughty and idle persons' – squatters, vagabonds and gypsies.[6] As travellers do today, vagabonds from outside squatted on unenclosed wastes; in the sixteenth and seventeenth centuries these came to be seen as nurseries of beggars and thieves. Such allegations helped to incline many respectable villagers to accept enclosure.[7]

The Act of 1589 against cottagers was, in the words of William Hunt, an 'important reversal of social policy', which has 'received less attention than it deserves'. It was followed by a campaign against cottagers, aided by judgments against squatters in the royal courts, and by the ruling that destroying an enclosure constituted a riot. R. B. Manning has calculated that the vast majority of Elizabethan anti-enclosure riots were in fact attempts to maintain rights on wastes, commons and woodlands. They increased sharply in the famine years of the 1590s.[8]

Large numbers of cottages were erected in the late sixteenth and early seventeenth centuries. Sometimes industrialists needing cheap labour would positively encourage vagrants to build cottages on waste lands.[9] Forest hamlets afforded some stability and freedom to landless peasants, to vagabonds and gypsies. But enclosure in general increased the dependence of labourers on landlords.[10] Kerridge suggests that in the early seventeenth century fen-drainage was even more significant in its social effects than deforestation. Between 1626 and 1640 forest and fen riots against enclosure were particularly large in scale.[11]

Profits in Tudor and early Stuart England were made in agriculture

5. Thirsk, 'Enclosing and Engrossing', in *The Agrarian History of England and Wales*, IV (1500–1640), (ed. J. Thirsk, Cambridge U.P., 1967), pp. 224–5.

6. Thirsk, 'The Farming Regions of England', ibid., IV, p. 11.

7. Manning, *Village Revolts*, p. 316.

8. Hunt, *The Puritan Moment: The Coming of Revolution in an English County* (Harvard U.P., 1983), pp. 70–71; Manning, *Village Revolts*, pp. 27, 30, 57, 79.

9. Thirsk, 'Enclosing and Engrossing', p. 204; D. Underdown, *Revel, Riot and Rebellion: Popular Politics and Culture in England, 1603–1660* (Oxford U.P., 1985), p. 37; Manning, *Village Revolts*, p. 272.

10. Everitt, 'Farm Labourers', in *Agrarian History*, pp. 408–9, 412.

11. Kerridge, *The Agricultural Revolution* (1967), Chapter 4; Manning, *Village Revolts*, p. 313.

rather than in industry. Brian Manning dates from the revolutionary decades the replacement of agriculture by industry as 'the engine of economic growth'.[12] Between 1580 and 1620, Professor Bowden tells us, there was 'a massive redistribution of income in favour of the landed class', though some yeomen shared in this prosperity. But for the poor 'the third, fourth and fifth decades of the seventeenth century . . . were probably among the most terrible years through which the country has ever passed'.[13] The victory of the capitalist economy involved a moral revolution, the assertion of the sanctity of private property and its absolute right to overrule the traditional customary rights of the poor. Wage labour alone 'could not support a viable household'; Hunt is quoting from a treatise by the radical Puritan Richard Rogers which reached its third edition by 1614.[14]

Violence played a large part in this process. In Henry VIII's reign John Palmer bought a former monastic manor. 'Being a man of great power', he grabbed their copyhold pastures from several tenants and enclosed them to make a park. And 'through like power took . . . all their commons and made of them fishponds' for his private use. He also seized houses, grounds, lands, tenements and orchards, pulling down houses and driving some of the occupants 'out of the said lordship by force and violence'. Lands which he had given them in alleged compensation were of inferior quality; and anyway were not his to give. The unfortunate tenants ('very poor men . . . and in great fear of their lives' as well as of their property) 'dare not return home into their country' without the King's 'most gracious speedy remedy' in Star Chamber.[15]

During the revolutionary decades radical Parliamentarians vainly tried to find an electorate which would return a reforming Parliament capable of meeting the demands of men of small or no property. Only an extremely oppressed segment of the poor, those who had no hope of finding

12. B. S. Manning, *1649: The Crisis of the English Revolution* (1992), pp. 98–9.
13. P. Bowden, 'Agricultural Prices, Farm Profits and Riots', in *Agrarian History*, IV, pp. 619–22, 695; R. C. Allen, 'Enclosure and the Yeoman', in *The Agrarian Development of the South Midlands, 1450–1850* (Oxford U.P., 1992), passim; G. Batho, 'Landlords in England', *Agrarian History*, IV, p. 305; M. W. Barley, 'Rural Housing in England', ibid., IV, p. 766.
14. W. Hunt, *The Puritan Moment*, p. 137, quoting Richard Rogers, *Seven Treatises containing such directions as is gathered out of the Holie Scripture* (1603).
15. Tawney and Power, op. cit., I, pp. 19–21. More subtly, another gentleman 'after the corn be inned and harvest done, bringeth his cattle in great numbers and eateth up the corn' (ibid., p. 45).

employment, perhaps no wish to, turned to the freedom of the road. Those who thought freedom lay outside the law had no solution until Gerrard Winstanley published his *The Law of Freedom* in 1652; and that was the last cry of a defeated minority.[16] England's future lay with the men of property, and they made the most of it. It was two centuries before the trade union movement returned to the quest for liberty through community, and it has not got very far yet.

Agricultural prosperity was accompanied by poverty for the producers. In the late sixteenth and early seventeenth centuries go-ahead landowners and commercial farmers could enjoy unearned profits, irrespective of their efficiency. Enclosure was a main cause of windfall wealth. 'Enclosure' is a catch-all term, signifying different things at different times and in different places. In the sixteenth and early seventeenth centuries it was mainly of common and waste lands for pasturing the sheep who were 'eating up men'; by the eighteenth century enclosure was aimed more at 'engrossing' agricultural lands of other villagers for food production. By then the complicity of the law with enclosers was more open. Previously the route had been via private bullying, bribery and lobbying to get a majority of those who mattered in the village. But for our purposes what matters is the effect on the poor of the villages. Either type of enclosure tended to be 'depopulating'. Whole villages were destroyed in the interests of large-scale production for the market, or to create congenial surroundings for a prospering family.[17] Piecemeal enclosure of the waste was followed by the imposition of competitive rents; copyholds were converted into leasehold. In legal theory customary tenants enjoyed some protection; in practice they had little prospect of taking advantage of the redress legally open to them. Smaller tenants had no financial resources and were not credit-worthy: they were at mercy when rents were racked or fines increased. Anyway they could not afford the capital outlay which improved farming demanded. Cottagers received no compensation at enclosure. Enclosure 'by agreement' was often forced on unwilling villagers.[18] When Henry Percy, ninth Earl of Northumberland, was

16. See Chapter 23 below.

17. For examples see Allen, *Enclosure and the Yeoman*, Chapters 3–5, 11–14; J. T. Cliffe, *The Yorkshire Gentry: From the Reformation to the Civil War* (London U.P., 1969), pp. 364–5; Cliffe, *The Puritan Gentry: The Great Puritan Families of Early Stuart England* (1984), pp. 111–12, 160.

18. Alan Everitt, 'Farm Labourers', in *The Agrarian History of England and Wales*, IV (1500–1640), pp. 417–25, 462–3; E. Kerridge, *Agrarian Problems in the 16th Century and After* (1969), pp. 125–6, 184, 187, 200–203; J. Thirsk, 'Agrarian Problems and

advised by his lawyers against evicting his numerous copyholders at Petworth, he had no difficulty in finding other ways of overthrowing manorial customs that stood in the way of improving his income.[19]

The overall result was polarization in the villages. A section of the peasantry – those with capital or with access to credit – might be lucky enough to thrive to yeoman status: others were depressed into poverty, having lost the not inconsiderable assets provided by common land – peat and wood for fuel, fruits, berries, mushrooms etc., the right to glean after harvest and to pasture sheep or cattle, geese or ducks, on the waste.[20] Sir Francis Bacon's definition of liberties included 'liberty to take timber or other materials in . . . woods'.[21]

David Underdown quotes a parish in Berkshire where a meadow once 'allotted to the youth of the parish there to make merry' was by 1611 let for a monetary return. A custom permitted the inhabitants of Eynsham to cut down trees at Whitsuntide; but they had no legal right to this privilege, and in 1677 'the chiefest of the parish' agreed to end it'.[22] Miners in the Forest of Dean could produce no evidence to establish the lawfulness of the privileges which they claimed. If they ever existed, they were overruled by mine law as laid down in a seventeenth-century Exchequer case.[23] In general the law did not recognize rights to common, or to compensation on the extinction of such rights by enclosure of forests. It is not surprising that the main opposition to forest enclosures came from cottagers.[24]

---

the English Revolution', in *Town and Countryside in the English Revolution* (ed. R. Richardson, Manchester U.P., 1992), p. 195; R. B. Manning, *Village Revolts*, pp. 88, 110, 114–16; L. A. Parker, 'The Agrarian Revolution at Cotesbach, 1501–1612', p. 62.

19. R. B. Manning, *Village Revolts*, p. 137.

20. For the value of wastes for villagers see J. M. Neeson, *Commoners: Common Right, Enclosure and Social Change in England, 1700–1820* (Cambridge U.P., 1993), pp. 17–24, 29–30, 34, 39–42, 47–50, 205–7, 223, 234, 251–4, 259, 279–80, 288–9, 313–19.

21. Bacon, 'Considerations touching the plantation in Ireland', *Works* (1826), III, p. 332.

22. Underdown, *Revel, Riot and Rebellion*, p. 61. Cf. ibid., p. 22: end of tolerance of poaching on land which the parish controlled by agreement with the King.

23. Buchanan Sharp, *In Contempt of All Authority: Rural Artisans and Riot in the West of England, 1586–1640* (California U.P., 1980), pp. 176–8, 207.

24. B. Sharp, 'Popular Protest in Seventeenth-Century England', in *Popular Culture in Seventeenth-Century England* (ed. B. Reay, 1985), p. 292.

II

As long ago as 1960, a seminal article by Eric Hobsbawm pointed out that the Scottish historical school – Adam Smith and others – had derived from English experience a general model of the transition to capitalism in agriculture. Two things were essential: first, the establishment of absolute property rights in their land for big landowners, and the transformation of copyhold and similar customary tenures into leasehold. Second, the abolition of all legal force for customary land rights, which would have had the effect of driving into vagabondage a large part of the underemployed poorer peasantry hitherto immobilized on the land. Henceforth they were available for employment elsewhere to greater profit (to their employers) as wage labourers in industry.[25]

In Scotland two acts of 1695 permitted any proprietor to force a division of common lands and wholesale enclosure. A statute of 1746 deprived 'custom' of all legal force in land tenancy. The forcible clearance of Highland crofters to make way for sheep was only the culmination of these processes. The Scottish school summarized lessons drawn from English experience. Enclosure, the ending of legal validity for customary rights in common lands, wastes and forests, had made continued existence in most villages impossible for landless small peasants, had driven them to vagabondage in search of employment. Britain's future lay with the men of property, and they made the most of it.

With Hobsbawm's article we may compare S.[ilvanus] T.[aylor]'s *Common-Good: Or, The Improvement of Commons, Forests and Chases, by Inclosure.* He faces head on the objection to enclosure that it 'is the undoing of many poor, who have their livelihood out of them' by the benefit of grazing cows and sheep, and of free fuel and sustenance. His answer is that if the poor man moved to some other place where himself, his wife and children 'might be employed in some manufactory', or they took to spinning at home ('which a child of 6 years old may profitably be employed in'), 'it would be much more comfortable for them and much better for the Commonwealth' than to continue 'lazying upon a common to attend one cow and a few sheep'. In unenclosed villages children are

---

25. Hobsbawm, 'Scottish Reformers and Capitalist Agriculture', in *Peasants in History: Essays in Honour of Daniel Thorner* (ed. E. J. Hobsbawm and four others, Oxford U.P., 1960), pp. 7–19.

nursed up in idleness and become 'indisposed for labour'; then 'begging is their portion or thieving is their trade'.[26]

J. M. Neeson's recent valuable book, *Commons, common rights, enclosure and social change in England, 1700–1820*, gets behind the guess-work statistics usually employed in this area to give an imaginative assessment of what enclosure meant to commoners. Before enclosure, an effective local system of by-laws and common rights offered some protection. In many common-field villages perhaps one-third of the villagers were entitled to common grazing. It was the poorest commoners who suffered most from enclosure as they became utterly dependent on miserable wages: rents were often doubled or trebled at enclosure. Those who defended enclosure as well as those who opposed it argued that one reason for ending common rights was to create an agricultural proletariat, subject to wage discipline. It ended commoners' right to work when and as they chose, and with it their independence. To the outsider commoners were 'lazy', wasted their time. It made as much sense to preserve the traditional economy as it would to leave North America to the Indians. Enclosure destroyed the old peasant economy, more completely separating the agricultural practice of small and large farms, pushing smaller occupiers into the market and expropriating smaller commoners.

Land sales were accelerated: it marked the end of the English peasantry. Many of those enclosed against became dependent on poor relief – or became vagabonds. Francis Trigge in 1604 wrote that 'Inclosers take upon them, as though they were not Lords of Mannours but rather kings, and doe make, as it were, a new Commonwealth and a new forme of governement'.[27] Professor Neeson gives much evidence for thinking that there was more resistance to eighteenth-century enclosure than historians have recognized.

John Taylor wrote some indignant lines about landlords who pushed up rents in order to be able to live life more extravagantly:

> One man now in garments he doth wear
> A thousand acres on his back,
> Whose ancestors in former times did give
> Means for a hundred people well to live.

Others

26. Op. cit., pp. 7–8.
27. Trigge, *The Humble Petition of Two Sisters: the Church and Commonwealth*, Sig. F–F5.

> Wear a farm in shoe-strings edged with gold,
> And spangled garters worth a copyhold:
> A hose and doublet, which a lordship cost
> A gaudy cloak (three manors' price almost) . . .
> For which the wearers are feared and abhorred.[28]

A turning-point came with the confiscations and land sales of the Revolution. Bishops' and Dean and Chapter lands were confiscated and sold; some royalists' lands too: others were allowed to 'compound' for their lands – in effect to buy them back. In all cases the new (or restored) owners had to recoup their highly speculative investments, since they suspected (rightly) that their tenure might not be permanent. So they racked rents, evicted tenants who were unable to pay or who proved otherwise troublesome. 'Papists and malignants compound', said Richard Heyricke in a sermon preached in 1646, 'and they oppress their poor tenants that have engaged themselves in the public cause for the Lord against their lords'.[29] Tenants everywhere complained of purchasers 'exacting such a rate . . . as they cannot bear without utter ruin'. Viscount Stafford's tenants petitioned for relief from taxes because their landlord had compounded and raised their rents 'to extreme rack rents'. Others spoke of 'rents lately increased from £200 to £400' between 1646 and 1652.[30]

III

Edward Thompson and others have revised our estimate of the *income* value of commons, over and above their social advantages. Neeson shows how the right to collect from the waste fuel, food and other aids to existence made commoners of squatters without land. Bought fuel was very expensive. Neeson lists the many products of the commons – reeds for thatching, rushes for lights and for floor covering, furze for fuel and for winter feed for cattle, peat for fuel, beech mast for feeding hogs,

28. Taylor, *Workes* (1630), I, p. 32; *The Old, Old, Very Old Man* (1635), pp. 19–20, both quoted by Bernard Capp, *The World of John Taylor the Water-Poet, 1578–1653* (Oxford U.P., 1994), p. 100.
29. Heyricke, *Queen Esther's Resolve*, quoted by R. Halley, *Lancashire: its Puritanism and Nonconformity* (Manchester, 1869), I, p. 421.
30. *Calendar of the Committee for Compounding*, III, pp. 1925, 2085; IV, p. 2731; cf. my *Puritanism and Revolution*, pp. 158–81. See also H. E. Chesney, 'The Transference of Lands in England, 1640–1660', *Trans. Royal Historical Soc.*, 4th series, XV (1932).

stones for building. As well as nuts, berries, mushrooms, truffles, herbs, watercress, leaves for salads, there were bilberries, crab apples, birds, rabbits, hares. In addition to its many other uses, burnt bracken made ash balls for lye for soap. There was sand for strewing on floors, and as an abrasive for scouring pots and pans. Even loose sheep's wool caught on bushes could be used to make clothes and blankets. All these products of the commons were useful; some were vendible – flowers, berries, rushes for mat-making. Common rights could double a family's income.[31]

Above all, the commons fostered a way of life away from the market – encouraging thrift and frugality. They offered insurance against destitution, a hidden reserve of wealth, which made regular waged employment unnecessary. They left commoners with time to spend on things other than work, gave them freedom to reject the drudgery of wage labour, left opportunities for recreation and celebration. And sharing the commons created bonds of mutual obligation through exchange or sharing of goods with other commoners.[32]

Neeson appropriately quotes Clare. The ending of 'the kindred bond', the eradication of old customs which enclosure brought, were among the causes of the mental disturbance which Clare suffered at the loss of 'joy' – a favourite word – and freedom in village life.

> Enclosure came and trampled on the grass
> Of labour's rights, and left the poor a slave.[33]

The two centuries from the reign of Elizabeth I to the mid-eighteenth century are often depicted as England's golden age: from being a third-rate state on the margin of Europe we became the world's greatest power. At the beginning of the period England was a corn-importing country which could not feed its growing population. There was starvation in the bad harvest years of the 1590s, 1620s and 1640s. By the end of the seventeenth century England was *exporting* corn, and when in the 1690s there was starvation in Scotland and France, there was none in England. Enclosure of commons, forests and fens had produced more food, more sheep, and more wool for the clothing industry. The abolition of feudal tenures and wardship in 1646 gave big landowners absolute ownership in their estates, but denied it to their copyhold tenants. Confirmed after the restoration this act made possible long-term planning on big estates. Copy-

31. Neeson, op. cit., pp. 168–9, 176–7, 183, 315.
32. Ibid., pp. 158–64.
33. Ibid., pp. 285, 297, quoting Clare; cf. p. 290. For Clare see also Chapter 26 below.

holders could be evicted when that suited the convenience of their land-lords, continually expanding production for the market.

There were similar advances in trade. Under Charles I English mer-chants had found in the Mediterranean area a potential market for the 'new draperies' – lighter cloths which ultimately replaced the heavy cloths whose export to Germany and the Baltic area was interrupted by the Thirty Years War (1618–48). But Charles ordered English merchants to keep out of the Mediterranean because he was unable to give them naval protection there. By 1655, after the overthrow of the monarchy, Blake was commanding a powerful fleet which destroyed piracy in the Mediter-ranean and made it safe for English merchants to make profits there. With Parliamentary control of foreign policy confirmed after 1660, taxes were regularly voted for the strongest navy in Europe, which was used to extend England's colonial empire. The Navigation Act of 1651 (confirmed in 1661) had restricted colonial trade to English merchants. Their trade with America and the Far East boomed, and England's naval power ultimately gave them a virtual monopoly of the lucrative slave trade. The wealth of the British Empire was founded on slavery and the employment of slave labour in the West Indies and North America; and in military conquest and exploitation of the Indian subcontinent.

For most of the propertied classes it was indeed a golden age. Expanding trade led to increased customs revenue, which nearly paid for the navy without increasing taxes. Yet looked at from the point of view of the lower classes, the years between Elizabeth and the elder Pitt look more like a series of disasters. In 1550 an act of Parliament had given protection to small cottagers building on wastes and commons. In an increasingly mobile society this was an attempt to create a permanent pool of cheap labour for employment in industrial expansion. (It was wrong for children not to follow the same occupations as their parents.) With population increase labour lost its fifteenth-century scarcity. The Statute of Artificers of 1563 treated those without property as semi-servile: they had a duty to work for their betters. Entry into skilled occupations was restricted to children of the relatively well-to-do. During a period of rising prices a wage-freeze was enforced. In 1597 Parliament voted that no new cottages should be erected without four acres of land attached – i.e. not by homeless vagabonds, who most needed them. In 1605 a judicial decision laid it down that inhabitants as such had no common rights in the waste.[34] In

34. A. E. Bland, P. A. Brown and R. H. Tawney, *English Economic History: Select Documents* (1914), pp. 268, 325.

Charles I's reign there were whipping posts for beggars every few hundred yards in London.

Enclosure solved England's food problem at the expense of the poorest villagers. There were riots against enclosure in 1607, in the late 1620s and 1630s, and in the 1640s. At Enfield, where there had been riots in 1589 and 1603 to preserve the inhabitants' rights on enclosure, in 1659 these inhabitants had to be suppressed by armed force when they threw down enclosures again.[35] After 1660 class divisions became wider as richer peasants producing for the market prospered at the expense of landless wage labourers. Enclosure led to a rapid increase in national wealth, to an agricultural revolution which enabled England to feed its rapidly growing population (and would – in the eighteenth century – feed an expanding industrial proletariat). By then agriculture was, in Edward Thompson's words, England's greatest capitalist industry.

But the agricultural revolution destroyed the livelihood of fenmen, forest dwellers, squatters on commons and wastes. In the late fourteenth and fifteenth centuries serfs had found freedom by taking to the roads. Where were they to go now? The authorities' only answer was to flog them back to the parishes from which they had originally fled. The effect of the harsh poor law may have been to thrust solidarity upon groups of vagabonds.

The growing army of landless peasants faced a hunted existence. Expansion of the navy and the mercantile marine was manned by impressment, of which vagabonds were the first victims: gentlemen of course were not liable to conscription.[36] Vagabonds and others surplus to the requirements of the labour market were dumped in the colonies. The rapid expansion of the clothing industry and of cloth exports was accompanied by stricter laws abolishing traditional perquisites and enforcing wage rates which were regarded as little better than slavery. In London one child in ten survived to the age of five; John Graunt in 1662 calculated a London child's life expectation at birth as seventeen and a half years.[37]

35. Buchanan Sharp, 'Rural Discontents and the English Revolution', in *Town and Countryside in the English Revolution* (ed. R. Richardson, Manchester U.P., 1992), pp. 267–8.
36. See [Anon.], *The London Prodigall* (1605), Act I, scene ii, in *The Shakespeare Apocrypha* (ed. C. F. Tucker Brooke, Oxford U.P., 1967), p. 198. For impressment, see Chapter 13 below.
37. See my 'Pottage for Freeborn Englishmen: Attitudes to Wage-Labour', in *Change and Continuity in 17th-century England* (Yale U.P., 1991); John Graunt, *Observations upon the Bills of Mortality* (5th ed., 1676).

Enclosure benefited the economy as a whole by its rationalization of agriculture. But the poorer peasantry lost innumerable customary rights thanks to the legislation of Parliaments composed of enclosers, implemented by J.P.s many of whom were also enclosing landlords. In 1677 the Statute of Frauds turned all interests in land, except short leases, into tenancies at will unless written evidence to the contrary could be produced. Most tenants relied on custom, not written evidence. Traditional rights to collect fuel, fruits and berries from the waste, to pasture cattle and birds on the commons, to glean after harvest, meant the difference between a viable life and starvation to villagers who had no assets but their labour. They were effectively expropriated and turned loose. Tawney pointed out that the custom of the manor, on which the rights of villagers depended, assumed village solidarity. 'Customary tenants are trade unionists to a man', he inimitably put it: they stood by their 'ancient customs and liberties'. Manorial custom rather than the authority of the state formed their political environment and supplied their political ideas. But as the peasantry polarized into rich and poor, employers and wage labourers, village solidarity broke down and the smaller men lost their protection. A poor copyholder had little hope of defending his legal rights: those who had no credit or savings were at mercy when fines or rents were increased, or when enclosure 'by agreement' was being mooted. Yeomen with capital might share in the benefits. As Fuller put it, 'rich men . . . to make room for themselves would jostle the poor people out of their commons'.[38]

Until the absolute rights of private property in land – or as it is polite to call them these days, the doctrine of possessive individualism – were established during the revolutionary decades by abolition of feudal tenures and Star Chamber, and the subordination of forest courts to the common law, until then kings and their favourites could override the customary property rights – or what were believed to be rights – of even powerful landowners. Gentlemen and even peers often put themselves at the head of popular movements against enclosure and forest laws until the rights of property became sacrosanct even against royalty and its favourites.[39]

---

38. R. H. Tawney, *The Agrarian Problem in the Sixteenth Century*, pp. 131, 139, 160–61, 244–7, 301; M. Campbell, *The English Yeoman*, pp. 133–4, 139–42; W. G. Hoskins, *Studies in Leicestershire Agrarian History*, pp. 57–76; quoted by Joan Thirsk, *English Peasant Farming: the Agrarian History of Lincolnshire from Tudor to Recent Times* (1957), p. 37.

39. R. B. Manning, *Hunters and Poachers*, Chapters 3 and 4.

Absolute property of this sort had been proclaimed by Cain in the Wakefield mystery play, *The Killing of Abel*, last performed in Mary's reign. Cain withheld his tithes from God because (he claimed) his property was his alone. It was appropriate that the tithes were due to God and not to a mere clergyman. In a final anticipation of the future, Cain justified his refusal by the words 'Reason only rules me still'.[40] Sections of the gentry who became involved in production for the market carried some of its values into their villages. This is relevant to Sidney's remark in *Arcadia*: 'The peasants would have all the gentlemen destroyed; the citizens . . . would have them reformed'.[41]

But the concept of absolute property took some time to triumph over customary liberties. Ultimately the law came to reject 'unreasonable customs'. A right to glean after harvest came to be seen as 'inconsistent with the nature of property, which imports exclusive enjoyment'.[42] A Jacobean, probably an M.P., referred in this context to 'the preposterous wills of perverse men who may, and will not, understand reason nor entertain a benefit offered them'.[43] Brian Manning asserts that 'the central issue of the 1630s and 40s, and of the English Revolution, . . . was to decide whether the landlords and big farmers or the mass of the peasantry were to control and develop the wastes and commons'.[44]

As the market developed, so increasing numbers of yeomen farmers came to see the advantages *for them* of enclosure; and 'enclosure by agreement' became easier to push through. But it took time. Edward Thompson makes the valid point that the great age of Parliamentary enclosures was delayed till 1760–1820 because 'agreement' on enclosure had been blocked by 'humoursome' or 'spiteful' fellows, 'holding out to the last for the old customary economy'.[45]

Proverbs tell the story. On the one hand, 'custom without reason is but

40. Ed. M. Rose, *The Wakefield Mystery Plays* (1961), pp. 66–71.
41. Sir Philip Sidney, *The Countess of Pembroke's Arcadia* (ed. H. Friswell, 1867), p. 226.
42. E. P. Thompson, *Customs in Common* (1991), p. 139.
43. Quoted by F. J. Fisher, 'Tawney's Century', in *Essays in the Economic and Social History of Tudor and Stuart England, in Honour of R. H. Tawney* (Cambridge U.P., 1961), p. 5.
44. B. S. Manning, *The English People and the English Revolution, 1640–1649* (1976), pp. 119, 283–4; cf. Bob Bushaway, *By Rite: Custom, Ceremony and Community in England, 1700–1880* (1982), pp. 214–17.
45. Thompson, *Customs in Common*, p. 110; cf. p. 106.

ancient error'. 'Custom is the plague of wise men and idol of fools'. On the other hand, 'He that is warm thinks all are so'; 'in a thousand pounds of law there's not an ounce of love'. 'Laws grind the poor, and rich men make the law'.[46]

When the Ludlows enclosed the common fields of Hill Deverill, Wiltshire, many of the tenants were turned into day labourers and/or paupers. Joshua Sylvester, in his translation of Du Bartas, was thinking of England when he wrote of

> the needy, hard-rack-rented hind,
> Or copyholder, whom hard lords do grind . . .
> Who scarce have bread within their homely cotes.[47]

'Only the large farmer', wrote Joan Thirsk grimly, 'did well out of the famine'. She was speaking of 1594; but famines were frequent in the 1620s and 1640s as well as the 1590s.[48]

A series of especially violent enclosure riots occurred around Malmesbury between 1590 and 1610: the corporation had enclosed the town's commons in order to discourage immigration by unemployed clothiers.[49] The struggle in the borough of Huntingdon, in which Oliver Cromwell took the part of the commoners against the ruling oligarchy, arose in part because a new charter granted by Charles I permitted the oligarchy to restrict rights of common pasture. This is one of many examples which expose the attempt of some modern historians to revive belief in the benevolence of Stuart absolutism towards the poor.[50]

46. S. C. Johnson, *The Book of Proverbs and Epitaphs* (n.d.), p. 19; [Anon.], *Proverbial Folk-lore* (Dorking, n.d.), p. 126; G. L. Apperson, *English Proverbs and Proverbial Phrases* (1979), p. 353; R. Chisty, *Proverbs, Maxims and Phrases of All Ages* (1888), I, p. 609.
47. D. Underdown, *Revel*, p. 114; Sylvester, *The Complete Works* (ed. Grosart, Hildersheim, 1969), I, p. 50.
48. Thirsk, 'Enclosing and Engrossing', p. 229.
49. R. B. Manning, *Village Revolts*, pp. 104–5.
50. For some corrections of this hoary Cavalier myth, recently revived, see Thirsk, 'Enclosing and Engrossing', pp. 213, 237; 'Agrarian Problems and the English Revolution', pp. 172–3; R. B. Manning, *Village Revolts*, p. 117; E. P. Thompson, *Whigs and Hunters* (1975), pp. 169–89.

RACK RENTS — EXTORTIONATE RENTS

IV

Literary evidence is overwhelming. Take for instance Michael Drayton on 'the country rook' complaining of 'his ravenous lord', who

> Raising new fines, redoubling ancient rent,
> And by the enclosure of old common land,
> Racks the dear sweat from his labourer's hand,
> Whilst he that digs for heath out of the stones
> Cracks his stiff sinews, and consumes his bones.[51]

Shakespeare's *Coriolanus*, Annabel Patterson has reminded us, is about famine as the cause of peasant revolt. It was only 'once we stood up about the corn' that Caius Martius 'stuck not to call us the Many-Headed Monster' (Act II, scene iii). The word 'power' occurs twice as often in that play as in any other work by Shakespeare.[52] We may compare Benlowes, writing of rural 'Nimrods',

> Whose vast designs engross the boundless land
>   By fraud or force; like spiders stand
> Squeezing small flies.[53]

When Don Jamie in Beaumont and Fletcher's *The Spanish Curate* deplores landlords who

> rack your poor tenants
> Till they look like so many skeletons
> For want of food,

the audience might think of England as well as of Spain.[54]

Of all the laws which the lower classes regarded as contravening their liberties, the most conspicuous and the most resented were the Game Laws, which I discuss in Chapter 7. Shakespeare, according to a persistent and highly plausible tradition, for which there is only late, rather gossipy evidence, is said to have got on the wrong side of the law by stealing

---

51. Drayton, *Poems* (1969), p. 417.
52. Patterson, *Shakespeare and the Popular Voice*, pp. 127, 144 and *passim*. Cf. epigraph to this chapter.
53. Edward Benlowes, *Theophila*, Canto I, stanza xxxviii, in *Minor Poets of the Caroline Period* (ed. G. Saintsbury, Oxford U.P., 1905), I.
54. Beaumont and Fletcher, *Plays* (Mermaid Series), II, p. 220.

deer from Sir Thomas Lucy's park. This was not necessarily an act of youthful indiscretion, nor 'a usual rite of passage for the youth who wanted to assert his manhood or lay claim to genteel status'. Manning notes, dampingly, that there is no evidence that Lucy possessed a deer park in Warwickshire, only a rabbit warren. But he adds that 'it is not easy to document the existence of deer parks'. And he notes that Shakespeare 'displayed a technical mastery of hunting terms'.[55] Lucy was a notorious encloser, hated by the local peasantry; robbing his property could be seen as a popular gesture. We should take this in the context of Shakespeare's attitude towards the law as revealed in his plays. Portia shows up Shylock's attempt to manipulate the law against a poor debtor, as so many rich men did. She turns the tables on him by a piece of legal trickery, also familiar enough, though normally used by the rich against the poor. In Dogberry the law is made to seem an ass, unworthy of its lofty claims. Lear in his madness reveals the law as permitting the rich to punish in the poor the crimes they themselves commit. As he observes, authority has thought too little about them.

Lear's madness makes a point. The reason for the prevalence of fools and madmen in Jacobean drama is that they were licensed to say the unsayable. For the same reason aristocratic households kept a fool, a jester, who could tell the truths which everybody was aware of and nobody admitted. Charles I's fool, Archie Armstrong, naturally was persecuted by Archbishop Laud, but he had a satisfactory last laugh after the Long Parliament had caught up with Laud. 'Who's fool now?' Archie asked him. During the revolutionary decades the truths which only jesters and fools could utter were every day in print: fools became superfluous. They did not reappear when kings, lords and bishops returned: restoration comedy took over their function.

George Wither returns to these social points again and again in *Brittans Remembrancer* (1628), denouncing racking of rents and eviction of tenants, usury, projects and spendthrift courtiers.

> The land is . . . poor indeed, and yet I do believe
> Few kingdoms are so rich . . .
> 'Tis poor, if we on those reflect our eyes
> On whom the labours of this kingdom lies;
> Those people, whom our great and wealthy ones

55. R. B. Manning, *Hunters and Poachers*, pp. 182–3.

> Have racked, oppressed, and eaten to the bones
> To fatten and adorn their carcases:
> The land (I must confess) is poor in these . . .
> If we had peace with God, and could agree,
> This kingdom, which so needy seems to be,
> Might with her superfluities maintain
> Far greater armies than the King of Spain.[56]

George Herbert, in a simple analogy, contrasted the enclosure of common lands (bad) with the fence of holy matrimony which prevented a man (or woman) from grazing on the common (good).[57] When it came to civil war, John Corbet thus described those in Gloucestershire who supported Parliament: they were not powerful gentry who were prepared to 'render themselves the slaves of princes' if they 'also might rule over their neighbours as vassals'; but rather they were 'yeomen, farmers, petty freeholders and such as use manufactures.' These and 'the whole middle rank of the people were the only active men', 'a generation of men truly laborious, jealous of their properties, whose principal aim is liberty and plenty'. Such men 'continually thwart the intentions of tyranny' acceptable to 'gentlemen in a corrupted age', those who 'do eat their bread in the sweat of other men'.[58]

The civil war did not completely solve these rivalries and inequalities. Moses Wall, writing to Milton in May 1659, assumed that the English people were not free; lords were tyrants and copyholders had no security of tenure. Fuller made the point succinctly. 'Tell the fenmen who object to the loss of freedom which enclosure of the fens entailed of the great benefit to the public because where a pike or a duck fed formerly, now a bullock or sheep is fatted; they will be ready to return that if they be taken in taking that bullock or sheep, the rich man indicteth them for felony; whereas the pike or duck were their own goods, only for the pains of catching them'.[59] In many areas where it did not get as far as

56. Wither, *Brittans Remembrancer* (Spenser Soc., 1880), II, pp. 393–7, 428–9, 476, 480; cf. pp. 393–7, 428–9.

57. S. Gottlieb, 'The Social and Political Backgrounds of George Herbert's Poetry', in *'The Muses Common-Weale': Poetry and Politics in the Seventeenth Century* (ed. C. J. Summers and T.-L. Pebworth, Missouri U.P., 1988), pp. 112–14.

58. John Corbet, *Historical Relation of the Military Government of Gloucester* (1645), in *Bibliotheca Gloucestrensis*, I, pp. 9–16.

59. D. Masson, *Life of Milton* (1859–80), V, pp. 602–3; for Fuller see my *Reformation to Industrial Revolution* (Penguin, 1967), p. 153, where I comment, 'This too was a loss of freedom for the poorer classes'.

rioting, the ruling gentry and yeomen were able quietly to prevent the building of cottages without adequate land, to close the parish to immigrants, to reduce customary rights like gleaning in order to encourage their poor to try their luck elsewhere.[60]

Ballads make no bones about the fact that 'the poor man pays for all'. The rich grind the faces of the poor and make them toil for inadequate wages. Usurers, bribed courtiers, lawyers, brewers and bakers all take advantage of the poor. A character in the anonymous play, *The Puritaine Widdow* (1607), complained that usurers 'keep our money in their hands and make us to be hanged for robbing of 'em'.[61] Contrast another Roxburghe Ballad, 'An Invitation to Lubberland', which they say is

> not above
> Two thousand leagues from Dover . . .
> There is no law, nor lawyer's fee, . . .
> They have no landlord's rent to pay;
> Each man is a freeholder.

Or another, 'I know what I know',

> There be many rich men
> Both yeomen and gentry
> That for their own private gain
> Hurt a whole country [county]
> By closing free commons,
> Yet they'll make as though
> 'Twere for common good,
> But I know what I know.[62]

The disruption which enclosure caused became an ironical proverb: 'they hold together as the men of Marcham when they lost their common.' To quote Fuller again, depopulating enclosure 'is a canker to the commonwealth; woeful experience shows how it unhouses thousands of people, till desperate need throw them on the gallows. Long since had this land been sick of a pleurisy' but for emigration to the western plantations.[63]

---

60. M. Ingram, *Church Courts, Sex and Marriage in England, 1570–1640* (Cambridge U.P., 1987), pp. 82–3.
61. *The Puritaine Widdow*, Act I, scene i, in *The Shakespeare Apocrypha*.
62. Roxburghe, *Ballads*, quoted in Ashton, *Humour, Wit and Satire*, pp. 34–7, 246–51.
63. [George Sandys], *Anglorum Speculum, or The Worthies of England* (1684), p. 453; Fuller, *The Holy State* (1841), p. 91. First published 1642.

V

When Hartlib said 'there are fewest poor where there are fewest commons', he was making two points. It was not that commons *created* paupers. But if there were no commons, many of the poor would be unable to remain in their villages because they could not earn enough to live on; and where commons survived they attracted vagrants to squat there in the hope of being able to live on pickings from the waste. It was their last resort. The influx of squatters was often resented by older inhabitants. In the early seventeenth century the common-law courts began limiting common rights to tenants, with the object of preventing vagabonds squatting.[64] The poet Henry Vaughan – no radical – put it forcibly: 'the rich and the great amongst us not only feed upon and live by the sweat, the slaughter and the blood of the poor and oppressed, but esteem them (of all others) their choicest dainties; for they are swallowed without much chewing, and there is none to deliver them'.[65]

Popular opposition to enclosure is found everywhere. R. B. Manning's table shows riots in every county from the reign of Henry VIII to that of James I, despite savage sentences on the leaders of the Oxfordshire rising of 1596.[66] John Morrill found evidence of enclosure riots in twenty-six English counties between 1640 and 1644. David Underdown speaks of a mass invasion of deer parks in south-western England in the early years of the civil war.[67] Brian Manning describes riots in Windsor and Waltham Forests in 1642–3. 'The rioters often had little sympathy with Parliament or interest in the disputes between the King and the two houses'. Their motives were simpler: attacks on landlords and their deer were continued by the rank and file in Parliament's armies: landlords who supported Parliament were not spared.[68] It was a class gesture, not a political one.

64. Hartlib, *His Legacy of Husbandry* (1655), p. 43; R. B. Manning, *Village Revolts*, p. 20 and Chapter 4.
65. Vaughan, *Works* (ed. L. C. Martin, Oxford U.P., 1914), II, p. 554; cf. 'The Bee', ibid., p. 652: 'the rich eat the poor like bread'.
66. R. B. Manning, *Village Revolts*, pp. 323–9; John Walter, 'A "Rising of the People"? The Oxfordshire Rising of 1596', in *Past and Present*, No. 107, esp. p. 141.
67. J. S. Morrill, *The Revolt of the Provinces: Conservatives and Radicals in the English Civil War, 1630–1650* (1975), p. 34; Underdown, *Revel*, p. 160.
68. B. S. Manning, *The English People and the English Revolution*, pp. 190–93. For Waltham and Windsor Forests see Chapter 7 below. Cf. Buchanan Sharp, *In Contempt of All Authority*, p. 264.

'This is no time to prosecute the enclosures of commons', said a gentleman in 1641, 'whilst the common people are at so much liberty'.[69] Liberty against law again, we note.

R. B. Manning observes that an influx of artisans and labourers into the west midlands and Welsh borderlands – for coal mining, iron manufactures, cloth weaving – made new demands upon the agricultural and fuel resources of those regions, and contributed to the possibility of enclosure riots. 'The development of rural industry may be nearly as significant a cause of social protest as agrarian change'.[70] It is perhaps an interesting coincidence that the early Quaker movement was especially successful in attracting converts in forest, woodland and fen areas.[71] Pressure on land resources added to the growing tendency to exclude from pasture rights all but freeholders, and copyholders with a well-established claim to such rights. Mere 'inhabitants' with no land were less fortunate.

At a later date, the poetess Mary Leapor in 'The Month of August' contrasted the exotic products of the new improved agriculture with simpler products of the traditional communal system with its customary rights. Richard Greene distinguishes her approach from that of Stephen Duck: 'Whereas Leapor seeks to retain freedoms which are threatened . . . Duck belongs to a section of society which has already seen its rights cut away'. He quotes Robert Bloomfield in 'The Farmer's Boy' who remarks on 'the widening distance which I daily see', and asks,

> Has Wealth done this? . . . then Wealth's a foe to me;
> Foe to our rights, it leaves a powerful few
> The paths of emulation to pursue.[72]

Bunyan's *Pilgrim's Progress* is, among many other things, an anti-enclosure allegory. Christian *en route* for the Celestial City found that Immanuel's Land was common for all the pilgrims. But he and his companion Hopeful soon get to a land which has been enclosed by Giant Despair, who threateningly asks 'what they did on his grounds?', arrests them and takes them away to his lock-up – just like an enclosing Justice of the Peace. Ultimately they escape, and proceed to the Delectable Mountains, where the vineyards are free for all to help themselves. After

---

69. Lipson, *Economic History of England*, II, pp. 406–7.
70. R. B. Manning, *Village Revolts*, p. 59.
71. Underdown, *Revel*, pp. 250–51.
72. R. Greene, *Mary Leapor: A Study in Eighteenth-Century Women's Poetry* (Oxford U.P., 1993), pp. 134–6; cf. pp. 142–5.

further adventures they reach the land of Beulah, where again orchards, vineyards and gardens belonging to the King are open for the solace of pilgrims. When Christiana follows her husband she learns that after crossing the River of Death a house was given to him in the Celestial City, where he dines at the table of the King. Her party is stopped by lions belonging to Giant Grim, who also claims that they are trespassing on his property. But Great-Heart tells him that he is obstructing the King's highway and that they have a right to proceed. They come to blows, and Great-Heart slays Giant Grim. They pass through the Valley of Humiliation, in which 'many labouring men have got good estates'. Finally they seek out another giant, Slay-Good, who did 'much annoy the King's High-way'. Great-Heart fights and kills him too – the invariable fate of enclosers in Bunyan's allegory – and the pilgrims proceed on their way to the Celestial City.[73] Commons and wastes could preserve families from falling into the slavery of full-time wage labour; but the pressures were very great. Capitalism in all its brutality was stalking the land, convincing of its liberating role those who wished to be convinced. Propagandists were upset by the failure of the poor to understand that it was in their own interests to quit the relative but familiar security of the village in order to work for others elsewhere. Silvanus Taylor tells us that he had many times offered to many of these idle persons, both men and women, 6d. by the day to work, and they have answered: 'they cannot live on it, and as good play for nothing as work for another'. He blamed 'blind alehouses' for 'these drones'.[74]

When enclosure came, the illusory freedom of the road offered itself; but vagabonds were exposed to the savagery of the law. It would ultimately drive them into full-time wage-labour, in which they had no control over their own lives or their own time. Before enclosure commoners worked in their own time – finding food and fuel from the waste, carrying water (often over long distances), herding sheep and cattle – all when and how they chose. Wage labour created an entirely new distinction between *free* time and working time.

Wage labourers sold their time to their employers. Such 'free time' as they had was rationed in small driblets. By contrast the time over which they were not master – 'enslaved time' – formed the bulk of the working day. Before enclosure the life of the poor had been hard, but their toil was

73. Bunyan, *The Pilgrim's Progress* (ed. J. B. Wharey and R. Sharrock, Oxford U.P., 1960), pp. 55, 113, 119, 155, 182, 218–19, 237, 266.
74. S[ilvanus] T[aylor], op. cit., p. 37.

self-imposed, or imposed by the weather and the seasons; not forced on them by their fellow men. By forcing peasants into wage labour, enclosure ended their freedom to decide how and when they worked, ended freedom of choice.[75] The dictionaries do not tell us when 'free time' became differentiated from unfree working time, when time too was reduced to the subjection of the market.[76] We are so used to the tyranny of the alarm clock and the factory whistle that it is difficult for us to think ourselves back to the 'free time' of our pre-capitalist ancestors.

Gay, interestingly enough, wrote a fable about the way in which the idle rich find that 'time hangs heavy'. In this fable Time, competing with Plutus and Cupid, has the last word.

> Though little prized and seldom sought
> Without me love and gold are nought . . .
> By me all useful arts are gained,
> Wealth, learning, wisdom is attained. . . .
> He spoke. The gods no more contest,
> And his superior gifts confest:
> That Time (when truly understood)
> Is the most precious earthly good.[77]

But with Parliament's victory over the King came confiscation and sale of church, crown and royalists' lands, which led inevitably to 'the racking up of rents of '51 and '52'.[78] With the abolition of feudal tenures and the Court of Wards more absolute conceptions of the rights of property came to prevail, with disastrous consequences for traditional customary rights which often lacked formal legal backing though they had been accepted for centuries. Ancient custom could be abolished by agreement among 'the chiefest of the parish'.[79]

Many who were not themselves victims of enclosure sympathized with those who were. The leader of the 'diggers' who in 1614 opposed the enclosure of open fields at Welcombe, Warwickshire, was a friend of Shakespeare. The bard himself declared that 'he was not able to bear the

75. See now an interesting article by Peter Burke, 'The Invention of Leisure in Early Modern Europe', in *Past and Present*, 146 (February 1995), esp. p. 148.
76. Neeson, op. cit., pp. 27–34.
77. Gay, Fable XIII, Plutus, Cupid and Time.
78. J. Thirsk and J. P. Cooper, *17th-Century Economic Documents* (Oxford U.P., 1972), pp. 70, 72, 140–44; my *Puritanism and Revolution*, pp. 161–72, 184–6.
79. Underdown, *Revel*, p. 61.

enclosing of Welcombe', though he would have lost nothing by it.[80] When Lord Gerard enclosed the waste at his manor of Nether Wyresdale in 1602 the ensuing riot was led by sixteen women encouraged by a local gentleman who declared that the women 'might boldly without any fear of punishment pull down the hedges and ditches'.[81]

During and after the civil war, 'Clubmen' revolts often involved the whole of a community. Clubmen had their own vision of Parliament's 'liberty and property', and meant something rather different from their betters when they hailed 'a time of liberty' in the 1640s. The class division became particularly alarming when Clubmen won backing from at least some rank and file parliamentarian soldiers.[82] The men of property did not feel secure until after 1660.

The decline of the smallholder became pronounced only in the later seventeenth century.[83] There was a great power of inertia behind traditional village customs. They survived so long as they did not seriously impede the economic activities of powerful members of the community. This meant that capitalist values spread slowly and irregularly, some areas leaving others behind. It was a long time before the new standards came to dominate the whole society; it needed the shake-up of the Revolution to expedite the process. As enclosure 'by agreement' of the powerful figures in the village became easier, many well-off peasants joined their betters in supporting the growing power of the state and its laws in the village.[84] Quaker acceptance of the law and lawyers was a symbol of the victory of the new standards. Upper-class solidarity was consolidated by the new game legislation.[85]

Cato's Letters (1720–23) followed Harrington in asserting that 'the first principle of all power is property, and every man will have his share of it in proportion as he enjoys property'. Since property in England was unequally divided, he thought democracy was impossible.[86] Oliver Goldsmith summed up the new view of liberty and law – after the law had won. The lines are familiar, but that perhaps makes its own point.

---

80. R. B. Manning, *Village Revolts*, p. 92.
81. Ibid., pp. 115–16.
82. Underdown, *Revel*, pp. 157–82, 228–31, 275–80.
83. Manning, *Village Revolts*, p. 152.
84. John Walter,₁'A "Rising of the People?"', p. 141.
85. See Chapters 7 and 24 below.
86. Op. cit. (3rd ed., 1733), III, pp. 151–62; Staughton Lynd, *Intellectual Origins of American Radicalism* (1973), pp. 21–2.

Even liberty itself is bartered here.
At gold's superior charms all freedom flies.
The needy sell it, and the rich man buys. . . .
Laws grind the poor and rich men make the law. . . .
That independence Britons prize too high
Keeps man from man, and breaks the social tie. . . .
[They] call it freedom when themselves are free.[87]

87. Goldsmith, 'The Traveller' (1765), in *Works* (1845), I, pp. 89–91.

II. LAWLESSNESS

3. Vagabonds

Thou hast a title in the common. . . . How do men strive . . . for their commons? They will raise a mutiny, do anything, keep somewhat on it for possession's sake, rather than lose it, if it were but to keep one poor cow upon it. . . . Whatever thou be, maintain thy title in this common.

Richard Sibbes, 'The Knot of Prayer Loosed', in *Works* (Edinburgh, 1862–4), VII, p. 249.

Serve God and make much of your own; and as these new leases fall out, raise your old rents according to my directions, that you may have something to live on like other neighbour gentlemen.

Ed. T. Heywood, *The Moore Rental* (Chatham Soc., 1847), p. 119. Advice of John Moore to his son, written just after the restoration.

Liberality is the most beneficial traffic that can be; it is bringing our wares to the best market; it is letting out our money to God, Who repays with vast usury: and 100 to 1 is the rate He allows at present, and above a hundred millions to one He will render hereafter.

Isaac Barrow, *The Duty and reward of bounty to the poor* (1671), in *Theological Works* (1859), I, p. 91. Barrow was an eminent mathematician, so his calculations are to be trusted.

I

Vagabondage had a long history. The catastrophe of the Black Death was followed by a century of declining population. There was a shortage of labour, land was unoccupied, and so a splendid opportunity was offered to serfs to liberate themselves by running away and settling elsewhere on uncultivated land. Vagabondage was then the route from serfdom to liberty.[1] A Commons petition of 1376 complained bitterly of the ease with

1. Cf. Zwi Ravi, 'The Myth of the Immutable English Family', in *Past and Present*, No. 140 (1993).

which runaways 'are taken into service immediately in new places, at such dear wages that example and encouragement is afforded to all servants to depart into fresh places, and go from master to master as soon as they are displeased about anything'.[2] In 1391 a Lollard, William Swinderby, said that we are 'not to give alms to each shameless beggar, strong and mighty of body to get his livelihood leaefull [lawful] and will not'.[3] Vagabondage may have been the price for being able to do your own thing, 'out of sight or out of slavery', as the Digger Gerrard Winstanley was to put it in the seventeenth century.[4] By the sixteenth century serfdom was virtually extinct. But by then the population had been restored, and roaming vagabonds presented new social problems.

A statute of 1495 laid it down that all beggars not able to work must return to the place where they last lived, without benefit of trial by jury. That was the beginning. The reformation created new vagabonds. Burnet tells us with some pleasure that the Vagabonds Act of November 1547 was 'chiefly levelled at the idle monks and friars' expelled from their monasteries. In Elizabeth's reign itinerant sectaries began to be treated as vagabonds. In 1593 Abraham Pulburye, pursemaker, a Sussex Brownist, was burnt in the ear and then pressed for a soldier as a vagabond.[5] The statute of Artificers (1563) declared that any man or woman without an agricultural holding could be condemned to semi-servile labour in industry or agriculture; children of paupers were to be compulsorily apprenticed. No labourer might leave his employment without the consent of his employer, under penalty of imprisonment. All these provisions naturally depressed the wages and status of workers. Organized resistance was impossible, since combination to raise wages was treasonable. Vagabonds were liable to conscription for overseas service in the army or navy. But wage labourers were not allowed to serve in the militia, the praetorian guard of the propertied.

A 'dangerous and incorrigible rogue' was to be marked in the left shoulder with a capital R. Whipping, never a very successful remedy, declined after 1660, when greater prosperity meant a greater demand for

---

2. Quoted by John Hatcher, 'England in the Aftermath of the Black Death', in *Past and Present*, 144 (August 1994), p. 19.

3. This was quoted by John Foxe in his *Book of Martyrs* (*Acts and Monuments*, ed. J. Pratt, n.d.), III, p. 118.

4. Winstanley, *Works* (ed. G. H. Sabine, Cornell U.P., 1941), p. 359.

5. Gilbert Burnet, *The History of the Reformation of the Church of England* (1825), III, p. 59; Champlin Burrage, *The Early English Dissenters in the light of recent research (1550–1641)* (Cambridge U.P., 1912), II, pp. 48–9; cf. pp. 134–7.

labour, and so an encouragement to the mobility which had characterized the revolutionary decades.[6] But the 1662 Settlement Act authorized J.P.s to convey any newcomer occupying a tenement worth less than £10 per annum to the parish where he was last legally settled, unless (if challenged within forty days of arrival) he gave security to the parish against any obligation to support him.[7] An M.P. in 1675 declared that 'under the late act [of 1662] the poor are hunted like foxes out of their homes'. In 1687 the period within which the newcomer could be challenged was extended from six weeks to life.[8]

All wandering persons with no means of subsistence were vagabonds. This included sailors, ex-soldiers, pedlars, jugglers, palm-readers, drovers, tramping artisans, freemasons, begging university undergraduates and scholars, travelling actors, singers or minstrels, Welsh bards. The fact that play-actors were technically vagabonds[9] explains why they had to obtain the protection of a great aristocrat or King.

Diggers claimed that they were not vagrants because they were not 'idle wanderers, begging up and down the country'. They thought that gentlemen rather than laborious poor men should be punished as 'persons who wander up and down idly'.[10] 'Men want the work, and the work men', declared Roger North; but they 'are by laws kept from accommodating each other'.[11]

In real life I do not suppose that many people chose to be beggars, then as now. But the open road and the greenwood offered more romantic possibilities than today's city pavements. Politicians and pamphleteers who had themselves never had to face beggary, then as now, portrayed them as idle scroungers. Those whose unemployment and begging had been forced upon them had to make the best of a bad job. I suspect that plays and ballads in praise of a beggar's life were not often composed by beggars.

Enclosure created vagabonds by abolishing customary rights of sustenance to poor persons, driving them on to the road. It was a legal offence

6. *Sir Henry Whithed's Letter Book*, I, *1601–14* (Hampshire Record Series, I, 1976), p. 105.
7. A. L. Beier, *Masterless Men: the vagrancy problem in England, 1560–1640* (1985), pp. 170–73.
8. Lipson, *Economic History of England*, III, pp. 457–9; B. Osborne, *Justices of the Peace for the Counties of England* (Shaftesbury, 1960), pp. 129–30, 187.
9. Cf. Justice Clack in *A Jovial Crew*, quoted on p. 54 below.
10. Gerrard Winstanley, *An Humble Request to the Ministers of both Universities and to all Lawyers in every Inns-a-Court*, in *Works*, pp. 431–2.
11. Quoted by Lipson, *Economic History of England*, III, p. 466.

to be a vagabond, however involuntarily. Vagabonds had no legal rights; begging and stealing were forced upon them. Bunyan phrased it well: they were 'kicked to and fro like footballs in the world'.[12] The law destroyed their liberty. Anyone who *threatened* to run away from his or her parish could be treated as a vagabond and be conscripted to forced labour. The under-class of permanent poor was dependent on charity.

Sir Walter Ralegh thought it important to distinguish between 'vagabonds and beggars', for whom he had nothing good to say, and the poor – 'those that labour to live', the old, 'poor widows and fatherless children, ... poor tenants that travail to pay their rents and are driven to poverty by mischance'. As Professor Underdown puts it, 'the member of even the poorest household inhabited a completely different world from that of the "masterless" man or woman'. In the later seventeenth century even paupers paid the hearth tax.[13]

Vagabonds came to be seen as outside society. They were 'cut off from God's face', wrote Ralegh. Beggars, William Perkins said, are 'for the most part a cursed generation', since they 'form not themselves to any settled congregation for the obtaining of God's kingdom'. They 'are as rotten legs and arms that drop from the body'. They had no calling: 'to wander up and down from year to year to this end, to seek and procure bodily maintenance, is no calling but the life of a beast'. 'Every man must be subject to the magistrate for conscience sake'; wandering beggars 'are to be taken as main enemies of this ordinance of God'. Perkins accordingly thought that the statute of 1597 was 'in substance the very law of God, ... never to be repealed'.[14] Richard Sibbes said that vagabonds 'lived without laws, without church', and 'have no order taken for them'. Thomas Shepard in New England argued that vagabonds were outside the covenant.[15]

Richard Yonge in 1654 made a similar point. Most vagabonds are unbaptized, outside the church, and so without God. There was a danger

12. Bunyan, *The Desire of the Righteous Granted* (1692), *Miscellaneous Works*, XIII, p. 134.

13. Ralegh, *Works* (1751), II, p. 354; Underdown, *Revel*, p. 11; cf. pp. 28, 34–6; *Wiltshire Quarter Sessions Records* (ed. B. H. Cunnington, Devizes, 1932), p. 243.

14. Ralegh, *History of the World* (Edinburgh, 1820), V, p. 154; Perkins, *Works* (1616–18), I, p. 755; III, p. 539; cf. III, pp. 92, 191. Francis Bacon said something very similar. The word 'civilized' is first encountered in 1601.

15. R. Sibbes, *Works* (Edinburgh, 1862–4), III, pp. 40–41. Note that order should be taken *'for* them'; Shepard, Preface to Peter Bulkeley, *The Gospel Covenant, or the Covenant of Grace Opened* (2nd ed., 1651), Sig. B 1.

that they would infect others with their 'licentious liberty'. They did not marry but consorted together like beasts; woodland and pasture areas were 'breeders and nurseries' of 'thieves, rogues and beggars', and of gypsies.[16] Even the Quaker Edward Burrough had no sympathy for 'sturdy beggars and rogues and idle and disorderly persons'. The laws against them should be duly and justly executed. (Quakers were perhaps sensitive about vagabonds, with whom they were often identified. In 1656 Devon J.P.s issued a declaration against Quakers and vagrants. Like vagabonds, Quakers were alleged to threaten property and the social order.)[17]

The fact that vagabonds were of no settled *community* was regularly held against them. Donne, whose religious perspective was very different from Perkins's, asked 'How many beggars were ever in church, how few ever christened or ever married?' He spoke of them as 'dogs' and 'vermin'; everyone must have a job. Donne rejected, on religious grounds, 'a sordid life, . . . a beggarly, a negligent abandoning of all ways of preferment, or riches, or estimation in the world'. The Dean of St Paul's was not himself negligent of preferment: he had a special dispensation to hold more than the regulation number of livings in plurality.[18] But not everyone found it so easy: Durham miners remained outside society.[19]

There was much denunciation of the 'false pity' which many felt towards vagabonds. 'Foolish pity moving many to make provision at their doors (hoping to do good)' was thought to have increased the problem of poverty in Norwich in 1571, where deacons withheld relief from those whom they judged to be the 'idle poor'.[20] A 'good' character in Thomas Heywood's *If You Know Not Me* (1605–6) explains that

> He makes a beggar first that first relieves him:
> Not usurers make more beggars where they live
> Than charitable men that use to give.[21]

16. P. A. Slack, 'Vagrants and Beggary in England, 1598–1664', in *English Historical Review*, XXVII, 3, 1974, pp. 360–75.
17. Burrough, *The Memorable Works of a Son of Thunder and Consolation* (1672), p. 358; Roberts, *Devon*, pp. 57–8. See Chapter 24 below.
18. J. Carey, *John Donne, Life, Mind and Art* (1981), pp. 96, 114, 196; R. C. Bald, *John Donne: A Life* (Oxford U.P., 1970), p. 456.
19. M. E. James, *Family, Lineage and Civil Society* (Oxford U.P., 1974), p. 95; D. Levine and K. Wrightson, *The Making of an Industrial Society: Whickham, 1560–1765* (Oxford U.P., 1991), *passim*.
20. Tawney and Power, *Tudor Economic Documents*, II, pp. 318, 322–5.
21. Heywood, *Dramatic Works* (1874), VI, p. 60; cf. P. Bayne, *An Entire Commentary upon the Whole Epistle of St Paul to the Ephesians* (1866), p. 295.

The relationship was ambiguous. Vagabonds who tried to squat on village commons roused resentment. In the early seventeenth century the royal courts began to limit common rights to *tenants*. It became a criminal offence to feed beggars.[22] Biblical authority could be quoted: in Genesis 4:14 Cain is described as a fugitive and a vagabond: 'everyone that finds me shall slay me'.

Samuel Butler, interestingly for our purposes, thought that the object of whipping vagabonds back to their parishes was to end 'the freedom they enjoyed' and to keep them 'from straggling about the country, to infect the people with dislike of the government'. They 'raised so much compassion of the common people by bewailing the unusual condition they were in' that without the statute of vagabonds 'they were in probability to raise insurrections.'[23]

We need not take this too seriously, but it was a widely held opinion. As the number of vagabonds increased from the 1570s, alarm grew. Their number was estimated at 80,000 in the early seventeenth century.[24] Edward Hext, Somerset J.P., in 1596 wrote an alarmist letter to Lord Burghley about the increase of rogues and vagabonds. They will not work, he said, 'neither can they without most extreme pains, by reason their sinews are so benumbed and stiff through idleness as their limbs, being put to any hard labour, will grieve them beyond measure. So as they will rather hazard their lives than work. . . . Some confessed felonies unto me by which they hazarded their lives, to the end they would not be sent to the house of correction, where they should be enforced to work'. The danger from vagabonds is that their example may spread socially subversive ideas, animating the poorest peasantry 'to say boldly, they must not starve, they will not starve'. 'Most commonly the simple citizens and women' are soft on vagabonds: they 'are of opinion that they would not procure a man's death for all the goods in the world'. Vagabonds stir up contempt in the lower classes for noblemen and gentlemen, 'continually buzzing into their ears that the rich men have gotten all into their hands and will starve the poor'. 'They have bred that fear in Justices and other inferior officers that no man dares to call them into question'. This makes them a potential danger to government.[25] Vagabonds were

22. Manning, *Village Revolts*, p. 20.
23. Butler, *Prose Observations* (ed. H. de Quehen, Oxford U.P., 1979), p. 106.
24. P. Clark, *The English Alehouse: A Social History, 1200–1800* (1983), p. 129.
25. Tawney and Power, op. cit., II, pp. 339–46. Cf. Slack, *Poverty and Policy*, pp. 23–4, 93–4, 98.

compared with the masterless Irish, with American Indians, and with gypsies.[26]

George Wither was brutally unsympathetic to vagabonds.

> They who delight from door to door
>   Of hunger to complain,
> Mere want of honesty made poor
>   Or want of taking pain.

His sympathies went to poor but industrious labourers.[27] But on the whole poets and dramatists were less harsh than were the godly. In *Coriolanus*, as we have seen, the rebels were given some shrewd remarks (see p. 34 above). In *The Tempest* Caliban represents the under-class. Lear's words are famous:

> Poor naked wretches, whereso'er you are,
> That bide the pelting of this pitiless storm,
> How shall your houseless heads and unfed sides,
> Your looped and windowed raggedness, defend you
> From seasons such as this? O, I have ta'en
> Too little care of this. (Act II, scene iii)

But then Lear had himself been exposed naked to the storm; and anyway he was mad. And players themselves were vagabonds.

II

It is worth recalling how large a proportion of the population was still itinerant. The profession of itinerant poet was held in great reverence by early Danish tribes, and minstrels and harpers were no less popular among the Anglo-Saxons than later among the Welsh and Irish. In 1469 Edward IV created a guild of minstrels in England; travelling actors, minstrels and singers continued to walk the roads in Elizabeth's reign and later. But they were losing much of their original dignity; in 1572 'minstrels wandering abroad' were included in the statute of 14 Eliz. cap. 5 among those to be punished as rogues, vagabonds and sturdy beggars – unless they

26. See 'Radicals in Ireland', in my *A Nation of Change and Novelty* (1990), pp. 135–6, and see Chapters 11 and 12 below.
27. Wither, *Hallelujah, Or Britains Second Remembrancer* (ed. E. Farr, 1857), p. 349. First published 1641.

belonged 'to any baron ... or ... any other prominent personage of greater degree'. And there were other patrons. Nearly every town had 'waits' whose 'freedom' included a monopoly of performing music for pay within the town; they were also allowed to travel to augment their income. Wandering, 'roguing' minstrels provided a large part of the music heard in rural England. 'Persons commonly called fiddlers or minstrels' were still being legislated against in 1656.[28]

Jugglers, tinkers, peddlars and players were denounced as vagabonds in the act of 1597. Hence the need for royal or aristocratic patronage. The stigma of idleness, of vagabondage, was often used against actors. 'However he pretend to have a Royal Master or Mistress, his wages and dependence prove him to be a servant of the people'.[29] Players were hirelings, idlers, of no fixed abode. 'Hirelings' included all players who were not shareholders in their companies; hence Shakespeare's reinsurance by getting himself a family tree and the status of a gentleman. As Robert Weimann reminds us, there were social distinctions to be drawn here. The English players who toured the continent to great acclaim were not 'vagabonds'. Nevertheless the word was a useful term of abuse for enemies of the stage.[30] Justice Clack could use it in *A Jovial Crew*: 'Vagabonds, that is to say ... strolling players' (Act V, scene i). In 1648 the Leveller journalist John Harris was denounced as 'sometimes a Players' Boy, a Rogue by the Statute'.[31] The fact that the spreading of the plague was often attributed to the 'base sort of people', and particularly to vagrants, was an added slur.[32]

In *The Pilgrim's Progress* the hero is a poor itinerant, perhaps a tinker, perhaps an evicted peasant. He is a man in rags, with a burden on his back; he has no property, no ties. He is free to leave his house and family

28. T. Percy, *Reliques of Ancient Poetry* (Everyman ed.) I, pp. 10–12, 22–63, quoting Puttenham among others; W. L. Woodfill, *Musicians in English Society from Elizabeth to Charles* I (Princeton U.P., 1953), *passim*, esp. pp. 5–8, 56–8, 67–73, 99–108, 131–2, 139.

29. 'J. Cocke', 'The Character of a Common Player', in *Satyrical Essays, Character and Others* (ed. J. Stephens, 1615), quoted by M. C. Bradbrook, *John Webster, Citizen and Dramatist* (1980), p. 168; cf. Phoebe Sheavyn, *The Literary Profession in the Elizabethan Age* (Manchester U.P., 1967), pp. 96–7.

30. Weimann, *Shakespeare und die Tradition des Volkstheaters* (Berlin, 1967), pp. 99–101.

31. *Mercurius Impartialis*, 12 December 1648, quoted by Nigel Smith, *Literature and Revolution in England, 1640–1660* (Yale U.P., 1994), p. 65.

32. Cf. P. Slack, *The Impact of Plague in Tudor and Stuart England* (1985), pp. 304–9.

on a moment's impulse. He tramps everywhere on foot. In Bunyan's *The Holy War* it is Incredulity, speaking for Diabolus, who told the captains of Mansoul that 'We take you to be some vagabond runagate crew, that . . . have gotten together in tumultuous manner and are ranging from place to place' looking for support. But in fact the vagabonds sided with Diabolus.[33]

Shakespeare throve to gentility, and actresses might become duchesses under the merrie monarch, but strolling players long remained of doubtful status. Goldsmith has a sad story of the ups and downs of one of them in Essay VI, published in 1765.[34] Crabbe in *The Borough* (1810) depicted players as

> A wandering, careless, wretched, merry race,
> Who cheerful looks assume . . .
> Slaves though ye be, your wandering freedom seems.

When the reckless Frederick Thompson

> first abused and then abjured his home,
> And when he chose a vagabond to be,
> He made his shame his glory – 'I'll be free . . .'
> Against a youth so vicious and undone
> All hearts were closed, and every door but one:
> The players received him.

Naturally he came to a bad end.[35]

Contemporary interest in vagabonds is demonstrated by the existence of a considerable Elizabethan pamphlet literature on the subject, of which the most important was *A Caveat for Common Cursitors* by the Kentish gentleman Thomas Harman (1566), which was plundered by many later writers. Harman, whose hostility appears to derive from real social anxiety, emphasizes the sexual promiscuity of vagabonds ('Not one amongst them is married'), and he (like Luther before him) is clearly prepared to believe any discreditable story about vagabonds and their swindling tricks. Interesting for our purposes are the many writings of Robert Greene on 'Cony-Catching', in which beggars are credited with a considerable degree of organization, forming a society within society, with its own conventions and rules, its own system of professional training. Beggars

33. Op. cit., ed. R. Sharrock and J. F. Forrest (Oxford U.P., 1980), pp. 48, 199.
34. Goldsmith, *Works* (1845), II, pp. 156–60.
35. G. Crabbe, *Poetical Works* (ed. A. J. and R. M. Carlyle, Oxford U.P., 1914), pp. 156–60.

have a private 'canting' language, in which they can converse with one another without being understood by outsiders. Ben Jonson's Puritans had a similar private 'canting' language: so had gypsies.[36] The total effect, almost certainly unintended, is to glamorize the fraternity of rogues, and to make it appear more of a fraternity than it really was.[37]

Thomas Hariot and others discussed the native Indians in America in a rather similar way – sympathetically at first, but the barbarous practices of 'savages' become more prominent as settlers intent on grabbing native lands came into closer contact with them. 'The noble savage' arrived on the scene much later, and in the mother country, not in the plantations. Literature on beggars likewise becomes increasingly hostile (and more fictitious) as the vagabonds' threat to propertied society was taken more seriously. There are no noble beggars in this literature.

But, just as vagabondage had been the way to freedom for fifteenth-century serfs, so sixteenth-century vagabonds were in some sense 'freer' than landless peasants. The popularity of the Robin Hood ballads in the late sixteenth and early seventeenth century may have struck a chord, restoring something of human dignity to society's outcasts. But they scared their betters, and were given an increasingly bad name. They were outside church and state, free from the church marriage ceremony being imposed on the population; they were in consequence regularly described as promiscuously licentious. Even Levellers called for laws to reclaim the 'thousands of men and women who are permitted to live in beggary and wickedness all their life long'.[38] This makes the relatively sympathetic picture given in Brome's play – of beggars as innocent victims rather than idle trouble-makers – all the more noteworthy. But by the time of *The Beggar's Opera* capitalism had established itself in England. Attempts at social reform during the revolutionary decades had been defeated. Brome's vagabond beggars had become the permanent poor.

The Robin Hood ballads were about a lost world of apparent freedom: hence their appeal to those trapped in the increasingly disciplined society of wage-labour for the lower orders. Robin Hood's world was in the remote past; vagabonds were an unpleasant reality, but they were also mysterious, alien, like the natives of North America.[39]

36. For Luther see p. 62 below.
37. Harman and Greene are conveniently reprinted, with others, in *Cony-Catchers and Bawdy-Baskets* (ed. G. Salgado, Penguin, 1972).
38. *The Large Petition* (June 1647), in Haller, *Tracts on Liberty*, III, pp. 401, 405.
39. See Chapter 12 below.

4. The Poor and Wage Labour

This is the best charity, so to relieve the poor as to keep them in labour. It benefits the giver to have the labour; it benefits the commonweal to suffer no drones, nor to nourish any in idleness; it benefits the poor themselves.

Richard Stock, *Commentary upon the Prophecy of Malachi* (1865), II, p. 56. First published 1641. Stock died in 1626

Without a class of persons willing to work for wages, how are the comforts and refinements of civilized life to be procured?

Lord Goderich, Colonial Secretary, 1831, quoted by E. P. Thompson, *Customs in Common* (1991), p. 167

I

Poverty was so old that it seemed natural in a fallen world. What was new in the sixteenth and seventeenth centuries was the sudden cleavage of the peasantry into rich and poor, the successful and lucky on the one hand, the unsuccessful on the other. In this newly mobile society 'the poor were no longer the destitute victims of misfortune or old age, but a substantial proportion of the population living in constant danger of destitution . . . In both town and country a permanent proletariat had emerged, collectively designated "the poor".[1] The wealth of the rich was seen to derive from the labour of the poor. 'The poor hate the rich', Deloney's Jack of Newbury told the King, 'because they will not set them on work; and the rich hate the poor because they seem burdenous'.[2] Under Elizabeth the permanent existence of the poor was institutionalized by the poor law: but the rich grudged the miserable doles necessary to prevent the landless unemployed from starving in bad years. 'Poverty *alone*' (said Robert Burton – my italics), 'makes men

---

1. K. Wrightson, *English Society, 1580–1680* (1982), pp. 141, 148, 154, 220.
2. Thomas Deloney, *Jack of Newbury* (1597), in *Shorter Novels, Elizabethan and Jacobean* (Everyman ed.), p. 50.

thieves, rebels, murderers'.[3] The very poor were demoralized, not least vagabonds.

A turning point came when those of the poor who had survived in their villages found their conditions little better than those of vagabonds. 'The fourth part of most of the inhabitants of England are miserable poor people, and (harvest-time excepted) without any subsistence'. 'The great cause of begging did proceed from the low wages for labour' rather than from the wanton idleness of the lower classes.[4] The permanent poor saw vagabonds sometimes as competitors, as when they tried to squat on other people's commons. But they could also see them as victims of forces beyond their control, not as shiftless idlers.

Not all of the poor could accept the teaching of men like Richard Baxter, that it was their duty to starve rather than steal, even to feed their families.[5] Baxter was a good man according to his lights, strongly opposed to slavery except as a just punishment for crimes; but for him idleness was the worst of sins. He thought that labour in the calling in which God had placed you was a religious duty, and he had no mercy for those who did not work – unless they were gentry. The years 1620–40 were exceptionally hard for the poor, and there was constant fear of popular revolt.[6] Since it did not happen, the alarm may be thought exaggerated. But there is evidence to support it. A pamphleteer in 1580 observed that 'the poorer sort of people . . . daily do harken [i.e. expect] when the world should amend with them. They are indifferent in what sort, so that their state were relieved; and so perhaps apt to assist rebellion, or to join with whomsoever dare invade this noble island . . . and so procure martyrdom with murder to many wealthy persons, for their wealth'.[7] In 1596 Oxfordshire rebels told themselves (wrongly) that 'the poor once rose in Spain and cut down the gentry, since when they have lived merrily'. The apparent imminence of a Spanish invasion might not

3. Burton, *Anatomy of Melancholy*, I, p. 354; cf. J. A. Sharpe, *Crime in 17th-century England* (Cambridge U.P., 1989), pp. 199–200; Tawney and Power, *Tudor Economic Documents*, III, pp. 452–3.

4. Anon., *Considerations Touching Trade* (1641), quoted by Lipson, *Economic History*, III, p. 484; ibid., pp. 153–5, quoting John Cary, *An Essay towards Regulating Trade* (1695), from edition of 1719.

5. Baxter, *Chapters from A Christian Directory* (ed. J. Tawney, 1925), pp. 26–35, 64–72. First published 1673.

6. P. Slack, *Poverty and Policy in Tudor England* (1988), pp. 49–52.

7. R. Hitchcock, *A Politic Plat* (1580), in Arber, *An English Garner* (1896–7), II, p. 159.

seem very terrible to such desperate men, who were 'ready to cut their masters' throats'.[8]

In the bad years of the 1620s capitalism had developed sufficiently for there to be mass unemployment in the clothing counties. In the early 1640s many expected economic crisis and unemployment to lead to lower-class revolts. Such fears helped to produce the splits in the ruling class which led to civil war.[9] Some foreign ambassadors and many Englishmen spoke openly of such dangers.[10] 'There be more poor than rich', said a weaver in 1624, predicting revolt by the poor. Five years later the well-to-do of Bocking feared that the unemployed would make it unsafe for them to live there.[11] When civil war came, the houses of rich papists were often plundered when being searched for arms; and the populace was apt sometimes to assume that all rich men were papists.

Lawrence Clarkson struck a class-war note when he warned 'the commonalty' against the nobility and gentry: 'Your slavery is their liberty, your poverty is their prosperity'.[12] After 1640 parishes were left much more independence in dealing with their poor. But the settlement laws established the right of the parish to expel *all* newcomers *likely to become* chargeable (my italics). The attempt to 'put the poor on work' was abandoned, and the workhouse took its place. The poor became increasingly a sub-class who alone were subject to the settlement laws.[13]

In the inflationary decades before 1640 the price of food rose faster than that of other commodities, prices of necessities more sharply than those of the food of the rich. Landlords met rising prices by racking rents, by enclosing or over-stocking commons, and by other devices from which the poor suffered. Enclosure by agreement between the richer occupants of a village increased their power over the community. 'Rich men had never more money, and covetousness had never less pity', said 'a countryman' in an anonymous pamphlet of 1608, attacking especially rack-renting

8. *C.S.P.D.*, 1595-7, pp. 316-17, 319, 343-5.

9. B. S. Manning, *The English People and the English Revolution*, Chapters 5-7.

10. W. R. Scott, *The Constitution and Finance of English, Scottish and Irish Joint-Stock Companies* (1910-12), I, p. 167; Lipson, *Economic History*, III, pp. 305-6; cf. Robert Weimann, *Shakespeare und die Tradition des Volkstheaters* (Berlin, 1967), pp. 65-8, 76, 110-11, 257-8.

11. I take these two examples from Sharpe, *Crime*, p. 208.

12. Clarkson, *A General Charge or Impeachment of High Treason* (1647).

13. Lipson, *Economic History*, II, p. cxlvii, III, pp. 426-7, 454-5. For examples see P. Styles, *Studies in 17th-century West Midland History* (Kineton, 1978), pp. 176-7, 186, 190, 204.

landlords.[14] In the 1660s the victims of plague, Clarendon tells us, were mostly the poor (and sectaries, almost all from the lower classes).[15]

The poor were no longer the casual victims of unpredictable crises and accidents but were a permanent class with no hope of escape from their poverty. The Biblical 'the poor always ye have with you' appeared to accept the inevitability of their fate, just as the poor law recognized the existence of mass poverty. Tyndale – not an unsympathetic man – had had no illusions about the state of the poor. They must propitiate their landlords in every possible way, anticipating their unreasonable demands. 'Yea, poll thyself and' prevent other; and give the bailiff or like officer now a capon, now a pig, now a goose, and so to thy landlord likewise', and then 'they shall be thy shield and defend thee, though they be tyrants and care not for God, that no man else shall dare· poll thee'.[16] (Note in passing Tyndale's assumption that in the early sixteenth century the poorest man kept some livestock on the waste.)

The class of permanent poor established itself whilst some fortunate peasants were thriving to gentility. Education was vital to crossing the barrier. The sixteenth century had experienced what has been called an educational revolution. But the poor could not afford to lose the labour of their children, and so could not afford to send them to school. Children of the gentry usurped free places in schools originally designed for children of the poor. The latter had no access to the educational ladder up which some of the children of their betters were busily scrambling. It was almost impossible for a pauper to escape from the lowly status into which he was born. As the advocate of women's education, Bathsua Makin, put it in 1673: 'Women are of two sorts: the rich, of good natural parts; the poor, of low parts'.[17] The mobile society had a static base.

Plague, when it came, hit the poorest classes hardest, especially in the overcrowded and insanitary towns. It 'exaggerated an established feature of metropolitan life'. 'No man could suspect a lady to die of the plague',

14. [Anon.], *The Great Frost* (1608), in *An English Garner* (ed. E. Arber, 1877), p. 88; M. Campbell, in *The English Yeoman*, pp. 374–6, quotes Fuller's and John Taylor's contrasting versions of yeomen as industrious patriots or greedy exploiters trying to do down the poor.
15. Clarendon, *Life* (1759), III, p. 420; for the social effects of the revolutionary period as seen by a royalist, see ibid., II, pp. 39–41.
16. William Tyndale, *Exposition of Chaps v, vi and vii of St Matthew's Gospel*, in *Expositions and Notes on Sundry Portions of the Holy Scriptures* (Parker Soc., 1849), p. 59.
17. Makin, *An Essay to Revive the Ancient Education of Gentlewomen* (1673), p. 22.

it was remarked in 1631.[18] William Gouge thought God intended the chief victims of plague to be 'the poorer and meaner sort, . . . because they are not of such use . . . and may better be spared' – an interesting example of God's care for humanity. Robert Harris agreed: some said the plague was a blessing, since it killed off 'the baser and poorer sort, such whose lives were burdensome, whose deaths were beneficial' to their society.[19]

Religion was a great consolation to those who had property. It was wrong to try to abolish poverty, reflected Sir Thomas Browne, for then there could be no charity.[20] Baxter's advice to the poor, starve rather than steal, was perhaps less consoling to them. Most theologians agreed that the abolition of poverty was impossible: charity was the only Christian answer. Usurers use their ill-gotten gains to build alms-houses, suggested Joseph Hall ironically. Puritans thought that if beggars could be subjected to congregational discipline they would disappear: a view which Bacon regarded as very plausible.[21] But it was not until 1644 that Parliament ordered 'every rogue and vagabond' to attend church worship each Sunday.

The author of *The Whole Duty of Man* wrote of charity as a form of social insurance, 'a kind of rent charge' which God had laid on landlords' estates. We should choose the fittest objects of charity carefully, ignoring the slothful and the lewd: loans might be better than gifts.[22]

Even Bunyan, always staunchly on the side of the poor, thought that idleness was the enemy of godliness. Those 'who have no need to work for meat or cloth / Should work for them that want', to feed and clothe them. Nevertheless, he described an importunate beggar as resembling 'them that pray / To God for mercy, and will take no Nay'.[23] *The Pilgrim's*

18. Slack, *The Impact of Plague in Tudor and Stuart England* (1985), Chapters 5–7.
19. Gouge, *Gods Three Arrows* (1625), p. 25; Harris, *Hezekiah's Recovery* (1626), p. 42, both quoted by Slack, op. cit., pp. 239–40.
20. Browne, *Works* (ed. S. Wilkin, 1852), II, p. 449.
21. Hall, *Characters of Virtues and Vices* (1608), in *Character Writings of the Seventeenth Century* (ed. H. Morley, 1891), p. 131; J. Spedding, *Letters and Life of Bacon* (1861), I, p. 100.
22. Op. cit., (1704), I, pp. 138–42; II, p. 72; cf. Stock, quoted as epigraph to this chapter. There is an interesting discussion of the two types of charity, indiscriminate and selective, between Springlove and Randal in Brome's *A Jovial Crew* (Act I, scene i).
23. Bunyan, 'A Discourse of the Building . . . of the House of God' (1688), in *Miscellaneous Works*, VI, *Poems* (ed. G. Midgley, Oxford U.P., 1980), pp. 305–6, 242; cf. p. 290.

Progress is the story of a man in rags, a poor itinerant, but 'Christ makes princes of beggars'.[24] 'The poor, because they are poor, are not capable of sinning against God as the rich man does', for a poor man 'can more clearly see himself preserved by the providence of God than the rich, for he trusteth in the abundance of his riches'.[25] In *The Holy War* the good characters are normally 'mean men': aristocrats supported Diabolus.

Beggars were associated with popery, with the indiscriminate charity of the monasteries and with the medieval mendicant orders. Wenceslaus Linck's *On Work and Begging: How one should deal with Laziness and Make everyone Work* was published in 1523. 'There appears to have been an affinity between the egalitarian strains in protestant theology and the social mobility of both rising urban élites and impoverished working people, both of whom had something to gain from change and joined the Reformation in disproportionate numbers'.[26]

Poverty was no longer regarded as a holy state. Luther's Preface to *The Book of Vagabonds and Beggars* (1525) deals almost exclusively with the fraud and knavery of beggars (ed. D. B. Thorn, translated by J. C. Hotten, 1932, p. 63). Similar points were made in England in Elizabeth's reign by John Awdeley, Thomas Harman and others.[27] Labour, the curse of fallen man, has become a religious duty.[28] George Wither denounced people who 'pity those who justly punished be' under the vagabond laws, 'as if their rigour injured the poor'.[29] Some charitable trusts stipulated that vagrants and idlers should receive nothing from them.[30] By 1711 *The Spectator*'s Sir Andrew Freeport could refer to alms given to the poor simply as 'the wages of idleness'.[31]

Samuel Butler suggested with provocative irony that society was maintained at the expense of the poor:

24. Bunyan, *The Pilgrim's Progress* (ed. J. B. Wharey and R. Sharrock, Oxford U.P., 1975), pp. 52–3; cf. pp. 199–200, 231, 237–8.
25. Bunyan, *The Life and Death of Mr Badman* (ed. J. Forrest and R. Sharrock, Oxford U.P., 1986), p. 94. Cf. p. 50 above.
26. Steven Ozment, *Protestants: the Birth of a Revolution* (1993), pp. 73, 230; cf. p. 54.
27. Reprinted in *Cony-Catchers and Bawdy Baskets* (ed. G. Salgado, 1972). Cf. p. 55 above.
28. See my *Puritanism and Revolution*, pp. 215–16.
29. Wither, *Juvenilia: Poems* (Spenser Soc., 1871), I, p. 159.
30. H. Jenkins, *Edward Benlowes (1612–1676)*, p. 4. Benlowes's friend, Clement Paman, however, wrote a treatise on 'the devout soul' who was charitable 'even to the loose and impious' (ibid., p. 159).
31. *The Spectator* (Everyman ed.), II, pp. 236–9. A year later *The Spectator* took a more sympathetic view (ibid., III, pp. 125–6).

> How various and innumerable
> Are those who live upon the rabble!
> 'Tis they maintain the Church and State,
> Employ the priest and magistrate;
> Bear all the charge of government,
> And pay the public fines and rent;
> Defray all taxes and excises,
> And impositions of all prices;
> Bear all th'expense of peace and war,
> And pay the pulpit and the bar . . .
> Support all schismatics and sects,
> And pay them for tormenting texts . . .
> All statesmen, cutpurses and padders,
> And pay for all their ropes and ladders.

. . . and many more.[32] Swift on the other hand suggested that 'the bulk of farmers, cottagers and labourers, with their wives and children, . . . are beggars in effect'.[33]

Tithes were due on wages, which did not endear the established church to poverty-stricken labourers. Levellers and other radicals won support, among other reasons, for their demand that tithes be abolished: so did Quakers. Blyth remarked caustically that 'the minister hath seemed to be the opposer' of enclosure, since the depopulation which enclosure entailed would decimate his income.[34]

The Rev. George Crabbe thought that in giving charity to the poor the rich were demonstrating rational self-interest.[35] The profane Burns, perhaps more realistically, wrote of the poor

> The fear o'hell's a hangman's whip
> To haud the wretch in order.[36]

II

The concomitant of the capitalist freedom established from the middle of the seventeenth century was enforcement of the discipline of wage labour.

32. Butler, *Poetical Works* (ed. G. Gilfillan, Edinburgh, 1854), II, pp. 241–2.
33. Swift, *A Modest Proposal for Preventing the Children of Poor People from being a burden to their Parents or Country* (1729).
34. W. Blyth, *The English Improver Improved* (1652), pp. 77–8.
35. Crabbe, *Poetical Works*, p. 172.
36. Burns, *Poems and Songs* (Everyman ed.), p. 130.

Traditionally J.P.s had fixed wage rates: since they themselves came from
the employing class this helped to keep wages down. But some employers
evaded the regulations by giving bonuses and perquisites to bribe their
employees.[37] In setting wage rates J.P.s tended to assume that they were
not the employee's sole resource: it was taken for granted that they also
enjoyed rights of commonage. When these were taken away by enclosure,
it was still assumed that all members of the family would contribute to
the household. Poor relief might be necessary in addition: full-time wage-
earners were assumed to be paupers. As David Ogg put it, 'Neither
contemporary nor modern economists can explain how they lived'.[38]
When the expectation that employers should keep employees at work in
time of depression lapsed from about the mid-seventeenth century there
was no safeguard against dismissal: the poor law had to relieve those
totally unemployed. In 1690 the Commissioners for Foreign Trade and
Plantations struck a modern note by arguing that labour must be cheap in
order to keep foreign markets. There were frequent complaints in the
House of Commons of the 'dearness of labour'. There was pressure to
work long hours, and for child labour to make up for lost common-field
rights or industrial perquisites.

Children had to be put to work so early in life that there was no
possibility of sending them to school.[39] Locke's charitable suggestion that
all children over the age of three should attend 'working schools' so that
they should be 'from infancy . . . inured to work' was not intended as a
soft option. Bread and 'in cold weather, if it be thought needful, a little
warm water gruel' should be given to the children; if money was given to
parents they would only waste it on drink.[40]

By the end of the century life-long wage-labourers were probably a
majority of the population. Mandeville summed up the new attitudes.
'*We* have hardly poor enough to do what is necessary to make *us* subsist'.
(The distinction between 'us' and 'the poor' who work for 'us' is revealing.) Mandeville drew the necessary conclusion. 'It would be easier, where
property was well secured, to live without money than without poor; for

37. Eleanor Trotter, *Seventeenth-century life in the country parish* (Cambridge U.P.,
1919), pp. 140, 146–7. On labour discipline see especially E. P. Thompson, 'Time,
Work-Discipline and Industrial Capitalism', in *Customs in Common* (1991).
38. Ogg, *England in the Reign of Charles II* (Oxford U.P., 1934), I, p. 85.
39. Joan Simon, *Education and Society in Tudor England* (Cambridge U.P., 1966),
pp. 195, 212.
40. H. R. Fox Bourne, *Life of John Locke* (1876), II, pp. 378–84.

who would do the work?' 'The poor . . . ought to be kept from starving', but 'should receive nothing worth saving'. 'It is the interest of all rich nations that the greatest part of the poor should never be idle, and yet continuously spend what they get'. Consequently, 'to make the society happy and people easy under the meanest circumstances, it is requisite that great numbers of them should be ignorant as well as poor'. 'People of the meanest rank' should not be educated; otherwise they might 'know too much to be serviceable to us'. Educating some of the poor, if it stops them labouring, 'may prove to be cruelty to others'.[41] Arthur Young was to put it more succinctly later: 'Everyone but an idiot knows that the lower class must be kept poor or they will never be industrious'.[42]

Pamphleteers shared the disagreeable habit of our present government in blaming begging on to the wicked idleness of the unemployed – confusing symptoms with causes. When men were offered what employers thought a reasonable wage, the reply was 'they cannot live on it, and as good play . . . as work for another.'[43] Defoe said the same in *Giving Alms no Charity* (1704): there is a shortage of labour, but the poor prefer idleness so long as their money lasts.[44] From Fynes Moryson's *Itinerary* of 1617 to Sorbière's *Voyage to England* (1709), the story was the same, though Sorbière blamed tobacco rather than ale-houses, the usual target.[45] Silvanus Taylor thought that ale-houses and commons were 'the two great nurseries of idleness and begging in the nation'. Ale-houses were 'fit for nothing but to uphold drunkenness, idleness, roguery, whoredom, and to increase begging'. Closing ale-houses would reduce the number of beggars.[46] Ale-houses were seen as the centre of opposition to ruling oligarchies of villages, where religious and political discontents could mutter sedition.[47]

41. Mandeville, *The Fable of the Bees* (3rd ed., 1724), I, pp. 212, 385–6, 356; II, pp. 424–6, I, 328–30. Italics mine. Cf. p. 171 below.

42. Sir John Clapham, *A Concise Economic History of Modern Britain* (Cambridge U.P., 1951), pp. 212–13; C. B. Macpherson, *The Political Theory of Possessive Individualism* (Oxford U.P., 1962), Chapter 4.

43. S.[ilvanus] T.[aylor], *Common-Good*, p. 37, quoted on p. 40 above.

44. Op. cit., in *English Economic History: Select Documents* (ed. A. E. Bland, P. A. Brown and R. H. Tawney, 1914), pp. 649–50.

45. Moryson, op. cit., p. 147; Samuel de Sorbière, op. cit., p. 537, both quoted in H. T. Buckle, *Miscellaneous and Posthumous Works* (1872), III, pp. 575, 537.

46. T.[aylor], op. cit., pp. 51, 56.

47. P. Clark, *The English Ale-house: a social history, 1200–1830* (1983), Chapters 7 and 8.

Acceptance of wage labour was the last resort open to those who had lost their land, but many regarded it as little better than slavery. There was no protection against abuses like payment of wages in kind, or in arrears. In James I's reign workers in Sir Arthur Ingram's Yorkshire alum works often had to wait nine months for payment.[48] In the Stannaries of Cornwall free miners fought long and hard in the sixteenth and early seventeenth centuries to avoid the wage system: 'they have no profit of their time if they be hired men'.[49]

There were many complaints that the introduction of a new industry into an area would bring 'a number of lewd persons, the scum and dregs of many [counties] from whence they have been driven'.[50] Industry creates poverty, for 'in those parts of [Suffolk] where the clothiers do dwell or have dwelt, there are found the greatest number of the poor'.[51] Though industry 'sets the poor on work where it finds them, yet it draws still more to the place; and their masters allow wages so mean that they are only preserved from starving whilst they can work; when age, sickness or death comes, themselves, their wives or their children are most commonly left upon the parish; which is the reason why those towns (as in the Weald of Kent) where the clothing is departed have fewer poor than they had before'.[52]

Nef suggested that the falling standard of living of wage-labourers led to differences in physical appearance – greater incidence of rickets among children, premature loss of teeth in adults. Coal miners were set apart by their dirtiness.[53] Immigrant squatters and cottagers often lived outside the traditional village community, far from church or chapel. (Anyway, they had no suitable clothes for going to church.) The Weald and the Forest of Dean were traditional areas of religious radicalism.[54] Propagandists for colonization argued that 'swarms of our

48. A. F. Upton, *Sir Arthur Ingram* (Oxford U.P., 1961), pp. 112, 128–32.
49. G. R. Lewis, *The Stannaries: A Study of the English Tin Mines* (Harvard U.P., 1924), pp. 211, 198.
50. J. U. Nef, *War and Human Progress* (1950), p. 231, quoting tenants of Broseley, Shropshire, in 1606.
51. Robert Reyce, *The Breviary of Suffolk* (ed. Lord F. Hervey, 1902), p. 57.
52. [Anon.], *Reasons for a Limited Experiment of Wooll*, quoted by Alice Clark, *Working Life of Women in the Seventeenth Century* (1919), p. 149.
53. Nef, op. cit.,ıp. 229.
54. Thirsk, *Agrarian History of England and Wales, 1500–1640*, pp. 112, 411–12, 463; Wallace Notestein, *The English People on the Eve of Colonization* (New York, 1954), p. 85.

rank multitude' starving in the streets of London might be got rid of by emigration.[55]

Wage labourers, like vagabonds, had no political rights. Sir Thomas Smith in 1565 declared that the 'commonwealth consisteth only of free-men'. 'Day labourers' and others with no free land 'have no voice nor authority in our commonwealth, and no account is made of them but only to be ruled'. Those who are 'hired for wages . . . be called servants'.[56] In 1624 an M.P. attributed to Magna Carta, cap. 30, the statement that 'he that hath no property in his goods is not free'.[57] Harrington denied citizenship to servants, a class outside the commonwealth.[58] Wage-labourers and paupers had lost their birthright by becoming economically dependent on others.

In 1640 it was 'the sense of the House' of Commons that 'no beggar or man that received relief or is not subject to scot and lot is capable of giving his voice in election of burgesses'. This appears to have been normal practice in Parliamentary boroughs.[59] In parish elections those who did not pay poor and church rates had no vote. In 1659, when such matters were under discussion, Richard Baxter observed that, since 'in most parts the major vote of the vulgar' is 'ruled by money and therefore by their landlords', those whose poverty is 'so great as to make them the servants of others and deprive them of ingenuous freedom' should have no right to vote.[60]

Both Henry Parker and the Leveller Richard Overton thought that loss of property in one's self – i.e. becoming a wage-labourer – was 'a

---

55. W. Strachey, *For the Colony of Virginea Britannia* (1612), quoted by E. G. R. Taylor, *Late Tudor and Early Stuart Geography* (1934), p. 163; P. Copland, *Virginia's God be Thanked* (1622), quoted by Perry Miller, *Errand into the Wilderness* (Harvard U.P., 1956), p. 110.

56. Smith, *De Republica Anglorum, A Discourse of the Commonwealth of England* (ed. L. Alston, Cambridge U.P., 1906), pp. 20–22, 46, 138. For 'freemen' see Chapter 21 below.

57. *Commons Journals*, I, p. 759.

58. C. B. Macpherson, *The Political Theory of Possessive Individualism: Hobbes to Locke* (Oxford U.P., 1962), pp. 122–3, 140–41, 182–3; Harrington, *Works* (1771), pp. 77, 409.

59. M. R. Frear, 'The Election at Great Marlow', in *Journal of Modern History*, XIV (1942), p. 435; M. F. Keeler, *The Long Parliament: A Study of its Members* (American Philosophical Soc., Philadelphia, 1954), pp. 33, 35; D. Hirst, *'The Representative of the People'? Voters and Voting in England under the Early Stuarts* (Cambridge U.P., 1975), Chapter 5; H. Prideaux, *Directions to Churchwardens* (Norwich, 1701), p. 51.

60. Baxter, *A Holy Commonwealth*, pp. 243, 218–19.

condition of servility'.[61] Levellers accepted the exclusion of paupers and
servants from the franchise because of their unfreedom.[62] On this the
appropriate comment is that of a leader of the Oxfordshire rebels of 1596:
'servants were so held in and kept like dogs that they would be ready to
cut their masters' throats . . . We shall have a merrier world shortly'.[63]
'Will you be slaves and beggars still when you may be free men?' the
Diggers asked in 1650.[64]

In 1647 it was argued that in the Army, which claimed to be representative of the people, very many were 'servants and prentices not yet
free' and so incapable of representing anybody.[65] In Scotland Patrick
Gordon distinguished between 'a freeborn gentleman and a servile or
base-minded slave'.[66] The poet Robert Heath contrasted 'freeborn birth'
with 'peasant blood':[67] cf. John Day: 'Verses though freemen born are
bought and sold Like slaves'.[68] When in 1652 Virginia abandoned resistance to the Commonwealth government, by the articles of surrender 'all
the inhabitants' were guaranteed 'such freedoms and priviledges as belong
to the freeborn People of England'[69] – perhaps a deliberately ambiguous
phrase.

Gerrard Winstanley, who described himself as a 'servant', argued that
'if the common people have no more freedom in England but only to live
among their elder brothers and work for them for hire, what freedom
then have they in England more than we can have in Turkey or France?'[70]
The relations between employer and wage-labourer, wrote Dean Tucker
in George II's reign, 'approach much nearer to that of a planter and slave
in our American colonies than might be expected in such a country as

61. Parker, *Observations upon some of his Majesties late Answers and Expresses* (1642),
in Haller, *Tracts on Liberty*, II, p. 186; Overton, *An Arrow against all Tyrants* (1646),
pp. 3–4.
62. Macpherson, op.cit., Chapter 4 *passim*.
63. *C.S.P.D.*, 1595–97, pp. 317, 343–5.
64. Winstanley, *Works*, p. 408.
65. [Anon.], *The Case of the Army Soberly Discussed*, p. 6.
66. Gordon, *A Short Abridgment of Britanes Distemper* (Spalding Club, Edinburgh,
1844), pp. 76, 78.
67. Heath, 'To one blaming my high-minded Love', in *Clarastella* (1650), p. 13. For
'freeborn' see my *Change and Continuity in 17th-Century England* (1991), pp. 226–31
passim, and pp. 243–5 below.
68. Day, *Works* (ed. R. Jeffs 1963), p. 568.
69. *Mercurius Politicus*, 20–27 May 1652, No. 103, p. 1616; in *Newsbooks* (ed.
P. Thomas, 1971), V, p. 44.
70. Winstanley, op. cit., p. 288.

England'.[71] An exchange in one of Southerne's plays, *Sir Anthony Love* (1690), makes the point:

SIR ANTHONY. – We are Englishmen, and never think of the poor out of our own parish.
VALENTINE. – Nor there neither, but according to law, and when we cannot help it.
ILFORD. – Charity is a free-will offering, and we part with nothing we can keep, I assure you.[72]

I have tried to illustrate the fact that hatred of wage labour and the discipline which accompanied it was widespread.[73] The ultimate answer to labour discipline freely imposed by employers was the creation of trade unions to establish class solidarity and thus liberty against the iron laws of capitalist society. But industrial organization was a novel idea, and took a long time to realize. The right of freeborn Englishmen to combine against the laws of the free market which set man against man is a new (and different) example of the theme of this book. Employers had been trying to overcome the 'idleness' of the poor since at least the fourteenth century. Defoe argued in 1704 'there is in England more labour than hands to perform it'. No one need be without employment. 'It is a regulation of the poor that is wanted ... not a setting them to work.' The problem arises from idleness and sloth: 'English labouring people eat and drink, but especially the latter, three times as much in value as any ... foreigners'. The labourer 'will tell you honourably, he will drink as long as it [his money] lasts, and then go to work for more'.[74] How could England become the workshop of the world without labour discipline? How could the landless poor be made to accept wage labour as a permanent system?

Poor relief backed up by religious pressure had been one way of imposing labour discipline. In Chelmsford in 1622 poor relief was to be given only to those who had satisfied the pastor in the fundamentals of Christianity.[75] Bolingbroke in 1717 pointed out 'the prodigious inequality between the condition of the moneyed men and the rest of the nation'.[76]

71. Josiah Tucker, *Instructions for Travellers* (1757), p. 25.
72. Thomas Southerne, *Works* (ed. R. Jordan and H. Love, Oxford U.P., 1988), I, p. 181.
73. See 'Pottage for freeborn Englishmen: Attitudes to wage labour', in *Change and Continuity in 17th-century England* (Yale U.P., 1991).
74. Defoe, *Giving Alms no Charity*.
75. Hunt, *The Puritan Moment*, p. 142.
76. Bolingbroke, *Letters to Sir William Windebanke and Mr. Pope* (1894), p. 23.

Tawney summed up the difference between having wage labour thrust
upon one and being able to choose between that and working on the land
as a squatter. 'The former is slavery: the latter is freedom'.[77] By George
III's reign Horace Walpole had come to see the rationality of trade union
organization.[78] The expansion of industry and trade necessitated regular
wages as against perquisites; the former ensured regular employment as
against working only when cash was needed.

   Trade unions gave discipline to the undisciplined, the free. But there
had been solidarity among servants and runaways (and pirates) long before
trade unions. When they had developed sufficiently to permit working-
class bargaining, that marked *acceptance* of the permanence of wage labour,
abandonment of liberty to work for wages only when workers chose:
regular wages had become necessary to enhance purchasing power in the
world of the competitive market.[79] To that extent the poor accepted the
loss of a sort of freedom. Individual contracting out was seen to be no
longer a viable alternative. Trade union discipline was an answer to the
discipline of wage labour.

77. Ed. J. M. Winter, *R. H. Tawney's Commonplace Book* (Cambridge U.P., 1972),
p. 75.
78. Ed. E. F. Carritt, *A Calendar of British Taste: From 1600 to 1800* (n.d.), pp. 303,
325: cf. Holstun, *A Rational Millennium*, p. 301.
79. Joyce Appleby, *Liberalism and Republicanism in the Historical Imagination* (Harvard
U.P., 1992), pp. 109, 176.

5. Robin Hood

In ancient times, no matter where,
   A nation lived of wise men . . .
Who made good laws to guard a hare,
   A partridge or a pheasant;
But left the poor to nature's cares –
   Say was not this right pleasant? . . .

Who to this country, would not run,
   Where only freedom's got at?
Where birds escape the fatal gun,
   And men alone are shot at?

Anon., *London Magazine*, April 1776, in R. H. Lonsdale, *New Oxford Book of 18th-century Verse*, p. 643

In my first chapter I suggested that the background to *A Jovial Crew* is the proliferation of roving bands of vagabonds and beggars in the two generations before 1640. The same two generations saw wide popularity for ballads about Robin Hood and his outlaws, which also stand behind *A Jovial Crew*. Historians have worked hard to locate Robin Hood in a single historical period, or in a single region, but have found it impossible to agree in their conclusions. The first three chronicles to mention Robin Hood were Scottish.[1] There are so many variant stories of Robin Hood's origins even before 1500, and the places involved are spread so widely, from Aberdeen to Exeter, that the simplest explanation is that the name was applied to, or adopted by, a series of outlaws or rebels. John Major spoke in 1521 of Robin Hood as 'celebrated in songs throughout Britain'. From about the same date onwards sayings about him were quoted in legal cases. His popularity is also demonstrated by the number of proverbs about him.

No Robin Hood ballads were printed in the sixteenth century, so this popularity must have been entirely oral. From the early seventeenth

---

1. Stephen Knight, *Robin Hood: A Complete Study of the English Outlaw* (Oxford, 1994), p. 33.

century 'tales of Robin Hood' came to be regarded as plebeian, perhaps in reaction to the attempt of Munday and others to make him a peer.[2] Ten ballads on Robin Hood were registered in 1656–7[3] – at a time when radicals were looking backwards for historical predecessors. *Robin Hood's Garland* (1656) was a popular chapbook, reprinted in 1663 and many times later.[4] It was one of the first books that John Clare read.[5]

For our purposes it does not matter whether Robin Hood ever existed, and if so whether he lived in the thirteenth or fourteenth century. What concerns us is what people believed in the sixteenth and seventeenth centuries. Richard Tardif suggested that the early ballads appear to be linked with small towns, and may have appealed to evicted peasants who had migrated in search of employment: Susan Brigden tells us of outlaws who sought shelter and sanctuary in London.[6] The carefree life of outlaws in the forests, so unlike the starved and hunted existence of real outlaws, may represent the ideal kind of life that the audiences of the ballads would have liked to live. Tardif points out that the word 'yeoman' can mean journeyman tradesman as well as a relatively prosperous peasant, and suggests that the ballads may have helped to create a cultural and class consciousness for discontented former peasants compelled to work for wages in an urban money economy – if they were lucky. Knight refers to the early ballads' emphasis on 'the value of solidarity' and 'contempt for financial concerns'. 'The Jolly Pinder' Knight sees as 'a matter of straightforward seduction of a [town] legal official into the band' of outlaws. In 'Robin Hood and Alan-a-Dale' the outlaws reject the authority of the church, preventing a lady being forcibly married to an old knight whom she disliked: she 'shall choose her own dear'. The forest was always seen as an area of imagined freedom adjacent to a town. After fighting Robin, the Pinder of Wakefield agrees to join the outlaws as soon as he receives sums due from his master. Knight thinks this 'a distinctly subversive

2. Ritson, *Robin Hood: A Collection of Poems, Songs and Ballads* (1884), pp. 70–77; R. B. Dobson and J. Taylor, *Rhymes of Robin Hood: An Introduction to the English Outlaw* (1976), p. 46.

3. H. E. Rollins, *Cavalier and Puritan, Ballads and Broadsides Illustrating the Period of the Great Rebellion* (1923), p. 70.

4. Ritson, op. cit., p. 81; Dobson and Taylor, op. cit., p. 51.

5. Ed. J. W. and A. Tibble, *Prose of John Clare* (1951), p. 14. Cf. Chapter 26 below.

6. Susan Brigden, *London and the Reformation* (Oxford U.P., 1991), p. 140; Knight, op. cit., pp. 51, 55–60.

response to town rule', illustrating an 'overarching sense of the repressive character of town rules'[7].

There were other ballads and plays at about this time dealing with 'banished men', who through no fault of their own had been outlawed – e.g. the hero of 'The Nut-Brown Maid' – 'I must to the greenwood go ... I am a banished man'. In *As You Like It* sylvan liberty is romanticized: the banished Duke lives in 'the forest of Ardenne, and a many merry men with him; and there they live like the old Robin Hood of England. They say many gentlemen flock to him [the Duke] every day, and fleet the time carelessly, as they did in the golden world' (Act I, scene i). Rosalind and Celia went 'in content' into the forest, 'to liberty, and not to banishment' (Act I, scene iii). Robin Hood, William Warner tells us, often asked his merrie men 'What juster life than ours?'[8] Massinger's *The Guardian* (licensed 1633) paints a grimmer picture of the life of Italian outlaws, but stresses that they steal only from four categories of persons – those who grind the faces of the poor by hoarding grain, enclosers of commons, builders of iron mills who grub up forests for fuel, and cheating shop-keepers and vintners – characters more familiar perhaps in England than in Italy. Among those to be spared are poor scholars, soldiers, rent-racked farmers, jobless labourers, carriers and above all women. Suckling's *The Goblins* (1638) has a similar band of outlaws, who are compared with courtiers. On a proposal to turn beggar the comment was 'That's the same thing at court; begging is but a kind of robbing the exchequer'.[9]

The intelligentsia had long affected to despise the vogue of 'tales of Robin Hood'. In the mid-fourteenth century John Fordun, the Scottish historian, denounced 'the foolish vulgar' who enjoy plays and ballads about Robin Hood. In Langland's *Piers Plowman* Sloth knows 'rhymes of Robin Hood', and not much else. Walter Bower in the 1440s spoke of the famous murderer Robin Hood, and of Little John, 'with their accomplices from among the dispossessed and banished'. William Tyndale

7. Richard Tardif, 'The "mistery" of Robin Hood: A New Social Context for the Texts', in *Words and Worlds: Studies in the Social Role of Verbal Culture* (ed. S. Knight and S. N. Mukherjee, Sydney Association for Studies in Society and Culture, 1983); Knight, op. cit., pp. 28–9, 63–5, 68, 120–1.

8. Warner, *Albions England* (1602), p. 132; cf. A. Munday, 'A Song of Robin Hood to his Huntsmen', in *The Civic Garland* (ed. F. W. Fairholt, Percy Soc., 1845), pp. 15–16.

9. Suckling, *Poems, Plays and other Remains* (ed. W. C. Hazlitt, 1892), II, p. 40.

spoke slightingly of 'a tale of Robin Hood'.[10] So did another protestant martyr Hugh Latimer, as well as the Roman Catholic Bishop Stephen Gardiner. They did not agree on many matters, but they may all have disliked a secular rival for popularity. The Puritan Nicholas Bownde, who preached to Oliver Cromwell in his youth, complained that Robin Hood was better known than the Bible.[11] By 1619 Henry Hutton wrote of the production of a hack writer:

> 'Twas made of Robin Hood and Little John,
> 'Twill be discovered e'er 't be long
> Under the bottom of a pipkin pie.[12]

These comments may refer to the popularity of the May games with which Robin Hood was associated rather than to the ballads, which derive from a separate tradition. But the games also offered open defiance to authority, an alternative to the rule of gentry, freemen of boroughs, and the hierarchy of the church. The ballads incorporated elements from the May games featuring Robin Hood and Maid Marian.[13] It is significant that the games were suppressed under Queen Mary no less than under protestant rulers.

Ballads give us the history which commoners knew, history from the commoners' point of view. Robin Hood incorporates features previously attributed to King Arthur of popular memory.[14] He recalls Davydd ap Siancyn, a Welsh Lancastrian captain, who clothed his outlawed followers in green during the civil wars of the mid-fifteenth century. He was greeted by a Welsh poet as a hero defying his enemies, generous to the poor and weak, 'an agent for moral good who righted society's wrongs'.[15]

---

10. Dobson and Taylor, op. cit., pp. 1, 5; Tyndale, *The Obedience of a Christian Man* (1528), in *Doctrinal Treatises*, pp. 161, 220, 306, 328; *Prologue to the Book of Genesis* (1530), ibid., p. 400; *Prologue to Jonas* (c. 1531), ibid., p. 450.

11. Ritson, op. cit., pp. 73, 90; M. M. Knappen, *Tudor Puritanism: A Chapter in the History of Idealism* (Chicago U.P., 1934), p. 68; Bownde, *Sabbatum Veteris et Novi Testamenti* (2nd ed., 1606), quoted by K. V. Thomas, *Religion and the Decline of Magic* (1971), p. 164.

12. Hutton, Dunelmensis, *Follies Anatomie: or Satyres & Satiricall Epigrames* (Percy Soc., 1840), p. 20.

13. D. Wiles, *The Early Plays of Robin Hood* (Cambridge, 1983), pp. 20, 56–7; Ritson, op. cit., pp. 90, 104–6.

14. Helgerson, *Forms of Nationhood*, pp. 231, 237–8.

15. Glanmor Williams, *Renewal and Reform in Wales, c.1415–1642* (Oxford U.P., 1993), pp. 48–9.

The outlaws' Lincoln green was the Levellers' colour in the 1640s, though this is commonly attributed to craftsmen's green aprons. Gay tells us that peasants still sang about Robin Hood in the early eighteenth century.[16] Some say that Robin Hood disappears from English literature between the seventeenth century and *Ivanhoe*, and there were indeed no plays about him between 1640 and the eighteenth century.[17] But in the late eighteenth and nineteenth centuries Robin Hood appealed especially to radicals. Ritson, his best editor, was known as a free-thinker and Jacobin.

There are controversies about the type of audience to which the Robin Hood ballads appealed. They address themselves sometimes to gentlemen, sometimes to yeomen:

> 'Lyth and listen, gentlemen,
>   That be of high-born blood.'

> 'Kind gentlemen.'

> 'All gentlemen and yeomen good.'

> 'Both gentlemen and yeomen bold.'[18]

Maurice Keen has pointed out that the fourteenth-century long-bow is a plebeian weapon, not that of a gentleman.[19] But gentlemen might well appreciate skill in archery, especially after the triumph of the long bow in the French wars.

In the early ballads Robin himself is always described as a yeoman. Perhaps he was an appropriate hero for newly-aspirant social groups after the Black Death? But, as we shall see,[20] many gentlemen also resented the forest laws and the attempt to monopolize hunting. They would appreciate infringing *the sheriff's* laws. Leadership in arms was their privilege,

---

16. Gay, *Poems*, p. 54.
17. W. F. Simeone, 'The Robin Hood of *Ivanhoe*', *Journal of American Folklore*, p. 74, Supplement 4, 1961. For the audience for Robin Hood ballads see P. R. Coss's useful article, 'Aspects of Cultural Diffusion in Medieval England', *Past and Present*, 108 (1985).
18. Ritson, op. cit., *passim*. The last example is from Martin Parker, 'A True Tale of Robin Hood', in *Samuel Pepys's Penny Merriments* (ed. R. Thompson, Columbia U.P., 1977), p. 57. See pp. 71–2 above.
19. M. Keen, 'Robin Hood – Peasant or Gentleman?', *Past and Present*, No. 19 (1961), p. 9.
20. See Chapter 6 below.

fighting their vocation, hunting their pastime and their *right*. But whatever the social origins of the outlaws and their leaders, they are not now landed gentry. In the forests

> They lived by their hands
> Without any lands,

just like expropriated peasants. Or rather, as another ballad put it,

> We live here like squires, or lords of renown
> Without e'er a foot of free land.[21]

The outlaws' attitude towards the state was feudal. 'The outlaw Murray', in his 'fair castle' in the forest, told an emissary from Scotland's monarch that he owned no king in Christendom; he had won his lands 'from the enemy', the English, when there was no royal power in the region. He would not recognize Scotland's king though 'landless men we a' will be'.[22] Outlaws were outside the king's law. They did not claim his protection, so there could be no question of allegiance. Robin Hood might feel personal loyalty to a king but he had no loyalty to or respect for the probably corrupt sheriff who mediated the king's law, just as the outlaw Murray claimed to be sovereign over his lands.[23] When it came to a showdown the king (in the ballads) was often impressed by the outlaws' honest integrity, and took them into his favour. There were thus two kings. One was the abstract external power in whose name evil local rulers oppressed outlaws and the poor; the other was the human being with whom direct personal contact could be made. We recall M.P.s in the 1620s insisting on their devotion to the King whilst attacking the 'evil councillors' whom he had chosen.

For centuries Robin Hood was a symbol of independence, of resistance to authority in church or state. This concept is central to the whole saga, and particularly prominent in the early ballads. 'The outlaw in an unjust society embodies truly the ideals which that society professes'.[24] In the interlude *Thersytes*, dating probably from the end of Henry VIII's reign,

---

21. 'Robin Hood and Maid Marian', in Ritson, op. cit., p. 392; 'Robin Hood and Little John', ibid., p. 379.
22. Quiller-Couch, *Oxford Book of Ballads*, pp. 374–80. Cf. the pirate Ward quoted on p. 115 below.
23. Ibid., pp. 372, 379, 384; cf. Ritson, op. cit., p. 4.
24. Douglas Gray, 'The Robin Hood Poems', *Poetica*, 18 (1984), pp. 1–39; Knight, op. cit., pp. 15, 45, 51–2, 58–60.

the eponymous hero is exposed as a 'great boaster'. After challenging 'King Arthur and his Knightes of the Rounde Table' and 'Robin John and Little Hode' ('outlaws' who 'take . . . away abbottes purses') he fails to conquer even a snail and runs away from a knight who challenges him.[25] Over a century later, at elections in Somerset for what turned out to be the Short Parliament of 1640, an opposition group known as 'Robins' and 'Little Johns' had a candidate to whom they referred as Robin Hood. They took the side of Parliament when civil war came. A comedy acted at Nottingham in 1661 'on the day of his sacred majesty's coronation' was entitled *Robin Hood and his crew of soldiers*. In this Robin and his men (soldiers, no longer outlaws) defended their support for the Good Old Cause of Parliament – 'this gallant attempt we've boldly followed' – but now that they have a law-abiding and a pious and really good king, it is no loss of freedom to obey his commands.[26]

In one of the Douce Ballads 'the father of Robin a forester was',[27] and he is described as a yeoman in other early ballads. But from Elizabeth's reign, if not earlier, attempts were made to upgrade him socially. Grafton tells us in a paragraph following the date 1569 that Robin, 'being of base stock was advanced to the noble dignity of an earl'. Soon his peerage becomes inherited. It is the culmination of his transformation from Latimer's 'traitor and thief'. It countered Sir Edward Coke's use of 'a Robin Hood, a Kett or a Cade' as the ultimate denigration of Sir Walter Ralegh in his trial. The best-known versions of this story are Anthony Munday's *The Downfall of Robert Earl of Huntingdon* and *The Death of Robert Earl of Huntingdon*, dated 1597–8 by Ritson.

Gentrification created a different Robin Hood. He ceases to be merely a subversive anti-authoritarian. I think Knight exaggerates when he says that in consequence Robin 'is gentrified out of any real activity'. 'He loses all humour, all sense of resistance, is bound in service to the crown and its officers; he forgives those who would do him most wrong'. The 'new ideology' is epitomized in *Albions England*, for instance, where Robin's men are 'merry', rather than being grim bandits or noble sufferers, as (according to Knight) the tradition has before envisaged; they live in 'the

---

25. *Thersytes*, in *English Miracle Plays, Moralities and Interludes* (ed. A. W. Pollard, Oxford U.P., 1927), pp. 136–45. The reference to the outlaws taking abbots' purses suggests that even at that date popular sympathies were with protestantism as well as with outlaws.
26. Underdown, *Revel*, p. 135; Ritson, op. cit., pp. 67–8.
27. *Douce Ballads*, 3, p. 112; Wiles, *Early Plays*, p. 49.

greenwood' rather than in forests. Robin Hood is sentimentalized as not so much the defender of the poor but rather as a founder of alms-houses and dispenser of charity to the poor.[28]

Why were the ballads so popular in the sixteenth and early seventeenth centuries? A shift did indeed take place in the image of Robin Hood, but it is perhaps a shift in audience attitudes resulting from socio-economic changes rather than in the ballads themselves. Robin may have been made more respectable socially, but the ballads remained popular. Why? Many reasons may be suggested – the spread of cheap printed matter, an expanding literary market based on increasing literacy. The market for broadsheets and ballads was presumably better in towns than in forests. Robin Hood and his outlaws may have appealed to recent urban immigrants in search of employment and independence.[29] Robin and his men preferred the freedom of the forest to the tyranny of a law in whose making they had no share. The sylvan liberty depicted in the ballads, in Shakespeare's Forest of Arden and in the 'wild men' of Elizabethan and Jacobean pageants, may be an idealization by town-dwellers of the semi-criminal existence of masterless men in sixteenth- and seventeenth-century forests, often former peasants who had been driven from their villages by enclosures.[30]

Robin Hood became the paradigm for those whom Eric Hobsbawm has called 'social bandits' – 'peasant outlaws whom the law and the state regard as criminal but who . . . are considered by their people as heroes, as champions, avengers, fighters for justice, perhaps even leaders of liberation, . . . men to be admired, helped and supported'. He calls Robin 'the international paradigm of social banditry'. 'Robin Hoodism, whether they believe in it or not, is useful to bandits'.[31] 'Robin with his courtesy/So won the meaner sort' that they would never help to capture him.[32] Robbing the rich and distributing some of the loot to the poor was attributed to many later figures who enjoyed a degree of popularity outside the law.

As Hobsbawm observed, outlaws after Robin Hood understood the

28. Knight, op. cit., pp. 127, 136, 143.
29. Brigden, *London and the Reformation* (Oxford U.P., 1991), p. 140.
30. D. M. Bergeron, *English Civic Pageantry* (1971), esp. pp. 56, 70–71, 82.
31. Hobsbawm, *Bandits* (1969), pp. 17–19, 92–3, and *passim*; also his *Primitive Rebels: Studies in Archaic Forms of Social Movement in the 19th and 20th centuries* (Manchester U.P., 3rd ed., 1971), pp. 20–23 and *passim*.
32. Matthew Parker, *A True Tale of Robbin* (1631).

advantages of doing good deeds – not robbing the poor, respecting women. This made sense, because outlaws needed friends within the society, and mediators, middlemen, if they were not to become totally isolated. John Major in 1521 is said to have been the first man of letters to express admiration for Robin Hood – because he would not rob the poor, and allowed no women to suffer injustice. He described him as the most humane of all robbers. In consequence the rich feared him and the poor loved and protected him. He built alms-houses for the poor – a practice later attributed less kindly to usurers. Many highwaymen allegedly imitated Robin Hood in this respect.[33] The rebellious miners of Dean in 1612, on the other hand, were described by the Earl of Northampton as no better than Robin Hoods.

Gamaliel Ratney, a highwayman executed in 1605, was said to have given 40 s. to a poor man whom he had intended to rob. He explained that he helped the poor, 'for the rich can help themselves'. Hobsbawm found himself relying for evidence about social bandits on poems and ballads.[34] The Robin Hood ballads hint at other lower-class attitudes. The outlaws were fiercely anti-clerical. Robin Hood's 'chiefest spite to the clergy was', 'who lived in monstrous pride', as a ballad put it, even suggesting that the outlaws 'did geld / All [clergymen] that came in their way'.[35] 'These bishops and the archbishops / Ye shall them beat and bind'.

> We'll not want gold, nor silver, behold,
> While bishops have ought in their purse.[36]

'Robin Hood and the Frere', a play of uncertain date, is particularly anti-clerical: it may derive from an earlier May-game play.[37] Abbots were the money-lenders of their time: they were fair game. Drayton in *Polyolbion* writes about Robin Hood:

> From wealthy abbots' chests and churls' abundant store
> What oftentimes he took he shared amongst the poor.[38]

---

33. Warner, *Albions England* (1589), p. 118; Riton, op. cit., pp. 7, 37, 249–50, 255. See Chapter 10 below.
34. Manning, *Village Revolts*, pp. 275–6; cf. Underdown, *Revel*, p. 110; ed. S. H. Atkins, *The Life and Death of Gamaliel Ratney* (1935); Hobsbawm, *Bandits*, p. 1.
35. 'A True Tale of Robin Hood', Ritson, op. cit., p. 241.
36. 'Robin Hood and his Meiny' (*Oxford Book of Ballads*), p. 499; 'Robin Hood and Little John', in Ritson, op. cit., p. 379.
37. Dobson and Taylor, op. cit., pp. 208–14.
38. Op. cit., Song XXVI.

Since the clergy in question had been Roman Catholics, they deserved no sympathy in newly-protestant England. Anti-clericalism was strong in other sixteenth-century ballads, and it reappears after 1640, in ballads and almanacs. It took the form mostly of anti-Catholicism. The Spanish Ambassador was a natural hate-figure in the 1620s, and the return of Prince Charles from Spain in 1624, unmarried, was the occasion for much spontaneous popular rejoicing. The tradition continues on to the Exclusion crisis, the Popish Plot and the ejection of James II.[39]

Another insufficiently remarked lower-class attitude was resentment of enforced church marriage. One ballad emphasizes that Robin Hood had only an informal marriage contract with Maid Marian: he had paid no fees for a church ceremony. The explanation of this given by the obsequious Munday is that outlaws could not legally marry.[40] But it is difficult to suppose that Friar Tuck could not have arranged something. More probably it was a deliberate gesture, linking up with the plebeian opposition to church marriage which I discuss in Chapter 16 below. We may compare the contempt for church ceremonies shown when Little John performed the marriage ceremony for Alan-a-Dale and the lady whom the outlaws had rescued for him. Robin Hood proclaimed that the old man whom her parents had chosen for her was 'no fit match'. 'The Birth of Robin Hood' suggests that Robin himself was born outside wedlock 'in the gude greenwood'.[41] In the eighteenth century a Robin Hood Society was a weekly mechanics' discussion group in London, where deists, Arians, Socinians and Jews were said to air doubts about the resurrection, the incarnation, the Trinity ('their everlasting butt'), the authenticity of the Scriptures and of the Gospel miracles.[42]

'The plays of Robin Hode, very proper to be played in Maye games' were printed in Ritson's Appendix, from an edition of 1634. First printed in 1562, Ritson thought it might date from as early as the fifteenth century.[43] Robin Hood figures in many plays from Edward VI's reign

39. Buchanan Sharp, 'Popular Protest', in Reay, *Popular Culture*, pp. 219, 302.

40. *Oxford Book of Ballads*, p. 465; Briggs, *Pale Hecate's Team*, p. 201.

41. 'Robin Hood and the Bishop of Hereford', in *Oxford Book of Ballads*, pp. 612–20. See also ibid., pp. 465–8: 'They made up their love-contract / Like proper paramours', not in church.

42. Richard Lewis, *The Robin Hood Society, A Satire by Peter Pounce* (1756), esp. pp. v–vi, 19, 79. There had been a political and philosophical Robin Hood Club meeting in a City tavern in James I's reign (V. L. Pearl, *London*, p. 233).

43. Ritson, op. cit., pp. 412–17; Wiles, *Early Plays*, p. 78.

onwards, as well as in May games.[44] There was a spate of plays from the 1590s on Robin Hood or other outlaw themes. One wonders whether these may be linked with the famine conditions which prevailed in that decade and form the background to *Coriolanus*. I list the most obvious of these plays:

George Peele, *Edward I* (1593). In this play 'Robin Hood of the Mountains' appears to be Llewellyn Prince of Wales in disguise.

The anonymous *George a Greene* (?1592, printed 1599).

Three lost plays – *A Pastoral Comedy of Robin Hood and Little John* (1594); *Robin Hood and the Friar* (1596 or 1597); *Robin Hood's Penniworth*, by William Haughton (1600).

Munday's *The Downfall of Robert Earl of Huntingdon* and *The Death of Robert Earl of Huntingdon* (dated 1597–8 by Ritson, p. 46).

[Anon.], *Look About You* (1604), a sex comedy in which Robin Hood plays a minor role – partly disguised as a woman in order to help a lady preserve her chastity. He claims, nevertheless, 'I can raise 2,000 soldiers in an hour'.

Metropolis Coronata, a Lord Mayor's pageant (1615) (Ritson, pp. 62–5).

Dekker, *The Welsh Ambassador* (c. 1620).

Ben Jonson, *The Sad Shepherd* (posthumously printed 1641).

To these we should add the references in Shakespeare's *Two Gentlemen of Verona* (IV. i. 36–7; V. iv. 156–7) and *As You Like It*; *I Henry IV*, III. iii; *II Henry IV*, V. iii; Beaumont and Fletcher, *Philaster* (1608); Middleton, *The Spanish Gypsy* (1623); Massinger, *The Guardian* (1633), V. ii; (Fletcher and ?Massinger), *Two Noble Kinsmen* (1634), Prologue; Suckling, *The Goblins* (1638).[45]

Robin Hood's popular reputation lasted as long as the first enclosure movement, against which he may have been seen as a symbol. After that his memory gave rise to a lament. Keats's 'R. H. to a Friend' looked back to the time, long since, when 'men knew nor rent nor leases'. But now Robin Hood sees that

44. Boris Ford, *The Age of Shakespeare* (Penguin, 1955), pp. 61–6; Ritson, op. cit., pp. 95–6, 102–3.
45. See Knight, op. cit., pp. 116–34.

> all his oaks,
> Fallen beneath the dockyard strokes,
> Have rotted on the briny seas.[45]

Robin belongs to a lost, better, pre-capitalist age.

Peacock in his *Maid Marian* referred with heavy irony to 'what was in those days called social order, namely the preservation of the privileges of the few who happened to have any, at the expense of the swinish multitude who happened to have none, except that of working and being shot at for the benefit of their betters, which is obviously not the meaning of social order in our more enlightened times'.[46]

Clare wrote of 'The Village Minstrel' who 'hung enraptured on . . . ancient songs' of Robin Hood and Little John. Like Clare himself, the Minstrel had a 'sense of freedom among the open fields'.[47] But to Clare in his lunatic asylum it appeared that law had overcome liberty.

Robin Hood still lives.[48] In February 1995 the British press was full of stories of 'Marcos', 'Mexico's Robin Hood' – a thirty-seven-year-old rebel who had the support of the peasantry and of the urban poor.

45. Keats, *Poetical Works* (ed. H. Buxton Forman, Oxford U.P., 1937), pp. 243–5.
46. T. L. Peacock, *Maid Marian*, in *Novels* (ed. David Garnett, 1948), pp. 489.
47. J. and A. Tibble, *John Clare: His Life and Poetry* (1956), p. 13.
48. See Knight, op. cit., Chapter 6.3.

6. Robin Hood, Possessive Individualism and the Norman Yoke

The Norman bastard William himself, his colonels, captains, inferior officers and common soldiers ... still are from that time to this day in pursuit of that victory, imprisoning, robbing and killing the poor enslaved English Israelites.

Gerrard Winstanley, *The True Levellers Standard Advanced*, April 1649, in *Works*, p. 259.

The Norman bastard did subject England to tyranny, and now Englishmen have freed themselves again.

Tyranipocrit Discovered (anonymous, 1649, ed. A. Hopton, n.d.), p. 53.

James I and Charles I (like William the Conqueror, or Pilate in the New Testament) were foreigners. They tightened the forest laws for their own fiscal purposes, and thereby provoked considerable opposition among gentry as well as commoners. Parliament, the representative assembly of the gentry, was no less aware than the government of the national significance of forests for timber for the navy, whose growing importance they had begun to appreciate. But the gentry had their own interest in forests. Here I am following R. B. Manning, who has illustrated at length the battles for forest and other waste land in the sixteenth and early seventeenth centuries.[1]

Under the first two Stuarts Star Chamber and the Exchequer revived royal prerogatives unknown under the Tudors, rejecting the idea of absolute and unqualified property rights for owners of enclosures in forests. When Charles I proclaimed new boundaries for the Forest of Essex he in effect cancelled all the disafforestation promised by Magna Carta and the Charter of the Forests, which the ancestors of the present holders

---

1. Manning, *Hunters and Poachers*, pp. 1–21. All references to Manning in this chapter are to R. B. Manning.

had purchased at considerable expense and had enjoyed for generations. This was 'contrary to divers Acts of Parliament'. When he extended Hampton Court Chase in the 1630s the King was accused of taking away 'men's estates at his pleasure', as Clarendon put it. Even when Charles offered compensation to persons whose property was confiscated, he did not always pay up. Expansion of royal forests and chases deprived tenants of their common rights and imposed on parishes a greater burden of poor relief for those who had been deprived of grazing rights. Charles's proposed solution was to have a workhouse built at the expense of the local community.[2] Freeholders who had land within purlieus or disafforested royal forests believed they were defending the Ancient Constitution when they resisted efforts of early Stuart kings to deny them hunting rights even on their own property. These rights were believed to have been secured by the Charter of the Forests, and had hitherto been respected.[3] It is characteristic of the geographical insouciance of Jacobean drama that one character in Beaumont and Fletcher's *Philaster* should say of another 'He hunts too much in the purlieus; would he would leave off poaching!'[4] Hardly a Spanish problem: but it makes a point relevant to our discussion.

The assumption that kings could regulate hunting privileges by licence or proclamation came into conflict with spreading ideas of possessive individualism: deer were chattels and could be stolen. But this cut both ways: landowners claimed that, for instance, a traditional liberty of free warren (right to hunt on their own land) extinguished the right of royal rangers to recover deer which had strayed on to their land. Drayton in *Polyolbion* had praised Kent for its courage in resisting the Norman Yoke after the Conquest,

> And with a high resolve, most bravely didst restore
> That liberty so long enjoy'd by thee before,
> Not suffering foreign laws should thy free customs bind.[5]

The legal rights of 'purlieu men' became involved in the constitutional struggle between the royal prerogative and statute law. Manning suggests that Peter Wentworth's defence of the hunting rights of purlieu men may have contributed to his notions about the privileges and powers of Parlia-

2. Ibid., pp. 92–3, 121, 230, 208.
3. Ibid., pp. 21, 57–8, 81.
4. Op. cit. (1611, played probably 1608), Act IV, scene i.
5. Ibid., pp. 25, 79, 88; *Polyolbion*, the eighteenth song, in *Works*, II, p. 282.

ment.[6] Sir Edward Coke invoked the Ancient Constitution as restored by Magna Carta and the Charter of the Forests to defend the hunting rights of purlieu men on their own land against the encroachments of forest law.[7] Star Chamber, in 'a veritable flood of prosecutions', overrode the common law and juries to enforce the game laws by denying the rights of purlieu men. The latter came to be seen as guardians of the first line of defence of the Ancient Constitution. Even Blackstone thought the game laws were a remnant of the Norman Yoke.[8] When the Long Parliament met, the Act 16 CI, for the 'Certainty of Forests', restricted royal forests to their borders as they had existed before 1603.[9]

In Robin Hood's day to be free meant escaping from the law, a law imposed on the native English by the Norman Conqueror, protecting the rights and liberties of the conquerors and holding the conquered in subjection. Over the centuries the distinction between Englishmen and Normans had become less clear-cut, but the distinction between rich and poor, powerful and powerless, free and unfree, remained. Villeinage, serfdom, no longer existed as an effective legal category. But as Tawney grimly remarked, 'villeinage ends, the poor law begins'. The poor had no rights, no freedoms. The idea of being free from the law incorporated the theory of the Norman Yoke, just as Robin Hood incorporated many of the legends originally attached to King Arthur.[10] By the seventeenth century the story of the Norman Yoke was well-established and had acquired mythical elements; Levellers and others generalized the rights of 'the free Anglo-Saxons' to the whole population. But this was mostly rhetoric. When pressed many Levellers thought that the Parliamentary franchise should be restricted to men of some property – not servants or paupers or beggars.

Francis Freeman in 1650 asked Oliver Cromwell to 'take away all the laws in one day and give us such wholesome laws the next, . . . the most suitable to what they were before the Norman Conquest'. John Rogers

---

6. Manning, op. cit., p. 187. Manning defines 'purlieu men' as freeholders possessing estates worth 40 s. p.a. within purlieus or disafforested areas once part of the royal forests. They were permitted the limited right to course deer on their own holdings provided they employed only hounds and no other hunting weapons' (*Hunters and Poachers*), p. 238.

7. Ibid., pp. 83–93, 105–8.

8. Ibid., pp. 68–70, 78, 87–8.

9. Ibid., pp. 81, 208.

10. Ritson, p. 95; Briggs, *Pale Hecate's Team*, pp. 214–17.

spoke of 'the Norman Yoke of corrupt lawyers'.[11] Lilburne thought that
England had been under oppressing bondage ever since the Norman
Conquest, under the common law whose complexity enabled William
the Conqueror to seize the lands of the conquered English. Statute law is
better, but it too has its defects: even Magna Carta 'falls short of Edward
the Confessor's laws, which the Conqueror robbed England of'. 'It is a
badge of our slavery to a Norman Conqueror', Lilburne wrote in 1648,
'to have our laws in the French tongue; and it is little less than brutish
vassalage to be bound to walk by laws which the people cannot know'.[12]
John Cook, prosecutor against Charles I, thought Englishmen were long-
ing for freedom from the Norman Yoke.[13] The anonymous author of
Tyranipocrit Discovered proclaimed in 1649 that victory in the civil war
had freed Englishmen again (see epigraph to this chapter). In 1651 prisoners petitioning for liberty said 'the law was the badge of the Norman
bondage'.[14] Milton too spoke of 'their gibberish laws, . . . the badge of
their ancient slavery'; but in *Eikonoklastes* (1649) he feared that the English
people were 'ready to be stroked and tamed again into the wonted and
well-pleasing state of their true Norman villeinage'. In *Samson Agonistes*,
as Empson observed, the hero acts for 'an underprivileged class'.[15]

As population increased, and with it the demand for game, the forest
laws were increasingly used against those who sought game for sale on
the market. Here forest laws conflicted with the interests of the business
sector of the general public. Common lawyers began to argue that if deer
were not wild animals available for all, but private property, then it must
be assumed that they existed only in *enclosed* game reserves, not in unenclosed forests. But popular belief denied that wild animals could be owned,

11. Freeman, *Light Vanquishing Darkness*, p. 58; Rogers, *Sagrir, or Doomes-day drawing
nigh* (1654), Sig. A. 4; Lilburne, *The Just Mans Justification* (1646), pp. 11–15. Edwards
quotes this tract at length in Part III of his *Gangraena* (1646), adding Overton's phrase
'Magna Carta . . . being but a beggarly thing' (III, p. 194).
12. Lilburne, *A Declaration of some Proceedings of Lt.-Col. John Lilburne*, articles 5 and
6; cf. Nigel Smith, *Literature and Revolution*, pp. 145–6, 199. See also R. B. Seaburg,
'The Norman Conquest and the Common Law: the Levellers and the Argument
from Continuity', *Historical Journal*, 24 (1981), pp. 791–806.
13. Cook to the Lord Deputy of Ireland, quoted by Ogilvie, *The King's Government
and the Common Law*, p. 166.
14. Whitelocke, *Memorials of the English Affairs* (1853), II, p. 362.
15. Milton, *The Tenure of Kings and Magistrates* (February 1649), in *Complete Prose
Works*, III, p. 193; *Eikonoklastes*, ibid., III, p. 581; Empson, *Milton's God* (1961),
p. 213.

or that places where they lived could be enclosed.[16] The near-Digger pamphlet *Light Shining in Buckinghamshire* complained of the loss of liberty when 'all the land, trees, beasts, fish, fowl are enclosed into a few mercenary hands; and all the rest deprived and made their slaves, so that . . . if they hunt a fowl it is imprisonment because it is gentlemen's game, as they say'.[17]

In the period from 1603 to 1640, Manning has shown, there was much resentment and private warfare over hunting rights, often in gangs led by gentlemen against peers or the crown. Aristocratic and gentry feuds were an inescapable part of the social and political scene in Tudor and early Stuart England, often with the connivance of local magistrates, themselves interested parties as gentlemen. Juries were tolerant of raids on the deer of papists.[18]

The Game Laws of 1603 and 1605 excluded from these privileges many lesser gentry who held their land by copyhold tenure. Attorney-General Noy's suggestion of *selling* an extension of hunting liberties proved superfluous: Star Chamber came more and more to prop up the social privileges of the greater aristocracy. But after the turmoil of the revolutionary decades and widespread attacks on deer parks in which Parliamentarian soldiers often joined local rioters, the post-restoration gentry became more conscious of the need for class solidarity. There is much less gentry-led deer-stealing; it becomes an exclusively plebeian practice. In any case, so many deer had fallen victims to popular resentment and hunger during the revolutionary decades that many gentlemen could not afford to restore their deer parks after the civil war. They became an expensive status symbol. Fox-hunting rose in favour as a gentlemanly sport, and the existence of a standing army offered an alternative outlet for the energies of young gentlemen.[19]

The revolutionary decades saw wide discussions about many matters, including the Biblical statement that God created Adam and Eve and bade them 'have dominion over . . . every living thing that moveth upon the earth' (Genesis 1:28). As early as 1381 peasant rebels had demanded that 'poor as well as rich might take wild beasts' and hunt hares. This divinely appointed dominion, men pointed out, was not given only to rich men. But a statute of 1392 specifically forbade 'any kind of artificer

16. Manning, op. cit., pp. 197, 237, 61; Sabine, *Works of Winstanley*, p. 612.
17. Ibid.
18. Manning, op. cit., pp. 159, 169, 209–10, 230, 232–3, 148, 162, 220–1.
19. Ibid., pp. 38–9, 209–10, 81, 230, 107, 56, 234, 124.

or labourer' to participate in this 'or other sport of gentlefolk'.[20] Nevertheless, it was popularly believed that all men had from time immemorial a
customary (as well as Biblical) right to natural products on waste and
common lands. Any modern laws which subverted such customary rights
were of dubious authority, were – in this case – part of the Norman Yoke
which radicals thought the civil war was designed to cast off. John Aubrey
commented on the way discussions of the Bible 'set their wits a-running
and reforming'.[21]

Freeholders who resisted attempts by early Stuart kings to deprive
them of their hunting rights believed – or said they did – that they were
defending the Ancient Constitution. So did some lawyers. R. B. Manning
not unreasonably claims that historians have failed to recognize the constitutional and legal significance of this belief for the seventeenth-century
struggle to limit the royal prerogative; royal claims conflicted with absolute property rights.[22] The Venetian Ambassador in October 1637 thought
that the question of the forests was 'more difficult and odious' than Ship
Money, 'because of the threat to rights of property'.[23] Historians might
ponder the implications of that remark. Constitutional matters seemed to
the Ambassador, a shrewd observer, less important than property rights.
We can see how Robin Hood came to be seen as a champion not only of
the populace but also of traditional justice: forest law was an aberration
devised by the King's evil councillors.[24]

Customary rights were easily transformed into the rights of man, of all
men. In 1601 the Rev. Peter Simon, examined by his bishop on a charge
of participating in an anti-enclosure revolt in the Forest of Dean, had also
been accused of preaching the equality of all mankind.[25] As Sir Henry
Slingsby put it, 'the common people judges not with things as they
are with reason or against; but long usage with them is instead of all'.
They had 'their own ill-defined yet deeply felt version of the Ancient

20. Quoted by John Hatcher, 'England in the Aftermath of the Black Death', *Past
and Present*, 144 (August 1944), p. 18.
21. Ed. J. E. Jackson, *The Topographical Collections of John Aubrey* (Devizes, 1862),
p. 246.
22. Manning, op. cit., pp. 2, 58, 75, 83–6, 107–8.
23. W. Hunt, *The Puritan Moment: The Coming of Revolution in an English County*
(Harvard U.P., 1983), p. 273.
24. Manning, op. cit., p. 63.
25. *C.S.P.D., 1631–3*, p. 36. Peter Simon had been presented to his living by the
Haberdashers' Company of London, not by a local gentleman.

Constitution.[26] During the mid-century revolution Gerrard Winstanley generalized the political consequences of the Norman Yoke, which it must be the task of Parliament, victorious in the civil war, to remove: 'Those that buy and sell land, and are landlords, have got it either by oppression, or murder, or theft'. All landlords are in breach of the seventh and eighth commandments, thou shalt not steal nor kill. Yet they are chosen as J. P.s, to sit in judgement on poor men who resist being swindled out of their rights to the land. When 'any Trustee or state officer is to be chosen . . . who must be chosen? but some very rich man, who is the successor of the Norman colonels or high officers. And to what end have they been thus chosen? but to establish the Norman power the more forcibly over the enslaved English, and to beat them down again, whenas they gather heart to seek for liberty'. 'The present powers of England' [i.e. the rulers of the Commonwealth] 'still lift up the Norman Yoke and slavish tyranny, and hold the people as much in bondage as the Bastard Conqueror himself'. The Diggers hold their land in common; it and its produce 'are not to be bought and sold among us'. So 'What need have we of imprisoning, whipping or hanging laws, to bring one another into bondage?' When private property has been abolished in Winstanley's utopia, there will be no need of 'outward, selfish, confused laws, made to uphold the power of covetousness, whenas we have the righteous law written in our hearts, teaching us to walk purely in the Creation'.[27]

Winstanley and his ideas had long been forgotten when in 1713 Alexander Pope in 'Windsor Forest' gave a rather different version of the ending of the Norman Yoke. He looked back to a distant time when England was

> To savage beasts and savage laws a prey,
> And kings more furious and severe than they . . .
> The swain with tears his frustrate labour yields,
> And famished dies amidst his ripened fields . . .
> But while the subject starved, the beast was fed . . .
> Our haughty Norman . . .
> Makes his trembling slaves the royal game.
> The fields are ravished from th'industrious swains . . .
> The levelled towns with weeds lie covered o'er . . .
> Awed by his nobles, by his commons cursed,
> Th'oppressor ruled tyrannic where he durst.

26. Quoted by Underdown, *Revel*, pp. 124–5; cf. p. 145.
27. Winstanley, *Works*, pp. 258–9, 282–5. See Chapter 23 below.

But all ended happily:

> Succeeding monarchs heard the subjects' cries
> Nor saw displeased the peaceful cottage rise . . .
> The forests wondered at th'unusual grain,
> And sacred transport touched the conscious swain.
> Fair Liberty, Britannia's goddess, rears
> Her cheerful head, and leads the golden years.

Sea power and empire bring wealth 'in Albion's golden days', and Pope concludes by looking forward to world prosperity, when 'free as seas or wind / Unbounded Thames shall flow for all mankind . . . / Till conquest cease, and slavery be no more'.

It is an interesting anticipation of present-day dreams of *pax Americana*.[28]

---

28. Pope, 'Windsor Forest', in *Poems, Epistles and Satires* (Everyman ed.), pp. 23–32.

7. Forests and Venison, Game Laws and Poachers

===

In forests I, at liberty and free,
Liv'd in such pleasure as the world ne'er knew . . .
Till this last age, those beastly men forth brought
That all those great and goodly woods destroyed.

Drayton, 10th Nymphall, in *Minor Poems*, ed. C. Brett, Oxford
U.P. (1970), p. 228.

I

Forests and fens had been from time immemorial the uncultivated and uncultivable areas of England. William the Conqueror had preposterously claimed that all forests were royal property, reserved for his hunting. But for a long time there was no effective machinery for enforcing royal ownership. The laws of the forest were always very different from the common law; many forest offences were felonies, carrying a sentence of death or outlawry.[1]

Forests and fens were almost by definition the last areas worth bringing under the control of the centralized state. Most areas called forests had no settled agriculture worth taxing: much of the terrain was impassable, sheltering outlaws and misfits in roving bands, living on game, fruits and berries. So long as the main military weapon was cavalry, the forest was impenetrable. The long bow was the foresters' weapon, and became the strength of English infantry: but it was no use against the superior skill of the outlaws.

Fens supplied fish and fowl for a few scattered settlers. In the forests, the bands acquired leaders, sometimes members of a higher class who for one reason or another had become outlaws. The commoners of the fens were organized, if at all, into democratic communities of relatively equal persons. Both existed as semi-independent communities with internal

---

1. Ed. W. Nelson, *Manwood's Treatise of the Forest Laws* (1740).

loyalties but no necessary subordination to the government of the state. The fens were more easily subjugated once their economic potential was recognized. Fen drainage called for capital, but once that was available resistance by fenmen was fairly easily overcome. But there was no economic incentive to do more than nibble at the edges of forests until a growing demand for timber – for ship-building or as fuel – began to make itself felt from the sixteenth century. Outlaws naturally gravitated to forest areas where the king's law did not effectively prevail. They enjoyed a freedom which lasted for longer than that of the fenmen but which was becoming precarious.[2] Outlawry was in fact an admission of the government's weakness – rather as excommunication was the rusty sword of the church.

Possession of land was a symbol of prestige, of social status. But from the sixteenth century uncultivated land was becoming scarce, more profitable in an increasingly market-conscious world. Deer and other game acquired commercial value. As the financial problems of Stuart kings mounted, forests mounted too in economic significance. The navy was becoming increasingly important as an instrument of foreign policy, and the national significance of forests as suppliers of timber for ship-building came to be appreciated both by governments and by Parliament.

The forest laws had been pretty notional from the start. Given the limited resources of the medieval state, the king's exclusive right to hunt in the vast forest areas of the country could be enforced only sporadically in areas where a particular king wished to hunt. With the breakdown of central authority in the fifteenth century, and royal lack of enthusiasm for hunting between 1547 and 1603, many of the gentry had established effective rights of hunting in royal forests in their localities. Harrington's theory that political power follows property, and that the gentry's rise to landed preponderance over the king underlay the political revolution of the seventeenth century, comes perhaps nearest to the truth in the gentry's effective assumption of hunting rights, and in Charles I's desperate effort not to reassert royal rights but to use forest fines to prop up his failing Exchequer.[3]

Hunting was the sport of the gentry. It was a training for war, and it supplied venison. So gentlemen living near forests strove to obtain royal

2. The anonymous 'The Wood-mans walke' (possibly by Anthony Munday) expatiates on the freedom of the woods (in *England's Helicon*, ed. H. Macdonald, The Muses Library, 1962, pp. 197–8, 229). First published in 1600.
3. See pp. 83–7 above.

authorization to hunt there, or hunted without licence. Not until the late sixteenth century did there begin to appear a royal policy for the forests. The motive for this was the growing importance of forests as sources of naval supplies, rather than as previously for the pleasures of the chase.

Pressure groups in the Commons advocating a forward commercial–colonial foreign policy were critical of the royal practice of leasing forests (or selling them outright) to commercial speculators who cut down trees – e.g. for iron smelting in the Forest of Dean, a notorious example. Commoners in the forests found their traditional rights disregarded by businessmen intent on making profits. Gentlemen and yeomen found hunting rights in forests called in question which they had long taken for granted. Buchanan Sharp sums up many pages explaining that poor foresters either had no rights or were swindled out of them: 'There were two types of forest inhabitants, those with land who went to law to protect their rights', and those with little or no land who rioted to defend their interests. The law could be broken when it favoured commoners; Keith Lindley gives examples of cottagers and squatters being out-manoeuvred.[4]

In *Polyolbion* Drayton repeatedly bemoaned 'the vile decay . . . of whole forests . . . in these impious times'.

> Where the goodly herds of high-palmed harts did gaze
> Upon the passer-by, there now doth only graze
> The gall'd-back carrion jade, and hurtful swine do spoil
> Once to the Sylvan powers our consecrated soil.[5]

For now the forests and the deer 'are by vile gain devour'd: So abject are our days'. 'Wise Chiltern' is now of 'his beechen woods bereft that kept him from the cold.' The forests of the Weald, 'poor woeful woods, to ruin lastly sold', 'under the axe's stroke fetch'd many a grievous groan', as they were cut down in the interests of mining.

> What should the builder serve, supplies the forger's turn,
> When under public good, base private gain takes hold.
> And at this hour we see the share and coulter tear
> The full corn-bearing glebe, where sometimes forests were;
> And those but caitiffs are, which most do seek our spoil,
> Who having sold our woods, do lastly sell our soil.

4. Sharp, *In Contempt of All Authority*, p. 144; Lindley, *Fenland Riots and the English Revolution* (1982), pp. 28–32, 49–51.
5. Op. cit., Fifth-Seventeenth Songs, in *Complete Works* (ed. R. Hooker, 1876), I, pp. 132, 180–83, II, pp. 183, 227.

The sales did not even benefit the sellers, he suggested, many of whom soon ran through the purchase price and were reduced to beggary.[6]

The disafforestation of Pewsam Forest in the 1620s led to riots and a poem by William Davenant in which he celebrated 'The Countess of Anglesey led captive by the rebels'.[7] Disafforestation hit marginal small-holders and cottagers hard: mostly they got no compensation for their rights of common either from the crown or from its lessees, who were often speculative strangers intruding into the life of the forest communities. There were riots and revolts in many forests in Dorset, Wiltshire, Gloucestershire and Worcestershire. The main opposition in these areas came from cottagers, whose resentment was directed against violation of traditional rights by outsiders – courtiers or Londoners who disrupted the forest communities in the name of improvement and private profit, Scots, and the hangers-on of the Duke of Buckingham, including the disreputable Sir Giles Mompesson.[8] But popular opposition often had the tacit support of a wider social circle.

The crown hoped to ally with property owners in the forests against cottagers by stressing the social dangers which their resistance involved. In the Parliament of 1610 James I drew M.P.s' attention to the fact that 'great numbers and multitudes of cottages have been daily more and more increased upon waste grounds and commons in many parts of this realm, especially near unto his Majesty's forests, chases and parks, and thereby the game and woods are daily spoiled and destroyed'. Local magistrates connive at this, but 'such cottages . . . are breeders, nurseries and receptacles of thieves, rogues and beggars and other malefactors and disordered persons'.[9]

The crown also began to put its ownership of the forests to fiscal purposes: hunting rights were a privilege whose price could be raised. Some gentry were fined for traditional practices which they had long enjoyed without question. The rising prosperity of many towns, and immigration of landless squatters to industrializing rural areas, stimulated the spread of enclosure for capitalist agriculture – as well as emigration.[10]

6. Ibid., Twelfth Song, I, p. 132; Fifteenth Song, II, p. 183; Seventeenth Song, II, pp. 227–8; Nineteenth Song, III, p. 3.
7. Davenant, *Shorter Poems and Songs* (ed. A. M. Gibbs, Oxford U.P., 1972), pp. 125, 402–3.
8. Underdown, *Revel*, pp. 108–12.
9. Ed. E. R. Foster, *Proceedings in Parliament, 1610* (Yale U.P., 1966), II, pp. 280–81.
10. Underdown, *Revel*, pp. 18, 34, 108, 128, 136.

There were rational arguments to suggest that opening up forests and fens to cultivation would benefit the nation; but they had to be set against the loss of traditional sources of livelihood for free men. Iron works began to be licensed in the Forest of Dean in 1612, and within a couple of decades there were eleven blast furnaces and eleven forges in action there.[11] Sir Giles Mompesson of ill-repute was enclosing for coal-mining in the Forest of Dean; others were licensed to enclose in forests in Wiltshire, Dorset and Gloucestershire.[12] Drayton painted a dire portrait of the consequences for the next generation of the destruction of forests:

> The little infant on the mother's lap
> For want of fire shall be so sore distressed
> That whilst it draws the lank and empty pap
> The tender lips shall freeze unto the breast.

Cattle would freeze to death, and 'men wanting timber wherewith they should build' would have to live in holes in the ground.[13] Mildmay Fane tactfully attributed the destruction of timber to the monarchy of the wind, whose 'violent reign hath done the forest mischief'; but the words 'monarchy' and 'reign' might suggest that others were blameworthy.[14]

The government feared that 'the Western Rising' might lead to a national insurrection. It was in connection with riots in the Forest of Dean that the Rev. Peter Simon proclaimed his belief in the equality of all mankind. Constables, trained bands and deputy lieutenants all proved

11. G. Hammersley, 'The Crown Woods and their Exploitation in the 16th and 17th Centuries', *Bulletin of the Institute of Historical Research*, XXX (1957), pp. 158–9; S. D. White, *Sir Edward Coke and 'The Grievances of the Commonwealth', 1621–1628* (North Carolina U.P., 1979), pp. 210–11; J. C. Cox, *The Royal Forests of England* (1905), pp. 77–8, 177, 281.

12. E. Kerridge, 'The Revolt in Wiltshire against Charles I', *Wiltshire Archaeological and Natural History Magazine*, 57 (1959), pp. 64–73. For the danger of 'a troublesome rising' in Essex, see Hunt, *The Puritan Moment*, p. 266.

13. Drayton, 10th Nymphall, *Minor Poems*, p. 229. The passage quoted is a continuation of that cited as epigraph to this chapter.

14. Fane, 'The Change', quoted by James Turner, *The Politics of Landscape* (Oxford, 1978), p. 98. But cf. Evelyn's account of the storm of November 1703, in which over 3,000 oaks were blown down in the Forest of Dean alone – 'the choicest ship-timber in the world' (*Diary*, ed. E. S. de Beer, Oxford U.P., 1955, III, p. 343, V, pp. 550–51). Evelyn had advised the King that cattle should be kept out of young plots on commons and private lands to let trees grow, even if this was 'to the detriment of a few clamorous and rude commons' (quoted by Carolyn Merchant, *The Death of Nature: Women, Ecology, and the Scientific Revolution*, San Francisco, 1979, p. 239).

reluctant to act against such rioters. So did soldiers when they were called in.[15]

The power of the royal government was put behind the enclosure movement. 'The drainage of the Isle of Axholme', Clive Holmes tells us, 'was a formidable example of the deployment of royal authority to crush a peasantry who were forced to watch the dismemberment of this traditional economy'.[16] There are many examples of the crown exercising pressure on legal processes.[17] In Windsor and Waltham Forests there was large-scale slaughter of deer in the troubled months before the outbreak of civil war,[18] and the revolutionary decades continued the process. The poorer classes must have eaten more meat than ever before.

Looking back in 1692, S.[ilvanus] T.[aylor] supposed a forest-dweller to say that thirty years earlier we lay 'under forest-laws. . . . We cannot make the best advantage of our enclosures, . . . for if we do, what with hunting and the deer's feeding, we have most of our corn spoiled; and if 500 deer lie in our corn all night, and we kill any one of them, that is a hanging matter. And if we keep but a dog . . . to hunt them out, upon any displeasure taken by an under-keeper . . . our punishment would be greater than the loss of all our corn'. Taylor could not understand why people failed to appreciate the advantages of enclosure of forests, which would 'give employment for many hundred thousand labouring hands' who now emigrate. Taylor's real interest in enclosing forests seems to be not the welfare of forest-dwellers but the provision of timber for the navy; his desire to discourage emigration was in order to retain 'an auxiliary of 20,000 men, able and ready to oppose any foreign enemy, either by sea or land'. He admitted that at enclosure cottages newly erected received no compensation; but if these many idle persons were set to work, it would not only be an enrichment but a great honour to our nation.[19]

15. Buchanan Sharp, *In Contempt of All Authority*, Chapters iv–ix; Sharp, 'Popular Protest in Seventeenth-Century England', in *Popular Culture in Seventeenth-Century England* (ed. B. Reay, 1985), pp. 300–302, 132–3. For Peter Simon see p. 88 above.
16. Holmes, *Seventeenth-Century Lincolnshire*, pp. 126–30.
17. Cf. K. Lindley, *Fenland Riots and the English Revolution* (1982), pp. 26–32, 42, 49; and W. J. Jones, *Politics and the Bench: The Judges and the Origins of the English Civil War* (1971), pp. 95–8, for 'the outrageous behaviour of Crown lawyers and the intimidation of juries' in the crown's exploitation of forests in the 1630s.
18. *C.S.P.D., 1640*, p. 34.
19. S.T., *Common-good: Or, The Improvement of Commons, Forests and Chases by Inclosure* (1692), pp. 29–38.

In the 1640s, as in the rebellion of 1549, there was much slaughter of deer. Riots were resumed in the fens and in all the western forests where they had occurred between 1626 and 1632.[20] But the revolutionary decades also produced many schemes for developing forests economically to the advantage of their inhabitants. Vegetable-growing around London, tobacco-growing in Gloucestershire, hop-gardens in Kent, Surrey and Devon, saffron, liquorice, teasels, herbs, flax and hemp all flourished, though governments opposed tobacco plantations.[21] In the 1640s common-ers in forests, as in fens, seem to have received fairer treatment when they were sold outright to purchasers who possessed the capital sums necessary for improvement.[22] But with the growing conservatism of the 1650s, attitudes towards former royal forests became 'exactly as they had been in the reigns of James I and Charles I'. They were regarded as potentially profitable but underdeveloped resources that bred 'idle, vagrant, pilfering and pernicious persons'. Consequently the forest policy of the Protectorate inherited the unpopularity of that of the Stuarts. Disafforestation, it was said, would result in great misery for 'thousands of indigent persons', far more than could be maintained by poor relief.[23] In 1655 it was proposed that part of a Staffordshire forest should be cut down, the proceeds from sale of the timber to be used to pay soldiers' wages.[24]

II

The game laws criminalized what most villagers regarded as traditional customary rights. The Bible was taken to confirm custom. Genesis 1:26–8 legitimated poachers' belief that God intended animals and natural prod-ucts for all men, not just for the rich who passed laws to give themselves a monopoly. In *The Merry Devil of Edmonton* (1608) Sir John, a priest, goes poaching on Enfield Chase. In the same play knights steal deer, and an inn-keeper steals venison (Act IV, scenes i and ii).

20. R. B. Manning, *Hunters and Poachers*, p. 17.
21. Thirsk, 'Agricultural innovations and their diffusion, 1640–1750', in *Agricultural Change* (ed. Thirsk), pp. 289, 312; cf. Thirsk and Cooper, *Documents*, pp. 135–40, and B. Sharp, 'Popular Protest', in *Popular Culture in 17th-century England* (ed. B. Reay), pp. 298–300.
22. Thirsk, *Agricultural Change*, pp. 142–3.
23. Ibid., pp. 250–52; Sharp, *In Contempt of All Authority*, p. 251.
24. Osborne, *Justices of the Peace*, p. 123.

Poachers, like smugglers, enjoyed considerable sympathy in their localities. They retained something of the Robin Hood spirit. But in many cases poaching was necessary to their physical existence. Peter Clark attributes an outbreak of poaching in Kent in the 1590s to sheer hunger in those starvation years.[25] The game laws became part of the new absolute property rights of big landowners, at the expense of what had been common rights justified by the custom of the manor. In consequence stray deer ate the corn in their fields, rabbits cropped the corn where villagers pastured their sheep. Game-keepers had a legal right to search cottages for nets or venison, a right naturally resented – and abused.

The breakdown of government in 1640 led to outbreaks of poaching as well as of looting. In Essex poachers were very selective, confining their activities to the parks of royalists and recusants, and to royal forests, Waltham Forest being the especial favourite of Parliamentarian soldiers. The very valuable oyster beds of the monopolist Earl of Sussex were also raided.[26] The poor of Colchester stole wood which they sold 'as they must do for the maintenance of their family'.[27] After 1660 legislation concerned itself with restocking deer parks destroyed during the Revolution, and making the game laws even harsher. Enclosure had reduced the area of waste and woodland over which game could roam, and it had also reduced the dangers of famine. Parks were needed to restore, preserve and build up stocks of deer. Grain surpluses could now safely be fed to game and horses.[28]

But the issues became less clear-cut. Before 1640 fen-drainage and enclosure of forests had notoriously often been to benefit court parasites and their hangers-on. During and after the Revolution propagandists for agricultural improvement like Hartlib and Worledge were able to stress the real advantages to the community of bringing new land under cultivation. And after the upheaval of the revolutionary decades, Joan Thirsk

25. Clark, *English Provincial Society from the Reformation to the Revolution: Religion, Politics and Society in Kent* (Hassocks, Sussex, 1977), p. 234. The same correlation is made for the eighteenth century by J. M. Beattie, 'The Pattern of Crime in England', *Past and Present*, 63 (February 1974), pp. 92–5.

26. W. Hunt, *The Puritan Moment*, pp. 300–309.

27. Brian Manning, *1649: The Crisis of the English Revolution* (1992), p. 95. Labourers from Enfield, a frequent scene of agrarian disturbance, poached deer (ibid.).

28. Thirsk, 'Enclosure and Engrossing, 1500–1640', in *Agricultural Change in Policy and Practice* (ed. Thirsk, Cambridge U.P., 1990), pp. 204–8.

tells us, landlords were more cautious in their treatment of tenants.[29] ' "Improvement of the wastes and forests" became the slogan of the age', as Brian Manning puts it; but with the difference that after 1640 more attention had to be paid to the interests of the poor. Manning insists that 'whether the wastes and forests would be improved for the benefit of lords of manors and richer farmers or for the benefit of the poor with little or no land' was 'a crucial issue of the English Revolution'.[30]

'The rich men are fed, and clothed, and grow rich, by what they get out of the poor's labour', declared Peter Chamberlen in 1649. This rudimentary labour theory of value was to be elaborated by Gerrard Winstanley.[31] Christopher O'Riordan has drawn attention to examples of collaboration between Parliamentarian troops and tenants against landlords, and of local sequestration commissioners conniving at 'squatting' in sequestrated royalist houses.[32] Here landless peasants were exercising freedom against the law. When enclosed, the virgin soil of the waste was more fruitful than any other land.[33] It was ideal for experimenting with new crops – if you could afford it. But because enclosure deprived the poor of the use of commons and waste land for pasture, fuel and fruits, and of gleaning rights 'according to the custom in harvest time', it increased the dependence of the poor on wages. They were forced to work harder and more regularly, no longer able to choose their own time for labour.

The common law did not recognize deer and hares as game: they were wild beasts, nobody's property, everybody's property. Despite this, between the fourteenth and eighteenth centuries Parliament made every conceivable circumstance in which a commoner might hunt deer or hares

29. A. Low, *The Georgic Revolution* (Princeton U.P., 1988), pp. 152, 235–6; Thirsk, *Seventeenth-century Agriculture and Social Change, Agricultural History Review*, XVIII, Supplement (1970), pp. 167–77.

30. B. S. Manning, *1649*, pp. 99–102.

31. Chamberlen, *The poore Mans Advocate* (1649), p. 30; for Winstanley see Chapter 23, below.

32. Christopher O'Riordan, 'Popular Exploitation of Enemy Estates in the English Revolution', *History*, 253 (1993), pp. 196–7. But cf. B. Osborne, *Justices of the Peace, 1361–1848* (Shaftesbury, 1960), pp. 120–21, for an interregnum campaign against squatters on commons.

33. John Houghton, *England's Great Happiness* (1677), quoted by E. Lipson, *The Economic History of England* (1943), II, p. 396; Thirsk, 'Making a Fresh Start; 16th-century Agriculture and the Classical Inspiration', in *Culture and Cultivation in Early Modern England* (ed. M. Leslie and T. Raylor, Leicester U.P., 1992), p. 243.

a crime. The law was extended to include deer parks and fish-ponds as private property – provided they were hedged: but this interfered with traditional communal access to streams or ponds – for instance for watering cattle.[34]

The game laws had always been openly class-specific. From 1544 no one with less than £100 a year freehold might possess, carry or hunt with handguns or cross-bows. Legislation of 1603 and 1605 limited the possession of dogs, nets and guns to the armigerous gentry and their heirs, or copyholders worth £30 a year. Even higher property qualifications were necessary for shooting partridges or pheasants; sale of such game was prohibited. 'Poaching was the act of outlawry which most significantly injured and insulted the King'.[35] 'Every outbreak of popular unrest', R. B. Manning writes, 'brought new and more restrictive game laws'.[36] James I, with his usual shrewdness and his usual lack of sensitivity, summed up the class nature of the game laws when he said that it was 'not fit that clowns should have these sports'.[37] His son used Star Chamber to punish those who unlawfully hunted game birds with dogs or nets.

III

After the restoration there seems to have been no systematic attempt at fiscal or economic exploitation of forests. Instead the crown granted hunting rights and the privilege of erecting deer parks to members of the aristocracy (at a price, of course) and so ensured their opposition to popular poaching. Gentlemen built deer parks for prestige reasons, and for profits from market sales.[38] The basic qualification of £100 a year

34. Unless otherwise annotated, all the evidence cited in the following paragraphs comes from D. Hay, 'Poaching and the Game Laws on Cannock Chase', in *Albion's Fatal Tree*, from R. B. Manning's *Village Revolts*, Chapter 11, or from his *Hunters and Poachers* (Oxford U.P., 1993).

35. Robert Kevelson, *Studies in Semiotics: Inlaws/Outlaws. A Semiotics of Systemic Interaction* (Indiana U.P., 1977). I couldn't resist quoting from a book so far removed from my interests. But I am not altogether happy about the author's dictum that 'there is an obvious relation between the card game of poker and the etymologically allied "poacher"'. My dictionary does not support this theory.

36. R. B. Manning, *Hunters and Poachers*, p. 57.

37. Ibid., p. 65.

38. Sharp, *In Contempt*, pp. 290–91, 303; Thirsk, *Agricultural Change*, pp. 142–3.

freehold was in 1750 between five and ten times the annual income of a labourer, and fifty times the qualification to vote for a knight of the shire. The penalty for keeping dogs or snares, or for killing rabbits in warren, was £5 or three months in gaol for those who could not pay; £30 or a year's imprisonment for killing deer; transportation or death if they were killed in the owner's park. The Game Act of 1719 declared deer-stealing a felony punishable by transportation. Four years later the Black Act made many hunting offences capital felonies. 'Liberty and forest laws are incompatible', wrote the Rev. Will Waterson in George II's reign.[39]

The traditional property qualification for the right to hunt was £2 per annum. This was raised by the early Stuarts to £40 for freeholders, £80 for copyholders. One effect of this was to exclude many *nouveaux riches* gentlemen who had purchased copyholds. No one without a sufficient estate might keep a hunting dog which had not been 'expediated' – i.e. prevented from chasing game by having two of its toes amputated. A statute of 1671 prohibited all freeholders with land worth less than £100 a year (or ninety-nine-year leaseholders worth £150 per annum) from killing game, even on their own land.[40] The qualified could hunt where they pleased. The emphasis on hunting as special privilege of a revived aristocracy gave a sharper edge to social protest.[41] Game, as P. B. Munsche puts it, 'became the property, not of the owner of the land on which it was found, but rather of an entire social class, the English country gentlemen'. Their supremacy was accentuated after 1671 by the reduction, from two to one, of the number of J.P.s required to impose a penalty under the game laws, and by legal acceptance of the evidence of a single witness as sufficient for a conviction. From the beginning of the eighteenth century those accused of offences against the game laws were increasingly tried by J.P.s without a jury.[42] Deer stealers were drawn into organized armies, recalling Robin Hood and his outlaws; they were 'armed foresters, enforcing the definition of rights to which the "country people" had become habituated'. Either because of the severity of the new sentences,

39. Quoted by E. P. Thompson, *Whigs and Hunters: The Origin of the Black Act* (1975), p. 49.
40. Thirsk, op. cit., pp. 194–8; G. M. Trevelyan, *Social History of England* (1942), pp. 279–82.
41. Sharp, 'Popular Protest', in Reay, *Popular Culture*, pp. 301–2.
42. P. B. Munsche, 'The Game Laws in Wiltshire, 1750–1800', in *Crime in England, 1550–1800* (ed. J. S. Cockburn, 1977), pp. 210–12.

or more probably through fear of reprisals, even J.P.s were often unenthu-
siastic about enforcing these laws.[43]

Resistance to the game laws was widespread and popular. In the second
half of the eighteenth century some 800 poachers were dealt with on
Cannock Chase, of whom 200 were known by name to the estate
stewards. 'The solidarity of the villagers was virtually complete' against
game-keepers: there were almost no informers. Poaching was a form of
social protest. There was a steady market for poached game – especially
among inn-keepers and butchers, who asked no questions. Many very
respectable characters bought stolen game, including parsons and Sir
Robert Walpole.[44]

'It is the common defence of a poacher', said Judge Christian, 'that it is
very hard that he should be punished for taking what he had as good a
right to as any other man.'[45] A steward complained that juries have 'a
strong bias . . . in favour of poachers, being professed enemies to all penal
laws that related to the game'. On the other hand, as another judge put
it, the commoner could not be allowed 'to destroy the estate of the lord
in order to preserve his own small right of common'.[46] But whatever
judges and preachers told them, some men must have felt that their
highest moral duty was to keep wife and children alive, even if it meant
breaking the law which protected the dubiously-acquired 'property' of
the rich.

Prudently, Parliament made most game offences punishable by J.P.s
acting without juries. In Surrey and Sussex, and no doubt elsewhere,
there was a trend away from court hearings in favour of summary convictions.[47] But even J.P.s could not always be relied on. When necessary,
Hay shows us, great landlords used their wealth to compel justices to do
what they wished. Village solidarity against the game laws was over-

43. Quoted by Edward Thompson, *Whigs and Hunters*, pp. 49–52, 59–67, 298–300.
44. Hay, op. cit., pp. 198–200, 207–9, 217, 241–7.
45. Edward Christian, *Charges delivered to Grand Juries in the Isle of Ely* (1809), quoted
by Hay, op. cit., p. 207. Judge Christian was 'always a frank defender of the unre-
formed law' (Hay, 'Property, Authority and the Civil Law', in *Albion's Fatal Tree*,
p. 58). A character in Smollett's *Humphry Clinker* agreed with Christian (op. cit.,
Navarre Soc., n.d., I, p.17).
46. Hay, 'Poaching and the Game Laws on Cannock Chase', ibid., pp. 211, 234; cf.
pp. 237, 248–9, 262–3.
47. Ed. A. Fletcher and J. Stevenson, *Order and Disorder in Early Modern England*
(Cambridge, U.P., 1985), pp. 19–26.

balanced by understandings among the members of the propertied class, in whose minds 'the game laws had little enough to do with any abstract idea of justice'. If disputes arose, the rich could always carry a case to a higher court, which would be immune to local opinion. M.P.s could bring trespassers before the House of Commons, which would rarely fail them.

A further social consideration was that the game laws helped 'to prevent persons of inferior rank from squandering that time which their station in life requireth to be more profitably employed' – more profitably of course to their potential employers. The poor must be protected from idleness. Poaching made labour discipline more difficult to enforce, because it helped the poor to feed their families without being forced into wage labour. Revolts against the game laws were 'among the few *free* expressions of the labouring poor'.[48]

IV

Venison became a social and prestige symbol. It was essential to hospitality, and for giving as gifts – to foreign ambassadors, to the Lord Mayor and aldermen of London, or to special friends. It had the prestige of the privileged hunt. 'Nobody would care for a present which everybody could give', said Lord Londonderry as late as 1827. Game could not legally be bought or sold, so venison was 'a special currency of class based on the solid standard of wealth, untainted by the commerce of the metropolis'. Those fortunate enough to be able to do so made regular gifts of venison to J.P.s and to judges on circuit. 'They sealed the bonds of class' and helped magistrates to remember the social importance of game laws. (Not of course with any idea of influencing verdicts, but it was useful for owners of game to be known to those who administered the law.) Poachers were therefore 'not only stealing a peculiarly valuable kind of social capital: they were also debasing its coinage. By supplying the black market they allowed tradesmen and Londoners to play the country gentleman at the dinner table'.[49]

Goldsmith's irony makes the point neatly:

48. Hay, in *Albion's Fatal Tree*, pp. 247, 191, 252.
49. Ibid., pp. 246–7.

> I get these things often . . .
> Some lords, my acquaintance, that settle the nation
> Are pleased to be kind – but I hate ostentation.[50]

The ancient punishment for killing the king's deer was loss of eyes and castration.[51] Early ballads about the outlaws stress that they

> Live by our Kinges deer;
> None other shift have we.[52]

In the ballad 'Robin Hood and Queen Katherine' the Queen wagered 'three hundred of the fattest harts / That run on Dallom-lee', in what the King agreed is 'a princely wager'.[53] From the sixteenth century the human population of England was increasing, the deer population contracting. So venison became more valuable and deer-stealing more profitable. This led to enclosing the deer in parks, established by royal licence, and protected by game-keepers. Trade in venison to meet the insatiable demand of the London market was too profitable to be stopped by Parliamentary statutes or royal proclamations.[54]

In the second half of the eighteenth century meat became too expensive for the poor to buy: if they could not poach game, bread and cheese had to replace it; and these too must be purchased. Venison could not legally be bought or sold; it was of course sold illegally, but peasants could not afford it anyway. Addison noted that yeomen qualified by the game laws could shoot hares or pheasants, and so could live much more cheaply than the poor.[55] 'What made directors cheat in South Sea year?' Pope asked. The answer was 'to live on venison when it sold so dear'.[56] 'A salmon from the pool, a wand from the wood, or a deer from the heath are thefts which no man was ever ashamed to own' ran the proverb.[57] The glorification of 'the roast beef of old England' came only after venison had been exhausted.[58]

50. Goldsmith, 'The Haunch of Venison', in *Works* (1845), I, p. 114.
51. Percy, *Reliques* (Everyman), I, p. 115.
52. 'A Little Geste of Robin Hood and his Meiny', in *Oxford Book of Ballads*, p. 561.
53. Ritson, op. cit., p. 333.
54. R. B. Manning, *Hunters and Poachers*, pp. 7, 70, 89, 133, 163.
55. *The Spectator*, 20 July 1711.
56. Pope, 'Epistle to Bathurst', in *Poems, Epistles and Satires* (Everyman ed.), p. 238.
57. Thomas Fielding, *Proverbs of all Nations* (1826), p. 7.
58. See Chapter 7 below.

So the statute of 1671 which made it a criminal offence for even freeholders (if they were worth less than £100 per annum) to kill deer linked the well-to-do against the rest. Poachers in breaking this law believed themselves (and were believed by many in their villages) to be exercising a traditional right which the rich had attempted to monopolize by usurping an exclusive *legal* privilege against customary rights. 'They came for venison, and venison they would have', said rioters in Waltham Forest in April 1642, *'for there was no law settled at this time'*. They were said to be led by a parson.[59]

Poaching continued after the defeat of freedom by property and its laws. Buchanan Sharp speaks of a newly 'self-conscious edge of social protest' in poaching after the restoration.[60] There is no need to glorify a past golden age of a prosperous peasantry: I doubt if it ever existed. What persists is the poverty amidst plenty of the eighteenth and nineteenth centuries – 'the rich man in his castle, the poor man at his gate' as the hymn put it. The fact that 'God made them high and lowly, and ordered their estate' is taken for granted: there will be short shrift for anyone upsetting this order.

'The eighteenth-century poor have not left a literature about the joys of poaching to match the gentry's eulogy of the hunt';[61] but the popular ballad 'The Lincolnshire Poacher' expresses something of the aesthetic satisfaction which poachers got from activities of which their betters tried to deprive them. The Lincolnshire poacher asserted a traditional right to take game where he found it, law or no law. 'Bad luck to every magistrate that lives in Lincolnshire'. 'In Robin Hood's bold Nottinghamshire' another ballad tells us of a sympathetic chairman of quarter sessions who dismissed a charge against a poacher.[62] We may compare

> Come all you gallant poachers
> That rambles devoid of care

commemorated in another ballad.[63]

---

59. R. B. Manning, *The English People and the English Revolution*, p. 190. My italics.
60. Sharp, 'Popular Protest', p. 302.
61. Hay, 'Poaching and the Game Laws', p. 201.
62. Ed. R. Bell, *Ballads and Songs of the Peasantry of England* (n.d.), pp. 214–17.
63. 'Van Dieman's Land', in *The Idiom of the People* (ed. J. Reeves, 1961), p. 217. The date must be after 1797, when Van Diemen's Land (Tasmania) was first colonized.

V

One of George Crabbe's *Tales* (1812), 'Advice, or the 'Squire and the Priest', throws retrospective light on the attraction of poaching for high-spirited young men. The tale combines concern for the poor with whole-hearted defence of the social order, which religion justifies. In this tale, the Squire told his young parson nephew, just about to preach his first sermon in the parish,

> There are sinners of a class so low
> That you with safety may the lash bestow;
> Poachers, and drunkards, idle rogues, who feed
> At others' cost, a marked correction need.
> And all the better sort, who see your zeal
> Will love and reverence for their pastor feel.

But the parson failed to take the point, and instead preached not on the wickedness of offences against property but exclusively on 'the power of grace' to redeem the worst of sinners – just like an enthusiastic dissenter. His uncle was horrified, and the parish was divided into factions, pro and con.[64]

Crabbe returned to the theme seven years later in *Tales of the Hall*. Here in 'Smugglers and Poachers' another young man, Robert Shelley (a foundling)

> would be a slave to no man – happy were the free
> And only they.

Crossed in love, Robert found that 'Danger only could repose produce', and he joined a gang of smugglers and poachers. Crabbe allowed the defender of unlicensed liberty to make a good case for smuggling. He made an even better case against those of the respectable godly who took advantage of the goods which smugglers and poachers supplied whilst reprobating the means by which they were acquired.

> He found that some, who should the trade prevent,
> Gave it by purchase their encouragement;
> He found that contracts could be made with those

64. Crabbe, *Poetical Works*, p. 301.

Who had their pay these dealers to oppose;
And the good ladies whom at church he saw,
With looks devout, of reverence and awe,
Could change their feelings as they changed their place,
And, whispering, deal for spicery and lace.

His goody-goody brother James, 'better taught',

> Sighed to think how near he was akin
> To one seduced by godless men to sin.

The attraction, Crabbe recognized, was in the risk involved:

> The smuggler cries
> 'What guilt is his who pays for what he buys?'
> The poacher questions, with perverted mind,
> 'Were not the gifts of heaven for all designed?'
> *This* cries 'I sin not – take not till I pay';
> *That* 'My own hand brought down my proper prey';
> And while to such fond arguments they cling,
> How fear they God? how honour they the king?

In the end James was killed in helping to round up poachers, among whom his brother Robert was also killed.

> 'Seized you the poachers?' said my lord. – 'They fled
> And we pursued not – one of them was dead,
> And one of us; they hurried through the wood,
> Two lives were gone, and we no more pursued,
> Two lives of men, of valiant brothers lost!
> Enough, my lord, do hares and pheasants cost?'

His lordship accepted the point, and no longer 'takes such dreadful vengeance for a hare'; and Crabbe, remembering his priestly function, tells 'the pious and the humble' that ''tis wisdom to be good, 'tis virtue to obey'.[65]

In Robert's bid for freedom by joining a gang of law-breakers Crabbe saw only an individual seeking excitement. He gives us no idea of what the community thought. The young man who sought liberty found death at the hands of property and law; the poet who seemed to be holding the balance even came down with a bump on the side of property and platitude.

65. Crabbe, op. cit., pp. 487–92.

Poaching, like smuggling, often had the approval of the community behind it; particularly when the poaching was directed against an unpopular landlord. The law against poaching, enforced by landowning J.P.s, seemed merely a weapon in the war between village solidarity and the class solidarity of landlords.[66] In December 1785 twelve poachers, after shooting as many pheasants in the woods of Mr Lane of Barmingham 'as they thought proper . . . drew up before his house, played several tunes on the German flute, fired a volley, wished Mr. Lane a good morning, gave three cheers, and then retired'.[67]

A recently published biography of 'the King of Norfolk Poachers' is a late example, but it gives his own account of his life and times. Its authenticity is open to question, since it was very self-consciously written by himself and edited for publication by Rider Haggard's daughter. But this is at least a guarantee that it had to be plausible; the poacher was a well-known character, on whom Sir Rider had sat in judgment on the bench. He had a sort of love-hate relationship with authority; a running battle with the police was punctuated by occasional unofficial deals – as when his poaching net was returned to him in exchange for a hare. 'The King of Norfolk Poachers' claims, reasonably, that in the later nineteenth century men were often driven to poaching by economic necessity. But 'some did it for the sake of sport and the excitement of the game. That was so in my case, and a great many more besides. – I loved the excitement. . . . You know the satisfaction of knowing that you had got keepers and police beat, and that went a big way towards recompence for the danger and risk run'. 'I did not mind paying these fines as long as I kept my liberty'.

It was not all good-natured fun, however. On one occasion he had to leave his area for a time, after badly beating up a game-keeper. At another time he did some research in the parish archives and led an agitation for the implementation of old charters benefiting the poor, and the restoration of land to charitable purposes. In order to get rid of him, he was offered a free passage to Canada. Instead he accepted a job as game-keeper for a newcomer to the village. He was naturally successful in this job; but he soon returned to poaching. 'I think it was born in me'. 'A poacher can most times make a living' provided he keeps a still tongue in his head and

66. Douglas Hay, 'Poaching and the Game Laws on Cannock Chase', in *Albion's Fatal Tree* (ed. Hay and others, 1975), p. 244. Cf. pp. 97–100 above.
67. E. A. Goodwyn, *Selections from Norwich Newspapers, 1760–1790* (1972), p. 26.

doesn't boast of his achievements. For the poacher was useful to the community: 'a great many people would be surprised to know what the Poacher is asked to do for other people; . . . they think he is an outlaw, and they make a tool of him as much as they choose'. Like many others, he found Biblical authority for his trade. 'Did not God say that he gave all the beasts and birds for the use of man, not the rich alone?' In World War I he volunteered and served in the army; but he disliked war memorials which said that the war had been fought 'for God and victory'. He was a social reformer: if there were more jobs for all as they left school there would be no crime. 'A poacher is a hard-worken man', but he gets much pleasure from his occupation, though he recognized that the day of the professional poacher was now over.[68]

The expression of some of these ideas has no doubt been improved by his editor; but she can hardly have attributed to such a well-known character views which were merely invented. 'Truth', said a late twentieth-century civil servant apropos answers to questions in parliament, 'is a difficult question'. The genre of ghosted autobiography recalls that of the memoirs of superannuated politicians which have proliferated since the reign of Lady Thatcher. They no doubt make the best case they can for themselves; but to tell obvious untruths would defeat their purposes.

An interesting article in *The Guardian*'s 'Society' supplement of 14 September 1994 describes the life of a full-time English poacher, recently semi-retired after a life-time of professional activity. The article is accompanied by approving comments on poachers from (among others) a bank manager ('It had a Robin Hood aspect to it') and a doctor whose father was 'almost spiritually diminished' when he stopped poaching. A passage is also quoted from an article by an Edinburgh Professor of Theology who cannot 'be persuaded that poaching is a crime, or even a sin'. 'The persecution of poachers', he claims, 'is one of the clearest symptoms of a continuing class war in Britain'. Even law-abiding citizens showed great tolerance for poachers who were useful to them.

68. Ed. Lilias Rider Haggard, *I Walked by Night*: . . . the Life and History of the King of *Norfolk Poachers* (1935), pp. 52, 68, 70, 108–11, 117, 139–40, 149–50, 161–4, 173–6, 179–80, and *passim*.

8. Smugglers

====

> The smuggler ... would have been in every respect an excellent
> citizen had not the laws of his country made that a crime which
> nature never meant to be so.
>
> Adam Smith, *The Wealth of Nations* (World's Classics), II, p. 563.
> First published 1776.

Smugglers have been dealt with very effectively by Cal Winslow, 'Sussex
Smugglers', in *Albion's Fatal Tree*. Here I shall add only a few points
relating them to my main theme.

Like poachers, smugglers could be seen as poor men's pirates. Items of
consumption as important as tea, salt, clothes, liquor, were taxed so
highly that the poor could not afford them.[1] Both poachers and smugglers
disregarded the law in order to supply cheaper commodities in general
demand – by eliminating customs officers' rake-off (i.e. the state's) in the
case of smugglers, by cutting out the middleman in the case of poachers.
In eighteenth-century France the smuggler Robert Mandrin was cast for
the role of 'noble robber' and became a popular hero.[2] After the passage
which I quoted as epigraph to this chapter Adam Smith continued: 'In
those corrupted governments where there is at least a general suspicion of
much unnecessary expense, and great misapplication of the public revenue,
the laws which guard it are little respected'. Could he perhaps have been
thinking of eighteenth-century England?

Smugglers carried to its logical conclusion the doctrine of individualism
preached in innumerable pulpits as well as by Adam Smith. Or – to take a
different argument – Robin Hood rejected William the Conqueror's
forest laws because they cut off sources of food and fuel to which Englishmen believed (on Biblical authority) that they should have free access.
Few young men of my generation returned from a trip to Paris without a
copy of Joyce's *Ulysses* concealed about their person, because they did not

---

1. Patrick Pringle, *Honest Thieves: The Story of Smugglers* (1938), p. 14.
2. Hobsbawm, *Bandits*, p. 57.

accept the justice of the law which forbade its importation. This law seemed irrational; eighteenth-century customs law seemed immoral because it was *class* legislation.

Smugglers were much less romantic than highwaymen or even poachers. The smuggler – like the poacher – got immediate cash returns for what became a routine business operation. Nevertheless, smugglers performed a socially useful service, at some risk to themselves; the penalties for those detected were severe – £50 fine under 19 George II c. 69. It cost a convicted purchaser of smuggled goods £10 for each purchase; the supplier could be released from his fine if he denounced the purchasers.[3] Some smugglers saw themselves as asserting traditional communal rights against the legislative encroachments of a state which represented the interests of a minority of rich property owners. Smugglers were claiming freedom from unpopular laws.

Smuggling in maritime counties of England was more than tolerated by local opinion, just as excisemen were always objects of popular hostility. The excise had been hated since its introduction in the 1640s when there were riots against it all over the country. In 1649 the Leveller rebel William Thompson 'plundered the holy treasures of the excise' in Northampton, and 'distributed it among the poor out of whose purses it was wrack't by the device of an ordinance'.[4] In a broadside poem of 1659 entitled 'A Dialogue betwixt an Excise-Man and Death' the conclusion is:

> Let all Excise-men hereby warning take,
> To shun their practice for their conscience sake.[5]

But a song published in the collection called *Rump* (1662) suggested that 'an Exciseman's conscience well seared', when mixed with other unpleasing ingredients, was 'a dish for the Devil and for his dam too'.[6] It was in a long tradition that over a century later Burns wrote a song attributed to 'ilka wife' in the town, the concluding lines of which ran

3. Ed. J. Beresford, *The Diary of a Country Parson – The Rev. James Woodforde* (Oxford U.P., 1981), III, p. 373n.
4. *Mercurius Pragmaticus*, 22–29 May 1649, No. 370. Usefully reprinted in *Making the News: An Anthology of the Newsbooks of Revolutionary England, 1641–1660* (ed. J. Raymond, Moreton-in-Marsh, 1993), p. 398.
5. Ed. R. Bell, *Ballads and Songs of the Peasantry of England*, pp. 30–32.
6. *Rump: or an Exact Collection of the Choycest Poems and Songs relating to the Late Times*, II, p. 164.

> The ae best dance ere came to the land
> Was the Deil's awa wi'th' Exciseman.[7]

It is doubtless no coincidence that both Burns and Paine had been excisemen.

Smuggling retained something of the Robin Hood Spirit. 'Tens of thousands of people were involved' in 'resistance, carried on by the poor, to the laws and institutions of their rulers'. In 1744 smugglers were 'got to an amazing height on the Kentish and Sussex coasts'. Twenty thousand smugglers was one contemporary estimate. 'The generality of people on the coasts are better friends to the smugglers than they are to the Customs House Officers'. 'Not one person in ten . . . but would give them assistance'. 'No magistrate, it was said, dared proceed against smugglers', or his house might be burnt down. It was calculated that more than three times the amount of legitimate tea imports was smuggled, until in 1745 the tea duty was slashed from 4 s. to 1 s. per pound. In 1744 soldiers in Sussex refused to assist the customs officers, and in some cases seem actually to have collaborated with the law-breakers. 'Smuggling was so common and involved so many people' that 'the Customs officers often had to face the open wrath of the entire community'. ('It was no sin to kill customs officers'.)[8] Female smugglers in Cornwall towards the end of the eighteenth century concealed spirits in 'bladders fastened under their petticoats . . . They were so heavily laden that it was with great apparent difficulty they waddled along' from the vessel to Plymouth, periodically interrupted by drunken sailors.[9]

The Ordinary of Newgate's statement that 'the common people of England in general fancy there is nothing in the crime of smuggling' is abundantly confirmed by other evidence. 'In some cases . . . entire communities supported the smugglers and would rise in their defence'. Smuggling was considered a legitimate part of the local economy, to which the poor – like poachers – claimed they had a right by custom and tradition. 'For the poor . . . smuggling often meant the difference between a bare subsistence and worse. Resistance of the plebeian smugglers . . . was also an aspect of the class struggle of the eighteenth century'. But 'only the poor

---

7. Burns, *Poems and Songs* (Everyman ed.), pp. 560–63.
8. Winslow, op. cit., pp. 148–60, in *Albion's Fatal Tree*.
9. George Lipscombe, *A Journey into Cornwall* (1799), pp. 227–8, quoted by Bridget Hill, *Women, Work and Sexual Politics in Eighteenth-Century England* (Oxford, 1989), p. 162.

went to the gallows, a fact that was not missed by the common people of Sussex'. After the government's bloody suppression, many smugglers 'took to the highway'. Dick Turpin had been a smuggler before he turned highwayman.[10]

Walpole admitted that the militia would protect rather than suppress smugglers. He himself used an admiralty barge to run his smuggled wine up the Thames.[11] Many of the clergy were deeply involved. Parson Wood-forde had regular dealings with a smuggler who kept him supplied with tubs of gin and brandy, each containing four gallons, plus the occasional pound of tea and Indian silk handkerchiefs. He recorded these transactions openly in his diary, lapsing into the decent obscurity of a learned language only when warning himself to be cautious. He sometimes worried about nasty rumours going round the parish, and in 1792 a smuggler was caught and fined. Fortunately he thought it would be wrong to inform on the parson.[12]

John Wesley's attitude was rather different. His mother had permitted her children, as soon as they had grown pretty strong, to drink small beer and eat as much as they wanted. Wesley was no teetotaller. But he was shocked to find in the 1750s and 1760s that many members of his congregations in coastal regions were deeply engaged in buying and selling smuggled goods. In July 1753 nearly all the members of the St Ives congregation in Cornwall were so occupied. In September 1762 Wesley reported with some satisfaction that there was now no more smuggling among members of the congregation at Port Isaac in the same county. He persuaded some 250 members of the Sunderland congregation to abandon the practice in 1757, though some refused. Wesley thought this as bad as highway robbery. In December 1765 he noted with satisfaction a reduction in smuggling activities by members of the Dover congregation.[13]

10. Winslow, op. cit., pp. 148–60.

11. I. Gilmour, *Riot, Risings and Revolution: Government and Violence in 18th-century England* (1992), pp. 94–5, 98, 163; Roy Porter, *English Society in the Eighteenth Century* (Penguin, 1982), pp. 114–15.

12. Woodforde, *Diary*, I, pp. 197, 282; II, ¡pp. 39, 45, 77, 292; III, pp. 30, 86; IV, pp. 99, 156, 362.

13. Wesley, *Journal* (1864–8), I, p. 364; II, pp. 285, 392, 410; III, pp. 109, 228, 419; IV, p. 251.

9. Pirates

Words said to have been spoken by a pirate to Alexander the Great: How darest thou molest the whole world? But because I do it with a little ship only, I am called a thief: thou, doing it with a great navy, art called an emperor.

St Augustine, *The City of God*, Book IV, Chapter iv.

In Gay's *Polly* Macheath found the transition from highwayman to pirate easy: the same rhetoric was used by both. In Elizabeth's reign piracy had become a relatively respectable occupation. Henry VII and VIII had established order of a sort by reducing the power of the aristocracy. Noble castles were destroyed, gangs of retainers disbanded. Younger sons of the gentry, of whom more were surviving as there was less and less land for them to inherit, had to find remunerative employment. On the continent younger sons could hope for jobs in the army or the growing bureaucracy of absolute monarchies. English younger sons had to look elsewhere for careers: but they had freedom of choice. Some took service in continental armies, where there was always employment for them. Elsewhere exploration – or piracy – offered exciting prospects. As Bacon observed, the mariner's compass and gunpowder had opened up the world to European trade, European plunder and European domination: 'To win new worlds, for gold, for praise, for glory', as Ralegh put it.[1] Starting with Ireland, colonization was a matter for private enterprise, not for the state until the days of Cromwell's Irish deportations and his Western Design. The Armada had shown how useful sea-dogs could be to an island without a strong navy: private enterprise defeated Spain, private enterprise colonized Ireland and began to expand English trade to Asia and America.

Sea-dogs, plunderers of the Spanish main, had a patriotic and protestant glamour. They brought much-needed bullion from Catholic Spain to

---

1. Ralegh, *Poems* (ed. A. M. C. Latham, 1951), p. 27. Some of the points in this chapter are developed further in my 'Radical Pirates?', in *People and Ideas in 17th-century England* (Brighton, 1986).

England. Queen Elizabeth found anti-Spanish pirates useful: she knighted Drake and Hawkins. James I, less sensitive to public opinion, had Sir Walter Ralegh executed – it was believed at the behest of Spain. Like Robin Hood, pirates saw themselves as rulers of a sphere independent of the English crown. A ballad from the early seventeenth century – apparently not published until after 1688 – had a pirate boasting

> Tell your king from me
> If he reigns king on all the land, Ward will reign on the sea.

Captain Ward consciously looked back to Robin Hood, renaming a captured French vessel 'Little John'.[2] If pirates sometimes plundered English merchants, the latter were members of privileged trading companies, profiting by a monopoly at the expense of the community. Pirates cut out those who had bought privileges from the state. Even after governments by the beginning of the eighteenth century clamped down on pirates who interrupted English trade, the author of *The History of the Pyrates* in 1724 emphasized the reluctance of juries to return guilty verdicts; and Tyburn crowds showed some sympathy for a pirate who died well.[3] We may compare the reluctance of juries to declare unmarried mothers guilty of infanticide: there may in both instances have been a recognition of overwhelming pressures bearing down on the accused.

The History of the Pyrates, sometimes attributed to Defoe, is not necessarily reliable as evidence of what pirates actually did or said. But it is evidence of what public opinion was prepared to believe. Pirate crews tended to be composed of men 'deeply alienated from their own societies'.[4] Their discipline, in contrast with that of naval or merchant vessels, was democratic. Like Robin Hood, many pirates were fiercely anti-clerical: they opposed the slave trade and liberated slaves.[5] The point was made by Gay's Polly in the West Indies. 'An open war with the whole world is

2. A. L. Lloyd, *Folk-Song in England* (1975), pp. 259–60; cf. 'The Seaman's Song of Captain Ward', *Douce Ballads*, No. 199; Peter Lamborn Wilson, *Pirate; Utopias: Moorish Corsairs and European Renegades*, p. 55. I am grateful to Peter Wilson for sending me a copy of this pioneering book.
3. Evelyn Berckman, *Victims of Piracy: The Admiralty Courty, 1575–1678* (1975), Chapter 6.
4. Cf. Marcus Rediker, '"Under the Banner of King Death": The Social World of Anglo-American Pirates, 1716–1726', *William and Mary Quarterly*, 3rd series, XXXVIII (1981), pp. 203–27.
5. R. C. Ritchie, *Captain Kidd and the War against the Pirates* (Harvard U.P., 1986), p. 233.

brave and honourable' – as opposed to a clandestine pilfering war against neighbours in civil society. "Tis only for poor people to be brave and desperate, who cannot afford to live'.[6] The name of the legendary Captain Kidd was coupled with that of Robin Hood, and in 1718 a pirate crew claimed to be 'Robbin Hood's men'.[7] There was an extensive imaginative literature associated with pirates and their islands, from 1534 down to the utopian settlement of Libertalia on Madagascar, described in *The History of the Pyrates*.[8]

The anti-Spanish tradition continued to be strong among English pirates, for whom the Caribbean and the route thence to Spain was most profitable. In the 1630s the Providence Island Company (Treasurer John Pym) set up a Puritan outpost on that island. Its originally proclaimed object was to bring true religion to native Americans, but its main occupation soon came to be plundering the Spanish mainland, where allies were found among the natives. The Providence Island Company got no support from Charles I's government, and the colony was finally overrun by Spain in 1641.[9] But things changed after Parliament's victory in the civil war, in which Cowley's 'The Publick Pyrat', the Earl of Warwick, had commanded the Parliamentarian navy. Cromwell's Western Design of 1655, which led to the capture of Jamaica, was the first move by the English state to acquire a stable base in the Caribbean. But there had been much unofficial emigration, 'many going to the West Indies for liberty of their consciences' as Walwyn put it in 1644.[10]

So pirates, like smugglers later, performed some socially useful functions: it was not an occupation to be ashamed of. Claydon House preserved a portrait of Sir Francis Verney, who had been a pirate for several years in James I's reign before dying at the age of thirty-one.[11] Pamphleteers in 1580 and 1615 noted that unemployment and vagabondage drove men to

6. Gay, *Polly: An Opera* (1729), Act II, scene v.
7. W. H. Bonner, *The Life and Legends of Captain Kidd* (Rutgers College, New Jersey, 1947), p. 203; Ritchie, op. cit., *passim*; ed. J. F. Jameson, *Privateering and Piracy in the Colonial Period* (New York, 1923), p. 304.
8. See my 'Radical Pirates?', esp. pp. 175–9.
9. Karen O. Kupperman, *Providence Island, 1630–1641: The Other Puritan Colony* (Cambridge U.P., 1993); cf. esp. p. 93 for anti-Spanish pirates; and Defoe, *The King of Pirates* (1895), p. 11. First published 1720.
10. Ed. A. Pritchard, *Cowley, 'The Civil War'* (Toronto U.P., 1973), p. 98; Walwyn, *Good Counsell to All*, in *The Writings of William Walwyn* (ed. J. R. McMichael and Barbara Taft, Georgia U.P., 1980), p. 128.
11. Verney, *Memoirs*, I, pp. 64–9.

piracy; both suggested state support for the fishing industry as a remedy.[12]

As soon as one starts to look for it, there is a good deal of literary evidence for pirates' libertarian sentiments. As early as 1534 Michael James of Hampton accepted the view that soon 'there shall be no clean man able to live within the realm of England, but that he shall be sought out and hanged up, till there shall be an insurrection within the realm'. His remedy was to turn pirate and 'obtain many great booties'; his crew would establish themselves on 'a certain island, whose name he remembreth not', where they would be able to live in freedom.[13] A pamphlet published in 1639 was entitled *A True Relation of the Lives and Deaths of the two most Famous English Pyrates, Purser and Clinton*. According to this account, they were common seamen who reflected 'what baseness it was in them to be no better than servants . . . who had the ability to command'. Thinking it high time to become 'freemen of the seas' they drew in several discontented sailors at Plymouth and formed a crew, seeing themselves as 'half lords at sea'. They had a brief but successful career, till Queen Elizabeth 'thought rather by her clemency to reclaim them' and offered a pardon. But 'they were then free commanders', and rejected the offer. In consequence they were proclaimed traitors, captured and ultimately executed.[14]

Mariners frequently deserted from naval or merchant vessels to join pirate crews. One attraction of course was the prospect of plunder. But perhaps more immediately appealing was the relatively democratic discipline on pirate vessels. Sir William Monson in James I's reign declared that mariners preferred the 'liberty' (his word) of service on a privateer, where risks and profits were shared, to the irregular wages and floggings of the king's ships. Pirate crews had a 'rough, improvised but effective egalitarianism that placed authority in the collective hands of the crew'. Captains were often elected, and were answerable to their crews; decisions on policy and disciplinary punishments were democratically taken. This contrasted very sharply with the despotism of naval captains, the rule of the lash, the ultimate possibility of a death sentence for mutiny.[15] By

12. Robert Hitchcock, *A Politic Plat for . . . relief of the poor, preservation of the rich, reformation of rogues and idle persons . . .* (1580), in Arber, *An English Garner*, II, esp. p. 160; E. S., *Britain's Buss, or A Computation, as well of the Charge of a Buss Herring Fishing Ship; as also of the Gain and Profit thereby*, Arber, op. cit., III, p. 652.
13. *Lisle Letters* (ed. Muriel St Clare Byrne, Chicago U.P., 1980), II, p. 113.
14. Op. cit., esp. Part I, Chapter 5, and Part II, Chapter 1.
15. Ed. M. Oppenheim, *The Naval Tracts of Sir William Monson* (Naval Records Soc., II, 1902), p. 237.

contrast with the slavery of a naval vessel to which the poor were forcibly
– but legally – press-ganged, a pirate ship offered freedom. 'Laws and
hierarchy did not exist on board [a pirate] ship or in the pirate settlements'.
Captain and crew wore the same type of garments.[16] It was the difference
between a factory and a co-operative. Captured slaves were liberated; in
Gay's *Polly* plantation slaves desert to the pirates (Act III, scene xiii) – as
they might well have done in real life.

The pirate Captain Misson is reported as saying that all men are born
free, but 'the greater part of the inhabitants of the globe' were 'born and
bred in slavery, by which their spirits were broken'. 'Ignorant of their
birthright and the sweets of liberty', they 'dance to the music of their
chains'. His crew 'were resolved to assert that liberty which God and
nature gave them', and 'owned no subjection to any, further than was for
the good of all'. Captain Bellamy 'would not submit to be governed by
laws which rich men have made for their own security . . . They rob the
poor under cover of law, forsooth, and we plunder the rich under the
protection of our own courage'. One of his crew claimed to have joined
'those marine heroes, the scourge of tyrants and avarice, and the brave
assertors of liberty'. Such sentiments were no doubt handed on from tract
to tract. In Captain Misson's ship officers were elected, captured slaves
were liberated and encouraged to join the crew on equal terms.[17]

Words like those I have just quoted, when I first read them, seemed to
me too dramatic to be true; and no doubt they were improved in the
recording. But after taking into account the evidence which I collected in
'Radical Pirates?' and in this chapter I am more prepared to believe that
they represent thoughts which some Englishmen entertained. This helps
to explain why in 1584 the bishops added piracy to the list of 'other grave
crimes' for which excommunication might be imposed. That there were
theorists among pirates is suggested by the fact that on trial they were
denied benefit of clergy.[18]

16. Ritchie, *Captain Kidd*, p. 123.
17. Charles Johnson, op. cit., p. 597; Lincoln B. Faller, *Crime and Defoe: A New Kind
of Writing* (Cambridge U.P., 1993), p. 196; M. Rediker, 'Under the Banner of King
Death', pp. 203–27; R. C. Ritchie, *Captain Kidd*, pp. 123–4; my 'Radical Pirates?',
pp. 163–4. With 'Libertalia' compare 'Eleutheria' in the Bahamas in 1647 – not a
pirate settlement though very radical (Robert Brenner, *Merchants and Revolution:
Commercial Change, Political Conflict and London's Overseas Traders, 1550–1653*, Princeton U.P., 1993, pp. 523–8).
18. Ed. A. Sparrow, *A Collection of Articles of the Church of England* (1661), p. 251;
Rediker, 'Under the Banner of King Death', p. 218.

Peter Wilson draws attention to the interesting coincidence that the years 1640 to 1660 were the golden age of the republic of Salé in North Africa, which is the centre of his studies, as they were an age of experimentation and achievement in England. Salé had a treaty with the Dutch republic and was recognized by the government. Many European renegadoes moved into the relatively democratic corsair republic. Did any ideas of influence come back from there to England?[19]

Marcus Rediker also emphasizes the relatively democratic arrangements of pirate crews and settlements. 'Even more revealing', he writes in a phrase relevant to this book, 'pirates abolished the wage. They considered themselves risk-sharing partners rather than a collection of "hands" who sold their muscle on an open market'. He adds the valuable comment, 'the social organization of piracy was part of the tenacious tradition that linked medieval peasants, seventeenth-century radicals such as Ranters and Levellers, and the free wage labourers of the eighteenth century'. 'Pirates constructed a culture of masterless men'.[20] As opposed to merchants and captains who appealed to contract and law, seamen 'used custom to guarantee their privilege and their right to "the necessaries of life"'. 'By the middle of the eighteenth century the language of contract had in many ways supplanted the language of custom at sea'. The captain of a privateer denounced his crew as 'a gang of Levellers' when they mutinied and cut out the shares of the 'Gentlemen Owners' who had financed the voyage. Their 'new establishment was more like a Commonwealth than an absolute monarchy', it was said of a similar mutiny. This, Rediker insists, contributed to the ideology of the American Revolution, in which seamen played a prominent part. 'The seaman who defended himself against impressment felt that he was fighting to defend his "liberty", and he justified his resistance on grounds of right'. It led into the concept of the rights of man.[21]

When a group of pirates made what was intended as a permanent settlement on Madagascar in the 1690s, they called it Libertalia. There are many stories about this settlement, some no doubt fictitious. On Libertalia the booty and cattle were said to have been divided equally 'according to

19. Wilson, op. cit., Chapter VI.
20. Rediker, *Between the Devil and the Deep Blue Sea: Merchant Seamen, Pirates, and the Anglo-American Maritime World, 1700–1750* (Cambridge U.P., 1987), pp. 107–8, 118, 247, 261–4, 286.
21. Ibid., pp. 150, 233, 252, Chapter 6 *passim*. For impressment see Chapter 13 below.

the law of pirates', and money was held in a common treasury, 'being of no use where everything was in common, and no hedge bounded any particular man's property'. Government was democratically elected. 'In a free state as we were', it was reported from another settlement on Madagascar, 'everybody was free to go wherever they would'.[22]

Libertalia and Eleutheria in the Bahamas are the only examples known to me of post-Robin Hood communities which were not divided into two (or more) classes, based on property. Plantations in Ireland, America or elsewhere required capital to start them off, and so were dependent on men of property. Intending colonists were instructed to bring servants with them: there were two classes from the beginning. Hence laws were needed, discipline, to maintain control by men of property – all backed up by help from England when necessary. Some offshoots might set off with minimal capital – Mrs Anne Hutchinson and her followers after their banishment, for instance; but they could not last for long in that state. Pirates had from the start no master–servant relationship, no dependence on foreign capital such as bedevilled plantations in North America. If pirates were lucky, capital came in windfalls from fortunate captures, and would be communal property. When pirates did make settlements they would be likely to carry over into them the democratic organization to which they had become accustomed aboard ship, and the communal sharing of loot. A crew of privateers, former sympathizers with Monmouth's rebellion of 1685, in 1697 set up 'a little commonwealth' on Providence Island, with its own laws and an elected governor. The Dutch Governor of Mauritius complained, after encountering a pirate crew, that 'every man had as much to say as the captain, and each man carried his own weapon in his blanket'.[23]

Pirate freedom extended to sexual relations. Women were not unknown on board, and wife-sharing was reported. One crew traded a vessel to a slaver in exchange for sixty African women. The ship was renamed *The Bachelor's Delight*. Anne Berry and Mary Read were notorious women pirates who successfully pleaded their bellies when their crew was on trial for piracy. Homosexual relations were no doubt more common and were not subject to penalties as in the navy. Marlene Brant points out that a favourite metaphor for harlot was ship – cf. Milton's

22. 'Radical Pirates?', pp. 163–4.
23. *A Relation of the great sufferings and strange adventures of Henry Pitman*, in Arber, op. cit., VII, p. 366; Ritchie, op. cit., p. 124.

Dalilah in *Samson Agonistes*.[24] Homosexuality was especially associated with pirate crews. D. R. Burg suggests that homosexually-inclined men deliberately chose to leave England for environments in which there was a preponderance of men, such as early Virginia and the West Indies. In the latter women were long 'statistically insignificant'. But on pirate vessels they were even more scarce.[25]

The democratic structure was reproduced in pirate settlements ashore, notably in Madagascar, where *The History of the Pyrates* has stories of polygamy being permitted. Samuel Burgess returned to Madagascar to live after having been successively pirate, slave, merchant captain, privateer and condemned man. The island offered him more freedom than any other place.[26] The woman pirate Mary Read thought that if there were no death sentence for piracy, 'many of those who are now cheating the widows and orphans, and oppressing their poor neighbours who have no money to obtain justice, would then rob at sea, and the ocean would be crowded with rogues like the land'.[27] In Gay's second opera Polly, disguised as a man, told the pirates that she wished to join them because she hated 'the clandestine pilfering war that is practised among friends and neighbours in civil societies' (Act II, scene v). 'We are for a just partition of the world, for every man hath a right to enjoy life' (Act III, scene i).

Other pirate settlements were said to be no less democratic.[28] Defoe echoed Bellamy[29] when he spoke of the famous French robber Cartouche retiring 'as other wealthy merchants do'.[30]

Piracy on the Spanish main in the sixteenth and early seventeenth centuries was one thing: piracy in the English Channel was always another. By the later seventeenth century trade had become all-important

24. M. Brant, *The Literature of the London Underworld*, 1660–1720 (Newcastle Polytechnic M.Phil, 1982), pp. 155–68.
25. Ritchie, *Captain Kidd*, pp. 123–4, 161, 258, 276; Burg, *Sodomy and the Pirate Tradition: English Sea Rovers in the Seventeenth-Century Caribbean* (New York, 1984), esp. pp. 57–8, 67–8, 75–105, 111–17, 179. Professor Burg's statistics give cause for thought.
26. 'Radical Pirates?', p. 178; Ritchie, op. cit., p. 123.
27. Charles Johnson, *A General History of . . . the Pyrates* (1736), p. 228.
28. Defoe, *The King of Pirates*, p. 81; cf. pp. 27–8 and 281 of the same volume.
29. See p. 118 above.
30. Defoe, *An Account of the Cartoucheans in France* (1724), in *The King of Pirates*, p. 110. One retired pirate settled in a place which he named 'Ranter Bay' ('Radical Pirates?', pp. 178, 187).

to the English economy and standard of living. Piracy was suppressed. Smugglers survived into the modern world. When they successfully responded to the demands of the market they became capitalist big business men.[31]

---

31. When I was a small boy there was a shocked legend in my middle-class nonconformist family to the effect that one of our eighteenth-century ancestors had been a pirate. He was mentioned in the same hushed tone as 'Henry who married the Housemaid'. But after writing this chapter and the chapters in Part IV I am prepared to take the legend more seriously. Perhaps such myths preserve truths which history wishes to forget.

10. Highwaymen

=====

> The Scripture I fulfilled . . .
> For when the naked I beheld
> I clothed them with speed . . .
> The poor I fed, the rich likewise
> I empty sent away.
>
> *Pepys Ballads*, VII, p. 316. Words attributed to a highwayman
> named Bliss, executed in December 1695 – echoing words attrib-
> uted to Robin Hood. The same words were later given to Dick
> Turpin. For Robin Hood, see Chapter 5 above.

The word 'highwayman' is said to have first occurred in 1642.[1] But the
profession is much older. In the bellicose and unpoliced society of the
Middle Ages the strong naturally robbed the weak. Robin Hood held up
rich suspects as they travelled through the forests. But from the sixteenth
century onwards far more business was being conducted over wider
areas: the word 'highwayman' testifies to the existence of regular trade
routes on highways. A pamphlet of 1674 suggested that highwaymen
preferred to ply their trade on Sundays, when the only travellers were
those on urgent business, and so the roads were quiet and it was harder to
start up a hue and cry. Even avoiding Sundays, the author added, it was
better to choose side-roads and to travel at night.[2]

There had long been a good deal of freelance, part-time highway
robbery, in which Sir John Falstaff was not ashamed to take part (*I Henry
IV*, IV.i). A son of Colonel Thomas Blood, famous as the crown-stealer,
was a highwayman.[3] Chief Justice Sir John Popham (1531?–1607) was

---

1. C. V. Wedgwood, *History and Hope* (1987), p. 307. For highwaymen in general see
J. S. Cockburn, 'The Nature and Incidence of Crime in England, 1559–1625: A
Preliminary Survey', in *Crime in England, 1550–1800* (ed. Cockburn, 1977).
2. [Anon.], *Jacksons Recantation, or, the Life and Death of the Notorious High-Way-Man*
(1674), pp. 154, 167–9. A MS note in the Bodleian Library's copy attributes this
pamphlet to Richard Head.
3. L. Stone, *Broken Lives: Separation and Divorce in England (1660–1857)* (Oxford U.P.,
1993), p. 38.

said to have been in his youth 'wont to take a purse in the company of a number of profligate companions'. This was no doubt when he was an undergraduate at Balliol, but some say that the habit continued for a dozen years or so. Of him the story is told that, having to try one of his former 'profligate companions', he asked after old friends and was told, 'You and I, my lord, are the only ones left'. Popham is interesting for our purposes: Aubrey alleges that he stocked the Virginian plantations 'out of all the gaols of England'.[4] George Sandys, poet and later Treasurer of the Virginia Company, was found not guilty of four highway robberies, though his companion in three of them was hanged: one suspects that the son of an Archbishop was treated specially leniently.[5]

But highway robbery was becoming a full-time occupation. Soldiers returning from military service on the continent often found that survival depended on begging or robbery. The ballad 'The Low-Country Soldier: or His Humble Petition at his Return into England' put this point succinctly:

> The High-way is my hope:
> His Heart's not big, that fears a little rope.[6]

Highwaymen succeeded to something of the Robin Hood legend. But outlaws, like pirates, formed communities outside the law, with their own self-justifying ideologies, real or attributed. The shared excitement of their lives helped to bond them together. The highwayman, on the contrary, was an individualist, as befitted a more capitalist society. He might have assistants, but normally he was a loner. Elizabethan merchants, when successful, had been credited with the aristocratic virtues;[7] gentle-manly honourable feelings were attributed to highwaymen. In 1623 a highwayman died a popular hero, insisting that he had robbed a Spanish courier only to show his disapproval of the proposed marriage between Prince Charles and a Spanish Infanta.[8]

Many highwaymen in the mid-seventeenth century were, or claimed

---

4. Aubrey, *Brief Lives*, II, pp. 158–60; Lloyd, *State-Worthies*, II, pp. 45–7. For Popham, see p. 134 below.

5. Bridenbaugh, *Vexed and Troubled Englishmen, 1590–1642* (Oxford U.P., 1968), p. 389.

6. *Douce Ballads*, 2, No. 141.

7. Laura C. Stevenson, *Praise and Paradox: Merchants and Craftsmen in Elizabethan Popular Literature* (Cambridge U.P., 1980), Chapter 6.

8. T. Cogswell, *The Blessed Revolution: English Politics and the Coming of War, 1621–1624* (Cambridge U.P., 1989), p. 49.

to be, former royalist soldiers ruined by their loyalty to the King. Often unpaid for long periods, plundering had become for them a way of life; when demobilized with nothing but a horse and a gun, highway robbery was the natural resort. Two Verney cousins took to the road, and were hanged for it.[9] Radical Parliamentarians had little sympathy with highwaymen. Both Lilburne and Winstanley refer to the republican régime as 'the government of highwaymen'.[10] On the other hand the Ranter Abiezer Coppe saw God as a highway robber, threatening the wicked rich man: 'Thou hast many bags of money, and behold now I come as a thief in the night, with my sword drawn in my hand, and like a thief as I am − I say, "deliver your purse! Deliver Sirrah! Deliver or I'll cut thy throat!"'[11] Earlier in the same year Charles I had refused to acknowledge the legality of the court which was trying him: 'there are many unlawful authorities in the world, there are robbers and highwaymen'.[12]

Criminal biography started to flourish as a popular form of literature during the revolutionary decades.[13] Many pamphlets about highwaymen depict them as inheriting the Robin Hood image. 'Good' highwaymen, like 'good' pirates, are very much a literary creation. Some were careful to live up to the image. The French were later to note that in England 'it is useful for a highwayman, demanding money, not only to avoid barbarity but to behave with humanity and even complaisance'. This was attributed to the fact that in England 'the spirit of liberty had prevailed'.[14] But some highwaymen were more realistic. 'I follow the general way of the world, sir', Captain Hind explained to one of his victims, 'which now

---

9. Ed. Margaret E. Verney, *Memoirs of the Verney Family* (1892–9), IV, pp. 281–92. These pages contain some interesting anecdotes about gentlemen highwaymen. Cf. the anonymous *The Counterfeit Lady Unveiled* (ed. S. Peterson, New York, 1961), pp. 107, 111–12, 130–34, 141.

10. 'The Picture of the Councel of State', in *The Leveller Tracts, 1647–1653* (ed. W. Haller and G. Davies, Columbia U.P., 1944), pp. 205–7; Winstanley, *The Law of Freedom* in *Works*, p. 529.

11. Coppe, *A Second Fiery Flying Roule* (1649), in *A Collection of Ranter Writings from the 17th Century* (ed. N. Smith, 1983), p. 100.

12. Ed. Sir C. Petrie, *The Letters, Speeches and Proclamations of King Charles I*, p. 244.

13. Lincoln B. Faller, *Crime and Defoe* (Cambridge U.P., 1993), p. 10.

14. Mary Wollstonecraft, *An Historical and Moral View of the Origins and Progress of the French Revolution* (1794), in *Works* (ed. M. Butler and J. Todd), VI (1989), p. 232. I owe this reference to Bridget Hill.

prefers money before friends or honesty'.[15] The nostalgia is presumably for the pre-1640 world, for Hind had (or claimed to have) been an active royalist who was at the siege of Colchester in 1648 and joined Charles II in Scotland in time to fight at Worcester, where he was captured. He was executed in 1652 – for treason, not as a highwayman. Hind had been apprenticed to a butcher in Chipping Norton, but 'having a runaway pate' he found the work slavish and departed for London, where he hoped to find freedom. Like so many others, Hind was said to have robbed the rich to feed the poor. Honour, 'the virtue of the brave . . . made him scorn to be a slave'.[16]

An unusual highwayman was John Clavell, whose career ended in 1626 when he was twenty-three years old. He published *A Recantation* in fifty pages of rhymed couplets, with a grovelling Preface to the King, the Queen, Duchesses, Marchionesses, Countesses, etc., Privy Councillors, friends at Court, judges, doctors of divinity and clergy, J.P.s, gentlemen of quality, sergeants and counsellors at the bar – asking for release from jail. He claimed to have been a doctor, a lawyer and a poet as well as a highwayman in his short life. He had been condemned to death.

> Nor yet would the summe I had, when I was doomed to die,
> Pay for my buriall, and my Coffin buy.

He had been reprieved, as few were, by a royal pardon, and his death sentence was commuted to imprisonment. But his (unnamed) adversaries were still trying to get him. Many young gentlemen, well-connected, had been executed as highwaymen, he told his readers. Clavell had been disinherited by his uncle, Sir William Clavell, knight and baronet. His wife, for whom he expresses what appears to be real love, had struggled 'by strange importunity' to get him pardoned. He promises the King that he will never relapse: he wants to be released from prison only in order to fight for King and country. 'Set me at liberty or let me die'. Like Jackson,

15. 'The True Portraicture of Captain James Hind' (?1652), in *Samuel Pepys's Penny Merriments* (ed. R. Thompson, Columbia U.P., 1977), pp. 215–20; Charles Johnson, *A General History of the Lives and Adventures of the Most Famous Highwaymen* [and pirates] (1736), pp. 86–90.
16. [George Fidge], *The English Gusman*, . . . *that Unparallel'd Thief James Hind* (1652), pp. 1, 24, 37, 40; *Lives . . . of the most Famous Pyrates*, pp. 70–78; *Samuel Pepys's Penny Merriments*, pp. 215–20; cf. *We Brought our Hogs to a Fair Market . . . Narrative of Captain James Hind* (1651[–2]).

he gives some useful advice to travellers on how to avoid highwaymen.[17]

A ballad on John Nevinson, hanged in March 1684–5, also said that he gave to the poor from what he robbed from the rich.[18] Richard Dudley, son of a Leicestershire gentleman whose fortunes were declining, became an officer in the King's army during the civil war, and later 'the Great Highway-man'.[19] A 'biography' of Colonel James Turner, highwayman, describes him as an ex-royalist, son of a clergyman whose wife was 'descended from a family of repute in Dorsetshire'. Turner was 'very charitable to poor distressed royalists', though he himself often had difficulty in making ends meet. He was nostalgic for a lost society: 'it is a new world, a world of malice and difference'.[20]

A life of Richard Hainam claimed that he sprang from an ancient family, and that he was a high-class thief who robbed the King of France. But when he found on another occasion that he had stolen from a poor man, he returned the money, saying 'there, honest man, take your moneys; I come not to rob the poor'.[21] The author of *Jacksons Recantation* tells his readers that 'the way for a highwayman to get off is to say you were well-born but your family fell into decay and you were exposed to great want: you took to highway robbery rather than starve'. There is 'a kind of proverbial saying amongst Scout-Masters of the Road, "he can't be hang'd (without treason or murder) who hath £500 at his command"'.[22]

Evelyn has an unromantic account of being robbed in 1652. Interestingly, he did not want the highwayman, who was soon caught, to be hanged, and so did not give evidence against him in court.[23] There are suggestions that dissenters may have been involved in highway robberies in the dark days after 1660.[24] Any itinerant of whom the authorities

17. John Clavell, Gent., *A Recantation for an Ill-Led Life: Or, A Discourse of the Highway Law*, (3rd ed., 1634), *passim*].
18. *Pepys Ballads*, III, quoted by Macaulay in his *History of England*, I, pp. 339–40.
19. [Anon.], *The Life and Death of Captain Dudley, the Great Highway-man* (1669), pp. 1–2.
20. Richard Head, *The Triumph of Truth* (1664), in *The Counterfeit Lady Unveiled*, pp. 109–36; cf. [Anon.], *The Life and Death of James . . . Turner* (1663). See also *The Life and Death of Captain George Cusack* (1676), p. 3. He was in the highway trade for twenty-five years, beginning *c*.1650.
21. E. S., *The Witty Rogue, . . . History of . . . Richard Hainam, thief* (1656), pp. 1, 8, 23.
22. Op. cit. (1674), no pagination.
23. Evelyn, *Diary* (ed. E. S. de Beer, Oxford U.P., 1955), III, pp. 69–74.
24. R. L. Greaves, *Enemies under his feet: Radicals and Nonconformists in Britain, 1664–1677* (Stanford U.P., 1990), pp. 201–2.

disapproved might be accused of being a highwayman. George Fox was taken for one in 1657, and the young Bunyan was rumoured to be 'a witch, a highwayman and the like'.[25] Of Bunyan's Mr Badman 'some have muttered as if he could ride out now and then, about nobody but himself knew what, overnight, and come home all dirty and weary next morning'.[26] Bunyan thought that the parable in Luke XIV implied that Christ struggled hard for 'hedge-creepers and highwaymen'.[27] And in *Seasonable Counsel*, commenting on Luke XVIII, Bunyan appears to compare God to a thief, a cheater and a defrauder.[28]

We hear much of highway robbery in the 1690s. As Macaulay put it, 'it should seem that, at this time, a journey of fifty miles through the wealthiest and most populous shires of England was as dangerous as a pilgrimage across the deserts of Arabia'. After the peace of Ryswick in 1697 disbanded (and unpaid) soldiers created an even greater crisis. 'Every newspaper contained stories of travellers stripped, bound, and flung into ditches'. On the Newmarket road 'robbery was organized on a scale unparalleled in the kingdom since the days of Robin Hood and Little John'.[29] Yet 'The Notorious Robbers Lament; or Whiting's Sorrowful Ditty' is a 'Farewell to all my Jovial Crew'.

> The life which once I had
> By law is now controlled.

Whiting was hanged on 1 February 1694–5.[30]

There are some interesting examples of female highway robbers. In 1613 a 'lusty spinster' of Ingatestone, found guilty of highway robbery, was hanged after her claim to benefit of pregnancy had failed.[31] Mary Frith claimed to have helped to plan Captain Hind's attacks on 'committee

25. Fox, *Journal* (8th ed., 1902), I, p. 378; Bunyan, *Grace Abounding* (ed. R. Sharrock, Oxford U.P., 1977), p. 93.
26. *The Life and Death of Mr. Badman*, pp. 87–8.
27. Bunyan, *Good news for the vilest of men* (1688), in *Miscellaneous Works*, XI (ed. R. L. Greaves, Oxford U.P., 1985), p. 29. There is in fact no specific mention of highway robbery in the text: Bunyan may have recalled 'highways and hedges' in Luke XIV:23.
28. Bunyan, op. cit., 1684, in *Miscellaneous Works*, X, p. 88; cf. W. Y. Tindall, *John Bunyan, Mechanick Preacher* (New York, 1964), p. 174.
29. Macaulay, *History of England from the Accession of James II* (World's Classics), IV, p. 359; V, pp. 328–30.
30. *Bagford Ballads*, II, pp. 556–60; *Pepys Ballads*, VI, pp. 309–13; cf. pp. 322–8.
31. Bridenbaugh, *Vexed and Troubled Englishmen, 1590–1642*, p. 380.

men' and Commonwealth officials as a form of political revenge 'since public combating of them would not prevail'.[32] The nameless 'English Rogue', whose biography was published in 1688, after returning from transportation encountered a female highway robber in man's clothes, and joined forces with her. A ballad records a woman highwayman *c*.1690. There was a highway-woman in Essex in the 1730s.[33]

The highwayman whose name is best remembered is Claud Du Val, who had a special way with the ladies. On one occasion he stopped a lady's coach, in which there was £400. But after dancing a coranto with her he returned £300. In prison 'dames of high rank visited him', and with tears interceded for his life. But in vain: he was hanged in 1670 at the age of twenty-seven.[34] The crowd at his execution, as at that of Hind and other notorious highwaymen, contradicts Sir William Davenant's statement that 'only the rabble were seen at executions.'[35] Samuel Butler devoted an ode to Du Val's memory, comparing his activities to those of a manorial lord, who in his court

> seized upon
> Whatever happened in his way
> As lawful waif and stray
> And after, by the custom, kept it as his own.

Dealing with lawyers, merchants, priests, he made them

> to the smallest piece restore
> All that by cheating they had gained before.[36]

Butler's last line became an eighteenth-century commonplace, relating especially to lawyers. The ballad 'On Hounslow Heath as I rode o'er' ends with the words

> But Turpin robbed him of his store
> Because he knew he'd lie for more.

32. *The Life and Death of Mary Frith* (1662), p. 150.
33. [Anon.], *The English Rogue*, p. 17; *Pepys Ballads*, V, pp. 291–4; Bridget Hill, *Women, Work and Sexual Politics* (Oxford, 1989), p. 162.
34. [Anon.], *Memoires of Monsieur Du Val* (1670); a manuscript note in the Bodleian copy says 10,000 copies of this work were printed.
35. Davenant, *Gondibert* (ed. D. F. Gladish, Oxford U.P., 1971), p. 15 – Author's Preface.
36. Butler, *Poetical Works* (ed. G. Gilfillan, Edinburgh, 1834), pp. 195–9.

The word 'knew' indicts the whole legal profession. It recalls the glee
with which the despoiling of bishops and abbots by Robin Hood was
celebrated. As the higher clergy have lost power, lawyers have succeeded
them as hate-figures. In the Robin Hood ballads abbots were fair game
because they took advantage of knights in financial difficulties. 'O rare
Turpin hero' avenges some men of affairs against the lesser hate-figures of
his day by beating lawyers at their own game of double cross and taking
'all that by cheating they had gained before'. The target has shifted down
the social scale, but the tone of contempt is the same. What kept the
highway trade going was the fact that the rich had to conduct their long-
distance financial transactions in coin of the realm. The career prospects of
many a promising young highwayman must have been ruined by the
invention of cheques.

11. *'Gypsy Liberty'*

====

Gypsies, who every ill can cure
Except the ill of being poor.

Charles Churchill, *Poems* (ed. J. Lane, 1933), I, p. 77.

Gypsies appear to have arrived in England in the early sixteenth century. They were not welcomed by the authorities. Their arrival in significant numbers coincided in time both with an increase of vagabondage in England – escaped villeins, friars, pedlars, tinkers – and with the spread of heretical groups among the populace. Gypsies – vagrants, ideologically very unsound – were trapped between the reformation and the poor law. On their first arrival in Europe they travelled widely and successfully on forged papal briefs, which declared them to be 'Egyptians' on pilgrimage. But these soon lost their usefulness in protestant countries. Laws against sturdy beggars (victims of enclosure or of the dissolution of the monasteries) were being enforced especially strictly soon after their arrival in England. But the effectiveness of legislation in sixteenth-century England depended on the active cooperation of unpaid local administrators, and gypsies benefited from the fact that this was not always forthcoming. Even where J.P.s were entitled to keep a half of any gypsy goods and chattels seized, they could not be relied on.[1]

Gypsies were vagabonds *par excellence* and on principle. They were a standing offence to those who wished to see the English lower classes set to work as wage labourers making profits for employers and wealth for the country.[2] Gypsies put up a very strong resistance to any attempt to make them abandon their travelling life and settle down in one place as wage labourers. Although a small minority, gypsies could be seen as enjoying a liberty which poor Englishmen and women lacked. Resolutely mobile, gypsies never had a fixed abode. They were thus difficult to fit

1. A. Fraser, *The Gypsies* (Oxford, 1993), pp. 117, 128–35, 140; H. M. G. Grellman, *Dissertation on the Gypsies* (trans. M. Raper, 1787), p. 181.
2. Cf. the Scottish School's analysis of early English agrarian capitalism as set forth by Eric Hobsbawm – p. 25 above

into the English system for dealing with vagabonds – flog them back to
their villages of origin and force them to labour. Gypsies raised a standard
of libertarianism. Some English vagabonds joined them, though it is
difficult to be sure in what numbers. Gypsies normally accepted into their
bands only those who had at least one gypsy parent,[3] but we do not know
how rigidly this rule was enforced in their early days in England. Samuel
Rid in *The Art of Juggling or Legerdemaine* (1612) says that 'many of our
English *loyterers* joined' the gypsies, who had 'purchased themselves great
credit among the country people'.[4] There are many stories of daredevil
boys joining the gypsies.

Their defiance of the wage labour system set a bad example. It may
have helped to focus opposition to 'wage slavery' which many must have
felt.[5] Fierce laws were passed against them. 22 H. 8 c. 10 (1531) ordered
them to leave the realm forthwith on pain of imprisonment. In 1536
gypsies were ordered to be proceeded against as thieves. 2 P. and M. c. 4
made any gypsy found in the country who would not renounce 'that
naughty, idle and ungodly life and company' liable to execution. This
was modified by a statute of 1563 which exempted native-born gypsies
from the death sentence. But 2 P. and M. was not repealed until 1783.
The last execution of a gypsy simply for being a gypsy dates from the late
1650s. Convicted gypsies could plead for the death sentence to be commuted to hard labour, often accompanied by a severe flogging. The
Vagrancy Act of 1597 made gypsies liable to transportation – as was the
practice in France and Spain.[6]

In 1596 Edward Hext, Somerset J.P., suggested that gypsies were never
as dangerous as vagabonds: he estimated that there were not more than
thirty or forty in a county.[7] Dekker in 1608 alleged that gypsies moved
commonly in 'an army four-score strong', though dividing into smaller
groups. He described them as 'outlaws'.[8] Magistrates reported groups of
up to 140. Despite persecution, some early gypsies seem to have done
fairly well. In 1544 a group of them offered £300 in order to obtain a

3. Judith Okeley, *The Traveller-Gypsies* (Cambridge U.P., 1983), p. 67.
4. Op. cit., quoted in Sir Thomas Overbury's *Miscellaneous Works* (ed. E. F. Rimbault, 1890), pp. 288–9.
5. See Chapter 4 above.
6. Fraser, op. cit., pp. 117, 128–30, 169–72; Beier, *Masterless Men*, pp. 61–2; John
Hoyland, *A Historical Survey of the Customs, Habits and Present State of the Gypsies*
(1861), pp. 78–81.
7. Tawney and Power, *Tudor Economic Documents*, II, p. 345.
8. Dekker, *Lanthorne and Candle-Light*, Sig. G. 5v.

pardon for two of their number who had been arraigned for felony. Significantly, the government accepted the offer: money was difficult to come by.[9] As with most Tudor laws, those against gypsies were enforced as and when local authorities thought fit; rarely in their full rigour. We do not know whether this was due to popular sympathy for gypsies or to the inefficiency of the state machine. In 1596, of 196 gypsies imprisoned in York, 106 were condemned to death, of whom only nine were executed. The rest were sentenced to forced labour in gaol.[10] Since it proved quite impossible to persuade gypsies to abandon their mobile existence, expulsion from the country was the only resource.

Gypsies penetrated Scotland too, possibly earlier than England. Many appear to have moved into Scotland when they were extruded from their old haunts in England by enclosure. In 1723 Billy Marshall, chief of the Galloway gypsies, was leader of a popular revolt by 'Levellers' against the landed proprietors who were enclosing grazing lands and dispossessing tenant farmers. In 1815 William Smith, Baillie of Kelso, said that 'a strong spirit of independence, or what they would distinguish by the name of liberty, runs through the whole tribe'.[11] Resolute opposition to a sedentary life of wage labour remained characteristic of English gypsies, and appears to have been a universal gypsy prejudice. In 1926 in Bavaria it was said that nothing 'hits them harder than loss of liberty, coupled with forced labour'.[12]

Failure to cope effectively with gypsies was replaced by a propaganda campaign against them. Like other vagabonds they were said to be unbaptized, not part of the English church and so not part of the English community. Gypsies nominally adopted the religion of the country they happened to find themselves in. They were said to be unmarried, consorting together as beasts.[13] They divorced and re-married as informally – though in fact their unions were stable while they lasted. Many traditional calumnies on Jews were transferred to gypsies. They were accused of

9. E. O. Winstedt, 'Early British Gypsies', *Journal of the Gypsy Lore Soc.*, N.S., VII (1913–14), pp. 6–10.

10. R. O. Jones, 'The Mode of Disposing of Gypsies and Vagrants in the Reign of Elizabeth', *Archaelogia Cambrensis*, 4th series, XIII (1882); Beier, *Masterless Men*, p. 58.

11. Judith Okeley, op. cit., p. 3; Fraser, op. cit., p. 184; Hoyland, op. cit., p. 97.

12. Fraser, op. cit., pp. 222, 253, 305.

13. Okeley, op. cit., pp. 159, 203; Paul Slack, 'Vagrants and Vagrancy in England, 1598–1664', *Journal of Economic History*, XXVII, 3, 1974, esp. pp. 360–75. Cf. Grellman, op. cit., pp. 45–6, 59.

stealing babies from their cradles and turning them into gypsies.[14] Sir
John Popham was said to have been stolen by a band of gypsies as a child.
He went on to become Lord Chief Justice.[15] In an unpublished play by
Cosmo Manuche, *Love in Travel*, a cavalier's daughter runs away to the
gypsies; she is reunited with her family only at the end of the play.
Manuche's *Banished Shepherdess* is about exiled courtiers who live idyllic
lives in the forest.[16] An anonymous pamphlet of 1688 tells of a boy who
ran away from boarding school and found a gang of gypsies who were
'glad of his company'.[17]

One theory of the origins of the gypsies is that they came from 'a low
caste living by singing and music', who left north-west India as a body
for reasons unknown – famine perhaps or war. When they first arrived in
Europe they were prominent as entertainers as well as fortune-tellers.
William Browne referred scathingly to 'gipsy jigs' . . .

> Dances or other trumpery to delight,
> Or take, by common way, the common sight.[18]

In 'The Shepherd's Week' (1714) John Gay described a girl whose hand
was read by three gypsies who

> Said that many crosses I must prove,
> Some in my worldly gain, but most in love.
> Next morn I missed three hens and one old cock,
> And off the hedge two pinnies and a smock.

This did not disillusion her sufficiently to refrain from begging – when
her boy-friend had slighted her –

> Help me, ye gypsies, bring him home again
> And to a constant lass bring back her swain.[19]

14. Grellman, op. cit., pp. 14–15. The calumny is refuted by Borrow in *The Zincali
or An Account of the Gypsies of Spain* (1841), pp. 83, 108–9. Cf. Hoyland, op. cit.,
p. 168.
15. *D.N.B.* See pp. 123–4 above.
16. Lois Potter, *Secret Rites and Secret Writing: Royalist Literature, 1641–1660* (Cambridge U.P., 1989), pp. 104, 106. Manuche had been a soldier in the royalist army
(ibid., p. 101).
17. [Anon.], *The English Rogue*, pp. 5–7.
18. Browne, *Poems* (ed. G. Goodwin, Muses' Library, n.d.), II, p. 316.
19. Gay, *Poetical Works* (Oxford U.P., 1926), pp. 37–8.

In 1786 a list of vagabonds included 'minstrels, jugglers or gypsies, . . . petty chapmen and pedlars not licensed'.[20] From earliest times the gypsies' speciality was prophesying and fortune-telling, in which their strangeness gave them an advantage over local wise men and women. Gypsy women made steady money out of this, but it was disapproved of on ideological grounds. Gypsies also won a reputation as healers.[21]

John Langhorne in 1766 warned maids to 'beware the gypsy's lines', after describing how two unmarried girls were led astray by a prediction that they would both have babies within ten months:

> Strife with fate is milking in a sieve;
> To prove their prophet true, though to their cost,
> They justly thought no time was to be lost.[22]

John Clare tells us how children

> on Sundays often strolled
> To gypsies' camps to have their fortunes told.

But 'truths told by gypsies and expanded dreams' were not always realized: in another poem Jane 'once believed them, but had doubts since then'. And the head of 'once-beguiled Kate' was perplexed by 'hopes of sweethearts . . . and charms to try, by gypsies told of late'.[23]

For our purposes literary material is as interesting as the scanty historical evidence. Gypsies made a sudden appearance in late Elizabethan and Jacobean drama. In Shakespeare's *As You Like It* (1600, not printed until 1623) occurs the apparently proverbial phrase 'both in a tune like two gypsies on a horse'. The mysterious word 'ducdame' in the same play (Act II, scene iv) has been claimed as Romany. Two gypsy words are alleged to be used in Fletcher's *Beggars Bush*, 'minche' and 'loni'.[24]

Ben Jonson appears to have had a gypsy phase in the 1620s. *The Masque of the Metamorphosed Gypsies* (1622), as so many other 'literary' representations of gypsies, was designed to be acted by courtiers. It suggests that of

20. Okeley, op. cit., p. 5.
21. See epigraph to this chapter.
22. Langhorne, 'The Country Justice: A Warning against Gypsies', in *The Penguin Book of Eighteenth-century Verse* (ed. D. Davison, 1973), pp. 125–6.
23. Clare, *Poems* (ed. J. W. Tibble, 1935), I, pp. 33, 396, 455–6, 458. For Clare, cf. Chapter 26 below.
24. Fraser, op. cit., p. 137; Charles Starkey, in *Journal of the Gypsy Lore Soc.* (New Series, III, No. 1, July 1891), pp. 96–9, 59.

the two groups, gypsies and courtiers, one is above the law, the other outside it, and that Buckingham and his family are really gypsies at heart. In Jonson's *The New Inn* (1629) Lord Frampul had lived for half a year with gypsies. Fly had been a strolling gypsy, and mine host declares that 'all my family indeed were gypsies'. Other servants at the inn had also been gypsies. It is all the more significant that Goodstock, the host, makes an indictment of Stuart society.[25] When the nurse asks Lord Beaufort 'Is poverty a vice?' he replies unhesitantly, 'The age counts it so'. The nurse retorts

> God help your lordship, and your peers that think so . . .
> And I must tell you now, young lord of dirt,
> As an incensed mother, she [the nurse's daughter] hath more
> And better blood running in those small veins
> Than all the race of Beauforts have in mass. (Act V, scene i)

The Witch in Jonson's *The Sad Shepherd* is 'a gypsy lady'. (Posthumously published 1641.)

Middleton's *The Spanish Gypsy*, based (among other sources) on Cervantes's *La Gitanella*, was acted at James I's court in 1623 or 1624, though not published until 1653. The 'gypsies' are disguised courtiers and their servants. 'Court and country flock' to the entertainments they provide. There is much generalized conventional reference to dishonesty and pilfering, but the pretended gypsies sing songs praising their freedom and honesty, presumably conveying the way in which Jacobean audiences sentimentalized gypsies. One of the disguised ladies says, in respect of marriage, 'I'll wear no shackles: liberty is sweet'. When she does marry, there is no church ceremony:

> Faith and troth I hope bind faster
> Than any other ceremonies can;
> Do they not, my lord?

To which the Corregidor of Madrid replies, somewhat dampingly,

> Yes, where the parties
> Pledged are not too unequal in degree,
> As he and thou art.

It is stressed that 'our gypsy wenches are not common':

---

25. Anne Barton, op. cit., pp. 261, 281, 315; Briggs, *Pale Hecate's Team*, p. 89.

> She to you the marigold
> To none but you her leaves unfold.
> (Act III, scenes i and ii; Act IV, scene i; Act V, scene iii)[26]

Sir Thomas Overbury in his *Character* of a tinker says that his 'foul sunburnt Queen is a gypsy who has recanted since "the terrible statute"' (presumably that of 1597).[27]

During the revolutionary decades, thanks to the collapse of censorship and the prevailing intellectual curiosity, we hear a good deal more about gypsies. Their image remains agreeably ambiguous. Sir Richard Baker, in his *Chronicle* of 1643, appears to compare the dispute between King and Parliament over Ship Money with a squabble between gypsies over a shilling.[28] Sir Thomas Browne has a chapter 'Of Gypsies' in Book VI of his *Pseudodoxia Epidemica* (1646) in which he speculates on their origins. A song, 'The Gypsies', published in *Witts Recreations* (1658), emphasized their singing, dancing, sleight of hand and fortune-telling.[29] Izaak Walton purports in *The Compleat Angler* (1653) to tell of an encounter with a gang of gypsies counting over their ill-gotten gains. He ends with them singing 'Frank Davison's song, which he made forty years ago':

> The beggars lord it as they please,
> And only beggars live at ease.
> Bright shines the sun; play, beggars, play!
> Here's scraps enough to serve to-day.[30]

Among radicals the Ranter Abiezer Coppe boasted of 'his most lowly carriage towards beggars, rogues and gypsies: together with a large declaration what glory shall rise up from under all this ashes'. Gypsies and gaol-birds Coppe described as 'mine own brethren and sisters, flesh of my flesh, and as good as the greatest lord in England'. But his behaviour with gypsy women was hardly fraternal: 'I sat down and ate and drank around on the ground with gypsies, and clipped, hugged and kissed them,

---

26. In John Day's *The Blind Beggar of Bednall-Green* (1600–1601) young Tom Strowd had his cloak stolen by an 'ill-fac'd gypsy' (Act II, scene ii) (*Works*, ed. A. H. Bullen, 1963), pp. 35–6.
27. Overbury, *Works* (ed. E. F. Rimbault, 1890), p. 90. This reprints the ninth impression of 1616.
28. I owe this interpretation, which seems plausible, to Nigel Smith, *Literature and Revolution in England, 1640–1660* (Yale U.P., 1994), p. 329.
29. Op. cit., II, pp. 439–45.
30. Op. cit. (ed. R. Le Gallienne, n.d.), pp. 131–6.

putting my hand in their bosoms, loving the she-gypsies dearly. . . .
When I was hugging the gypsies I abhorred the thoughts of Ladies, their
beauty could not . . . entangle my hands in their bosoms; yet I can, if it be
my will, kiss and hug Ladies, and love my neighbour's wife as myself,
without sin'.[31]

Bunyan, on a rather less excitable wing of radicalism, held a more
conventional and hostile view of gypsies. In *Grace Abounding* (1666) he
tells us that 'I often, when these temptations have been with power upon
me, did compare myself in the case of such a child, whom some gypsy
hath by force took up under her apron, and is carrying from friends and
country; kick sometimes I did, and also scream and cry; but yet I was
bound in the wings of the temptation, and the wind would carry me
away'.[32] Introducing the Second Part of *The Pilgrim's Progress* Bunyan
urged his book to stand firm against those who had been deceived by
counterfeit versions,

> Thinking that you like gypsies go about
> In naughty wise the country to defile,
> Or that you seek good people to beguile
> With things unwarrantable.[33]

The strongest impression of gypsy freedom is to be found in ballads. In
the late ballad, 'The Raggle-Taggle Gypsies', the lady, sitting alone in her
chamber at night, was no doubt typical of many neglected wives of
wealthy gentry. The sweet and shrill singing of the gypsies melts her
frozen heart. She discards her 'silken gown' and makes a break for liberty
by joining the gypsies. 'What care I for your goose-feather bed?' she says
when her husband, hotly pursuing his property on his 'milk-white steed',
tries to buy her back by reminding her of the luxury she is leaving behind
her. She dismisses it as 'all your show' – a show of which she was no
doubt part. The issue of property versus freedom is clearly posed.

This is no doubt a later version of 'The Gypsy Countess', in which the
singing of 'seven Egyptians', 'sae sweet' '(and wow, but they sang bonny!)'
'cast the glamourie owre' Earl Cassilis's lady. 'She's awa' with the gipsy
laddie', the Earl was told when he came home.

31. Coppe, *A Second Fiery Flying Roule* (1649), Chapter V.
32. Bunyan, *Grace Abounding to the Chief of Sinners* (ed. R. Sharrock, Oxford U.P.,
1962), p. 32.
33. Op. cit. (Oxford U.P., 1975), p. 168. First published 1678. Bunyan himself was
accused of being a gypsy. Cf. pp. 127–8 above.

> 'Come saddle for me the brown', he said,
>   'For the black was ne'er so speedy,
> And I will travel night and day
>   Till I find out my wanton lady.'
> 'Will you come home, my dear?' he said,
>   'Oh will you come home, my honey?'

But she replied,

> 'Yestreen I lay on a good feather-bed,
>   And my own wedded lord beyond me;
> And to-night I'll lie in the ash-corner,
>   With the gypsies all around me . . .
> The Earl of Cassilis is lying sick;
>   Not one hair I'm sorry;
> I'd rather have a kiss from Johny Faa's lips
>   Than all his gold and his money'.[34]

John Collop made an interesting comparison when he mocked at 'gypsies in religion', 'canting vagrants' who changed their beliefs with the political weather.[35] Fuller, in *Mixt Contemplations in Better Times*, also published in 1660, used 'the very gypsies, who generally have no good name (condemned for crafty cheaters and cozeners' but who 'would not take away what was given to their God in his ministers') as a stick with which to belabour those radicals who wished to abolish tithes.[36]

The Earl of Rochester's Artemisia attacked

> Our silly sex! who, born like monarchs free,
> Turn gypsy for a meaner liberty

in pursuit of promiscuity.[37] Defoe's Captain Singleton was stolen from his parents when two years old and 'disposed of . . . to a gypsy, under whose government I continued till I was about six years old'. He was 'continually dragged about . . . from one part of the country to another'. His adopted gypsy mother was hanged, and Bob was shifted from parish to parish as

34. 'The Gypsy Countess', in *The Oxford Book of Ballads* (ed. A. Quiller-Couch, Oxford U.P., 1927), pp. 781–3. Faa was a well-known Scottish gypsy surname.
35. Collop, 'Iter Satyricum' (1660), in *Poems* (ed. C. Hilberry, Wisconsin U.P., 1962), p. 169.
36. Op. cit., in *Good Thoughts in Bad Times; Good Thoughts in Worse Times; Mixt Contemplations in Better Times* (1830), pp. 299–300.
37. Rochester, 'A Letter from Artemisia', in *Complete Poems* (ed. D. M. Vieth, Yale U.P., 1974), pp. 105–6.

they disputed 'my supposed mother's last settlement', until finally he ran away to sea.[38] *Moll Flanders* begins with the heroine wandering among gypsies, but she does not stay long with them.

Captain Singleton's experience of being stolen from his parents and spending some years with gypsies recurs in the lives of pirates and highwaymen. The hero of the anonymous *The English Rogue* (1688) ran away from boarding school and joined a gypsy gang: he learnt a lot of their canting dialect. But his final career was that of highwayman.[39] Bampfylde Moore Carew (1693–1730), born of a good Devonshire family, with a number of his school-fellows fell in with a society of seventeen or eighteen gypsies: he was impressed by their 'great air of freedom, mirth and pleasure'. They knew no other use of riches than to enjoy them. Property was held in common. No people, he thought, enjoy so great a share of liberty. He remained loosely attached to the gypsy community for over forty years, and was elected their king. He led an independent roving life, robbing and swindling with great success – at one stage in the guise of a scholar of Balliol College disordered in his mind. He suffered transportation to Maryland, but escaped with the help of some friendly Indians and returned to England.[40]

The poet Cowper dismissed gypsies as 'a vagabond and useless tribe', 'self-banished from society', preferring 'squalid sloth to honourable toil'.[41] Very different were the views of John Clare, for whom gypsies had a fascination. He wrote several poems on 'The Gypsies' Camp', 'The Camp', 'Gypsies' and 'The Gypsy', 'Gypsy's Song', 'The Bousing Gypsy', 'The Gypsies' Evening Blaze'. Two poems are more personal – 'My love she was a Gypsy' and 'My own sweet Gypsy girl'. There are literally scores of references to gypsies in his poems and correspondence, including a prose account of a Gypsy wedding.[42]

Clare became acquainted with gypsies about the age of nineteen, in

38. Defoe, *The Life, Adventures and Pyracies Of the Famous Captain Singleton* (1720). I cite from the Oxford edition of 1840, pp. 2–3.
39. Op. cit., pp. 5–7.
40. [Anon.], *The Surprising Adventures of Bampfylde Moore Carew, King of the Beggars* (new ed., 1812), pp. 7–16, 56–68, 256–64 (first published 1745. On p. 69 there is an ode on the life of gypsies); [Anon.], *An Apology for the Life of Bampfylde Moore Carew, King of the Beggars* (1789), p. 137; first published 1749; [Anon.], *The Adventures of Bampfylde-Moore-Carew* (1871), p. 371.
41. William Cowper, *Poems* (1821), II, pp. 18–19.
42. Ed. J. W. and A. Tibble, *Prose of John Clare* (1951), p. 127. See Chapter 26 below.

1814, and saw a good deal of them in the next three years.[43] They taught him to play the fiddle, and he learnt dance tunes from them. He 'became so initiated in their ways and habits' that he was often tempted to join them. He defended them from their calumniators, who he said were often worse than the gypsies themselves – the latter being 'a quiet, pilfering, unprotected race'. He 'loved the gypsies for the beauties which they added to the landscape'.[44]

> The camp of the gypsies is sweet by moonlight,
> In the furze and the hawthorn and all out of sight –
> There'll be fiddling and dancing and singing to-night
> In the pale moonlight.[45]

It was one of Clare's many reasons for detesting enclosure that it kept gypsies 'ill provided with a lodging'. Unlike those whom I shall discuss later as opting out of the English state, gypsies refused to opt into it.[46]

> The gypsies' camp was not afraid . . .
> Till vile enclosure came.[47]

As we shall see later, gypsies and their freedom were part of the 'joys' of Clare's earlier life, whose loss contributed to his later mental illness.[48]

The gypsy image remained an ambiguous one. But their resolute rejection of wage labour must have appealed to many as wage-slavery seemed to become the inevitable fate of the poor.

43. Clare, *Selected Letters* (ed. M. Storey, Oxford U.P., 1990), pp. xxi.
44. Clare, *Autobiographical Writings* (ed. E. Robinson, Oxford U.P., 1986), pp. 31, 67–72; *Poems* (ed. J. W. Tibble, 1935), II, p. 379.
45. 'The Camp', *Poems*, ed J. W. Tibble (1935), pp. 158–9.
46. *Autobiographical Writings*, p. 72. See Chapter 26 below.
47. 'The Lament of Swordy Well', *Poems*, I, p. 420.
48. See Chapter 26 below.

III. Imperial Problems

12. 'Going Native': 'The Noble Savage'

=====

> We women, like weak Indians, stand
> Inviting from our golden coast
> The wandering rovers to our land;
> But she who trades with 'em is lost.

Thomas Southerne, *Sir Antony Love* (1691). In *Seventeenth-Century Lyrics* (ed. Norman Ault, 1950), p. 446.

Julio, a 'wild man' from the Amazon forests, 'a poor savage creature':

[In my country] we ... have no need for money to make us happy, no laws to make us wise. ... Your arts and your sciences ... are good for nothing ... but to give knaves an advantage over honest men, fools authority over wise men'.

James Miller, *Art and Nature* (1738), quoted by W. A. Speck, *Society and Liberty in England, 1700–1760* (1983).

I

As the discipline of wage labour closed in throughout England, some had thought that there might be more freedom in the open spaces of the New World, where in fact outlaws were to survive longer than they did in England: their legend lasted as well in America as did that of Robin Hood in England. But we must recollect that many who emigrated to Ireland or America were not volunteers. Some were taken as servants; others were sentenced to transportation, or shanghaied. Pauper and vagabond children were regularly shipped off to Virginia by the City of London, many of them against their will. Bridewell inmates were transported to Virginia or the West Indies.[1] A seventeenth-century ballad

---

1. I. Pinchbeck and M. Hewitt, *Children in English Society*, I, *From Tudor Times to the 18th century* (1969), pp. 106–7; R. B. Manning, *Village Revolts*, p. 169. Cf. pp. 165–70 below.

described how a man arranged to dispatch to Virginia the girl whom he had got with child. She trepanned him on board, gave him the slip, and he went to Virginia instead.[2] From the 1650s onwards servants formed an important part of Bristol's exports.[3]

We recall that on the Mayflower 'some of the strangers received at London' dropped 'some mutinous speeches as if there were now no authority over them'. In consequence 'the people, . . . before they landed, wisely formed themselves into a body politic'. 'The people' clearly excluded those who did not accept the authority of their betters.[4] In 1646 intending planters in the West Indies were advised to 'bring with you three or four labouring men, by whose pains and your managing of their endeavours you may do well'. They too were presumably not 'people'.[5]

Many migrants, dissatisfied with continuing subjection, 'went native', finding a freer existence among Irish or Indian communities. (I put 'going native' in quotation marks, because the phrase repeats contemporary beliefs. I shall be discussing its meaning later.) Nicholas Canny has emphasized that historians of early modern Ireland and colonial America have not appreciated that 'the English poor did not accept the English social and cultural superiority that were expounded by their betters', and were 'so indifferent to the extension of English civility that they happily integrated themselves into the indigenous society'. Some even came near to 'espousing the rights of the indigenous population against the intruders'. Hence the necessity for martial law – 'a feature of colonial settlement in Ireland and Virginia', though in Ireland it applied only to vagrants and masterless men.[6]

Ireland was England's first plantation, dating back to long before the seventeenth century. Elizabethan commentators were appalled to find that English settlers in Ireland had over the centuries absorbed many of

2. *Douce Ballads*, p. 255.
3. See p. 169 below.
4. Arber, op. cit., II, pp. 410–11.
5. *A Continuation of certain special and Remarkable passages*, No. 21, 6–13 February 1645[–6], in *Making the News* (ed. J. Raymond), p. 261.
6. N. Canny, 'The permissive frontier: social control in English settlements in Ireland and Virginia, 1550–1650', in *The Westward Enterprise: English Activities in Ireland, the Atlantic and America, 1480–1650* (ed. K. R. Andrews, N. P. Canny and P. Hair, Liverpool U.P., 1978), pp. 34–6; Ciaran Brady, 'The Framework of Government in Tudor Ireland', in *Natives and Newcomers: Essays on the Making of Irish Colonial Society, 1534–1641* (ed. Brady and R. Gillespie, Royal Irish Academy Press, 1986), p. 39.

the practices and ideas of the original Irish inhabitants. 'Wild Irish are as civil as the Russies [Russians] in their kind', wrote George Turberville in a poem of 1568. In 1612 Sir John Davies attacked Irishmen's 'contempt and scorn of all things necessary for the civil life of man'. None 'did . . . plant any gardens or orchards, enclose or improve their lands, live together in settled villages or towns'.[7] A writer of 1615, over the pseudonym 'E.S.', insisted that settlers in Munster must be strictly segregated from the native Irish, to whose 'barbarism' previous settlers had succumbed.[8] Barnabe Rich in the following year asserted that 'the planting of the Northerne parts of Ireland with the English cannot but be acceptable in the face of God', since it brings 'light and understanding to a blind and ignorant people'.[9]

So too in New England. Idleness, Professor Morgan reminds us, was 'a masculine virtue among Indians', whereas propertied Englishmen regarded it as a vice among their lower-class countrymen.[10] Robert Burton provocatively called idleness 'the badge of gentry', 'an appendix to nobility'.[11] In the 1620s Sir Thomas Dale complained that in Virginia 'not many give testimony besides their names that they are Christians'.[12] When Thomas Dudley, Deputy-Governor of Massachusetts, called in March 1631 for godly persons to emigrate from England ('they cannot dispose of themselves or their estates more to God's glory') he added with significant firmness 'but they must not be of the poorer sort'.[13] Clearly here 'the people' does not include 'the poor'. 'The savages' in Ireland and America were free in the sense that, having no property, they were not controlled by law.

The danger of Thomas Morton's settlement at 'Merrymount' in 1628 was its 'celebration of masterlessness and idolatry' – and acceptance of a 'more happy and freer life'. The settlers lived as vagabonds, not cultivating the soil. Plymouth's rulers 'saw they should keep no servants', since the latter found the Indian way of life 'enormously attractive': more

7. Sir John Hale, *The Civilization of Europe in the Renaissance* (1993), pp. 362–3.

8. Canny, 'Edmund Spenser and the Development of an Anglo-Irish Identity', *Yearbook of English Studies*, 13 (1983), pp. 16–17.

9. Barnabe Rich, *A New Description of Ireland* (1616), Sig. B ii.

10. E. S. Morgan, *American Slavery, American Freedom: The Ordeal of Colonial Virginia* (New York, 1975), p. 61.

11. Burton, *The Anatomy of Melancholy* (Everyman ed.), I, pp. 242–4.

12. William Bradford, *History of Plymouth Plantation* (Collections of the Massachusetts Historical Soc., 4th series, III, 1856), pp. 237–40.

13. Arber, op. cit., II, pp. 580–81.

Englishmen chose to live with the Indians than Indians with the English.[14] People 'delivered' from Indian captivity ran away again. An English serving-woman reported that life with the Algonquians had been hard but no harder than that of a serving-woman at home. Every colony condemned runaways to whipping; some imposed the death penalty – the Jamestown colony as early as 1610. For centuries the open frontier offered release from the slavery of wage labour to the hardy.[15] Joining a pirate crew might equally offer independence to the bold – an opportunity of which some women took advantage.[16] Spanish colonizers faced similar problems. A man who had lived for eight years as a slave in Yucatán refused to be 'liberated': he had married an Indian woman by whom he had three children. A Spanish soldier who deserted to live with the Mayas led his adopted tribe in an attack on his own countrymen.[17]

We still do not know enough about conditions of life among the North American Indians, but despite the degradation and deprivation to which they had been reduced, we know that they were far from being the barbarians depicted by the early settlers. The canard that they failed to cultivate the land appears to have been invented by settlers in order to claim Biblical authority for expropriating them. In fact they sold agricultural produce to the early settlers. Their marriage customs may have seemed to rank and file colonists more like those with which they were familiar in England than the church marriage being imposed there.[18] Sir Philip Sidney, in his abortive plan for a settlement in Central America, had appealed 'to the religious divines' by offering 'a large field of reducing poor Christians, misled by the idolatry of Rome, to their mother primitive church'. 'To the merchant' he offered 'a simple people, a fertile and unexhausted earth. To the fortune-bound, liberty. . . . Generally the word gold was an attractive Adamant'.[19]

14. Neal Salisbury, *Manitou and Providence*, pp. 160–63, 132–9, 177; R. B. Morris, *Government and Labour in Early America* (Columbia U.P., 1946), pp. 170, 454; K. O. Kupperman, *Settling with the Indians*, pp. 156–8. Cf. Arber, op. cit., II, pp. 483–4.
15. Stephen Greenblatt, *Marvellous Possession: The Wonders of the New World* (Oxford U.P., 1992), p. 146; M. Rediker, 'Good hands, Stout Heart, and Fast Feet'; The History and Culture of Working People in Early America', *Labour/Le Travailleur*, 10 (1982), pp. 139–42.
16. See Chapter 9 above.
17. Greenblatt, op. cit., pp. 140–41, 146.
18. See Chapter 18 below.
19. Fulke Greville, *Life of Sir Philip Sidney* (Oxford U.P., 1907), p. 119. First published 1652.

What few of the early settlers commented on was picked up by Montaigne from a servant who stressed the absence of class structure and servitude among the American Indians, as contrasted with the misery of oppression in the old world. Montaigne compared the alleged Indian habit of eating human flesh with the European customs of racking and burning heretics, throwing them to the dogs.[20] Nashe reported 'atheists' who alleged that 'the late discovered Indians are able to show antiquities thousands [of years] before Adam'; Marlowe supported this view.[21]

In the play *Eastward Hoe* (1605 – attributed to Marston, Chapman and Ben Jonson) a character sings the praises of Virginia, where 'they have married with the Indians', and venison is as common as mutton. 'You may be an alderman there, and never be a scavenger; you may be a nobleman and never be a slave; you may come to preferment enough and never be a pander . . . There we shall have no more law than conscience, and not too much of either'.[22] That was ironical: it is not yet a picture of the noble savage. But the contrast between 'law' and 'conscience' is noteworthy.[23]

In a most useful article, Richard McCabe has pointed out elements in the writings of Spenser which seem relevant to my thesis. Taking 'husbandry and urban settlement' as 'the essence of civility', Spenser 'persistently attacks as vagabonds, in the diction of the Elizabethan statute book', figures who enjoy 'the essential liberty of the pastoral life style'. On the basis of his experience in Ireland, Spenser is contrasting the native Irish with what he regards as the better elements in the relatively civilized English peasantry: 'to have the land . . . enclosed and well fenced,' well-tilled fields rather than common pasture. 'Private property inspires [Spenser's] civil aesthetic'. 'From the satyrs of Book One to the savages of Book Six, the landscape of *The Faerie Queene* is populated by . . . outlaws',

> lawless people . . .
> That never used to live by plough nor spade
> But fed on spoil and booty.[24]

20. Quoted by Greenblatt, op. cit., pp. 148–50.

21. Nashe, *Christ's Tears over Jerusalem* (1593), in *The Unfortunate Traveller and other works* (ed. J. B. Steane, Penguin, 1972), p. 479; Gordon Brotherton, *The Book of the Fourth World: Reading the Native Americans through their Literature* (Cambridge U.P., 1992), p. 364.

22. Op. cit., Act III, scene iii, in *The Plays of John Marston* (ed. H. H. Wood, Edinburgh, 1934–9), III.

23. See Chapter 19 below.

24. *The Faerie Queene*, Book VI, canto 10, stanza 39; Book II, canto 9, stanza 1; McCabe, 'Edmund Spenser, Poet of Exile', *Proceedings of the British Academy*, 80

So *The Faerie Queene* and *A Vewe of the Present State of Irelande*, taken together, give us a newcomer's explanation of why some of the original settlers have 'gone native'. Spenser is anxious to proclaim a superior ethos for the occupying race against the still prevailing ethos of the 'natives'; between the two there is sheer hostility. In *The Faerie Queene* Spenser describes a people who appear to be Irish:

> In these wild deserts . . .
> There dwelt a savage nation, which did live
> Of stealth and spoil, and making nightly road
> Into their neighbours' borders, ne did give
> Themselves to any trade (as for to drive
> The painful plough, or cattle for to breed,
> Or by adventurous merchandise to thrive)
> But on the labours of poor men to feed
> And serve their own necessities with others' need.[25]

Spenser argued that a people who failed to make full use of the land have no right to it – an argument used later against the American Indians. Spenser follows through the logic of this position. The roaming Irish, with no settled places of residence, no villages or towns, no private property, must be settled in one place to cultivate the soil. Barnabe Rich, who like Spenser knew Ireland at first hand, in his *New Description of Ireland* (1610) argued that wandering Irish tribes had been 'nuzzled from their cradles in the very puddle of Popery', and were ungovernable until they practised settled agriculture. They justified everything by 'custom'. 'The wild Irish and the Indians do not much differ', declared Hugh Peter, just back from New England in 1646.[26] The Indians did in fact cultivate the soil, but they left vast areas untilled – areas even greater than the forests in England. In *The Faerie Queene* Spenser drew on early English history, writing of the Ancient Britons,

> They held this land, and with their filthiness
> Polluted this same gentle soil long time

(1993), pp. 82–4. See also Anthony Low, *The Georgic Revolution* (Princeton U.P., 1985), esp. Chapter 2, 'Poet of Work: Spenser and the Courtly Ideal'.

25. *The Faerie Queene*, Book VI, canto 8, stanza 35.

26. Op. cit., Sig. B 2v–3, p. 15; Chapters 4, 6, 7, 19, 22 *passim*; *A True and a Kinde Excuse Written in Defence of that Booke entituled A New Description of Ireland* (1612), Chapters 1, 4; *Mr. Peters Last Report of the English Warres*, p. 5.

until representatives of the higher Roman civilization came 'and them of their unjust possession deprived'.[27] The moral for Ireland was clear.

In *The Faerie Queene* Spenser uses the words 'licentious' and 'liberty' in describing the native Irish, 'wallowing in their own sensual government', as Lord Grey put it. English lower-class settlers found this attractive. 'As it is the *nature of all men* to love liberty, so they become libertines and fall to all the licentiousness of the Irish'. Intermarriage (or 'licentious conversing') with the Irish 'posed the most serious threat of cultural assimilation'. 'How can such matching but bring forth an evil race?' Spenser asked. For him 'the phenomenon of assimilation betrayed the insecurity of English culture', the danger of 'degeneration'[28] Spenser *assumed* the total inferiority of the Irish and their culture. 'Their savage brutishness and loathsome filthiness . . . is not to be named', he wrote. He was referring especially to the clothes they wore, or failed to wear, to their sexual habits, to their lack of any fixed abode and to the fact that they have 'never yet been . . . made to learn obedience unto law, scarcely to know the name of law, but instead thereof they have always preserved and kept their own . . . Brehon law' – an unwritten law, delivered by tradition. The comparison with the rivalry of law and custom in seventeenth-century England is interesting for our purposes. Before Ireland can be civilized, Spenser concluded, the military power of the chiefs must be broken, and everybody must be drawn into labour.[29]

But when *Colin Clouts Come Home Againe* and Spenser hopes to cash in on the reputation won by the first three books of *The Faerie Queene*, the English court sadly disappointed him. 'What is particularly remarkable', McCabe comments, 'is that many of the adjectives applied to courtiers are identical to those applied to the "wild" Irish: "foul", "guileful", "idle", "wasteful", "lazy", even "lewd and licentious"'. Books IV–VI of *The Faerie Queene* were published soon after Colin Clout's (i.e. Spenser's) disappointed return from Ireland. 'The quality of violence in Book Five', McCabe comments, 'attests to the measure of Spenser's personal assimilation into the Irish problem, . . . man as political animal negotiating expedient stratagems of *realpolitik* while at the same time seeking a moral basis for moral compromise'. So Spenser rationalizes. 'Artegall's enchanted

27. *The Faerie Queene*, Book II, canto X, stanza 9.
28. McCabe, op. cit., pp. 86–8. He quotes *The Faerie Queene*, Book IV, canto 8, as an example.
29. Spenser, *A Vewe of the Present State of Ireland*, in *Works* (ed. R. Morris, 1924), pp. 632, 672–7.

"sword" allegorizes Lord Grey's "thorough" policy, and month by month, from 1580 to 1582, his private secretary took toll of the casualties, fully aware of the compromise with "civility" therein entailed: "seeing that by no other means it is possible to recure them, and that these are not of will but of very urgent *necessity*".' 'The words "wild" and "savage" occur more often in the sixth Book of *The Faerie Queene* than in any other, and its visions of pastoral tranquillity invariably degenerate into scenes of carnage'. 'It is, perhaps, indicative of Spenser's final state of mind that' [in the *Mutability Cantos*] 'he invokes the deity as Lord of Hosts (Sabbaoth God), as though heaven itself were a well-garrisoned civil plantation in an otherwise "savage" universe'.[30]

This looks forward to the new settlements in America, where the 'natives' are wholly alien and primitive, but they may be convinced by the superior virtues of European Christian civilization, provided only the new settlers made no compromises. Fraternization and miscegenation must be prohibited from the start. Others as well as Spenser advocated strict segregation between the English and the Irish until the latter had been freed from the tyranny of their lords and re-educated.[31] For our purposes the point to stress is that the liberty which some saw the native Irish and the American Indians as enjoying was connected with the absence of an alien state authority enforcing laws, and with freedom from wage labour and from marriage laws.

In Gay's opera *Polly* the European pirates join the Indians against their local exploiters, but King Pohetohee cross-questions Macheath (disguised as Morano): 'Would not your honest industry have been sufficient to have supported you?' To that assertion of the values of commercial nonconformity Macheath retorts, 'Honest industry! I have heard talk of it indeed among the common people, but all great geniuses are above it'.[32] Here the noble savage speaks for values which recall those of Gay's background.

II

In this context I was very impressed by a brilliant article by Peter Linebaugh and Marcus Rediker, 'Notes on *The Tempest* and the Origins

30. McCabe, op. cit., pp. 95–9.
31. Canny, 'Edmund Spenser and the development of an Anglo-Irish identity', *Year Book of English Studies* (1983), XIII, pp. 16–17.
32. *Polly*, Act III, scene xi.

of Atlantic Capitalism', which all Shakespeare scholars and seventeenth-century historians should read. It was a paper presented to a Conference on 'American Exceptionalism: The Formation of the American Working Class in International Perspective', held in University College, London, on February 17–18, 1995. What follows has been mostly pillaged from this paper, of which the authors kindly sent me a copy. (Forthcoming in a book entitled *The Many-Headed Hydra: Explorations in the History of the Atlantic Working Class*.)

They draw special attention to the opening scenes of *The Tempest*, in which the storm which has wrecked the voyagers also upsets accepted conventions of subordination. Faced with danger and disaster, the boat-swain takes command and issues the necessary orders. When Gonzalo, 'an honest old counsellor of Naples', tries to intervene, the boatswain curtly says, 'Out of our way, I say . . . You mar our labour. Keep your cabins; you do assist the storm'. To Gonzalo's 'Nay, good, be patient', the boat-swain replies, 'When the sea is. Hence! What care these roarers for the name of the king? To cabin! Silence! Trouble us not . . . Out of our way, I say'. 'Have you a mind to sink?' Gonzalo takes the point, and leaves the boatswain to go about his business. But Antonio, the usurping Duke of Milan, and Sebastian, brother to the King of Naples, try to assert their authority by shouting down the boatswain: 'you bawling, blasphemous, uncharitable dog!' 'You whoreson insolent noise-maker!' The ship goes down but they all get ashore. The boatswain was able to report that the vessel had been salvaged and was 'tight and yare and bravely rigged, as when / We first put out to sea'.

On the island they encounter Caliban, who claims that it belongs to him:

> By Sycorax my mother,
> Which thou takest from me.

Caliban has been enslaved by the European invaders, after he had shown them 'all the qualities o'th'isle'. 'Curst be I that did so'. 'The red plague rid you / For learning me your language', whose only use to him is that he knows how to curse. Sycorax had been dumped on the island by sailors after being banished from Algiers. Ariel, her servant, was rescued by Prospero from imprisonment 'in a cloven pine' and is also treated as Prospero's slave. Caliban initiates a plot to murder Prospero and recover control of the island. As Linebaugh and Rediker point out, there had been conspiracies of the lower classes in early Virginia, after which those who 'did run away to the Indians' were captured and hanged, burned, broken on the wheel or otherwise disposed of as an example to discourage others from fraternizing with Indians.

Caliban's conspiracy against the fear of continued exploitation apparently involved only himself, Stephano (a 'drunken butler') and Trinculo (a 'jester'). But it seriously alarmed Prospero (who turned out to be the Duke of Milan), though he succeeded in defeating it after getting the conspirators drunk. Ultimately his magic proved stronger than that of Sycorax.

The authors see this as a paradigm of European methods of conquest and rule in America. Prospero 'needed Caliban's sure grasp of the ecology of the island simply to survive. He needed Ariel, taught by Sycorax, to carry out his orders'. He 'had to learn how to deal with a slave such as Caliban. . . . But above all else Prospero's "art" now lay in understanding and manipulating social divisions, thereby controlling the likes of Caliban, Trinculo and Stephano, whom he collectively dubs "the rabble". He uses Ariel . . . as an agent provocateur', promising him freedom in return.

They draw attention, by contrast, to Gonzalo's vision of the 'commonwealth' which he would establish 'had I the plantation of this isle'. He would have no magistrates, no letters, no riches or poverty, no wage labour.

> all men idle, all;
> And women too, but innocent and pure:
> No sovereignty

and 'all things in common'. It is the Land of Cokayne, which some Europeans believed they had found in America, where 'there is not *meum* and *tuum* amongst them'.[33]

Linebaugh and Rediker suggest that Shakespeare drew heavily on Montaigne's essay 'Of Cannibals', published in English translation in 1603. But they also stress that Shakespeare, like very many of his contemporaries got his information and ideas from talking to mariners who had crossed the Atlantic. Shakespeare appears as a detached chronicler of the New World scene. Whatever his private views may have been, it would have been highly imprudent to depict the conspirators as heroic. He does nothing to associate himself with their aims. But his play, Gay's *Polly* and much other evidence suggests that the discovery and colonization of

---

33. Robert Rich, *Newes from Virginia, the Lost Flocke Triumphant* (1610).

America had put new ideas into people's heads, leading them to question the accepted authority of the law and the physical violence with which it was enforced when challenged.[34]

III

> I am as free as nature first made man,
> Ere the base laws of servitude began,
> When wild in woods the noble savage ran.

Dryden, *The Conquest of Granada*, Act I, scene i, in *Plays* (Mermaid ed., n.d.), I, pp. 47–8.

Literary reactions to the very different societies of America were mixed. Montaigne saw a primitive golden-age civilization 'ruined and defaced for the traffick of pearles and pepper'. Gonzalo in *The Tempest* envisaged (with Montaigne's help) an ideally virtuous primitive civilization: 'no kind of traffic' [i.e. trade], 'no name of magistrate', 'no sovereignty', 'riches, poverty and use of service, none', no contracts, no inheritance, no fenced off private property in land; and finally, 'no occupation, all men idle, all; and women too'; 'all things in common'.[35]

Advocates of colonization differed widely in the arguments they used to persuade the public. For William Crashawe the Virginia Adventurers were taking part in the establishment of Christ's kingdom. 'God is coming towards Virginia', where now Satan rules 'visibly and palpably . . . more than in any other known place in the world'. We go to enlarge the kingdom of God, and 'to accomplish the number of his elect'. The conversion of souls comes 'after they first be made civil men'. Crashawe drew more optimistic conclusions from Spenser's historical parallel: we English were once like the Indians; they are 'our brethren'. 'The same God made them as well as us; gave them as perfect and good souls and bodies as us; and the same Messiah and Saviour is sent to them as to us'. He argued that the colonists had no legal or moral right to use force to expropriate and convert the Indians. The Virginia Company must not put profits before

---

34. The authors cite William Brandon's *New Worlds for Old: Reports from the New World and their Effect on the Development of Social Thought in Europe, 1500–1800* (Athens, Ohio: Ohio U.P., 1986). I have not seen this.
35. Shakespeare, *The Tempest*, Act II, scene i.

building a godly colony.[36] A favourite metaphor was the Biblical one of the wilderness being transformed into 'a garden enclosed'. For this purpose 'Civility may be a leading step to Christianity'.[37]

The analogy between expropriating the unproductive Indians and enclosure in fens and forests was often drawn. In both cases some unfortunates had to lose out in the interests of rational improvement – or so it was argued. William Penington made the point with heavy irony: 'Let the poor native Indians (though something more savage than many in the fens) enjoy all their ancient privileges, and cultivate their own country in their own way. For 'tis equal pity, notwithstanding some trifling dissimilarity of circumstances, that they should be disturbed'.[38] The absurdity of respecting the rights of Indians justified ignoring those of fenmen.

Many were the rationalizations for expropriating the natives. As early as 1583 Peckham's *Discourse of the Necessitie and Commoditie of Planting English Colonies upon the North Partes of America* had concluded that the natives must pay for the advantages of Christianity and civilization being forced upon them. Sir Walter Ralegh thought that aggression was lawful against barbarians 'whose religion and impiety ought to be abhorred', especially if they are powerful: war against them is lawful, for the suppression of evil.[39] Bacon disagreed: 'make no extirpation of the natives under pretence of planting religion'. But a sermon preached in 1615 to the Lord Mayor, Aldermen and Sheriffs of London, and the commissioners for Plantations in Ireland and Virginia, asked 'Can you do God better service than in promoting his kingdom and demolishing daily the power of Satan' by 'furthering this great and glorious work of the gathering in of the Gentiles' by colonizing Ireland and Virginia?[40]

---

36. Crashawe, *A Sermon Preached . . . before . . . Lord La Warre, Lord Governour and Captain General of Virginea* (1610); *Good Newes from Virginia* (1613), Epistle Dedicatory to Sir Thomas Smith, and *passim*.
37. Cf. *The Song of Songs*, IV:12; K. Stavely, 'Roger Williams and the Enclosed Gardens of New England', in *Puritanism: Transatlantic Perspectives on a Seventeenth-Century Anglo-American Faith* (ed. F. J. Bremer, Boston, 1993), pp. 261–70.
38. Penington, *Reflections on the Various Advantages Resulting from the Draining, Enclosing and Allotting of Large Commons and Common Fields* (1769), pp. 34–5, quoted by J. M. Neeson, *Commoners and Common Right, Enclosure and Social Change in England, 1700–1820* (Cambridge U.P., 1993), p. 30.
39. Tawney and Power, *Tudor Economic Documents*, III, p. 265; Ralegh, *The Cabinet-Council*, in *Works* (ed. T. Birch, 1715), I, p. 79. First published by John Milton in 1658.
40. Bacon, 'Advice to Sir George Villiers', in *Works* (1826), III, p. 455; cf. ibid., pp. 33 and 471–2; T. Cooper, *The Blessing of Japheth, Proving the Gathering in of the Gentiles and Finall Conversion of the Jewes* (1615), Sig. A 2–3, pp. 33–5.

George Wither, in a hymn 'for those who intend to settle in Virginia, New England, or the like places', reverted to Peckham's view in versifying the settlers' duty towards the natives:

> So let their good be sought
> That they may room to us afford
> As due for what we brought.[41]

'The law of Nature', said the Rev. Richard Baxter, 'may bind a Christian nation in charity to rule over some Nations by force', if they will not receive the Gospel. Winthrop and John Eliot ('the apostle to the Indians') agreed.[42] The problem was solved for the Pilgrim Fathers when they found themselves in a land 'abounding with a multitude of pernicious savages, whereby they would have been in great peril of their lives, and so the work of transplanting the gospel into those parts much endangered and retarded. But God so disposed that the place where they ... settled was much depopulated by a great mortality amongst the natives ... whereby he made way for the carrying on of his good purposes in propagating of his gospel'.[43] God was much to be congratulated on arming the intruders with diseases hitherto unknown in America. Once the power of English settlers was established, John Cotton saw America as a theatre for experimentation: a place where 'free preaching of the word and the actual practice of our church discipline' would be possible for those deprived of it in England. In America 'we could offer a much clearer and fuller witness' than in English gaols or under forced conformity.[44]

There was much pro-settlement propaganda. The repertory of the Red Bull theatre, and Heywood's plays in particular, specialized in anti-Spanish themes, plays which dramatize citizen values, telling of fortunes to be made by trade with the New World and the Indies, of heroic sea-fights and defences of merchant shipping against pirates. Heywood's plays encourage young people without lands or prospects at home to join overseas

41. Wither, *Hallelujah* (ed. E. Farr, 1857), Hymn LXI, p. 388. First published 1641.
42. Baxter, *A Holy Commonwealth* (1659), p. 170; James Holstun, *A Rational Millennium: Puritan Utopias of Seventeenth-Century England and America* (Oxford U.P., 1967), pp. 107–8; cf. p. 143.
43. Nathaniel Morton, *New England's Memorial* (1669), in *Chronicles of the Pilgrim Fathers* (Everyman ed.), p. 20–21.
44. F. J. Bremer, *Congregational Communion: Clerical Friendship in the Anglo-American Puritan Community, 1610–1692* (Northeastern U.P., 1994), pp. 107, 117–19, 134–5.

exploration and trading ventures, or even emigrate to Virginia in the hope of making their fortunes.[45]

The idea of the noble savage is to be found in Erasmus.[46] Account had to be taken of the fact that many Europeans saw 'freedom' in the idle life of the Indians, preferring it to the hard labour expected of the lower classes in the early colonies. In 1649 an English newspaper reported on two American Indians who had been brought to France. One of them declared himself amazed at the contrast between the rich and costly apparel of some in Paris and the extreme poverty and near-starvation of others. He 'conceived them all to be equal in the balance of Nature'. In April 1649 this 'worthy expression' of 'heathen Levellers' made its own point.[47]

The sceptical Francis Osborn, in his *Advice to a Son* (1656), noted that 'some of the wild Indians, and other people by us styled barbarians, are yet more strangers to the unsociable sins of improbity, covetousness etc. than such as pretend to advance their conversion'. He suggested that this superiority might be due to Indian lack of belief in an afterlife and having no private property, 'and not one to be exalted above another'. Jesus Christ's advice to the young man to sell all that he had and give to the poor would be meaningless in such a society.[48] From early days the concept of native innocence had lurked behind contempt for sexually promiscuous native Indians. But when Walter Hammond, ship's surgeon, in 1640 published a tract *Proving That the Inhabitants of the Island, called Madagascar . . . (in Temporal Things) are the happiest People in the World* he had called this elevation of African noble savages *A Paradox*.[49] It was in the disappointed and frustrated society of the post-revolutionary later 1650s and 1660s that the cult of the noble savage developed.

The phrase is Dryden's (see p. 155 above), but the idea had been anticipated by Davenant in *The Cruelty of the Spaniards in Peru*, played before Oliver Cromwell's court.[50] It was Aphra Behn who gave literary form to the myth. Her *Oroonoko, or The Royal Slave* (1688) may derive

45. Margot Heinemann, 'Rebel Lords, Popular Playwrights, and Political Culture: Notes on the Jacobean Patronage of the Earl of Southampton', *Yearbook of English Studies*, 21 (1991), pp. 71–5.

46. J. Huizinga, *Erasmus of Rotterdam* (1952), p. 108.

47. *The Kingdomes Faithfull and Impartiall Scout*, No. 11, in Raymond, op. cit., p. 268.

48. Osborn, *Miscellaneous Works* (11th ed., 1722), I, pp. 100–101.

49. In *Harleian Miscellany* (1744–6), I, pp. 256–62.

50. Davenant, *Shorter Poems and Songs from the Plays and Masques* (ed. A. M. Gibbs, Oxford U.P., 1972), pp. 250–1.

from her own experience in Surinam; but her early biography is very mysterious. She was clearly an ambiguous character: she spied for Charles II but took lovers among former Parliamentarians. She uses her novel to air radical opinions. Of the Indians she wrote, 'These people represented to me an absolute *Idea* of the first state of innocence, before man knew how to sin: And 'tis most evident and plain, that simple Nature is the most harmless, inoffensive and virtuous Mistress'. 'Religion would here but destroy that tranquility they possess by ignorance; and laws would but teach 'em to know offences of which now they have no notion'.[51] In Oroonoko's country 'the only crime and sin against a woman is to turn her off, to abandon her to want, shame and misery: such ill morals are only practised in Christian countries, where they prefer the bare name of religion; and, without virtue or morality, think that sufficient. But Oroonoko was none of those professors'. 'He would never be reconciled to our notions of the Trinity, of which he ever made a jest.'[52]

Oroonoko was treated with the most outrageous treachery by the English captain who seized the Prince and all the other guests invited to dine aboard the English ship. They were all sold as slaves, Oroonoko included.[53] In Southerne's play of *Oroonoko* (1696) Aphra Behn's anti-religious attitudes are retained. Thus he makes the Prince say 'For his sake, I'll think it possible / A Christian may be yet an honest man.' The sentiment was repeated in Gay's *Polly*.[54] In her poem 'The Golden Age' Aphra Behn depicted a state of primitive freedom in which

> Lovers . . . uncontrolled did meet . . .
> Not kept in fear of gods, no fond religious cause,
> Nor in obedience to the duller laws.
> Those fopperies of the gown were then not known,
> Those vain, those politic curbs to keep man in,
> Who by a fond mistake created that a sin;
> Which freeborn we, by right of nature claim our own.
> Who but the learned and dull moral fool
> Could gravely have foreseen, man ought to live by rule?[55]

51. Aphra Behn, *Works* (ed. M. Summers, 1915), V, pp. 131–2.
52. Ibid., V, pp. 139, 175.
53. Ibid., V, pp. 161–6.
54. Thomas Southerne, *Works* (ed. R. Jordan and H. Love, Oxford U.P., 1988), p. 172; cf. p. 14 above. Aphra Behn's play, *The Widow Ranter* (posthumously published, 1690), also emphasizes the natural goodness of primitive man, contrasting it with the treachery and deceit of the 'civilized' colonists. The name of the widow is ostentatiously 'libertine'.
55. Behn, op. cit., VI, p. 141.

In a poem on the vegetarian teetotaller Thomas Tryon she wrote of

> that blest golden age, when man was young,
> When the whole race was vigorous and strong;
> When Nature did her wond'rous dictates give,
> And taught the Noble Savage how to live.[56]

Among the propertied classes it took a free-thinking libertine like Aphra Behn to appreciate the 'savage' virtues. There were those among the godless common people to whom it came easier. Proper sexual morality had to be imposed on them.

Gay looks back to Aphra Behn. 'You talk downright Indian', said Jenny Driver to a pirate who spoke of honour, 'as other great men do; but when interest comes in your way you should do as other great men do'.[57] 'How different are your notions from ours', said the Indian chief Pohetohee to the planter Ducat, who shrank from engaging in battle; 'we think virtue, honour and courage are as essential to man as his limbs or senses; and in every man we suppose the qualities of a man, till we have found the contrary'. Ducat replied, ''Tis time enough to own a man's failings when they are found out'.[58]

The libertine approach to noble savages must be distinguished from Christian humanitarian views, though they might lead to similar conclusions. William Penn in *The Peace of Europe* (1683) insisted that the Indians of Pennsylvania were not savages, and painted his own picture of their natural nobility. 'They care for little, because they want but little, and the reason is, a little contents them. In this they are sufficiently revenged on us; if they are ignorant of our pleasures they are also free from our pains . . . We sweat and toil to live; their pleasure feeds them'. Penn deplored the paganism of the Indians, yet stressed their belief in a God and immortality. He also praised their democratic system of government.[59] His 'Great Indian Treaty' – with the native inhabitants of the territory he was occupying – made arrangements for living peacefully side by side which survived so long as Quakers controlled the colony.

In *Oroonoko* Aphra Behn established a tradition which looks forward to Rousseau and the romantics. Her first-hand description of the brutalities

---

56. Ibid., IV, p. 380.
57. Gay, *Polly*, Act II, scene ix.
58. Ibid., Act III, scene i. Cf. pp. 14–16 above.
59. Penn, 'A Description of Pennsylvania' (1683), in *The Fruits of Solitude and other writings* (Everyman ed., 1942), pp. 284–8.

of slavery anticipated anti-slavery ideas which developed painfully slowly in England. Churchill, for instance:

> Happy the savage of those early times
> E'er Europe's sons were known, and Europe's crimes!
> Gold, cursed gold . . .
> Happy, thrice happy now the savage race
> Since Europe took their gold and gave them grace![60]

The heavy irony reminds us that Churchill left all his papers to John Wilkes.

Finally, we may ask whether in their plays Brome and Gay created an image of 'the noble beggar' parallel to that of 'the noble savage'. I think not. The latter concept is a view from the distance, and owes much to reported horrors of atrocities against Indians and other native peoples. Their nobility lay in their free-ranging absence. Beggars were too present to be idealized.

The Robin Hood ballads, together with Elizabethan and Jacobean plays about outlaws, anticipate *A Jovial Crew*: the lives of pirates and highwaymen anticipate *The Beggar's Opera* in criticizing the dishonesty of politicians and the propertied.

60. Charles Churchill, 'Gotham', in *Works*, (ed. J. Lavar, 1933), I, pp. 309–10, vii.

13. *Impressment and Empire*

=====

When Britain first, at heaven's command,
   Arose from out the azure main,
This was the charter of the land,
   And guardian angels sang this strain:
   'Rule, Britannia, rule the waves,
   Britons never will be slaves'.

James Thomson, *The Masque of Alfred* (1740). For the eighteenth-
century sense of 'charter' see pp. 242–3 below.

[The game laws are] almost as offensive to the peasantry as press
warrants to the mechanic.

Mary Wollstonecraft, *Works*, V, p. 17.

I

As the English Revolution consolidated, and radicals like Levellers, Diggers, Ranters and Fifth Monarchists were suppressed, liberty came to be
ever more closely associated with private property; and private property
came to be concentrated in the hands of fewer people. For these people,
freedom meant freedom to make profits, to accumulate capital. Britain's
future as a commercial state came increasingly to demand a forceful
expansionist imperial policy, with a strong navy to protect and expand
trade.

During the civil war, although 'liberty' was agreed to be the ultimate
object, individual liberties had gone by the board. There were large
numbers of principled volunteers on both sides, but Royalists and Parliamentarians alike had to resort to impressment. As the wars in England
ended, Parliament faced war with Scotland and the reconquest of Ireland;
and this led to resentment among the rank and file of the Army, few of
whom were enthusiastic about fighting outside England – especially not
in Ireland. For some there were principles involved. Walwyn was alleged
to have said that 'the Irish did no more but what we would have done
ourselves if it had been our case'. 'What had the English to do in their

kingdom?' 'Why should not they enjoy the liberty of their consciences?'[1]
Many soldiers were no doubt simply war-weary and anxious to get back
home:

'Freedom' came to be interpreted as meaning independence for the
British state rather than for individuals. Individuals are free through membership of that state, their incorporation into which is illustrated by the
frontispiece of Hobbes' *Leviathan*. The navy guarantees the freedom and
independence of the British protestant state against conquest by Spain or
France, and guarantees free access to the wealth of the East and West
Indies, to the African slave trade. Since the days of the sea-dogs and the
Providence Island Company the interests of English protestants and English merchants had seemed inextricably linked in face of the persecuting
great powers, Spain and then France. Conquest by either of these would
mean an end of protestantism in England, so the freedom of the state
guarantees that English men and women will not suffer the fate of the
Vaudois in Savoy or the Huguenots in Louis XIV's France – much publi-
cized in England.[2]

As so many Englishmen lost their hold on the land in Britain, the
appeal of free land across the Atlantic became greater. Professor Kupperman has convincingly shown that private property in land played a large
part in the success of the Massachusetts plantation. 'Security of tenure'
involved not only ownership but a representative system of government
to guarantee against unwarranted seizure of property. She quotes Captain
John Smith on Virginia. 'Here are no hard landlords to rack us with high
rents, or extorting fines, nor tedious pleas in law to consume us with their
many years' disputation for justice . . . as here every man may be master
of his own labour and land'. That was freedom.[3]

It would be interesting to trace the stages by which the word 'land'
acquired an additional meaning. The *O.E.D.* is not very helpful here.
'Native country' occurs frequently in the sixteenth century – for instance
Thomas Becon in 1543: 'I think there is no man so far estranged from
civil humanity which knoweth not how far every one of us is indebted to
our native country'. But there is nothing in *O.E.D.* about 'native land'.
An early example comes from the translation of *The Aeneid* made by

---

1. Thomas Edwards, *Gangraena*, Part II, p. 27.
2. See J. F. Bosher, 'The Franco-Catholic Danger, 1660–1715, *History*, No. 255
(1994), pp. 5–30.
3. Karen Ordahl Kupperman, *Providence Island, 1630–1641: The Other Puritan Colony*
(Cambridge U.P., 1993), pp. 141–6; cf. pp. 19–23, 127.

Gavin Douglas, Bishop of Dunkeld, in 1513: 'Banist and flemyt of my native land'.[4] Gerrard Winstanley in April 1649 said that 'the poor people . . . shall be the Saviour of the land'.[5] In 'Land of hope and glory / Mother of the free', or 'Land of our fathers' the word 'land' refers to the abstraction 'country'. Most citizens had been robbed of the land of their fathers. The brash triumphalism of Thomson and his like, who assumed that the propertied rulers *were* the people of England, gives way in the nineteenth century. In 'It is my own, my native land', the useful word 'native' makes it clear that individual landownership is not in question.

II

War was, among other things, an opportunity for setting the poor on work. Vagrants tended to be the first to be conscripted when an army or navy was being raised. Any community asked to supply a quota of men would naturally start with vagabonds or paupers, who would otherwise be a charge to that community. But the presence of large numbers in arms from the lower orders always alarmed the gentry. A combination of peasant soldiers with 'the meaner sort of people' presaged 'mutiny and rebellion'.[6] We have here an additional reason, not often emphasized, for the 'natural rulers'' dislike of standing armies.

'To wear some nobleman's badge' would save a waterman from being pressed.[7] The gentry were themselves of course immune from conscription. In the play *The London Prodigal* (1605) it was accepted that a rich man should not be pressed. 'Oh fie Sir Arthur, press *him*', said one shocked character to another. 'He is a man of reckoning.'[8] Ralegh in his *History of the World* considered that 'where most vile and servile dispositions have liberty to show themselves begging in the streets' they might

4. Becon, *The Policy of War*, quoted by John Hale, *The Civilization of Europe in the Renaissance* (1993), p. 69. I am indebted to Dr Bernadette Paton, senior editor of the *Oxford English Dictionary*, for the reference to Douglas. His is the first translation from a classical language into English (*D.N.B.*).
5. Winstanley, *The True Levellers Standard Advanced*, in Sabine, op. cit., p. 264.
6. Hunt, *The Puritan Moment*, pp. 173, 183–6, 190, 213, 240–44; cf. Tawney and Power, op. cit., II, p. 343; Slack, *Poverty and Policy in Tudor and Stuart England* (1988), pp. 13–14, 23–4, 98.
7. Wye Saltonstall, *Picturae Loquentes* (1631 and 1635). I cite from the Luttrell Society's reprint of 1946, p. 40.
8. Op. cit., Act I, scene ii, in *The Shakespeare Apocrypha*. My italics.

properly be pressed into the navy. From the example of Cain he argued that 'vagabond is taken for a man without protection, and cast out from the favour of God'.[9] In Elizabeth's reign some felons sentenced to death were reprieved for service in the galleys. In 1602 a special search was instituted for 'vagabonds and other evil, dissolute and masterless persons ... of whom this realm may well be disburdened'. They were to be sent 'with the utmost secrecy' to serve the Dutch in their war of liberation against Spain, together with any who might volunteer for this service. Under James I 'lesser offenders' were conscripted into the English armed forces.[10]

The Vagrancy Act of 1597 declared incorrigible or dangerous rogues liable to banishment overseas, which from 1603 was interpreted as meaning to the American plantations. The Virginia Company accepted such characters, though Bacon thought it a mistake to found a colony on the 'scum of people and wicked condemned men'.[11] Thousands of poor children were shipped off to Virginia from 1607 onwards. In 1620 the London Common Council ordered that parents refusing to allow their children to be extradited were to have their poor relief cut off. Many children died on the way or soon after arrival in Virginia, where they worked in conditions of virtual slavery.

In 1618 forty 'poor maidens' fled from one Somerset village alone to avoid transportation; there was a revolt in Bridewell by children unwilling to be sent to Virginia, but it was unsuccessful. A large proportion of these involuntary exiles, picked up in the streets of London, Bristol and Liverpool, failed to survive to adulthood. In 1622 the Virginia Company was told of labourers rising early, working all day, going to bed late, who are 'scarce able to put bread in their mouths at the week's end, and clothes on their backs at the year's end'. They formed a useful supply of labour for the plantations, of persons who otherwise would never be reclaimed from 'the idle life of vagabonds', as King James I put it to the Governor of Virginia.[12]

9. Ralegh, op. cit., V, p. 109, I, p. 154.
10. *Sir Henry Whithed's Letter Book,* I, *1601–14* (Hampshire Record Series, I, 1976), pp. 11–13; J. S. Cockburn, *A History of English Assizes* (Cambridge U.P., 1972), p. 129.
11. Bacon, 'Essay of Plantations', *Works,* II, p. 324.
12. Beier, *Masterless Men,* pp. 162–4, 169–70 and references there cited. See also R. C. Johnson, 'The Transportation of vagrant children', in *Early Stuart Studies* (ed. H. S. Reinmuth, Minneapolis, 1870), pp. 138–46; Ivy Pinchbeck and Margaret Hewitt, *Children in English Society,* I, *From Tudor Times to the Eighteenth Century,* p. 106.

In 1630 the Dutch were promised English vagabonds for their new colony on the Hudson.[13] An undated paper from the early days of the Long Parliament said that 'We must have a new press and send [the poor] to a new plantation'.[14] In 1642 Parliament discussed impressing 'loose persons' for service in their army against the King, and in 1656 several hundred London prostitutes were transported to the West Indies to boost the birth rate there. The penalty for killing or wounding deer in royal forests was increased in 1719 from a fine to seven years' transportation. Powers of arrest, judgement and punishment were entrusted to parish constables.[15]

Only the lowest classes were liable to impressment. In the Putney Debates of October 1647 Colonel Rainborough pointed out that 'we do find in all presses that go forth, none must be pressed that are freehold men. When these gentlemen fall out among themselves they shall press the poor scrubs to come and kill [one another] for them'.[16] The Leveller *Agreement of the People* of November 1647 contained a clause saying that the representatives of the people should not be empowered to impress or constrain any person to serve in war: 'it is against our freedom'. But after the execution of Charles I Parliament passed an act authorizing 'pressing of sea-men', threatening three months' imprisonment for any who resisted. (In the crisis of 1659 this was altered to the death penalty.) The Leveller *England's New Chains Discovered* rebuked Parliament for passing this act since it was directly contrary to the officers' *Agreement of the People* presented to Parliament.[17] In the *Agreement* of May 1649 the prohibition of impressment was reinforced by adding 'every man's conscience being to be satisfied in the justice of that cause wherein he hazards his own life or may destroy another's'.[18]

Pressing remained at the centre of Parliamentary policy for manning the navy. There was much evasive action – bribery, favouritism, rescues,

13. Noel McLachlan, 'Columbus and Australia: New World Natives and the Gulliver Complex', p. 11, an unpublished typescript which he kindly allowed me to read.

14. Ed. Maija Jansson, *Two Diaries of the Long Parliament* (Gloucester, 1984), p. 142.

15. *A Perfect Diurnall of all the Passages in Parliament*, No. 11, 22–9 August 1642, in *Making the News*, pp. 66–7; Beier, *Masterless Men*, p. 163; Thompson, *Whigs and Hunters*, pp. 59–63.

16. Woodhouse, *Puritanism and Liberty*, p. 71.

17. Ed. W. Haller and G. Davies, *The Leveller Tracts 1647–1653* (Columbia U.P., 1944), p. 162.

18. Ed. D. M. Wolfe, *Leveller Manifestoes of the Puritan Revolution* (New York, 1944), p. 405.

abscondings, organized resistance – often with the connivance of local officials. A seamen's petition of 1654 declared impressment inconsistent with the principles of freedom; a Council of War endorsed this by a large majority. In December 1659, in a public declaration of support for the Rump of the Long Parliament, Vice-Admiral Lawson called for impressment to be abolished except when immediately necessary for the safety of the country.[19]

Freedom from impressment here – for I believe the first time in England – took its place as an essential liberty. Before 1640 men had been pressed for military and naval service in time of wár; but these conscripts had normally been beggars or vagabonds, those whom parish élites were glad to be rid of. But now larger numbers were required – first in the conquest of Scotland and Ireland, then for naval and military wars against Spain and France. Under the 'liberty' which the men of property had established, England soon had a large navy, whose sailors were perforce mainly pressed men. Some men's freedom turned out to involve slavery for large numbers of less fortunate persons. Conscripts were no longer mainly rightless vagabonds; they included many who believed they had fought – and won – a war for freedom. So there was much principled objection to impressment, as slavery. The anonymous radical *Tyranipocrit Discovered* (Rotterdam 1649), sometimes (probably wrongly) attributed to Walwyn, suggested that 'all rich uncharitable persons, which have and hold an extraordinary portion of worldly goods, more than their poor neighbours have, . . . expostulate with the poor according to that which followeth: . . . you see that we rich hypocritical tyrants have gotten by fraud and force the most part of the goods of this world into our impious power, and we have made a law, as we call it, that if any poor persons do steal any of our goods which we have taken from them, that they shall hang by their necks till they be dead: but now you poor miserable wretches, if you will serve the devil and us, then we will employ you in his and our service. . . . Some of you shall serve by sea and some by land; . . . some of you shall rob the poor Indians for us, . . . and some of you shall kill our neighbour tyrant's slaves, for if we suppose that he hath done us any injury then we will send some of our slaves to kill some of their slaves and then one innocent shall kill another.'[20]

19. B. Capp, *Cromwell's Navy: The Fleet and the English Revolution. 1649–1660* (Oxford U.P., 1989), pp. 263–72.
20. Op. cit., ed. A. Hopton, n.d., ?1991, p. 21

It is worth recording that Gay's farce *The What D'Ye Call It* (1716) denounces various examples of social injustice – the game laws, the poor law, rural exploitation – and impressment.

> You press'd my brother – he shall walk in white,
> He shall – and shake your curtains ev'ry night.
> What though a paltry hare he rashly killed,
> That cross'd the furrows while he plough'd the field?
> You sent him o'er the hills and far away;
> Left his old mother to the parish pay,
> With whom he shared his ten pence ev'ry day.
> Wat kill'd a bird, was from his farm turn'd out . . .
>
> Now will you press my harmless nephew too?
> Ah, what has conscience with the rich to do?[21]

England's future, in the eyes of its new rulers, was tied to trade wars and colonial expansion. 'Liberty at home breeds wealth and power abroad', said Nedham in 1650. A great future opened up for newly liberated England. But this great future assumed the existence of a powerful navy with which to fight the wars necessary, among other things, to win England a virtual monopoly of the slave trade. Impressment was unavoidable, however much it might seem to conflict with the new ideology of British freedom. It was anyway an old British custom.

Fortunately trade and colonial wars demanded naval vessels, not the galleys which did service in the Mediterranean. Galleys manned by men chained to their oars were a form of slavery: much was made of this in anti-French propaganda. But it was not easy to maintain that pressed men sent to fight and die in the Pacific or Indian Oceans were free. The point had been eloquently made in *A Remonstrance of Many Thousand Citizens* addressed to the House of Commons in July 1646: 'We entreat you to consider what difference there is between binding a man to an oar, as a galley-slave in Turkey or Algiers, and pressing of men to serve in your war; to surprise a man on the sudden, force him from his calling, . . . from his dear parents, wife or children, against inclination, disposition to fight for a cause he understands not . . . for pay that will scarce give him sustenance; and if he live, to return to a lost trade or beggary, or not

---

21. J. F. Bosher, 'The Franco-Catholic Danger, 1660–1715', *History*, No. 255 (1994), pp. 20–21.

much better'. Overton – the presumed author – ended with a shrewd thrust. 'If ye would take care that all sorts of men might find comfort and contentment in your government, ye would not need to enforce men to serve your wars'.[22]

'The scum of people and wicked condemned men' continued to be a main source of rank and file colonists in the eighteenth century, when some 50,000 British and Irish convicts were transported to North America – at least a quarter of total immigrants, including one-third of the felons annually convicted at the Old Bailey. The colonists regarded this as a great grievance, and Americans today appear to be less proud of their convict inheritance than Australians, though no less a person than Benjamin Franklin (who should have known) said in 1759 that 'the most substantial men of most of the provinces are children and grandchildren of . . . thieves, highwaymen and robbers'.[23]

In the 1640s and 1650s prisoners of war were transported beyond the seas 'for the service of the states of Venice, or to the West Indian plantations'.[24] Some 4,500 convicted felons were sent to the colonies between 1655 and the end of the century.[25] After the restoration, under the 1662 Act of Settlement, large numbers of dissenters were transported to the colonies if they attended conventicles for a third time. Persons convicted of felony might pray for the favour of commutation to transportation. A great many persons were illegally spirited away to the American plantations where there was always a shortage of labour.[26]

Export of servants from Bristol to the American colonies 'reached enormous heights' in the 1650s and early 1660s, ranging from 884 in 1658–9 to an annual average of 250 in the 1670s. How far these were voluntary emigrants is uncertain. J.P.s (almost all of whom traded in the American colonies) were said to threaten petty criminals with hanging in order to get them to pray for transportation.[27] Early eighteenth-century

---

22. Op. cit., in Wolfe, op. cit., p. 125.

23. Roger E. Kirch, 'Bound for America', in *The Transportation of British Colonists to the Colonies, 1718–1755* (Oxford U.P., 1987), pp. 21–7.

24. *H.M.C., 10th Report*, Appendix, Part 4, pp. 93–4; *9th Report*, Part 2, p. 126; Gardiner, *Great Civil War*, IV, p. 193.

25. A. G. L. Shaw, *Convicts and the Colonies* (1966), p. 24, quoted by J. A. Sharpe, *Crime in seventeenth-century England*, p. 147.

26. B. Osborne, *Justices of the Peace*, pp. 139–46; Lipson, *Economic History*, III, pp. 161–4.

27. D. H. Sacks, *The Widening Gate: Bristol and the Atlantic Economy, 1450–1700* (California U.P., 1991), Chapter 9; my *Reformation to Industrial Revolution*, p. 178.

legislation of the Irish Parliament provided for 'loose and idle vagrants' to be pressed into the royal navy or shipped to the American plantations for up to seven years.[28] In 1776 the city marshals of Barnsley were searching public houses in order that 'such as could give no account of themselves might be sent to serve his Majesty'.[29]

The liability of dismissed servants to be treated as vagabonds put a powerful weapon into the hands of their employers. This is illustrated by two items from the *London Chronicle* in 1760. In the first 'a Country Gentleman' was 'resolved speedily to advance the wages of all my servants on condition of their taking money from no person of any denomination that enters my gates: if they do, that instant I turn them adrift to the mercy of a press gang'. In the second, when over fifty servants to officers in the army in Germany 'agreed amongst themselves to leave their masters if their wages and perquisites were not advanced, . . . the officers were obliged to discharge them. The servants procured passes to come over to England'. But when they landed at Sheerness the captain of the *Princess Royal*, who had been notified, sent his men to press them.[30] Solidarity among servants was matched by solidarity among their betters.

In Francis Place's youth pressed men were sworn in, whether they consented or not; a magistrate had to certify that it was 'voluntary', especially when it was not. 'Volunteers were then marched through the streets in handcuffs'.[31] Blackstone regarded pressing as part of the common law – another case of the law used against freedom.

From the later seventeenth century British freedom again became a catchword – now identified with Parliamentary sovereignty, limited monarchy, religious toleration. Attempts were made to play down memories of the 1640s. But as increasing numbers of pressed men were needed to fight wars against the Netherlands or France, a great deal of propaganda had to be devoted to glorifying the freedom of the British seaman.

The experience of Leveller-influenced army democracy in the 1640s helped to warn the English ruling class off standing armies. Both Charles II and James II were apprehensive about the possible social consequences of allowing large numbers of lower-class Englishmen to congregate with

28. Angus Fraser, *The Gypsies* (1992), p. 172.
29. *The Gentleman's Magazine*, 1776, p. 529. I owe this reference to Bridget Hill.
30. *The London Chronicle*, VII (1760), pp. 260, 441. I owe this reference too to the kindness of Bridget Hill.
31. [Ed. Mary Thale], *The Autobiography of Francis Place* (Cambridge U.P., 1972), p. 35.

arms in their hands. In the navy there were fewer democratic traditions. Beggars and vagabonds pressed as seamen lacked the experience of freedom of Cromwell's yeomen cavalry who knew what they fought for and loved what they knew.

III

As England got richer and richer behind her vast navy and with her near-monopoly of the lucrative slave trade, Mandeville's analysis began to make sense to the men of property. 'In a free nation', he wrote, 'where slaves are not allowed of, the surest wealth consists in a multitude of laborious poor. ... Men who are to remain and end their days in a laborious, tiresome and painful station of life, the sooner they are put upon it, the more patiently they'll submit to it *for ever after*'.[32] A tiny part of the newly acquired wealth trickled down to the lower orders – not much until trade unions got organized. But traditions of the 1640s also survived, especially in nonconformist congregations, still more perhaps among the lowest classes normally outside politics, as larger and larger numbers of them had to be pressed into the navy and the mercantile marine. We may perhaps relate this to the sympathy shown for pirates at Tyburn: pirates were mostly volunteers, and their ships' discipline was far more democratic than that of the navy. The mercantile marine was expanding *pari passu* with the navy, and there was much interchange of personnel. As more and more men had to be pressed into the navy, comparisons began to be drawn.

So we find new ideas of liberty in the patriotic songs and ballads of the eighteenth century. 'The roast beef of old England' is sentimentalized as stocks of venison give out and it becomes ruinously expensive. 'Britons never, never, never will be slaves'. Other nations, 'not so blest as we' will 'to tyrants fall / While thou shalt flourish great and free'. But Britannia ruled the waves thanks to enslaved sailors. 'Hearts of Oak', for instance, started

> Then cheer up, my lads, 'tis to glory we steer,
> To add something more to this wonderful year.
> 'Tis to honour we call you, not press you like slaves;
> For who are so free as the sons of the waves?

32. Bernard Mandeville, *The Fable of the Bees; or, Private Vices, Publick Benefits* (3rd ed., 1724), I, pp. 328–9, 345. The words which I have italicized are revealing.

'Jolly tars' needed a lot of cheering up under the lash. But of course such songs were aimed at reassuring those at home who profited by seamen's enslavement, at preventing them even thinking about the realities of England's sea power. These are no longer anonymous spontaneous ballads, but the self-conscious work of establishment poets like James Thomson. Eighteenth-century patriotic verse is unfailingly aggressive.

'Hearts of Oak' recalls the destruction of forests to provide timber for ship-building; 'jolly tars are our men' recalls the press-ganged rural swains whose livelihood had been destroyed with the forests and who had little alternative but to become dehumanized grinning puppets (*'jolly* Jack Tars') who spring into action at the word of command, always ready and steady to kill or be killed. John Bull with his cudgel personifies the aggressive English yeomanry on the quarter deck: poets produced an appropriately debased concept of liberty. 'We'll fight and we'll conquer again and again' sang 'Hearts of Oak' – the plural 'we' covering those buried at sea as well as the survivors.

We saw in Chapter 5 that a new interest in Robin Hood stressed his Englishness, his patriotism. In a Robin Hood play of 1730 the outlaws are 'hearts of oak'.[33] Even the radical Ritson, writing in 1795, when England was at war with revolutionary France, went out of his way to praise Robin Hood's 'patriotic sentiments'. Sir Walter Scott, who had no radical ideas to cover up, strongly emphasized anti-Norman patriotism in *Ivanhoe*.

Naval victories meant that England's population was satisfactorily culled, whilst the power of John Bull's state was extended. Echoes ring across the centuries, from the anonymous *Tyranipocrit Discovered*, published in the first year of the republic ('send some of our slaves to kill some of their slaves' – see p. 167 above) to John Clare, driven mad by loss of community freedom (see Chapter 26, below).

Thomson's complacency is pretty remarkable, notwithstanding England's military victories. It is worth contrasting his view of freedom with those which we have been considering hitherto. In his *The Castle of Indolence* 'freedom reigned without the least alloy' till 'Sir Industry' 'made for Britain's coast' ('my great, my chosen isle'), 'to freedom apt, and persevering pains'. In the poem 'Liberty'

> Crecy, Poitiers, Agincourt proclaim,
> What . . . people fired with liberty can do.

33. Knight, op. cit., p. 156.

Thomson has a very good Whig analysis of the revolution of the 1640s, after which Liberty, 'her bright temples bound with British oak' appeared as 'an island goddess now', to care for 'The queen of isles, the mistress of the main'.[34]

> Dreadful Blake . . .
> Awed angry nations with the British name.

Sea power and overseas trade made her 'The queen of nations'. But

> Oh! it much imports you, 'tis your all
> To keep your trade entire, entire the force
> And honour of your fleets.

Otherwise,

> o'er other lands
> The various treasure would resistless pour
> Ne'er to be won again.[35]

Thomson's insensitivity to the lives of the poor reaches its climax when he tells us that 'Britain's matchless constitution' was due to 'the several advances of Liberty, down to her *complete* establishment at the Revolution' (of 1688). Since then 'the poor man's lot with milk and honey flows'.

> Justice like the liberal light of heaven
> Unpurchased shines on all.

Consequently '*unfailing fields of freemen*' will rise to Britain's defence.[36] Freedom has come to relate to state power and a powerful navy, both used to win the commerce of the world for English merchants – including the slave trade. Alexander Hamilton and James Madison had no difficulty in persuading the early rulers of the American republic that a big navy was essential for protecting and expanding overseas trade, the basis of national wealth.[37]

It is a refreshing change to turn to Churchill's 'Gotham' (1764), in which the poet looks at the effects of Christian colonization on native peoples. 'Some roving buccaneer set up a post' in unknown territory,

34. Thomson, *The Castle of Indolence and other Poems* (ed. H. D. Roberts, Muses' Library, n.d.), pp. 12, 30, 54, 123, 128–32.
35. Ibid., pp. 155, 158, 160–61; cf. 151–2.
36. Ibid., pp. 98, 121, 133, 150–51. My italics.
37. S. H. Beer, *To Make a Nation: The Rediscovery of American Federalism* (1993), p. 354.

His royal master's name thereon engraved,
Without more process, the whole race enslaved,
Cut off that charter they from Nature drew
And made them slaves to men they never knew. . . .

Happy the savage of those early times,
Ere Europe's sons were known, and Europe's crimes! . . .
Happy, thrice happy, now the savage race,
Since Europe took their gold and gave them grace! . . .
Knowledge she gives, enough to make them know
How abject is their state, how deep their woe;
The worth of freedom strongly she explains,
Whilst she bows down and loads their necks with chains. . . .
And whilst she teaches, on vile interest's plan,
As laws of God, the wild decrees of man,
She makes them ten times more the sons of hell'.[38]

Churchill's view of England's history is rather different from Thomson's. But he concludes by praising monarchy under a patriot king.

Cowper, in *The Task*, whilst glorifying English freedom (Books II and V), criticized the exploitation of India (Book IV) and asked 'We have no slaves at home – Then why abroad?' (Book II). 'Grace makes the slave a freeman'. But then Cowper was cautious about monarchy:

> (King was a name too proud for man to wear
> With modesty and meekness).

He believed that

> He is a freeman whom the truth makes free
> And all are slaves besides (Book V).[39]

Marcus Rediker has shown that struggles against impressment intensified from the later seventeenth century. Admiral Peter Warren warned in 1745 that seamen 'have the highest notions of the rights and liberties of Englishmen, and indeed are almost Levellers'. His recollection of the 1640s was pertinent. Resistance to press gangs was, not unnaturally, particularly strong in the colonies. On St Kitts in 1743 a crowd threatened to burn a ship unless her captain released men whom he was pressing.

38. Op. cit., Book II.
39. Op. cit., Books II, IV and V. Cf. 'The Negro's Complaint' and 'Pity for poor Africans'.

Parliament passed an act in 1746 forbidding pressing in the Sugar Islands, presumably because the trade was too valuable to lose, and there was no occupying power to enforce impressment. Implementation of the act was called for in New England and elsewhere.[40]

The Rev. Jonathan Mayhew, in a sermon preached on the centenary of the execution of Charles I, 30 January 1749, declared it a day for remembering that Britons will not be slaves: he wished to go beyond passive resistance, which he described as 'slavery'. It was not a sin 'to transgress an iniquitous law'. Rediker suggests that cooperation between seamen and black slaves helped the evolution of a theory of the rights of man. 'All men are by nature on a level', declared Samuel Adams's weekly, *The Independent Advertiser*, in January 1748. They are 'born with an equal share of freedom'. Adams developed a new 'ideology of resistance', in which the rights of man were used for the first time in New England to justify mob activity. Rediker sees this as a major breakthrough in libertarian thought, that would ultimately lead to revolution – which started among sailors, 'the largest single occupational group' in American cities. Adams watched a motley crew of Africans, Scots, Irishmen, Dutchmen and Englishmen, and probably others, rioting: 'the rights of Englishmen' were hardly relevant there.

James Otis in 1761 spoke of 'the rights of man in a state of nature . . . subject to no law but the law written on his heart' or in 'his conscience'. Three years later, in *The Rights of the British Colonists Asserted and Proved*, he argued that all men, 'white or black . . . are by the laws of nature freeborn'. The inclusion of black men within 'men' proved embarrassing to propertied whites during the American Revolution and at the drafting of the constitution. J. Philmore in *Two Dialogues on the Man-Trade* in 1760 had justified forcible resistance by black slaves, and said it was the duty of others, white as well as black, to assist them. 'No legislature on earth, which is the supreme power in every civil society, . . . can alter the nature of things, or make that to be lawful which is contrary to law of God'. This looks forward to the anti-slavery movement. Sailors in 1769 'preferred death to such a life as they deemed slavery'. They could hardly not sympathize with the African slaves who rioted with them against the press gangs.[41]

40. Rediker, 'A Motley Crew of Rebels: Sailors, Slaves, and the Coming of the American Revolution', *passim*. The contents of this and the following three paragraphs derive from this important article.
41. Ibid., pp. 4–13, 20–22, 24–8, 39.

Popular violence played a crucial part in the events leading up to the war of independence. There was no police force or standing army in New England; local militia men tended to side with the mobs, the imperial authorities were far away. The real will of the people could express itself uncontrolled. Taken together, slaves, servants, prentices, seamen, labourers and poor craftsmen amounted to 50 to 60 per cent of urban working men. Rediker notes the interesting fact that throughout the eighteenth century the crew of a ship was known as 'the people'; once ashore they were on their 'liberty'.

When the American Revolution came the majority of the population who descended from involuntary emigrants needed little convincing that they were not 'virtually represented' in the English Parliament which taxed them. Traditions of popular liberty lived on, and passed to those who pushed the American frontier westwards – at the expense of the rights of Indians. In England in 1772 Wilkes began to argue for the right to resist impressment, following battles between seamen and press gangs in London.[42]

42. See Chapter 27 below.

IV. CHRISTIAN LIBERTY

===

14. *The Ambiguities of Protestantism*

Where there is law, there can be no discipline.

Samuel Taylor Coleridge, quoted by W. Lamont, 'The two "National Churches" of 1691 and 1829', in *Religion, Culture and Society in Early Modern Britain: Essays in Honour of Patrick Collinson*, p. 348; cf. p. 352.

If God be a Father and we are brethren, . . . it is a levelling word. . . . The word 'Father' is an epitome of the whole Gospel.

Richard Sibbes, *Works* (Edinburgh, 1862–4), II, p. 311, V, p. 25; cf. VI, p. 458.

So far I have been discussing those who broke the law of the land in order to make money or – more numerous – the poor and social outcasts who wanted to preserve traditional forms of livelihood to which they believed they had a customary right. Now I turn to a different category – those who deliberately broke the law on grounds of religious principle. There would have been no protestant Reformation in England if the first reformers had not been prepared to break the law, as William Tyndale did in smuggling into England his translation of the New Testament.

It was illegal to publish any translation of the Bible not authorized by the Roman church. Tyndale knew this very well; he failed to find respectable sponsors in England for his dangerous enterprise, and had to go into exile on the continent to get his New Testament printed. Smuggling it into England involved a whole army of coadjutors, some of whom were no doubt interested only in the money. The legalization of the printing of the Bible in English came not as a result of theological conviction but because Henry VIII wished to get rid of Catherine of Aragon and the Pope was not complaisant. The major contribution made by Anne Boleyn during her chequered career was when she gave Henry VIII Tyndale's *The Obedience of a Christian Man* to read, with passages of special interest marked in the margin. Henry presumably read those, and those only, before deciding that this was a book for all kings to read, since Tyndale exalted the authority of the king over all rivals. If Henry had been a more careful reader, or if Anne Boleyn had not chosen her marked passages skilfully, the result might have been different. For Tyndale not only exalted the authority of kings; he also said that we must obey God rather than man. Henry was perhaps unlikely to conceive of God disagreeing with anything that he might wish to do. But Tyndale had elevated the consciences of believers above the king when he broke the king's law by publishing the Bible in English, and he provided no satisfactorily convincing proof of how individuals knew what God wanted. For him it was enough that he felt a strong inner conviction, based on his faith. But he failed to convince other virtuous Christians – St Thomas More, for instance – and no satisfactory way was found to demonstrate that some actions of the state power might conflict with God's commands as interpreted by true believers.

Tyndale, accepting that God's commands might not always appear sensible to average unilluminated consciences, instanced the possibility of God inciting to murder or adultery. He would presumably claim that God had undoubtedly authorized such offences by godly characters in the Old Testament. No doubt God spoke to their consciences directly. But how could one know with absolute certainty in the seventeenth-century that God had authorized Clarkson's adulteries? How could one decide between Clarkson (and the many Ranters who agreed with him) and Tyndale? Protestantism had this teasing ambiguity from the start. It was not due to Tyndale. The Bible available in English opened up new possibilities of freedom which could be discussed only verbally before 1640 but which after that date could get into print and be discussed openly in religious congregations. Protestantism, the priesthood of all believers, led to all sorts of novel doctrines being preached, not only by ordained clergymen.

Tyndale, father of English protestantism, had stressed the secular liberating potential of free preaching of the gospel. The most part of men, he said, seek liberty, and are glad when they hear the 'insatiable covetousness of the spirituality rebuked', when 'tyranny and oppression is preached against, when they hear how kings and all officers should rule Christianly and brotherly', that they have 'no authority of God to tithe and poll as they do, and to raise up taxes . . . to make wars, they wot not for what cause'. He was careful to add that he was not justifying rebellion. 'It is the bloody doctrine of the pope which causeth disobedience'. But Tyndale offered entrancing prospects: 'faith setteth the soul at liberty'.[1]

---

1. Tyndale, *The Obedience of a Christian Man*, in *Doctrinal Treatises*, pp. 166–8, 54.

'The children of faith are under no law . . . but are free'. 'The spirit of Christ hath written the lively law of love in their hearts; which driveth them to work of their own accord freely and willingly'. They need 'no law to compel them'. 'He that may be free is a fool to be bound'. 'Let love interpret the law'. John Ponet had argued that St Peter's 'servants be subject to your masters' (I Peter 2:18) could not be applied to *free* subjects under a king.[2] Tyndale's famous (and more accurate) translation of *ekklesia* as 'congregation' rather than 'church' stressed the centrality of the demo-cracy of the congregation rather than the distant authority of a national or international institution. This translation was hotly contested by St Thomas More and by all who thought that the only successor to the international popish church must be a national church. The seeds of 'dissent' were there from the very beginning of the English reformation, sown by Tyndale.

In the sixteenth century the most persistent and determined law-break-ers were the godly, who – like twentieth-century conscientious objectors in wartime – claimed to be obeying a higher authority than that of the state. Protestants who believed that the correct ordinances for worship had been laid down in the New Testament thought that breach of them was idolatry, a breach of the second commandment. The idolatry of Anglican worship justified separation.[3] The rationale of this was set out clearly by Henry Barrow and John Greenwood, defending themselves in a series of examinations between 1589 and 1593.

'The Scripture hath set down sufficient laws for the worship of God and the government of the church, to which no man may add or diminish . . . Christ is only head of his church, and his laws may no man alter'. Greenwood therefore rejected the royal supremacy over the church.[4] No prince (nor anyone else, said Henry Barrow), 'may make any laws for the church other than Christ hath already left in his word'. 'If the civil magistrate . . . command anything contrary to the commandment of

---

2. Ibid., p. 297; *Prologue to the Book of Genesis* (1530), ibid., p. 403; Ponet, *A Short Treatise of Politique Power* (1642), p. 23. First published 1556: the date of the reprint is suggestive.

3. S. Brachlow, *The Communion of Saints: Radical Puritan and Separatist Ecclesiology, 1570–1625* (Oxford U.P., 1958), Chapter 1 *passim*, quoting Henry Barrow, Henry Jacob and many separatists as well as Thomas Cartwright, Walter Travers, William Perkins, William Ames and William Bradshaw.

4. Greenwood's Examination, 24 March 1588–9, in *The Writings of John Greenwood, 1587–1590* (ed. L. H. Carlson, 1962), pp. 28–9.

God', he ought not to be obeyed. 'The judgments due and set down by God for the transgression of the moral law cannot be changed or altered without injury . . . to God himself'. He too could not take the oath of supremacy. Barrow replied to a question, 'if the prince deny or refuse to [correct] abuses . . . the church of Christ . . . may, without staying for the prince, reform them'. The pastor of the appropriate church ought to pronounce excommunication on the prince 'if this is necessary for his salvation'.[5] Yet at the Hampton Court Conference in 1604 James himself told Puritans who objected to the use of the cross in baptism that such an appeal to private consciences 'smelled very rankly of Anabaptism'. He charged them 'never to speak more to that point (how far you are bound to obey) when the church had ordained it'. Laud in 1625 argued that the teachings of Calvin nullified the 'practice of piety and obedience' and were destructive of 'external ministry' in the church and 'civil government in the commonwealth'.[6] William Perkins, no separatist, proclaimed that no man's law can bind the conscience, an argument which he used to defend usury.[7]

When men felt that the worship enjoined by the state church was contrary to the Gospel, they had no alternative but to contract out of the church and form their own illegal congregations, either underground in England or in emigration. If they remained in England they had to break the law in order to be free to worship as they believed God demanded. The ministers who linked these congregations were likely to be regarded as vagabonds. On the other hand there were those, like the future Earl of Clarendon, who disliked divine-right bishops as they disliked divine-right monarchy, but who accepted them as part of the law of the land, as forces for stability. The 'enthusiastic' religion of the sectaries, on the other hand, offered to the classes excluded from power before 1640, and to women, means of self-expression. The congregations gave them a novel opportunity. But those taking advantage of it were a minority.

5. The Indictment of Barrow, 21 March 1592-3, in *The Writings of John Greenwood and Henry Barrow, 1591-1593* (ed. L. H. Carlson, 1970), p. 261; Barrow's Fifth Examination, in *The Writings of Henry Barrow, 1587-1590* (ed. L. H. Carlson, 1962), pp. 198-201.
6. Peter White, 'The *via media* in the early Stuart Church', in *The Early Stuart Church, 1603-1642* (ed. K. Fincham, 1993), p. 218, and Nicholas Tyacke, 'Archbishop Laud', in ibid., p. 65, quoting Laud's *Works* (Oxford U.P., 1847-60), VI, pp. 245-6.
7. See my 'William Perkins and the Poor', in *Puritanism and Revolution* (1993), pp. 167-70.

Bible reading, a private occupation, led some towards individualistic theories. The merchant Barterville in Dekker's *If this be not a good play, the Devil is in it* (1612) held that

> Nature sent man into the world, alone,
> Without all company, but to care for one,
> And that I'll do. (IV.i)

Lurchall, a devil who happened to be present, commented approvingly 'True City doctrine, Sir'. He felt that his task as tempter was superfluous. 'I came to teach, but now (methinks) must learn'.[8] Henry Barrow in 1590 defined 'Christ's church' as 'a holy free people, separate from the world' – something very different from 'parish assemblies'.[9]

The protestant doctrine of the priesthood of all believers offered laymen freedom from the monopoly rule of the clergy. From John Greenwood to Oliver Cromwell radicals referred to 'your popish term of laymen'.[10] A lay believer listened to the voice of God in his conscience, and that set him free from laws ecclesiastical or civil in so far as they dealt with religious behaviour. With separatists we are dealing not with people claiming the protection of tradition and customs which have been invaded by the legislation of an alien state power and its laws, but with congregations which set the consciences of the godly above the laws of church and state. Discipline was to be decided by the congregation, and was no business of any outside body. It was Charles I and Oliver Cromwell who insisted on the political necessity of a state church.

Separatists went further than those who tacitly contracted out of the state church as individuals. They believed that liberty of conscience meant freedom from constraint on the beliefs and practices of the congregation – if necessary by separating from the state and its church. This newly confident position contrasted the liberty of separatists with the subservience of Anglicans to the law of the church – which in many matters consisted of relatively new laws. Greenwood spoke in 1589 of 'entangling us by your law'. 'You go about to bring us within the compass of the law'. But 'Christ is the only head of his church, and his laws may no man

8. Op. cit., in *Dramatic Works of Thomas Dekker*, III, p. 179.
9. In *The Writings of John Greenwood, 1587–1590* (ed. L. H. Carlson, IV, 1962), p. 150; cf. pp. 185, 259.
10. Greenwood, *A Collection of Certaine Sclaunderous Articles gyven out by the Bisshops* (1590), in *Writings of John Greenwood, 1587–1590* (1962), p. 165.

alter'. A church subjecting itself to laws other than Christ's is a harlot. Set prayers 'upon commandment brought into the public assemblies ... bringeth our liberty in bondage'; the liturgy takes away 'the whole liberty, freedom and true use of spiritual prayers'. How could men talk to Christ in words dictated by others? Tyndale had asked. Outward bondage to 'such laws and officers as the Pope left' was the negation of Christian liberty, was subjection to Antichrist. So they claimed freedom to separate from a church upheld only by 'their penal law'. They would be obedient in civil matters, but 'the prince cannot make lawful what God forbids': they will undergo the penalties imposed by the magistrate rather than forsake God. They rejected the Queen's supremacy, her authority to make laws ecclesiastical.[11]

Radicals affirmed these positions in the 1640s and 1650s. Joseph Bau-thumley wrote that 'if men were acted and guided by that inward law of righteousness within, there need be no laws of man, to compel or restrain men'.[12] Roman Catholic recusants had their own, different, brand of freedom from the law. They too contracted out. The Pope could free them from the oath of allegiance; Jesuit doctrines of equivocation also opened doors of freedom from the laws of the English state.

G. S. Wood defined the gentry's freedom as 'freedom from material want, freedom from the caprice of others, freedom from ignorance, and freedom from having to work with one's hands'.[13] All negative forms of freedom, it will be noticed. The dictionary definition of 'free' is 'exempt from', or 'not subject to', 'self-sufficient' − free chapel or church, free bench, free denizen, freeborn, freehold, free-lance, free-living, freemason, free state, freethinker, freethought, free will. Or it can mean 'exempt from payment', as in free board, free quarter, free trade. Or it may refer to personal characteristics − free-handed, free-hearted, freespoken. To be free of a corporation is to enjoy the privileges or exemptions of. All these senses are negative. To be free *to* do something is a secondary meaning by implication from being free *from*. In the common law sense a 'liberty' is an exclusive royal prerogative in the hands of a subject.[14] In three stanzas of Drayton's *The Barons Warres* (1603), which neatly illuminate the radical

---

11. Greenwood, op. cit., pp. 24, 28, 86–92, 98–101, 114, 123, 126, 141, 179–80.
12. Bauthumley, *The Light and Dark Sides of God* (1650), p. 76.
13. G. S. Wood, *The Radicalism of the American Revolution* (New York, 1993), p. 33; Christopher Haigh, 'The Continuity of Catholicism in the English Reformation', in *Past and Present*, 93 (1981), p. 69.
14. Cf. Attorney-General Noy, quoted on p. 234 below.

concept of the Norman Yoke, the Norman barons in Edward II's reign expect their 'free birth' to bring them privileges. But they have fallen from the 'greatness, liberty and all' of their fathers. 'Then to what end hath our great conquest served?'[15]

Contracting out of the state and its church was something that religious heretics had long practised. From Lollards through Familists to Ranters, a popular reaction to the tightening up of religious discipline was quietly to evade it. Hermeticists, Rosicrucians, Familists, Muggletonians, outwardly conformed whilst effectively disregarding the church's demands. When necessary they would make public recantation, and then continue as before. 'From time to time a member of the congregation might need to take temporary refuge in the woods; that kind of rural Alsatia composed of varied sorts of outlaws, from occasional religious refugees to vagabonds created by Tudor England's economic stresses, to common criminals'.[16] Before Laud, even under Laud, there were still many mansions in the Church of England. In remote Yorkshire the Familist Roger Brearley lived and died a clergyman of the state church: his congregation at Grindleton continued his heresies. John Everard, in and out of prison, still retained his living.

For William Erbery separatism was a necessary religious duty, but he was not satisfied with the results: Antichrist, he thought, appears most visibly in particular (i.e. separated) churches. 'I am a man in Babylon', he admitted, 'with all the gathered churches and scattered saints'. Like Milton, he appears to have ended a member of no church at all.[17] Isaac Penington too rejected churches set up by kings and Parliaments – 'built by force, settled by force, her ministers maintained by force'. 'Babylon hath prevailed'. Penington was more directly political in his pre-Quaker days, when he called for 'universal freedom' and said that the 'right liberty and safety of the people consists in the choice of their government' and 'in enjoying the power of altering their government'.[18]

'Opting out' was always a second-best. Those who chose it helped one

---

15. Drayton, *Poems* (1969), pp. 6–7, reprinting the edition of 1619.
16. Joseph Martin, 'The Elizabethan Familists: A Separatist Group as perceived by their contemporaries', *Baptist Quarterly*, XXIX, no. 6 (1982), pp. 271–8; Martin, 'The Protestant Underground: Congregations of Mary's Reign', in *Journal of Ecclesiastical History*, 35, no. 4 (1984), pp. 530, 533.
17. *The Testimony of William Erbery* (1658), p. 315.
18. Penington, *A Question* (1659), in *Works* (3rd ed., 1784), I, p. 337; *The Scattered Sheep Sought After* (1659), p. 2; *The Fundamental Right, Safety and Liberties of the People* (1651), Sig. B–B4v, pp. 1–9, 26.

another to evade the law, but did not combine to change it.[19] They did not wish to become members of a 'sect'. They assumed that they represented Christ's church, and expected everyone else ultimately to follow them. But the process of separation revealed divisions among those who chose it, which in time became too wide to be bridged. 'Sects' began to form themselves into separate organizations before the Church of England was restored in 1660, and Bunyan organized local groupings of like-minded congregations – from jail, where most of the pastors found themselves. We do not know what genius spotted the usefulness of this to post-restoration governments. When Charles II offered 'indulgence' to separatist congregations it was conditional on their having a minister licensed by the government, and the congregation accepting a sectarian label. This was not by the choice of the 'sects', and caused difficulties. Bunyan's congregation on different occasions described itself as 'Congregational' or 'Baptist'. But it was a great coup for the government. Divisions among the sects were perpetuated, yet all were grateful to the government for 'indulgence'; and it was the King, not Parliament, who granted the indulgence and gained the credit. Organization within the law was forced on those whom we may henceforth begin to call members of sects.

While accepting indulgence, the sects disliked having to give themselves a sectarian name. Quakers referred to themselves as 'the people called Quakers'. Fox's preferred name for them was 'the children of the light'; 'friends in the truth' or 'Publishers of truth' were alternatives. But from the early 1650s Fox had addressed epistles of advice and encouragement simply to 'Friends'. The title ultimately preferred, 'The Society of Friends', contained no theological overtones. It was simply a way for Quakers to identify themselves as a group within the church of Christ.[20]

There might be economic reasons for separating from the state church.[21] Parish control of poor relief meant, as poverty increased, that the rich decided how much the poor were to receive, and on what conditions; whereas most separatist congregations had their own systems of poor relief – perhaps with less money to distribute, but with the distribution organized relatively democratically. Henry Ainsworth in 1617 distin-

19. F. Bremer, *Congregational Communion: Clerical Friendship in the Anglo-American Puritan Community, 1610–1692* (Northeastern U.P., 1994), pp. 55, 58, 60–61, 68–9 and *passim*.
20. See Chapter 24, below; cf. W. C. Braithwaite, *The Beginnings of Quakerism* (1912), p. 307.
21. On this see my *Puritanism and Revolution*, p. 191; *Society and Puritanism*, p. 286.

guished between poor relief 'not by the appointment of the church . . . but by the appointment of the magistrate' on the one hand, and the practice of separatist congregations on the other – 'collection by their deacons'. In the revolutionary year 1647 the city magistrates of Norwich were persuaded to double the poor rates; but it was admitted that the poor were better off in congregational churches.[22]

Those who rejected the Church of England would no doubt in time have been glad to accept the position of tolerated minorities; but after Charles II's reign they were separately licensed groups, the independence of each of which depended on retaining royal favour. I used to regard the words 'nonconformist' and 'dissenter' as interchangeable till I made the mistake of calling a distinguished Welsh scholar a nonconformist. 'I am not a nonconformist', he exploded; 'I am a dissenter from the Church of England'. Charles II has not received sufficient credit for creating and perpetuating the dissenting sects which have meant so much in English history, but who since that king's reign were incapable of united political action. Congregations disciplined their own members, but were themselves controlled by law and the state.

There was a good deal of *de facto* opting out, without bothering about the principles involved. The people of New and Windsor Forests, we are told in 1617, 'go ten times to an ale-house before they go once to a church'.[23] In the Forest of Knaresborough the inhabitants were believed to be more attached to wise men and wizards than to Christianity. Some northern parishes were so large that regular attendance was impossible: churches in some areas were not large enough to accommodate all the inhabitants.[24]

Before 1640 and after 1660 nonconformists broke the law by leaving their own parish church in search of true preaching. John Dod and Robert Cleaver advised their readers to do this in their best-selling *A plain and familiar Exposition of the Ten Commandments*:

22. B. Hanbury, *Historical Memorials* (1839–44), I, p. 348; J. Stoughton, *History of Religion in England* (1881), I, p. 498. For the generosity to the poor of the separatist churches, see Mrs Katherine Chidley, *The Justification of the Independent Churches of Christ* (1641) pp. 43–4.
23. P. Clark, 'The Alehouse and the Alternative Society', in *Puritans and Revolutionaries* (ed. D. Penington and K. Thomas, Oxford U.P., 1978), p. 65. But in the 1650s 'alehouses were haunted more by cavalier agents and disenchanted republicans . . . than by committed radicals' (ibid., p. 67).
24. E. Fairfax, *Daemonologie* (ed. W. Grainge, 1971), p. 35, quoted by B. Reay, 'Popular Religion', in *Popular Culture in Seventeenth-Century England*, pp. 95–6.

But if in place thou have abode where ignorance dark doth reign,
I wish thee further seek forth truth, or there do not remain.[25]

The alternative was emigration.

There was a different kind of intensity behind the religious motivation to reject some laws; but it lacked the spur of hunger, seeing one's children starving, which made anti-enclosure rioters so dangerous in crisis years.

In the 1640s congregations came up from underground, or spontaneously organized themselves. Their independence and the nature of the doctrines which they preached and discussed caused considerable alarm to the propertied classes. Quakers appeared the most frightening. George Fox in the 1650s gathered meetings of sympathizers in the streets, though often opposed by Ranters and others. Quakers were not pacifists until 1661; only exceptional personalities could control meetings which frequently led to disorder. The Quaker movement was one of outsiders. Originating in the north of England, 'The Northern Quakers' from 1654 onwards descended on the midlands and south, with startling results. They formed communities of dedicated friends, and had a wide penumbra of sympathizers. They picked up some of the ideas of Levellers, Diggers and Ranters, who had been suppressed with difficulty in 1649–52. Some alleged that Winstanley had founded the Quakers.

In New England Quaker missionaries were regarded as 'bent . . . especially against magistrates and ministers and all order and ordinances'.[26] They were thought to be 'turners of the world upside down', said William Penn, 'as indeed in some sense they were'. Their refusal to acknowledge social superiors or magistrates by doffing the hat, their egalitarian modes of address ('thou' and 'thee') were disturbing. So were their denunciations of woe to 'you that are called lords, ladies, knights, gentlemen and gentlewomen'.[27] In 1659–60, as restoration of monarchy threatened, Quakers rallied to the republican government; there was much alarmist talk of 'arming the Quakers'. And indeed, many Quakers rejoined the army from which they had been expelled because of their reluctance to accept military discipline. Nobody knew how many Quakers and Quaker sympathizers there were, so it was easy to create a panic that may have been exaggerated. Barry Reay has plausibly suggested that fear of Quakers was

25. Op. cit. (19th ed., 1662), Sig. A 3v.
26. *Mercurius Politicus*, no. 341, 18–24 December 1656, in *Making the News*, pp. 414–17.
27. Preface to Fox's *Journal* (1901 reprint), I, p. xxxiv; cf. pp. 391–3, 411, 418, 425–6, 467–8, 473–5, 533; B. Reay, *The Quakers and the English Revolution* (1985), p. 39.

a main reason for the rapidity with which Charles II was restored to the English throne – much to his own surprise.[28]

After the restoration, the problems became somewhat different. Milton and others had discovered during the 1650s that it was impossible to find an electorate the majority of whom would welcome the establishment of a godly society. 'How can the kingdom be the saints', when the ungodly are electors and elected to govern?' asked 'many Christian People' in Norfolk immediately after the execution of Charles II.[29] It proved an unanswerable question. The social force was lacking to carry through a revolution against the law by changing the law-makers. The disunity which led to the defeat of religious opposition was utilized by Charles II to tame dissent. Abandoning the hope of controlling the state or a state church, most dissenters in the years after 1660 pursued a policy of passive opting out. We do not know whether Milton or Winstanley conformed to the state church or not. Milton thought that the apostasy (which had started soon after the time of the Apostles) was likely to continue till the Second Coming: so why bother?

But although the religious revolution was defeated, dissenting pressures could be made effective by non-violent means, at least so long as no fundamental shifts of social power were involved. The history of dissent is not to be written in terms of winning total religious freedom from the law. The struggles which individual dissenters conducted in the reign of Elizabeth are recorded in the *Elizabethan Nonconformist Texts* edited by L. H. Carlson. Liberty from the law was sought first by individuals in the Netherlands, and subsequently by large-scale emigration to New England, whence the émigrés hoped to bring it back to England.

Charles II gave dissenters not abolition of the law which they detested, but exemption from its enforcement against certain licensed groups. This slowed down the flow of emigration. But dissenters and later the Liberal Party retained a partially effective check on governments throughout the nineteenth and early twentieth centuries. My father was a life-long Liberal because he thought it was the teetotal party. But in 1931, with the pound in danger, he decided that politics had become too serious to be determined by teetotal scruples, and he voted Conservative. In the heyday of the British Communist Party in the 1930s and 1940s it was a familiar jibe

28. Reay, op. cit., chapter 5.
29. [Anon.], *Certain Queries . . . Presented by many Christian People* (19 February 1649), in Woodhouse, *Puritanism and Liberty*, p. 246.

that its many middle-class members and intellectuals were of nonconformist origins. The latter were prominent again in the break-up of the British
C.P. in 1956–7, when the party leadership had tried to prevent free
discussion and criticism of Soviet armed intervention in Hungary –
although they had condemned analogous British action over Suez a short
time before. The result was a significant opting out of members.

   In the difficult days after 1660 a great deal of sympathy for religious
dissidents was often shown. Neighbours covered up for them. Frustrated
radicals who made their way to North America and the West Indies were
protected by the local population against the forces of the English state.
The regicides William Goffe and Edward Whalley lived for nearly twenty
years in hiding in Massachusetts, despite a proferred reward for their
capture.

   Discipline for the lower orders in nascent capitalist society could be
enforced by wage labour and unemployment, or could be instilled by the
religious congregations, which contrasted godly discipline with the licentious liberty that came naturally to fallen man. Paul Seaver has shown how in
the 1640s members of separatist churches were linked by trade, by marriage,
by correspondence: the congregations set standards of economic behaviour
for their members and offered shelter and protection in time of need.[30]

   The discipline of the market was accompanied by the discipline of
parish registers and parochial assumption of control over whether the
poor should be permitted to marry or not. Well-to-do parishioners had
an interest in seeing that the poor did not gain a 'settlement' for their
presumably unemployable offspring. Church marriage was enforced as
against traditional customary forms of union – handfast marriages,
broomstick marriages, marriages by plighting troth, etc.; and against
informal divorce by desertion or more formally by wife-sale – often the
consequence of poverty. Opposition on principle to church marriage,
already shown by the Lollards, was taken over by some of the sects – and
by Milton.[31]

---

30. Seaver, *Wallington's World: A Puritan Artisan in Seventeenth-century London* (1975),
passim.
31. Lollard suspects in the diocese of Norwich in the early fifteenth century were
routinely asked whether they recognized the necessity of church marriage (ed. N. P.
Tanner, *Heresy Trials in the Diocese of Norwich, 1428–31*, Camden Soc., 4th series,
1977, pp. 86–95, 111–17, 193–205). Cf. p. 202, Chapter 16, below. See Thompson,
Customs in Common, p. 458. For an example see Robert Greene, 'The Black Book's
Messenger' (1572), in *Cony-Catchers and Bawdy Baskets* (ed. G. Salgado, Penguin,
1972), pp. 235–6. For desertion, see Martin Ingram, *Church Courts, Sex and Marriage
in England, 1570–1640* (Cambridge U.P., 1990), pp. 186–7.

Another group which found freedom from the law by opting out was the Diggers (see Chapter 23, below). Durant Hotham in 1652 contrasted Ranters with Quakers who refused to compromise, whereas Ranters 'would have done as we commanded, and yet have kept their own principle still.'[32] Muggletonians – about whom we know more than about earlier opters-out – evaded the law by mobility, bribery, use of friends, legal stratagems, occasional conformity and other compromises. Since they did not proselytize and had no system of poor relief for their members, they had little need for organization. Since they believed that God takes no notice of our prayers, collective worship was not important for them. Their predestinarian beliefs precluded any necessity for martyrdom: suffering was to be avoided whenever possible. They raised flight and evasion to a moral principle.[33]

Milton in his *De Doctrina Christiana* discussed the legitimacy of prevarication, flight and evasion under persecution, preferring it to useless martyrdom 'except when not running away was more conducive to the glory of God'.[34] But he considered it to be 'the duty of every believer to join himself, if possible, to a correctly instituted church'.[35] We do not know whether he himself attended any church after the restoration. We must I think assume that he conformed to the Church of England sufficiently to avoid penalties. Similarly Toland later did not think it necessary to run serious risks in order to maintain his position of abstention from the state church.[36]

As in so many spheres, sectarian disagreements led to secularizing innovations. In 1646 Thomas Edwards in *Gangraena* alleged that 'the sectaries', instead of urging 'legal rights and the laws and customs of this nation, . . . talk of and plead for natural rights and liberties such as men have from Adam by birth'.[37] From asserting the rights of descendants of the Anglo-Saxons against the Norman Yoke to the natural rights of all men.

The protestant principle of the priesthood of all believers had a great liberating effect once *all* individual consciences were free to decide for

32. Fox, *Journal*, I, p. 95.

33. Reay, 'The Muggletonians: An Introductory Survey', in *The World of the Muggletonians* (ed. C. Hill, B. Reay and W. Lamont, 1983), pp. 43–6.

34. Milton, *Of Christian Doctrine*, in *Complete Prose Works* (Yale U.P.), VI, pp. 605, 762–5, 801.

35. Ibid., VI, p. 568.

36. Toland, *Pantheisticon* (English translation, 1751), p. 107.

37. Edwards, *Gangraena*, III, Sig. c 2v. Something has gone wrong with the pagination here.

themselves, as within the limits they were for a short time after 1640. Congregations could contract out of the state church, as squatters contracted out of the agrarian economy. After 1660 itinerant preachers were dealt with as vagabonds under the settlement laws. Those individuals who were not committed to a particular religious community would perforce be treated as members of the Church of England – Milton (perhaps), Wither, Winstanley, Stubbe. Many dissenters advocated occasional conformity with the national church.[38] In 1940, when I was enrolling for the army, the corporal who was filling up our forms announced that the man in front of me 'says he's an atheist, Sarge'. 'Put him down C. of E.' was the inevitable reply. Agnostic or atheist were not recognized categories: the C. of E. was still the church of the uncommitted, including unbelievers.

---

38. See my 'Occasional Conformity and the Grindalian Tradition', in *Religion and Politics in 17th-century England*.

15. *Church Courts and Fees*

═══

The division between the clergy and the temporal law is full of great peril to the state, as much as the discontents of the common people against the gentry.

Journal of Sir Roger Wilbraham (1607), in *Camden Miscellany* (ed. H. S. Scott, 1902), p. 96.

The government of Archbishops, and Lord Bishops, Deans and Archdeacons &c., with their Courts . . . hath proved . . . to be a maine cause of many foul Evills, Pressures and Grievances . . . unto his Majesties Subjects, in their own consciences, liberties and estates; . . . as in a Schedule of particulars hereunto annexed may in part appear . . . The great increase of Whoredoms and Adultery occasioned by the Prelates' Corrupt administration of justice, . . . [turning] all into moneyes for the filling of their purses.

The . . . Petition of the City of London . . . for a reformation in Church-government, 11 December 1640.

[Churchwardens] are wilfully resolved to be foresworn rather than they will present any justice or gentleman or rich neighbour, be they never so faulty.

A Buckinghamshire parson reporting to Sir John Lambe, Dean of the Arches, in 1635 (W. H. Summers, 'Some Documents in the State Papers Relating to Beaconsfield', *Records of Bucks.*, VII, pp. 99–101.

[The Court of High Commission] was grown from an ecclesiast-ical court . . . to a court of revenue, and imposed great fines . . . Thereby the clergy made a whole nation . . . if not their enemy, yet very undevoted to them.

Edward, Earl of Clarendon, *The History of the Rebellion and Civil Wars in England* (Oxford U.P., 1888), I, p. 372. First published 1702.

It is an excellent legal system, only nobody can afford it.

Words attributed to a judge, in *The Guardian*, April 1994.

The law of the English state church took over much from the law of the
Roman church. Many of those whom we later call dissenters felt that it
was their religious duty to reject the forms of worship laid down for the
church by law established, and to worship in what they believed to be the
manner laid down in the New Testament. This brought them into conflict
with the law enforced by church courts.

There was a whole hierarchy of these, quite distinct from and often
in conflict with common-law courts. But from the point of view of
non-privileged laymen, church courts were part of the legal establishment, one which bore especially heavy on the lower classes. Milton
summed up the business of church courts as being 'to prog and pander for
fees'. 'For their courts, what a mass of money is drawn from the veins
into the ulcers of the kingdom this way: their extortions, their open
corruptions, the multitude of hungry and ravenous harpies that swarm
about their offices, declare sufficiently. . . . Their trade being, by the same
alchemy that the Pope uses, to extract heaps of gold and silver out of the
drossy bullion of the people's sins. . . . What stirs the Englishmen . . .
sooner to rebellion, than violent and heavy hands upon their goods and
purses?'.[1]

The proceedings of church courts were conducted in Latin, which few
English laymen could understand. Men and women against whom accusa-
tions had been made were put on oath and then compelled to testify, if
necessary against themselves. Penalties for perjury were severe. This was
very different from common-law procedure, in which the accused were
deemed to be innocent until proved guilty on the evidence of at least two
witnesses. The oath *ex officio* was exacted regardless of social rank, Gouge
protested. 'This useth to be exacted of inferiors, as Gen. XXIV. 3, but not
so of superiors'. Lilburne told Star Chamber in 1638 that no freeborn
Englishman ought to take an oath *ex officio*.[2] It was a stigma of social
inferiority, denial of the right to trial by common law which was believed
to be granted to free men by Magna Carta. In what were popularly (and
significantly) known as 'the bawdy courts' one could be accused on
'common fame', and one could exculpate oneself by oath of compurgators
– neighbours prepared to swear not to the fact of your innocence, but to

1. Milton, *Of Reformation Touching Church-Discipline in England* (May 1641), in *Complete Prose Works*, I, pp. 590–92.
2. Gouge, *Commentary upon Hebrews*, II, p. 52; Rushworth, *Historical Collections*, II,
p. 463.

general belief in it. This cost money – either in bribing the compurgators or at least paying their expenses to the place of trial, which might be far distant.

The canons of 1604 laid it down that church courts should have cognizance of matters relating not only to religous belief but also to 'adultery, whoredom, incest, drunkenness, swearing' and any other 'uncleanness and wickedness of life'. Church courts claimed jurisdiction over wills, an important source of fees but also vital to the inheritance of property. Causes relating to tithe payments were disputed between common-law and church courts, since here too questions of property arose; since the reformation many laymen were recipients of tithes formerly due to monasteries. Procedure by 'oath *ex officio*' in matters affecting property was fiercely resented, though J.P.s regularly used similar procedures in dealing with the peccadilloes of the lower classes.[3]

Excommunication was a powerful weapon of the ecclesiastical courts. It could be imposed for heresy, schism, simony, perjury, usury, incest, adultery, 'or other grave crime'. In 1584 the bishops added to the list piracy, conspiracy against the government, wilful murder, sacrilege, bearing or suborning false witness. 'Working or opening a shop upon a holiday made one liable to excommunication', the Root and Branch Petition of December 1640 complained.[4] Midwives who practised without the bishop's licence were also liable: so were common scolds. 'The power of this excommunication', wrote Thomas Helwys in 1612, 'is of another especial use of profit in that by the power thereof are brought in all duties, tithes and court fees'. Even the saintly Lancelot Andrewes admitted that 'Church censures nowadays do only touch the purse. Evil-doers when they have paid their fees return scot-free. If no money, then have at the offenders with the episcopal sword'.[5] 'The number of excommunicates was immense', Craig Horle says. In the early seventeenth century, about 50,000, or 5 per cent of the population of the

---

3. For what follows see my *Society and Puritanism*, Chapters 8–10.
4. Ed. A. Sparrow, *A Collection of Articles . . . of the Church of England* (1661), p. 256; Cardwell, *Documentary Annals of the Reformed Church of England* (Oxford U.P., 1839), I, p. 428. Gardiner, *Constitutional Documents of the Puritan Revolution* (3rd ed., 1906), p. 142.
5. Helwys, *The Mistery of Iniquity* (1935 reprint), p. 20; first published 1612. Andrewes, quoted by William Ames, *A Fresh Suit against Human Ceremonies in Gods Worship* (?Rotterdam, 1633), p. 421. Ames unkindly translated from the Latin in which Andrewes had preached a sermon before Congregation.

dioceses of York, Norwich and Chester were habitual excommunicates'.[6]

Excommunication was notoriously used to impose *economic* penalties on the excommunicate, who could not buy or sell, be employed, sue or give evidence in courts (and so could not recover debts, give bail, make a will or receive a legacy or serve as administrator or guardian). An excommunicate could recover these rights only after he had done penance and paid substantial fees. If he had not submitted within forty days the secular authorities could be called upon to imprison him until he had been absolved. But the secular power did not always cooperate promptly. In 1570, 200 persons in the diocese of St David's stood excommunicate for immorality, but the sheriff would not execute the writs against them. Excommunication was compared to outlawry both by bishops and by William Prynne.[7]

Under Laud excommunication was used to enforce unpopular ceremonnies — for example against backwardness in railing in communion tables. Church tenants might be excommunicated for non-payment of rents. A whole parish was sometimes excommunicated for failing to obey the order of a church court, and had to pay substantial fees (and travelling expenses for its officers) before it was absolved. Absolution might be withheld from those too poor to pay their fees, even after penance had been done, 'whereby many poor people have been kept excommunicate to their deaths, without any other fault than want of money.' But for those with money 'fornication and adultery . . . for 4s.' posed no problem.[8] By such means the clergy could always secure 'money and such a sum of money as the poor man cannot reach unto'.[9] In Buckinghamshire in the 1630s there is no recorded instance of money offered for commutation of penance being refused; only the poor had to appear publicly in a white sheet. 'The richer may commute', wrote Richard Bernard in 1641, 'but the miserable poor . . . cannot be freed from their courts without

6. C. W. Horle, *The Quakers and the English Legal System, 1660–1688* (Pennsylvania U.P., 1988), p. 231. Barry Reay appears to agree (ibid., p. 250).

7. Penry Williams, *The Council in the Marches of Wales* (University of Wales Press, 1948), pp. 101–2; the bishops' answer to articles in Parliament, 1585, in Cardwell, op. cit., I, pp. 425–6; Prynne, *A Breviate of the Prelates intollerable usurpations* (1637), p. 142.

8. [Anon.], *A Petition presented to the Parliament . . . from the County of Nottingham* (1641), p. 7; [Anon.], *A Lordly Prelate* (1641), p. 3.

9. *Zurich Letters, 1558–79* (Parker Soc., 1842), p. 164; A. Gilbey, *A Pleasaunte Dialogue betweene a Souldier of Barwicke and an English Chaplaine* (1589), in E. Arber, *Introductory Sketch to the Martin Marprelate Controversy* (1895), pp. 30–33.

money though they beg for it, but must . . . be . . . given over to the devil for non-payment of money'.[10]

There were many ways in which the rich could make ecclesiastical punishments ineffective. Compurgation may or may not have been effective in a community of relative equals, where everybody knew everybody else's business; less so in a society riven by distinctions, and no doubt hatreds, between rich and poor. Putting the accused on oath severely strained the consciences of business men who made their money by outwitting competitors whilst nearly keeping on the right side of the law. They much preferred the common-law assumption of innocence until guilt was proven. The public humiliation of penance in a white sheet was more detrimental to a rich man than to a pauper; hence penance could be commuted for money, a practice to which other objections could be (and were) raised. That hostility to church courts was not confined to Puritans is illustrated by a play put on at the Red Bull in 1639 which 'scandalized and libelled the whole profession of proctors belonging to the Court of Probate'.[11]

Periodical visitations of parishes cost money. Richard Hooker, defender of the hierarchy, admitted that disciplinary matters are treated as a mere formality at visitations, 'fees and pensions being the only thing which is sought. . . . We are not to marvel if the baseness of the end doth make the action itself loathsome.' In 1621 a judge of the Prerogative Court was fined £20,000 for corruption: 'he would not only take bribes of both parties . . . but many times shamefully begged them'.[12] Alexander Leighton thought that men spent not less than £50,000 a year on matrimonial suits in church courts, £100,000 on probate of wills, and another £100,000 was 'drawn out of the people's purses for visitation fees, pleas and jangling matters'.[13] Officials and hangers-on of church courts were estimated at above 10,000 in 1641, their maintenance at £200,000 per annum.[14]

The clergy themselves were not immune. Entering into holy orders

10. E. R. C. Brinkworth, 'The Laudian Church in Buckinghamshire', in *University of Buckingham Historical Journal*, V, p. 53; Bernard, *A Short View of the Praelaticall Church of England*, p. 14.

11. C. I. A. Ritchie, *The Ecclesiastical Courts of York* (Arbroath, 1956), p. 60.

12. Hooker, *Works* (1836), III, pp. 386–7; *Diary of Walter Yonge* (ed. G. Roberts, Camden Soc., 1847), p. 37.

13. Leighton, *Sions Plea against the Prelacie* (?Holland, 1628), pp. 121, 263–4.

14. Sir R. Verney, *Notes of Proceedings in the Long Parliament* (Camden Soc., 1845), p. 75; Richard Bernard, *A Short View of the Praelaticall Church of England* (1641), pp. 8–9.

was expensive, since 'not only the bishop and his registrar, but also his usher, his chamberlain, his butler and porter, and almost all his menial servants, must have their fees before the poor clerk ... can pass the bishop's lodge'.[15] Alexander Leighton may have exaggerated when he suggested in 1628 that in one way or another the church courts extracted an average of £100,000 a year from ministers alone – over £10 a man.[16] But once ordained, licences and dispensations for pluralism, licences for non-residence, for eating meat on fast days and in Lent, could always be bought for cash. (I do not necessarily underwrite any of these figures, but they illustrate the order of magnitude that some contemporaries were prepared to accept.)

'Benefit of clergy' was another crying abuse. In the Middle Ages ability to read had ensured that clerics would be tried in church courts, by churchmen who would understand, not by secular courts. 'Clergy' could be claimed by anyone who could read, and after the reformation, as literacy spread, it became a class privilege. In 1613–14, 61 persons sentenced to death by Middlesex Quarter Sessions read the 'neck-verse' and so escaped with a branded palm. A Balliol freshman who killed a fellow-undergraduate in 1624 got off without even that. Ben Jonson pleaded clergy successfully after killing a man.[17] Benefit of clergy naturally did not apply to women.

Already in 1641 Archbishop Williams had called excommunication 'the rusty sword of the church'.[18] When it was used to extort money for minor or procedural offences, when the rich could buy themselves off, it was easy to rouse indignation and to call in question all ecclesiastical jurisdiction. In a changing world men appealed to the individual conscience against the church's traditional coercive powers. Perkins, for instance, held that all courts of men are inferior to conscience, the tribunal which God has erected in every man's heart.[19] This was a far-reaching principle, setting up the individual conscience against *any* court of law. It was in effect an appeal to the changing standards of the lay society in which these consciences had been formed – a newly commercialized society.

Under Land the common-law judges were told not to interfere in the

15. J. Nalson, *An Impartial Collection* (1683), I, p. 759.
16. Leighton, op. cit., p. 121.
17. My *Society and Puritanism*, p. 299.
18. *Cabala* (1654), I, p. 103.
19. Perkins, *Works*, I, p. 530.

ecclesiastical courts without the Archbishop's permission. 'Every lackey' of the Court of High Commission, in the words of Sir Anthony Weldon, 'might give a checkmate to any gentleman, yea to any country nobleman that was not in court favour'.[20] As Arise Evans put it, 'the bishops . . . thought to do all with the club'.[21] But this was changed by the Revolution. After 1660, with no High Commission to enforce their authority, church courts lost most of their functions except disciplining the lower orders. It was difficult to do much about the vices of the rich and influential. And even in dealing with drunkenness and bastards J.P.s took over from church courts. As separatist congregations established themselves legally, excommunication lacked any coercive power: an excommunicate from one congregation simply went elsewhere.

The disrepute into which the clerical courts, by general agreement, had fallen helped to create an atmosphere in which the law in general could be regarded with disrespect. Over a century ago John Stoughton suggested that historians have underestimated the significance of the ending of the effectiveness of the tribunals before which men and women could be cited for unchastity and other vices not cognizable at common law: it was 'a considerable judicial and social advance',[22] and a great liberation. Henceforth sin was distinguished from crime, and sin was left to the consciences of individuals. By the end of the century the Society for Promoting Christian Knowledge and societies for the reformation of manners thought it necessary to take up the campaign against sin. But in their case it was almost exclusively the lower class whose pleasant vices were prosecuted.[23]

One universal grievance against the law was its enforcement of the compulsory payment of tithes, mostly going to the maintenance of the minister of the parish, but quite often to a lay impropriator, the descendant of a man who was rich enough to buy monastic lands at the dissolution of the monasteries in Henry VIII's reign. Critics like Levellers who attacked tithes were denounced for 'their declared enmity to the ministers of the gospel' as well as to magistracy.[24] Milton's cry to Oliver Cromwell

20. Weldon, *The Court and Character of King James* (1651), p. 207.
21. Evans, *An Eccho to the Voice from Heaven* (1653), pp. 100–101.
22. Stoughton, *A History of Religion in England* (1881), I, pp. 473–5.
23. D. W. R. Bahlmann, *The Moral Revolution of 1688* (Yale U.P., 1957), p. 74.
24. John Owen, *Human Power Defeated*, a sermon preached before Parliament on 7 June 1649 to celebrate the defeat of Leveller-influenced mutinous regiments at Burford in May 1649.

Help us to save free conscience from the paw
Of hireling wolves whose gospel is their maw

must relate to enforced tithe payments. Milton thought that religious
freedom was impossible without the abolition of tithes. What worried
him most in 1659, when the restoration of monarchy was looming, was
his fear that the king would 'bring back again bishops, archbishops and
the whole gang of prelaty . . . – to keep their tithes?'[25]

25. Milton, sonnet to the Lord General Cromwell (1652); *The Likeliest Means to
remove Hirelings out of the church*, August 1659 (*Complete Prose Works*, VII, p. 283).
The passages from Milton which I have quoted in this chapter make me even more
surprised that Professor W. B. Hunter thinks Milton cannot have written his treatise,
De Doctrina Christiana, because it is insufficiently Anglican! (See articles in *Studies in
English Literature, 1500–1900*, Vol. 34, No. 1, winter 1994.)

16. Marriage and Parish Registers

We finde not in the Scriptures the gyving and joyning in matrimonie to be an action of the church.

John Greenwood, *A Collection of Certaine Sclaunderous Articles Given out by the Bisshops* (1590), in *Elizabethan Nonconformist Texts*, IV (ed. L. H. Carlson, 1962), p. 171.

The right joining in marriage is the work of the Lord only, and not the priest's or magistrate's, for it is God's ordinance and not man's. . . . Friends . . . marry none; it's the Lord's work, and we are but witnesses.

George Fox, *A Collection of Many Select and Christian Epistles*, II (1698), pp. 62–3, 281.

Too many historians carry their twentieth-century assumptions back with them into the past, and take for granted, without even asking the question, that church marriage was the universally-accepted norm in sixteenth- and seventeenth-century England. But was it? In legal theory of course it was. But legislation was enforced in those centuries, or not enforced, in accordance with the opinion of those who mattered in the localities. There is ample evidence, if we care to notice it, of varying marriage and divorce customs being accepted in different areas of the kingdom.

What was taking place in these centuries was an enforcement of church marriage as solely legitimate, overriding local customs familiar in 'bastardy-prone' areas, to use Mr Laslett's unfortunate phrase. For a long time the two practices might exist side by side. Formal church marriage might come after they 'were all night together, till the morn tide; / And they to church went'.[1] Gypsies married by pledging troth, without any other ceremony – like Adam and Eve in *Paradise Lost*. Despite hostile accounts of gypsy promiscuity, gypsy marriages were fairly constant –

1. 'The Turnament of Tottenham', in Percy, *Reliques*, I, p. 301. First printed 1631. Cf. p. 140 above.

while they lasted.[2] Clare had a happy phrase for informal marriage as opposed to the church ceremony: 'Not felon-like law-bound, but wedded in desires'.[3] The law isolated church marriage and regarded it only as legally binding (when properly performed and paid for), ignoring the many variant marriage customs which had been accepted by the communities.

In a traditional village, whether or not they liked the customs, people knew what they were. The advent of capitalism led some to wish to reject custom and regard rights (especially to property) as dependent on the law. For others the law seemed alien, abstract and tyrannical, imposing rules on a community which had regarded itself as self-governing: custom was known to all, not declared by state judges sitting far off, ignorant of local needs and habits. Custom is in a sense 'democratic'; there was no democracy about the state's law, no understanding. Its introduction marks a transition from what was accepted as 'freedom' to what was seen to be unfreedom. By the later eighteenth century the courts automatically rejected many local customs which imposed restraints on the rights of private property.

Opposition on principle to church marriage, as so much else in English protestantism, goes back to the Lollards. In the early fifteenth century Lollard suspects in the Diocese of Norwich were routinely asked whether they recognized the necessity of church marriage.[4] Contemporaries had little doubt that the main interest of the clergy was in the fees payable to them for marriage. From the point of view of the propertied class registered church marriages served several useful purposes. They established the legitimacy of marriages, births and deaths, and so guaranteed property transactions and the establishment of families. They declared who had and who had not a 'settlement' in any given parish, and so prevented false claims to poor relief. They ensured proper payment of fees to the incumbent, thus reducing the burden of his maintenance on parish funds.

The discipline of parish registers and parochial assumption of control over the marriage of the poor complemented the discipline of the market. Parish registers may have helped in identifying dissenters in the parish, those who did not want their marriages, births or deaths to be recorded. The importance which governments attached to the enforcement of

---

2. H. M. G. Grellman, *Dissertation on the Gypsies*, pp. 45–6.
3. Clare, *Poems*, I, p. 151; cf. p. 322 below.
4. N. P. Tanner, *Heresy Trials in the Diocese of Norwich, 1428–1431* (Camden Soc., 4th series, 20, 1977), pp. 86–95, 111–77, 193–208.

church marriage is shown by its prominence alike among the activities of the Council in the Marches of Wales under Elizabeth and of Devonshire petty constables in the reign of Charles I.[5] The introduction of parish registers was an essential part of this campaign to make a formal church ceremony the only legal form of marriage.

There was naturally considerable resistance, in literature as well as in life. Little John married Alan-a-Dale to his true love in the church where the bishop had intended to marry her to a wealthy knight.[6] This illustrates both the outlaws' devotion to social justice and their mockery of church marriage. Robin Hood himself could not marry Maid Marian because he was an outlaw. Lollard opposition to church marriage was inherited by some of the sects. (See epigraphs to this chapter.)

During the revolutionary decades there was much discussion of sexual liberty and of marriage, notably by Ranters. Lawrence Clarkson himself performed the ceremony which united him and his wife.[7] In *A Jovial Crew* it is the women who feel liberated. The two sisters took the initiative in persuading their men to join the beggars, and they stayed the pace better. A third girl joined them who had eloped with a clerk in order to escape from a marriage being forced upon her by Justice Clack, her guardian. The beggars in *A Jovial Crew* have no need for church marriage: their wedding celebrations are conducted by 'parson under-Hedge'. Ladies who deserted their husbands for the gypsies (see pp. 138–9 above), like Anne Bonny and Mary Read who turned pirate, all expected some sort of liberation. Mary Read thought that plighting troth was 'as good a marriage, in conscience, as if it had been done by a minister in church'. Anne Bonny changed husbands on the basis of a formally witnessed document. Pirates were notorious for their tolerance of all sorts of sexual freedom.[8] Marcus Rediker instances the two women pirates in speaking of 'an antinomian disdain for state authority' evident in the 'proletarian practice of self-marriage and self-divorce', as against 'the property-preserving practice of the middle and upper class.' Pirates also exercised the

5. Penry Williams, *The Council in the Marches of Wales under Elizabeth* (University of Wales Press, 1958), pp. 101–2, 135; S. K. Roberts, *Recovery and Restoration in an English County: Devon Local Administration, 1646–1670* (Exeter U.P., 1985), p. 186.
6. *Oxford Book of Ballads*, pp. 611–20.
7. A. L. Morton, *The World of the Ranters*, pp. 122–4.
8. My *People and Ideas in 17th-century England*, pp. 165, 178, 181. Cf. 'The Seaman's Song of Captain Ward' (*floruit* 1603–15); Charles Johnson, op. cit., pp. 277–8; Ritchie, *Captain Kidd*, pp. 123–4 258, 270.

'marital liberty' of wife-sale.[9] The Ranter John Robins changed his wife 'for an example'.[10] As Lord Brooke had sagely observed, 'communion of wives . . . takes away property'.[11] Pordage's reported remark that marriage was a very wicked thing may have referred to church marriage (with its attendant fees and expensive celebrations) as opposed to traditional customary forms of union.[12]

We must distinguish between theological principle and libertinism, though this is sometimes difficult. During the revolutionary decades royalist propaganda regularly linked sexual libertinism with political radicalism.[13] But after the restoration royalists were the libertines. It was Dryden who drew attention to the Biblical example of 'God-like David':

> In pious times, e'er priestcraft did begin,
> Before polygamy was made a sin,
> When man on many multiplied his kind,
> E'er one to one was cursedly confined,
> When nature prompted and no law denied
> Promiscuous use of concubine and bride,
> Then Israel's monarch, after heaven's own heart
> His vigorous warmth did variously impart
> To wives and slaves, and, wide as his command,
> Scattered his Maker's image through the land.[14]

One consequence of the tightening of marriage laws appears to have been a campaign against infanticide to which there are many references in contemporary literature. R. W. Malcolmson quotes Oliver Heywood, Bunyan, Defoe and Addison. The full rigour of the death penalty for infanticide was seldom enforced: midwives and juries were often sympathetic to girls who had little chance of marriage, or of being able to bring

9. Rediker, 'Liberty beneath the Jolly Roger: The Lives of Anne Bonny and Mary Read, Pirates', in *Iron Men, Wooden Women: Gender and Anglo-Saxon Seafaring* (ed. Margaret Creighton and Lisa Norling, Johns Hopkins U.P., 1993); A. L. Morton, *The World of the Ranters*, pp. 122–4. Cf. pp. 120–1 above.

10. My *Religion and Politics*, p. 171.

11. Brooke, *A Discourse . . . of Episcopacie* (1642), in Haller, *Tracts on Liberty*, II, p. 91.

12. John Pordage, *Innocencie appearing, Through the dark Mists of Pretended Guilt* (1655), p. 19.

13. Cf. S. N. Zwicker, *Lines of Authority: Politics and English Literary Culture, 1649–1689* (Cornell U.P., 1993), Chapter 5.

14. Dryden, 'Absalom and Achitophel', ll. 1–10. Milton might have approved of the lines as history, if not of their tone. Cf. Aphra Behn, quoted on pp. 158–9 above.

up a child alone.[15] It was a particular problem for domestic servants, often at the mercy of an employer or his son, or of other servants. Female servants were closely watched by their employers lest they become pregnant or left their employment to get married. This constant surveillance in what was often loneliness and isolation might well be counterproductive: sex would seem the only chance of freedom from a servile condition. The fact that the number of bastards appears to have peaked in the early seventeenth century may be explained by falling living standards, falling earnings, which made marriage impossible for many of the poor; or it may be a consequence of the campaign against non-church marriages being waged at the time.[16]

As Gerrard Winstanley pointed out, sexual liberty was for men only: the woman was often left alone to carry the baby.[17] But we should not underestimate the overall liberating effect for women of participation in the discussions and discipline of separatist congregations, and even of preaching themselves. Quaker women missionaries toured the countryside, sometimes unchaperoned; or even risked their lives trying to convert New England Puritans. For a time new vistas of freedom were opened up for women as well as for men. The monopoly of church marriage took a long time to establish: Hardwicke's Marriage Act of 1753 was resented, among many other reasons, because it made illegal practices which were still tacitly accepted in some areas: it posed law and property against customary liberties.

15. R. W. Malcolmson, 'Infanticide in the 18th Century', in *Crime in England, 1550–1800* (ed. J. S. Cockburn, 1977), pp. 187–209. Cf. pp. 337–9.
16. Paul Slack, *Poverty and Policy in Tudor and Stuart England* (1988), p. 102. I have benefited by discussing this matter with Bridget Hill.
17. See my *The World Turned Upside Down*, p. 319, and references there cited.

17. The Mosaic Law and the Priesthood of All Believers

=====

> Christ has redeemed us from the entire Mosaic law ... Christ himself broke the letter of the law ... Paul did the same.
>
> Milton, *Of Christian Doctrine, Complete Prose Works*, VI, pp. 529, 532; cf. pp. 525–6, 531.

> People are afraid to speak out of things that are Christ's for fear of giving liberty to people of sin ... So shall Christ be suppressed, for fear of giving liberty.
>
> The Rev. Tobias Crisp, *Christ More Exalted*, Vol. III (1648).

Tyndale's 'heresies' included a belief that the Mosaic law had been abolished by the gospel. 'The children of faith are under no law ... but are free'. 'To steal, rob and murder ... are holy when God commandeth them'.[1] Many protestants repeated similar views in the century after Tyndale wrote. Milton for instance approached the doctrine through his desire for a divorce. In *Tetrachordon* (1645) he insisted that 'the great and almost the only commandment of the gospel is to command nothing against the good of man, and much more no civil command against his civil good'. 'No ordinance, human or from heaven', he wrote in the *De Doctrina Christiana*, 'can bind against the good of man'. Those who, on the basis of the Mosaic law, 'burden us with imaginary and scarecrow sins ... enslave the dignity of man',[2] of which Milton was always very protective – though less so perhaps of the dignity of woman.

Milton argued that English protestant reformers had erred in not abolishing obstacles to a man divorcing what he regarded as an unsatisfactory

---

1. Tyndale, *The Obedience of a Christian Man* (1528), in *Doctrinal Treatises* (Parker Soc., Cambridge U.P., 1848), p. 297, and *Prologue to the Book of Genesis*, ibid., p. 407.
2. Milton, *The Doctrine and Discipline of Divorce* (1643), in *Complete Prose Works*, II, p. 228; *Tetrachordon* (1645), ibid., pp. 588, 638–9, 661–2; *Colasterion* (1645), ibid., p. 750.

wife. Milton blamed the Roman church for curtailing this freedom, thanks to the 'canonical tyranny of stupid and malicious monks, who . . . invented new fetters to throw on matrimony'. 'Popery and superstition . . . attempted to remove and alter divine and most prudent laws for human and most imprudent canons'.[3] Milton's attitude to divorce and polygamy may be a salutary reminder for us that when men in the seventeenth century spoke of 'freedom' they did not necessarily think of reforms which we today should regard as unequivocally desirable. A parallel example is medieval prohibitions on usury, which Milton linked with prohibitions on divorce. Both, divorce and usury, he thought, were permitted by 'the word of God' and 'the rule of charity'.[4] Calvin among other protestant reformers was anxious to render the prohibition of usury less absolute in practice than it was in the theory of Catholic canon law.[5] W. L. Letwin in *The Origins of Scientific Economics* (1963) sees 1640 as the dividing line in acceptance of usury in England. Henry Vaughan was one who remained hostile to 'damned usury', of which he had no doubt himself been a victim.[6]

As early as 1629 Milton in the 'Nativity Ode' associated the penalties of sin not with the Garden of Eden but with Mount Sinai 'altogether on a smoke' because an angry God 'descended upon it in fire . . . and the whole mount quaked greatly' (Exodus 19:18).[7] The Mosaic law expresses God's wrath, not Jesus's love for humanity. Thirty years later Milton announced his intention of writing against the validity of the Law of Moses – a promise which he fulfilled in the *De Doctrina Christiana*. Arguing that 'in matters of religion . . . church governors . . . neither can nor should use constraint', he proclaimed that 'the whole Mosaic law is abolished by the gospel'. 'Its purpose is attained in that love of God and of our

3. Milton, *The Judgment of Martin Bucer* (1644), ibid., II, pp. 430–40; cf. my *Milton and the English Revolution* (1977), Chapter 9.

4. Milton, *The Doctrine and Discipline of Divorce* (1643), II, p. 322.

5. See R. H. Tawney, *Religion and the Rise of Capitalism* (Penguin ed., 1940), *passim*, esp. pp. 150–57 and 284, and his Foreword to the 1930 translation of Weber's *The Protestant Ethic and the Spirit of Capitalism* (1930), reprinted in *History and Society: Essays by R. H. Tawney* (ed. J. M. Winter, 1978), pp. 189–97. Here Tawney gives a useful critique of Weber's pioneering work. See also my *Change and Continuity*, pp. 106–7.

6. Vaughan, *Works* (ed. L. C. Martin, Oxford U.P., 1914), pp. 14, 43–6, 525 (two volumes, continuous pagination).

7. Boyd M. Berry, *Process of Speech: Puritan Religious Writing and Paradise Lost* (Johns Hopkins U.P., 1976), p. 120.

neighbour which is born of faith through the Spirit'. 'The law of slavery having been abrogated by the gospel, the result is Christian liberty, God's law written in the hearts of believers'. Consequently 'we are released from the decalogue' – which Milton did not consider 'a faultless moral code': 'it contains nothing relevant to gospel worship'.[8] 'The works of the faithful . . . never run contrary to the love of God and of our neighbour, which is the sum of the law. They may, however, sometimes deviate from the letter even of the gospel precepts . . . in pursuance of the over-riding motive, which is charity'. 'The practice of the saints interprets the commandments'.[9] Milton concluded that 'anyone with any sense interprets the precepts of Christ in the Sermon on the Mount not in a literal way but in a way that is in keeping with the spirit of charity'. 'Christ our liberator frees us from the slavery of sin and thus from the rule of the law and of men, as if we were emancipated slaves'. (Galatians IV:7: 'No more a servant but a son'.) In *Paradise Lost* Michael admits to Adam that 'law appears imperfect' and looks forward to 'a better Covenant',

> From imposition of strict laws to free
> Acceptance of large grace, from servile fear
> To filial, works of law to works of faith.
> (*Paradise Lost*, XII. 285–314)

'Thus we are freed from the judgments of men, and especially from coercion and legislation in religious matters'. This could justify resistance to human authority, ecclesiastical or civil. Milton quoted I Corinthians 9: 19: 'I am free from all men', and adds 'and therefore of course from the magistrate, at any rate in matters of this kind'.[10]

The relish with which Milton proclaimed our freedom from the Mosaic law, from the divorce tracts to the *De Doctrina Christiana*, suggests that he felt himself in some way personally affronted. His frequent recurrence to this theme is one of the many reasons for attributing the *De Doctrina* to him.[11]

Calvin had opened a wide door when he wrote that since believers

---

8. *Of Christian Doctrines*, pp. 525–6, 531–8, 711.
9. Ibid., pp. 368, 646. I shall not waste space in refuting the eccentric suggestion made by Professor William B. Hunter that Milton is not the author of the *De Doctrina Christiana*. See Barbara Lewalski, 'Lewalski's refutation', in *Studies in English Literature, 1500–1900*, 32 (1992) and several articles in ibid., 34 (1994).
10. Milton, *Complete Prose Works*, VI, pp. 531–8; *Paradise Lost*, XII. 305–6. See also *A Treatise of Civil Power* (1659), in *Complete Prose Works*, VII.
11. See note 9 above.

'have derived authority from Christ not to entangle themselves by the observance of things in which he wished them to be free, we conclude that their consciences are exempted from all human authority'.[12] But what are the things in which he wished them to be free? Much depended on how they were defined.

What had Gerrard Winstanley in mind when he appealed to 'the law of liberty' in the *Epistle of James*? James praises especially works rather than faith, deeds rather than words, mercy rather than justice, the humble rather than the proud. He is unfriendly to the rich, and to those who respect persons.[13] In 1776 Granville Sharp made this *Epistle* basic to his arguments against slavery.[14]

The Bible's silences could be as significant as what it actually said. John Hall of Richmond declared that 'unto my strictest enquiry, there could not be found one text of the Bible containing and maintaining any other form' of government than monarchy, and none defending the power of the people or a representative assembly.[15] But James Harrington collected innumerable texts which he thought favoured a commonwealth.[16] Romans 13:1 was the favourite text of the royalists: 'The powers that be are ordained of God'. With Charles I and Parliament at loggerheads, this was no help. Calvinist doctrine justified revolt led by the magistrates, who were also 'powers that be'. For Samuel Rutherford kings were a consequence of the Fall of Man: God discouraged the Israelites from having a king until conditions had been imposed on him.[17] Hunton and others argued on Parliament's behalf that God bound no people to monarchy until they had bound themselves.[18] The irreverent Selden had the last word: 'When a man has no mind to do something he ought to do by his contract, then he gets a text and interprets it as he pleases, and so thinks to get loose'.[19] Ultimately the Bible proved indecisive.

Many difficult choices were forced on conscientious Bible-readers in

---

12. Calvin, *Institutes of the Christian Religion* (trans. H. Beveridge, 1949), II, p. 140; cf. p. 683.

13. *The General Epistle of James*, I. 25, II. 12. See pp. 276–7 below.

14. Granville Sharp, *The Law of Liberty* (1776), p. 30, and *passim*.

15. Hall, *Of Government and Obedience* (1654), Sig. b, pp. 434–5.

16. Harrington, *Political Works* (ed. J. G. A. Pocock, Cambridge U.P., 1977), pp. 174–8, 209–10, 279, 370–82, 411, 459–64, 485, 496–7, 572–7, 601, 614–53.

17. Rutherford, *Lex, Rex*, pp. 106, 142, 161ⲅ3, 173, 192–3, 232, 406.

18. Philip Hunton, *A Treatise of Monarchie* (1643), pp. 2, 5, 23; cf. Charles Herle, *A Fuller Answer to a Treatise Written by Doctor Ferne* (1642), pp. 2–4, 8, 13–15, 17.

19. John Selden, *Table-Talk* (1847), p. 196. First published 1689, posthumously.

post-Reformation England. John Greenwood in 1590 argued that set forms of prayer 'upon commandment brought into the public assemblies . . . bringeth our liberty into bondage'. 'Now to be in outward bondage to another outward government, other laws, officers and ordinances than Christ's, is to be by outward subjection servants of Antichrist'.[20] The canons of 1604 forbade fasts not authorized by public authority – i.e. ordered merely on the authority of the congregation. But Arthur Hildersham thought that Christians could lawfully participate in fasts arranged secretly in defiance of the magistrate, since 'these times may . . . be justly called times of persecution' when 'their Christian duty of public fasting . . . is not only not allowed but opposed and persecuted'. It was a *duty* to break the law.[21]

Milton shared with Quakers the conviction that 'God's law is written in the hearts of believers'. This lent itself to subjective interpretations by protestants. Melanchthon, for instance, thought that rulers had a duty to enact only the laws of God – one of which was to punish heresy and promote true religion, another never to infringe the property rights of subjects.[22] Bishop Bale thought that many ceremonies had been retained in England not because they were enjoined in God's Word but because they had long continued.[23] Bullinger had been careful to ward off the danger of antinomianism lurking in the doctrine of the priesthood of all believers. He rebuked those who abuse Christian liberty by claiming to be 'set free from all bodily debts and duties. . . . to their masters, creditors, magistrates and princes'; and those who 'when they are not as yet justified by Christ, do notwithstanding promise liberty to all men; and think that . . . they may do whatsoever it pleaseth them'. 'That licentious lust is not worthy to be called by the name of liberty'.[24] These forebodings were

20. Greenwood, 'An Answere to George Gifford's pretended defence of read praiers and devised litourgies', 1590, in *The Writings of John Greenwood, 1587–1590*, pp. 56, 86; cf. pp. 88, 91–2. This work was reprinted, significantly, in 1640 as *More Work for Priests*.

21. British Library, Addit. Mss. 4275, fol. 289, quoted by Stephen Foster, *The Long Argument: English Puritanism and the Shaping of New England Culture, 1570–1700* (North Carolina U.P., 1991), p. 98.

22. Quoted by Quentin Skinner, *The foundations of modern political thought* (Cambridge U.P., II, 1978), pp. 68–9.

23. John Bale, *The Image of Both Churches* (1550), in *Select Works* (ed. H. Christmas, Parker Soc., 1849), p. 427.

24. Henry Bullinger, *The Decades* (3rd ed., 1587; ed. T. Harding, Parker Soc., 1849–52), III, pp. 314–15.

to be justified during the 1640s and 1650s in England, when William Erbery rejected any state church. 'Godly ministers' in the Anglican church, he declared, were 'never more greedy of gain' than when he wrote.[25] 'Clergymen and common lawyers are the chiefest oppressors', he told Oliver Cromwell in 1652; the poor 'are the chief among the oppressed'. He proposed steeper taxation for 'rich citizens, racking landlords . . . and mighty moneyed men' to create 'a treasury for the poor'.[26] James Nayler agreed that 'carnal professors' are those 'most afraid of freedom, lest any of you should believe in the Son who leads to it'.[27]

Bunyan admitted that it was impossible for natural man to observe the Mosaic law.[28] It could lead 'carnal men' only to despair. We cannot appease God by trusting to our own righteousness, however hard we try. 'Christ's church is an hospital of sick, wounded and afflicted people'. 'He that seeth his own pollution . . . seeth he cannot answer the demands of the Law'. He can only be saved by Christ's imputed righteousness. 'Men are justified from the curse of the Law before God while sinners in themselves', not for their own righteousness but 'his Faith is counted for Righteousness'. 'The Christian man hath nothing to do with the Law . . . as it burdeneth the conscience to wrath and the displeasure of God for sin'. 'He must have regard to it, and count it holy, just and good . . .' But the believer 'may not, cannot, dare not make [the Law] my Saviour and Judge, nor suffer it to set up its government in my conscience; for by so doing I fall from grace'. The believer must 'remember that he who giveth it [the Law] is merciful, gracious, long-suffering and abundant in goodness and truth, etc.'[29]

'If thou wouldest be faithful to do that work that God hath allotted thee to do in this world for his name; labour to live much in the savour and sense of thy freedom and liberty by Jesus Christ . . . Thou art a redeemed one, taken out of this world, . . . out of the power of the Devil, . . . and placed in a Kingdom of grace and forgiveness of sins for Christ's

25. Erbery, *Testimony*, pp. 91, 197.
26. Ibid., pp. 42, 53, 90–91, 306–7; J. Nickolls, *Original Letters and Papers of State Addressed to Oliver Cromwell* (1743), pp. 88–9.
27. Nayler, *A Salutation to the Seed of God* (1656), p. 8. Nayler denied that the Bible was the Word of God: *A Publike Discovery of the Open Blindness of Babels Builders* (1656), pp. 9–10.
28. Bunyan, *Justification by an Imputed Righteousness* (1692), *Miscellaneous Works*, XII, *passim*. 'Now keep this law no mortal creature can', *Poems*, ibid., IV, p. 112.
29. *Justification by an Imputed Righteousness*, pp. 316, 286, 293, 313; *Of the Law and a Christian* (1692), *Miscellaneous Works*, XII, pp. 411–13.

sake'.[30] 'Our liberty is to hope'. 'Hope is the grace that relieveth the soul when dark and weary',[31] when tempted to despair. By the knowledge of Christ's love Christians 'may walk at liberty, and their steps shall not be straitened', though 'the best of men' are still 'sinners in themselves'.[32]

A clear trend in radical protestant thinking can be traced from Tyndale to Milton and Bunyan. This trend elevates the conscience of believers above the law, whether of church or state. There are really only two commandments, Tyndale said in the Preface to his translation of the New Testament (1534): 'love God and love thy neighbour'. And these two can be reduced to one commandment, since 'if we love our neighbours in God and Christ', then 'we have God himself dwelling in us, and all that God desireth'. 'Let love interpret the law', Tyndale wrote in the Prologue to his translation of the Old Testament. 'The very commandments of God bind not where love and need require'.[33]

Milton was to say similar things over a century later, about secular as well as religious law. He noted in his Commonplace Book that 'Lambard saith that laws were first devised to bound and limit the powers of governors', to avoid arbitrariness.[34] 'Faith, not law, is our rule', Milton wrote in the *De Doctrina Christiana*. 'It follows from this that, as faith cannot be compelled, the works of faith cannot be either'.[35]

Milton was free to express his unorthodox views in the unpublishable *De Doctrina Christiana* as he was not in published works liable to censorship. As Maurice Kelley and many others have demonstrated, the *De Doctrina* helps us to understand cryptic passages in Milton's other works. In *Paradise Lost* he managed to say that 'law appears imperfect', 'works of law' are to be replaced 'in full time' by 'works of faith' (*Paradise Lost*, XII. 300–306). Milton made Michael explain to Adam that thanks to Christ's sacrifice on the cross, their sins would never hurt 'them more who rightly trust . . . in this his satisfaction' (*Paradise Lost*, XII. 415–20).[36]

Rejecting the Mosaic law meant rejecting parts of the Bible – a momentous decision. Those godly protestants who had agonized over the rel-

---

30. *Paul's Departure and Crown* (1692), ibid., XII, p. 374.
31. *Israel's Hope Encouraged* (1692), ibid., XIII, p. 32.
32. *The Saints' Knowledge of Christ's Love* (1692), ibid., XIII, pp. 403–4, 413–14; *Justification by an Imputed Righteousness*, ibid., XII, p. 313.
33. Ed. David Daniell, *Tyndale's New Testament* (Yale U.P., 1989), pp. 4–8; *Tyndale's Old Testament* (Yale U.P., 1992), p. 10.
34. Milton, *Complete Prose Works*, I, p. 423; cf. II, pp. 38–9.
35. Ibid., VI, pp. 531–2, 536.
36. Cf. pp. 223–4 below.

evance of the law of Moses would find it relatively easy to conclude that the laws of the secular state were not sacrosanct. In this context it is worth citing Thomas Jenner's *The Path of Life* (1656), in which he looked forward to the withering away of the law. 'Sin hath set up a court in the conscience of man; in this court the debt or crime impleaded is sin, the pleader and informer is Satan, the rule of proceeding is the Law of Justice, the evidence given or witness is conscience, the Judge the Lord, the penalty is death and destruction . . . In what a pickle is man!' But Christ removes sin and guilt by 'the ranson of his blood, . . . delivers the soul from both the guilt and dominion of sin. The chief thing being gone, the rest fall off themselves'. The soul, freed from sin, 'fears no bailiff, no ill conscience, no Devil. . . . Christ redeemed us from sin and therefore from all bondage thereto and thereby'.[37]

37. Ed. Sidney Gottlieb, *The Emblem Books of Thomas Jenner* (Delmar, New York, 1983), pp. 39–40. Jenner was a printer and publisher. His authorship of this tract is not absolutely certain.

18. Antinomianism

The antinomian doctrine is the very same in almost every point
which I find naturally fastened in the breasts of the common
profane multitude. . . . The very work of preachers . . . is princi-
pally the cure of natural antinomianism.

*Richard Baxter's Confutation of a Dissertation for the Justification of
Infidels* (1654), p. 288.

Righteousness is that which puts a man away from Christ.

Tobias Crisp, *Christ Alone Exalted* (ed. J. Gill, 1932), p. 104.

Thou art no captive, but a child and free.
Thou wast not made for laws, but laws for thee.

Bunyan, *Poems*, p. 294.

The dictionary definition of antinomian is 'one who holds that the moral
law is not binding on Christians'. Tobias Crisp (1609–43) preached full-
fledged antinomianism before 1640. His main concern was to relieve
believers of 'horror in their consciences'. Many worried themselves sick
about their chances of salvation. Crisp was against hell-fire preaching
except to reassure believers that they are secure from hell. 'Even the most
blameless walking according to God's law, not only before but after
conversion, is truly counted but loss and dung'. 'Prayers, tears, fasting,
mournings, reluctancy and fighting against our own corruptions' move
not God a jot. God is moved only from himself. The elect upon the death
of Christ ceased to be sinners; their sins are the sins of Christ. Saving faith
is nothing but our persuasion that our sins are pardoned.[1] But God sees no
sin in believers, though he sees the fact. They ought not to charge
themselves with any sin, even when they commit the grossest wickedness.
'Suppose a believer commits adultery and murder', he can nevertheless be
'certain of forgiveness'. Crisp told his congregation that 'Sin is finished', a

---

1. Crisp, *Christ Alone Exalted* (1643), pp. 6, 34, 182: *Christ Alone Exalted*, Vol. III
(1648), pp. 129–30.

phrase eagerly taken up by Coppe and other Ranters. Clarkson attended
Crisp's sermons and read all his books. 'To be called a libertine is the most
glorious title under heaven', Crisp had said – another phrase put to good
use by Coppe. More directly to our purposes, Crisp said in so many
words 'if you be freemen of Christ, you may esteem all the curses of the
law as no more concerning you than the laws of England concern Spain'.[2]
All the elect are actually united to Christ, even before they are born.[3]
Every believer is as righteous as Christ: Christ being made sin, became as
completely sinful as we.[4]

Believers must 'stand fast in the liberty wherein Christ hath made you
free; . . . do not again entangle yourselves with such yokes of bondage
that neither you nor your fathers were able to bear'.[5] It is hardly surprising
that 'so many were converted by his preaching, and so few . . . by ours'.
The words are attributed to William Twisse, Prolocutor of the
Westminster Assembly of Divines.[6] Crisp, 'so magnified of many' was
accused (with others) of 'prostituting the free grace of God to all those
gross and graceless sinners that will not humble themselves'.[7] If it was
indeed true that Crisp said 'Nothing we do, though it be never so good, is
acceptable to God', why should one bother to be good?[8]

Roger Brearley of Grindleton thought that it was 'a sin to believe the
Word . . . without a motion of the Spirit', an idea which was repeated
almost *verbatim* by the Ranter Jacob Bauthumley in *The Light and Dark
Sides of God* (1650). John Everard appealed to the Christ in believers as a
check on 'the dead letter' of the Bible.[9] We may compare Milton's 'precise
compliance with the commandments . . . when my faith prompts me to
do otherwise . . . will be counted a sin'.[10]

2. Crisp, *Christ Alone Exalted*, and others of his writings quoted in my *The English
Bible and the 17th-century Revolution*, pp. 180–82; Clarkson, *A Single Eye* (1650); *The
Lost Sheep Found* (1660). For murder and adultery see Edwards, *Gangraena*, II, p. 8.
3. Daniel Williams, *Gospel-Truth Stated: Wherein some of Dr. Crisp's Opinions are
considered and the Opposite Truths Are Plainly Stated and Confirmed* (2nd ed., 1692),
pp. 2, 31, 61, 46, 146. Williams is a hostile witness, but he documents from Crisp's
own writings beliefs which he attributes to him.
4. Crisp, 1643, p. 89.
5. Ibid., p. 150.
6. Ed. J. Gill, *Crisp's Christ Alone Exalted* (1832), pp. vi–vii.
7. Stephen Geree, *The Doctrine of the Antinomians . . . Confuted* (1644), Sig. B 2v.
8. [Anon.], *Crispianism Unmask'd: or A Discovery of the Several Erroneous and Pernicious
Doctrines Maintain'd in Dr. Crisp's Sermons* (1693), p. 50, and *passim*.
9. Brearley, Bauthumley and Everard are quoted in my *The English Bible*, pp. 181–3.
10. Milton, *Of Christian Doctrine*, p. 639; cf. pp. 368, 521, 537–40, 711.

In New England Mrs Hutchinson created a furore by her antinomianism. Our main source for her beliefs is again hostile – Governor Winthrop. He was interested in what he saw as the social consequences of Mrs Hutchinson's views. 'It pleases nature well to have heaven and their lusts too'. She was alleged to think that 'there had been no magistracy since the Apostles times, nor could there'. That was hardly welcome to the plantation's chief magistrate.[11] Mrs Hutchinson was reported as saying that 'God loves a man never the better for any holiness in him, nor less if never so unholy'. 'Sin in a child of God must never trouble him'. 'Though I fall into murder or adultery, to question my assurance proves that I never had true assurance', but was in the covenant of works. 'We are not bound to keep up regular family prayers unless the spirit stirs us up thereunto'.[12] Samuel Gorton, a New England radical who became notorious in England in the late 1640s, held that 'every believer . . . is Christ', and that sin had been invented by the privileged classes to keep the lower orders down.[13] We can believe the suggestion that Harvard was founded to combat antinomianism after the Hutchinson affair.[14]

Richard Sibbes in 1639 was one of many who agreed with Baxter's remark quoted as an epigraph to this chapter. For Sibbes antinomianism was 'an error crept in amongst some of the meaner, ignorant sort of people'.[15] This frequently expressed view suggests that 'natural man' – as opposed to the godly – acted naturally: he preferred freedom to law. Radical Puritan theology converges with politics in opposition to law: antinomianism posed political as well as religious questions.[16] George Cranmer, in 'an excellent letter' to Richard Hooker in 1598, said that

11. Lyle Koehler, 'The Case of the American Jezabels' in *Anne Hutchinson: Troubler of the Puritan Zion* (ed. F. Bremer, Huntington, N.Y., 1981), p. 122.
12. Ed. D. D. Hall, *The Antinomian Controversy, 1636–1638* (Wesleyan U.P., 1968), pp. 212–14, 224, 232. 'God's love to David was not less because of his adultery and murder', said the accused in a case before the High Commission in 1632 (ed. S. R. Gardiner, *Cases in . . . Star Chamber and High Commission*, Camden Soc., 1886), pp. 270–71.
13. P. F. Gura, *A Glimpse of Sion's Glory: Puritan Radicalism in New England, 1620–1660* (Wesleyan U.P., 1984), pp. 85–6, 89, 294, 298–9.
14. L. Ziff, *Puritanism in America: New Culture in a New World* (Oxford U.P., 1973), p. 68.
15. Sibbes, *The Returning Backslider*, in *Works* (Edinburgh, 1862–4), II, p. 316.
16. Jonathan Dollimore aptly quotes contemporaries aware of this fact – Montesquieu, Bacon, Anatomy Burton and Hobbes (*Radical Tragedy: Religion, Ideology and Power in the Drama of Shakespeare and his Contemporaries*, Brighton, 1984, pp. 13–14).

Puritans were greatly to blame for criticizing 'outward and accidental matters in church government', especially because they took their complaints to 'the common people, judges incompetent and insufficient, both to determine anything amiss [and] for want of skill and authority to amend it'.[17] But the godly saw clear distinctions between themselves and others of the common people. 'We who are believers', wrote John Saddington, 'are both free-born and free by redemption'. Saddington, the 'eldest son' of the Muggletonians, was one of their earliest adherents. His *Articles of the True Faith* circulated in manuscript among the faithful in the eighteenth century.[18]

With the collapse of church courts and the censorship, antinomian doctrines could be freely discussed in the 1640s. In April 1643 Nehemiah Wallington got into an argument with a man whose views 'opened a very wide gap of liberty to sin'. 'He was too hard for me in reasoning and did puzzle me'. Wallington had to resort to his minister for reassurance.[19]

In 1649 the Leveller William Walwyn accepted the label 'antinomian': his 'heart was at much more ease and freedom than others', who were entangled with those yokes of bondage, unto which sermons mixt of Law and Gospel do subject distressed consciences'. No one, he said, 'should so much as doubt of your salvation'. John Saltmarsh, one of the most notorious antinomians, thought that a believer was 'as free from hell, the law and bondage ... as if he were in heaven'. Ranters believed that 'the moral law' was no longer binding on true believers.[20]

For antinomians not only the law of Moses but all human laws were inapplicable to the elect. Perfection is attainable on earth, believers can be in heaven in this life, all men can be saved, God is in all men, all men are Sons of God.[21] Hence antinomianism's attraction for the unprivileged, for 'natural man'. However austerely theological antinomians might claim to be, inevitably their ideas were taken up by men who wanted an excuse for disregarding laws which they found inconvenient.

---

17. In Hooker, *Of the Laws of Ecclesiastical Polity* (Everyman ed.), II, p. 553.
18. Saddington, *The Articles of the True Faith, depending upon the Commission of the Spirit* (1830), quoted by Thompson, *Witness against the Beast* (1993), pp. 73–4.
19. Paul S. Seaver, *Wallington's World: A Puritan Artisan in Seventeenth-Century London* (1985), p. 247.
20. *Walwyns Just Defence*, in *The Leveller Tracts, 1647–1653* (ed. W. Haller and G. Davies, Columbia U.P., 1944), p. 361; Walwyn, *The Power of Love* (1643), pp. 21, 27–8; Saltmarsh, *Free Grace* (10th ed., 1700), p. 111; A. L. Morton, *The World of the Ranters* (1970), p. 17 and *passim*.
21. Edwards attributed such views to Erbery (*Gangraena*, I, p. 78).

The group known as Ranters were widely condemned as sexual libertines. In September 1649 John Crouch in *The Man in the Moon* depicted Commonwealth London as Bedlam, where the social order is inverted and 'freedom' becomes a code name for brothel.[22] A newsbook of August 1654 invented a song pretended to have been sung 'in a parlour near Milk St.', which assumed that sexual promiscuity was all that Ranter ladies were interested in:

> Dear Sisters, you may freely do't.

'Is it not that liberty ye long looked for, to lie with whom you list, live merrily, eat, drink and sing, and enjoy the pleasures of the world?'[23] Ranters, like early Quakers, were accused of having 'no Christ but within, no Scripture to be a rule, no ordinances, no law but their lusts, . . . no sin but what men fancied to be so, no condemnation for sin but in the consciences of ignorant ones'.[24]

Seventeenth-century antinomians did in fact draw from the doctrines of the priesthood of all believers conclusions very different from those of Luther and Calvin. They argued that if the elect were known from all eternity, then their sins were forgiven in advance. Were they indeed sins? Lawrence Clarkson tells us that he concluded that 'there is no such act as drunkenness, adultery and theft in God . . . Sin hath its conception only in the imagination . . . What act soever is done by thee in light and love, is light and lovely, though it be that act called adultery . . . No matter what Scripture, saints or churches say, if that within thee do not condemn thee, thou shalt not be condemned.' 'None can be free from sin till in purity it be acted as no sin, for I judged that pure to me which to the dark understanding was impure; for to the pure all things, yea all acts were pure'. 'No man could attain to perfection but this way'.[25]

Coppe assured his public that he could 'kiss and hug ladies, and love my neighbour's wife as myself, without sin'. For 'sin and transgression is finished . . . Be no longer so horridly, hellishly, impudently, arrogantly wicked, as to judge what is sin, what not'. God's service is 'perfect freedom and pure libertinism'. God is 'in . . . everyone' said

---

22. Quoted by Raymond, *Making the News*, pp. 149–50.
23. *Mercurius Fumigosus*, ibid., pp. 158–9.
24. Thomas Collier, *A Looking-Glasse for the Quakers* (1657), p. 7.
25. Clarkson, *A Single Eye*, pp. 8–12, 16; *The Lost Sheep Found*, p. 25.

Richard Coppin, for whose *Divine Teachings* (1649) Coppe wrote a Preface.[26]

In the liberty of the 1640s Ranters like Coppe and Clarkson translated into noisy practice what for Crisp had been abstract ideas. Geneva, Scotland and English Puritans all struggled to curb the antinomianism which Luther had unwittingly unleashed, and to enforce godliness. But in the free-for-all of the 1640s this proved impossible. We recall the servant who told her master, 'I would have the liberty of my conscience, *not* to be catechized in the principles of religion,' and the 'female antinomian' who explained a theft with the words, 'It was not I but sin that dwelleth in me'.[27]

If conscience could liberate one from the moral law of the Old Testament it could also liberate one from the law of the land. John Reeve, founder of the Muggletonians, declared that 'whosoever hath the divine light of faith in him, that man hath no need of man's law to be his rule, but he is a law unto himself, and lives above all laws of mortal men, and yet obedient to all laws'.[28] Muggletonians carried over into the eighteenth and nineteenth centuries the ideas of mid-seventeenth-century antinomians. E. P. Thompson quoted many Muggletonians who said that believers are 'freed from the law'; he suggested that Blake was perhaps born of Muggletonian parents: he certainly was Muggletonian-influenced. It was A. L. Morton who saw Blake as 'the greatest English antinomian, but also the last.'[29] Morton demonstrated the many similarities between Blake's ideas and those of seventeenth-century antinomians. Thompson established that there were innumerable reprints of seventeenth-century antinomian books and pamphlets in the later eighteenth century.

Seventeenth-century antinomians clearly meant something different from what Luther and Calvin had meant by the freedom of the gospel. But their large and worrying claims were based on orthodox protestant doctrine. It is worth citing some of the early reformers' words, to show

26. Coppe, *A Fiery Flying Roll* and *A Second Fiery Flying Roll* (1649), in *A Collection of Ranter Writings from the 17th-century* (ed. N. Smith, 1983), pp. 86, 97, 107; Coppin, op. cit., p. 8. Cf. Blake, 'Thou art a man, God is no more' (*The Everlasting Gospel*, in *Poetry and Prose of William Blake*). Nonesuch ed., p. 138.
27. Edwards, *Gangraena*, I, p. 86, my italics; John Trapp, *Commentary on the New Testament* (1958), p. 501. First published 1647.
28. Reeve, *A Divine Looking-Glasse* (3rd ed., 1719), pp. 56-7. First published 1656.
29. Thompson, *Witness against the Beast*, pp. 92-3, 103-4, 160-61, 205; Morton, *History and the Imagination*, p. 124.

how easily their emphasis could be transformed. Thus Luther wrote of religious observances:

'Whatsoever thou shalt observe upon liberty, and of love, is godly; but if thou observe anything of necessity, it is ungodly'. 'If an adultery could be committed in the faith, it would no longer be a sin'. We may compare Tyndale: 'The children of faith are under no law (as thou seest in the epistles to the Romans, to the Galatians, in the first to Timothy), but are free'. Or Calvin: 'all external things [are] subject to our liberty, provided the nature of that liberty approves itself to our minds as before God. The consciences of believers may rise above the law, and may forget the whole righteousness of the law'. 'They are exempt from all power of men'.[30] Bullinger in 1543 found it necessary to guard against the dangers of antinomianism lurking behind the doctrine of the priesthood of all believers. He rebuked those who say that Christian liberty sets them free from all debts and duties – to master, creditors, magistrates and princes; those who (not being themselves saints) promise 'liberty to all men . . . to do whatsoever pleaseth them', abuse 'things indifferent' in their licentious lust.[31]

Luther's *'ama et fac quod vis'* was indeed all very well when preached in university lecture halls to aspirant academics with reasonable job prospects. It conveyed rather a different message to peasants with starving families. Luther's attack on the revolting peasants revealed a gulf between the haves and the have-nots which theology could not bridge. 'Love and do what you will' could be interpreted as a doctrine of complete liberation from all restraints – freedom from law and convention as well as from priestly control. It was heady doctrine, philosophical anarchism, which could call in question all earthly authority, all earthly law. In the 'wrong' hands it could be profoundly and intolerably subversive of law and order.

Contemporaries saw links between the antinomianism of the lower classes and their aptness to 'go native' in the plantations. Thomas Shepard associated the defeat of the Pequot Indians with the prosecution and

30. Luther, *Thirty-Four Sermons* (trans. W. Grau, 1747), p. 281; Tyndale, *The Obedience of a Christian Man* (*Doctrinal Treatises*, Parker Soc., 1848), p. 297; *Expositions and Notes on Sundry Portions of the Holy Scripture* (Parker Soc., 1849), p. 232 (the last item was first published in 1525); Calvin, *Institutes of the Christian Religion*, II, pp. 135, 227, 683. Cf. pp. 182, 208–9 above.
31. H. Bullinger, *Decades* (Parker Soc., 1849–52), III, pp. 314–15, 'Of Christian Liberty'.

exile of Mrs Hutchinson and other subversive 'antinomians'. 'Indians
and Familists . . . arose and fell together'. Some of the latter had refused
to serve in the army sent against the Pequots.[32] Cowley noted the paradox
in the support for Parliament shown by antinomians during the English
civil war:

> Such a Warre who would be listed in,
> But onely those who count no action Sinne?

Cowley listed libertines, Adamites, Pelagians and Arians together with
antinomians among the most enthusiastic supporters of Parliament. This
of course is royalist propaganda, not in itself reliable evidence; but some
Parliamentarians would have advocated greater religious freedom than
any royalists. Perhaps the most surprising antinomian sentiment comes
from Andrew Marvell in his 'Poem upon the Death of O.C.':

> But to the good . . .
> All law is useless.[33]

The Presbyterian state church set up by Parliament failed to establish
effective machinery for enforcing discipline. So did the Cromwellian
state church. Independent congregations tried to impose discipline on
their members, but what sanction had they? Excommunication, which
even in pre-revolutionary days Archbishop Williams had called 'the rusty
sword of the church', was now useless, since a choice of congregations
existed.

The impossibility of determining who the saints were contributed
greatly to the restoration of 1660, and to nonconformist quietism after
that date. The congregations could discipline themselves, within limits;
they gave solidarity and useful business contacts. But after the restoration
the godly no longer aspired to run the state. Christ's kingdom was
demonstrably not of this world. Closet antinomians survived into the
eighteenth-century: Blake consciously inherited from Milton, perhaps
from Ranters and Muggletonians, a tradition which set men and
women free from the law of the state as well as the church.[34] The ballad
which attributed Christian motives to Dick Turpin may link up with

32. Ed. M. McGiffert, *God's Plot: . . . the Autobiography and Journal of Thomas Shepard*
(Massachusetts U.P., 1972), pp. 66–8.
33. Abraham Cowley, *The Civil War* (ed. A. Pritchard, Toronto U.P., 1973),
pp. 110–11; Marvell, *Poems and Letters*, p. 128.
34. Morton, *History and the Imagination* (1990), pp. 124, 134–8. Cf. now Thompson,
Witness against the Beast, passim.

this tradition: so may the sympathy for pirates and highwaymen which we have noted. Marcus Rediker described the pirate Captain Bellamy's defence of plundering the rich who robbed the poor as 'the secularized eighteenth-century voice of the radical antinomians who had taken the law into his or her own hands during the English Revolution.'[35]

Continuities are difficult to establish. Naturally, aggressive lower-class antinomianism could not get into print after 1660. But the records of the Fenstanton Baptist congregation in the 1650s reveal a radical rejection of 'the Christ who died at Jerusalem' by a lady who 'trampled the Scriptures under her feet'.[36] John Wesley pays frequent tribute to antinomianism's survival in the mid-eighteenth century. Jonathan Edwards followed Milton in making the directly political point that when the millennium comes 'the absolute and despotic power of the kings of the earth shall be taken away, and liberty shall reign throughout the earth'.[37] The ethos of robbing the rich to give to the poor has a long popular history, going back at least to the Robin Hood ballads. But in the eighteenth century the state was more ruthlessly enforcing the rights of property against the unpropertied: we cannot visualize Sir Robert Walpole or the Duke of Newcastle fraternizing with Dick Turpin as the ballads make the King fraternize with Robin Hood and his men, or as Shakespeare's Prince Hal had enjoyed Falstaff's company.

Far more Englishmen in the eighteenth century became acquainted at first hand with waste wildernesses across the Atlantic, through piracy, service in army, navy or mercantile marine, through emigration or transportation. Simultaneously they experienced the violence associated with imperial conquest, and got to know victims of imperialism and slavery who came to London in large numbers. The latter ultimately contributed significantly to the revival of political radicalism at the end of the century. But by then Paine had succeeded the Bible as the radicals' handbook.

Between the Revolution and Blake's time the law had robbed many thousands of Englishmen of rights recognized as customary by

---

35. Rediker, 'Liberty beneath the Jolly Roger'.
36. *Records of the Churches of Christ gathered at Fenstanton, Warboys and Hexham* (ed. E. B. Underhill, Hanserd Knollys Soc., 1854), p. 90; cf. Burns, *Christian Mortalism*, p. 159.
37. Quoted by Ruth Block, *Visionary Republic: Millennial Themes in American Thought, 1756–1800* (Cambridge U.P., 1985), p. 19.

Deuteronomy XXIV. 19–21. The whip, the branding iron, transportation
and the gallows enforced new absolute rights of big property against
those from whom had been taken even that which they thought
they had. Bunyan, we recall, was always whole-heartedly and theo-
logically on the side of the poor and under-privileged. Defoe put it
strongly:

> The very lands we all along enjoyed
> They ravaged from the people they destroyed . . .
> 'Tis all invasion, usurpation all. . . .
> 'Tis all by fraud and force that we possess
> And length of time can make no crime the less. . . .
> Religion's always on the strongest side.[38]

The dangerous words of the Bible remained familiar to men and women
even when they had lost faith in the God of the church. 'Christ died
as an unbeliever', declared Blake. All Blake knew was in the Bible, he
himself said. But 'to defend the Bible in this year 1798 would cost a man
his life', he wrote. 'The Beast and the Whore rule without control'. Like
Ranters, Blake rejected Scriptural literalism: he understood the Bible in
the spiritual sense: 'as to the natural sense, that Voltaire was commissioned
by God to expose'. The title of Blake's 'The Everlasting Gospel' invokes a
seventeenth-century revolutionary theme. Blake contrasts radical
Christianity with formal orthodoxy:

> Both read the Bible day and night,
> But thou read'st black where I read white.[39]

When Blake wrote 'Jerusalem is called Liberty among the children of
Albion', he was echoing the Ranter Joseph Salmon.[40]

One of the most exciting things about Thompson's *Witness against the
Beast* is his demonstration not only of Blake's debt to seventeenth-century
antinomians but also to Milton and Bunyan, not always so clearly identified with the heresy. At the height of *Paradise Lost* Milton makes Michael
explain to Adam that by Christ's sacrifice

---

38. Defoe, *Jure Divino* (1706), pp. 206–17.
39. Blake, 'The Everlasting Gospel', in *Poetry and Prose* (ed. G. Keynes, Nonesuch
ed., 1927), p. 133. 'The Everlasting Gospel' is a key phrase in the radical vocabulary:
see Morton, *History and the Imagination*, pp. 106–46.
40. Morton, op. cit., pp. 120, 141; Salmon, *A Rout, A Rout: Or Some Part of the
Armies Quarters Beaten Up* (1649).

> To the cross he nails thy enemies,
> The law that is against thee, and the sins
> Of all mankind with him there crucified. (XII. 415–19).[41]

Bringing together Milton, Bunyan and Blake perhaps helps us to understand all three better.

For Blake 'The Gospel is Love, and then no law'. Law was driven out by love. 'The Gospel is forgiveness of sins and has no moral precepts'.[42] Blake's gospel stressed 'thou shalt', in particular 'thou shalt love' and 'thou shalt forgive' as against old Nobodaddy's invariable 'thou shalt not'. Wesley records meeting an antinomian in 1746 who said he had nothing to do with the law of God: 'I am not under the law; I live by faith'. When asked the obvious succeeding question, 'Have you a right to all the women in the world?' he replied, tactfully, 'Yes – if they consent.' 'To him that thinks it is a sin' this would be a sin; 'but not to those whose hearts are free'.[43]

Although my main concern has been with lower-class opposition to the law, we should not forget the very subversive line of thought which we find discussed verbally in Ralegh's circle in the 1590s, among Ranters in the 1650s, and which is inherited by Aphra Behn: the suggestion that religion, 'of itself a fable', had been deliberately invented by the upper classes to keep 'the baser sort' in fear and so protect private property. John Owen in 1655 was sure that unless the majority of men were 'overpowered by the terror of the Lord' and 'threats of wrath to come', 'the outrageousness and immeasurableness of iniquity . . . would utterly ruin all human society'. John Reeve observed that 'many thousands in these three nations . . . count the Scriptures mere inventions of wise men, to keep the simple in awe under their rulers'.[44] The Quaker Samuel Fisher confessed that there was much popular hostility to the doctrine of original sin, although – he added – the gentry accepted it.[45] The more radical Henry Denne alleged that opponents of the antinomian doctrine of free grace were motivated by socio-political considerations. They think 'it

41. See p. 212 above.
42. See E. P. Thompson, *Witness against the Beast: William Blake and the Moral Law* (Cambridge U.P., 1993), Chapters 2 and 12; Jack Lindsay, *William Blake* (1978), pp. 277–80.
43. John Wesley, *Journal* (1864–8), II, pp. 10–11.
44. Owen, *Works* (1850–63), XII, p. 587; Reeve, *A Divine Looking-Glass* (3rd ed., 1719), p. 94. First published 1656.
45. Fisher, *Baby-Baptism meer Babism* (1653), pp. 27–9, 34–8, 44, 105–6.

were better to hide this from the people, and to terrify them with hell-fire, with the wrath and judgment in order to keep them in bondage'.[46]

Fear of hell represented different ideological interests from the terrors of the Mosaic law, but it might lead to similar conclusions. Much of Ranter libertinism was taken over by restoration rakes. Etheredge, for instance, in *She wou'd if she cou'd* (1668) mocked both Ranter libertines and parsons. When the 'country knight' Sir Oliver Cockwood hints that the clergy's interest in church marriage is owed mainly to the fees to be derived from the ceremony, Mr Courtall, 'an honest gentleman of the town', replies 'Let 'em [the clergy] but allow Christian liberty, and they shall get ten times more by christenings than they are likely to by marriage.'[47]

For Blake abrogation of the Moral Law did not leave a vacuum. Law was driven out by love. This again is a seventeenth-century idea. Thomas Tany in 1653 declared that 'The Gospel is Love, and then no Law'. Blake wrote 'The Gospel is forgiveness of sins and has no moral precepts. These belong to Plato and Seneca and Nero'. Of the Mosaic law he wrote

> No individual can keep these laws, for they are death
> To every energy of man, and forbid the springs of life.[48]

In the Moral Law Blake 'challenged the entire superstructure of learning and of moral and doctrinal teaching as ideology: the Reason of the Seed of the Serpent now embodied in the temporal rulers of the earth'. Thompson refers to Blake's 'profound distrust of the 'reasons' of the genteel and comfortable, and of ecclesiastical and academic institutions . . . because they offered specious apologetics ['serpent reasonings'] for a rotten social order based, in the last resort, on violence and material self-interest'. 'Antinomians offered a central challenge to the Moral Law in a society whose legitimating ideology was precisely that of Law. . . . This same polite rule-governed society multiplied prohibitions and capital offences on every side, placing the altar of Tyburn at the centre of its institutions. Can we decide so easily on which side "reason" is to be found?' 'All Penal laws . . . are cruelty and "Murder",' wrote Blake.[49]

To the Moral Law Blake opposed the spontaneous impulses of faith

---

46. Denne, *Grace, Mercy and Peace* (1645), in *Records of the Churches of Christ gathered at Fenstanton, Warboys and Hexham, 1644–1720*, p. 398.
47. Sir George Etheredge, *Dramatic Works* (ed. H. F. B. Brett-Smith, Oxford, 1927), II, p. 95.
48. Thompson, *Witness against the Beast*, pp. 23, 30, 218–29.
49. Ibid., pp. 94, 109–13.

and love. Thompson saw antinomianism as an 'artisan or tradesman stance', embracing a lack of deference to what Blake saw as the propaganda and patronage of the propertied classes. 'The enquiry in England is not whether a Man has Talents and Genius. But whether he is Passive and Polite & a Virtuous Ass, & obedient to the Noblemen's Opinions in Art & Science'. 'If he is; he is a Good Man; if Not he must be Starved'. 'Christ and his Apostles were Illiterate Men. . . . Caiaphas, Pilate and Herod were Learned'.[50] Such words encapsulated what I suspect Clare thought but never formulated so precisely.[51]

Thompson suggested an influence upon Blake of Volney's deprecia-tion of the American Declaration of Rights, in which Liberty was allowed to precede Equality. Equality for Blake must be the basis upon which Liberty is founded. But Blake might have got the idea from Winstanley (see Chapter 23, below), or from Ranters – John Robins, for instance, who wished to see 'property disowned and charity embraced'.[52] 'You cannot have Liberty in the World without what you call Moral Virtue', wrote Blake, '& you cannot have Moral Virtue without the Slavery of that half of the Human Race who hate what you call Moral Virtue'.[53]

Blake's 'London' begins

> I wander thro' each charter'd street
> Near where the charter'd Thames does flow.

Thompson points out that 'chartered' relates to the monopolies of the 'chartered companies' – 'bastions of privilege within the government of the City'. 'A charter is, in its nature, exclusive'. 'London' is informed throughout by the antinomian contempt for the Moral Law and the institutions of the state, including monarchy and marriage. . . . A conjunc-tion between the old antinomian tradition and Jacobinism is taking place'.[54] Blake perhaps hoped that his ideal might be realizable in America if not in England. In one fragment he wrote:

> Though born on the cheating banks of Thames . . .
> The Ohio shall wash his stains from me;
> I was born a slave, but I go to be free.[55]

---

50. Ibid., pp. 112–13, 224.
51. See Chapter 26 below.
52. Thompson, op. cit., p. 200; *The Declaration of John Robins and other writings* (ed. A. Hopton, 1992), pp. 9, 34. First published 1651.
53. Blake, op. cit., p. 843.
54. Thompson, op. cit., pp. 174–83.
55. Blake, op. cit., p. 90.

V. SOCIETY, LAW AND LIBERTY

19. History and the Law

=====

We Englishmen behold
Our ancient customs bold
More precious than gold
   Be clean cast away . . .

Temporal lords be almost gone,
Households keep they few or none,
Which causeth many a goodly man
   For to beg his bread . . .

If he steal for necessity
There is none other remedy
But the law will shortly
   Hang him all save his head . . .

The great men now take no heed
How ill so ere the commons speed
The poor dare not speak for dread
   For nought they can recover.

Thomas Langdon, 'Nowadays', c.1537, in L. I. Gurney, *Recusant Poets*, I (1938), pp. 33–7.

Should I sigh because I see
Laws like spider webs to be?
Lesser flies are quickly ta'en
While the great break out again.

Barnabe's *Journal* (1638), p. 85.

God changes circumstances, assigns kingdoms and takes them away . . . through the agency of men.

Milton, *Defence of the People of England* (1651), in *Complete Prose Works*, IV, pp. 394–5.

Only Armed Pow'r can Law protect,
And rescue Wealth from Crowds, when Poverty
Treads down those Laws on which the Rich rely.

> Yet Law, where Kings are arm'd, rescues the crowd
> Even from themselves, when Plenty makes them proud.

Davenant, 'Upon His Sacred Majestie's most happy Return to His Dominions', *Shorter Poems and Songs from the Plays and Masques* (ed. A. M. Gibbs, Oxford U.P., 1972), p. 83.

> 'Tis liberty, liberty, liberty that wicked men long for.

Richard Baxter, *A Holy Commonwealth* (1659), pp. 92–4, 226–31.

I

In publishing his translations of the Bible Tyndale broke the law, with what seemed to him the higher purpose of bringing about a reform of the church. How is this higher purpose justified against the law? And how is it ascertained? For most protestants the ultimate authority was the individual conscience, even when it came to challenging the state and its laws. In the Netherlands, in 1589 D. V. Cornhaert had declared, à propos the Revolt against Spanish rule, that 'each common man may, yea should, judge whether a doctrine is true or false'.[1] A ballad justifying John Felton, awaiting sentence for assassinating the Duke of Buckingham in 1628, made the same appeal to conscience:

> Enjoy thy bondage, make thy prison know
> Thou hast a liberty thou canst not owe
> To such base punishment; keep't entire, since
> Nothing but guilt shackles thy conscience.[2]

Or as a ballad of January 1660 put it,

> 'We care not a straw
> For reason and law,
> For conscience is all in all'.[3]

Parliamentarians had to face the problem, after victory, of forcing other

---

1. Quoted by Martin Van Gelderen, *The Political Thought of the Dutch Revolt, 1555–1590* (Cambridge U.P., 1992), p. 253. But liberty of conscience did not necessarily mean liberty of worship.
2. *Witts Recreations* (1656), I, pp. 174–5. I quote from an undated reprint of the edition of 1817. I have corrected the original's 'They conscience'. Possibly 'the'?
3. 'A Psalm of Mercy', 20 January 1660, in *Political Ballads published in England during the Commonwealth* (ed. T. Wright, 1841), p. 252.

people to be free. William Erbery wanted 'to see how liberty may be settled in the whole earth'.[4] In 1650 Isaac Penington had urged his fellows to lose no opportunity to prosecute the cause of liberty, yet not by violence. The Army should ensure that 'every . . . sort of men might feel their oppressions broken and their just rights and liberties recovered' – though the word 'just' was hopelessly ambiguous.[5] William Sedgwick in 1661 agreed that the remedy for England's confusions was liberty of conscience – even for papists. 'Would you think to beat this freedom into the nation by force?'[6] Another Quaker, Howgil, asked equally pertinently, 'Was it only a form of government . . . that ye pursued after? Or was it not . . . freedom itself?'[7] Owen had asked meaningfully in 1649, 'Are not groans for liberty, by the warmth of favour, in a few years hatched into attempts for tyranny?'[8]

Bunyan had his own theological reconciliation of law and liberty. 'If thou wouldest be faithful to do that work that God hath allotted thee to do in this world for his name, labour to live much in the savour and sense of thy freedom and liberty by Jesus Christ' – the ground of all good works. 'Despair is a fall, a falling down from our liberty; our liberty is to hope'. 'By the knowledge of this [Christ's] love they may walk at liberty'. 'I am a Son of love, an object of love, a monument of love, of *free* love'.[9] Ned Ward, describing London clubs in 1709, listed the Atheists' Club which held 'that all men might set up to be their own master, and cast off the yoke of lawful authority which they deemed tyranny, and degenerate into a state of heathenish brutality, which they account freedom'; and the Thieves' Club:

> He that will no human laws obey
> Will ne'er be awed by what the priests can say.[10]

In the eighteenth century law replaced religion as the arbiter of the

---

4. *The Testimony of William Erbery* (1658), p. 32.
5. Penington, *Some Considerations Proposed to the City of London and the Nation*, in *Works* (3rd ed., 1784), II, pp. 332–3.
6. Sedgwick, *Animadversions Upon a Book Entituled Inquisition for the Blood of our late Soveraign*, pp. 193–6.
7. Howgil, *Works* (1676), pp. 335–8.
8. John Owen, *A Sermon Preached . . . on January 31* (1649), in *Works* (1850–55), VIII, pp. 147–8.
9. Bunyan, *Miscellaneous Works* (Oxford U.P.), XII, p. 374; XIII, pp. 32, 403–4, 413–14.
10. [E. Ward], *The Secret History of Clubs* (1709), p. 70.

community's morals. Where was liberty between public law and private conscience? Clarissa's conscience came up against the legalistic materialism of the Harlowes, and so she fell an easy prey to Lovelace. She was reluctant to invoke the law to prosecute him; we may contrast her family's compliance with and Lovelace's mastery of the legal system. – 'What an admirable lawyer I should have made!' 'In actual civil society', Zomchick comments, 'one is either with the law like the Harlowes, or against it like Lovelace, or one is nothing'.[11] Some, like the Quakers, held out for the sovereignty of the individual conscience.

In George I's reign the Blacks might be seen as standing for freedom against the law. The rule of law demands a more stable, more equal society than then existed. To assert the primacy of the law ultimately meant accepting that there could be universal values of law worth striving for – those of the market, for instance. Winstanley would have replaced the new market system with a new social system; others demanded a democratic electorate before the overriding authority of the law could be accepted.[12]

II

The old apophthegm, 'laws they are not which public approbation hath not made so' is roughly true if we read it as meaning 'laws are enforced unless public opinion resists them too hard'. But in the seventeenth century, with vast economic changes and the first beginnings of a public opinion wider than that of the gentry, law-making became newly contentious. Eric Hobsbawm, in a brilliant article,[13] showed how the eighteenth-century Scottish school, drawing on English experience, decided that two conditions were necessary for the successful introduction of capitalist agriculture – (1) absolute security of tenure for gentry and well-to-do peasantry; (2) removing most lesser tenants from the land where their subsistence economy contributed nothing to national wealth, and driving them into waged employment, whether in town or country, which would add to national wealth and to the wealth of those with

11. J. P. Zomchick, *Family and the Law in 18th-century Fiction* (Cambridge U.P., 1993).

12. Thompson, *Whigs and Hunters*, pp. 258–69, 49–52; cf. Chapters 14–20 below.

13. E. J. Hobsbawm, 'Scottish Reformers and Capitalist Agriculture', in *Peasants in History: Essays in Honour of Daniel Thorner* (ed. Hobsbawm and others, Oxford U.P., 1960).

capital. The first condition was established in England during the Revolution by the abolition of feudal tenures and wardship, with a concurrent refusal of security of tenure to copyholders. The second was ensured by refusing to respect traditional customary rights, whether of access to commons in the villages, or in the form of traditional perquisites and vails in industry. Both of these necessary conditions for capitalist production had the effect of driving subsistence peasants into regular wage labour. They breached long-standing customs and were fiercely resented, whether in agriculture or in industry. But they were ensured by *laws* passed by a sovereign Parliament, in which the poor were totally unrepresented. There could hardly have been a clearer case of law abolishing liberties. Its victims were unlikely to have much respect for such laws.

Hostility to the law may ante-date the examples I have so far given. Robert Weimann long ago pointed out that in the fifteenth-century Towneley plays Annas and Caiaphas insist that Jesus is an enemy to the law, tempting the people and turning them against its observance. Pilate describes Jesus as 'this traitor . . . that would destroy our law', and the Second Torturer agreed:

> if he reign any more
> Our laws are miscarried.

When Pilate heard of Jesus's resurrection, his comment was

> Alas, then are our laws forlore
> For evermore.

The law was defended by Pilate – the agent of foreign conquerors and oppressors. Are we intended to see an analogy here between the rise of Christianity and the overthrow of the Norman Yoke? The law of the conquerors is also defended by Annas and Caiaphas, described as 'bishops' and 'prelates'. (This incidentally suggests possible doubts about recent claims that the Church was a popular institution before the Reformation: the miracle plays offer the only glimpse we get before the development of printing of a view from below. The Towneley plays depict at least one Pope in hell for murder.)[14]

14. Weimann, *Shakespeare und die Tradition des Volkstheaters* (Berlin, 1967), pp. 106, 467; *York Mystery Plays* (ed. Lucy Toulmin Smith, Oxford U.P., 1885), pp. 255–69, 281, 288, 309; *The Towneley Plays* (ed. G. England, Early English Text Soc., Oxford U.P., 1897), pp. 174, 206–7, 222–37, 307, 322; cf. *The Chester Plays*, II (Early English Text Soc., Oxford U.P., 1916), pp. 280, 290, 313, 350, 428–48; *The Wakefield Mystery Plays* (ed. M. Rose, 1961), pp. 305, 308, 352–4.

For most villagers 'the law' was something imposed on them from far away and high above. Statute law was made by representatives of a small section of the upper classes, and related to their interests rather than those of the populace. 'Freedom' for the latter meant living according to traditional customary rules, accepted unquestioningly from time immemorial. In connection with enclosure new laws were introduced which blasted this freedom, these traditional rights – rights to pasture domestic animals and birds on the waste, to collect fuel, fruits, berries etc. from wastes and woods. The livelihood of many villagers depended on these rights; but now they were being stigmatized – and punished – as theft. This is the root cause of the widening gap between rich and poor in villages, and of vagabondage.

The law prevented people doing things which they believed they had a long-standing right to do. It could transform their lives, render them homeless. Sir Charles Ogilvie defines 'liberty' in the seventeenth-century as 'freedom to possess and acquire'; 'the Common law . . . was essentially a law of property, and especially of landed property', and was regarded by the gentry 'as its shield and buckler'.[15] But, as the Act abolishing Star Chamber put it, 'the Council Table hath of late times assumed to itself a power to meddle in civil causes and matters only of private interest between party and party, and have adventured to determine of the estates and liberties of the subject, contrary to the laws of the land and the rights and privileges of the subject'.[16] Judges had made the King's subjects mere tenants at will of their liberties and estates. Attorney-General Noy went so far as to claim that 'all liberties are derived from the Crown'. 'A liberty is a royal privilege in the hands of a subject'.[17]

Faced with the growing inequality of seventeenth-century English society, respectable commentators made no bones about the class nature of law in England. The judicious Hooker explained that laws 'are never framed as they should be . . . unless presuming man to be in regard of his depraved mind little better than a wild beast'.[18] This view extended to politics.

The Bible in English encouraged ordinary people to discuss politics,

15. Ogilvie, *The King's Government and the Common Law*, p. 6.
16. Gardiner, *Constitutional Documents*, pp. 181–2.
17. Noy, *Trentisẹ of the Principall Grounds and Maxims of the Laws of England*, quoted by Lawrence Venuti, *Our Halcyon Dayes: English Prerevolutionary Texts and Postmodern Culture* (Wisconsin U.P., 1989), p. 297.
18. Hooker, *Of the Laws of Ecclesiastical Polity* (Everyman ed.), I, p. 188.

and they sometimes found revolutionary arguments in God's Word. Christopher Goodman, writing in Mary's reign, thought that the Bible in some circumstances authorized the people to 'take unto themselves the punishment of transgressors'. The Scot George Buchanan in *De Jure Regni apud Scotos* (1579) noted that God 'many times' stirred up 'from amongst the lowest of the people some very mean and obscure man to revenge tyrannical pride. . . . If kings continue in their madness, whoever doth most obey them is to be counted their greatest enemy'.[19]

Religious arguments had to be used to counter such ideas. The *Homily on Disobedience* had rejected the possibility of resistance, even if 'the prince be indiscreet, and it is also evident to all men's eyes that he is so'. Richard Strier quotes several examples from *King Lear, Pericles, The Winter's Tale* and especially *Cymbeline* to show that 'Shakespeare offered an answer very different from the Homily'.[20] But traditional theology was strongly in favour of obedience to authority. The protestant John Ponet in 1556 thought that 'common and simple people' obeyed 'because their doings are counted tumultuous and rebellious', and 'therefore they suffer them- selves like brute beastes rather than reasonable creatures to be led and drawen where so ever their Prince's commandments have called'. He cited Biblical examples of refusal to obey 'the king's unlawful command- ment', in which behaviour they were 'yet the king's true servants and subjects'. In some cases, Ponet thought, Christians are free to kill male- factors, 'yea though they were magistrates'.[21]

Before 1640 it was difficult to get fundamental criticism of the law into print. We have to work from the implications of attack upon the advocates of liberty. Davenant in *Gondibert* spoke of 'this wild monster, the people', 'whose appetite is liberty' and their liberty 'a licence of lust'. Davenant suggested that 'obedience, like the marriage yoke, is a restraint more needful and advantageous than liberty'.[22] 'Liberty' for whom?

At an early date Melanchthon had made protestantism's position on property very clear: all rulers must punish heresy and promote true religion; they must also protect and never infringe their subjects' property

19. Goodman, *How Superior Powers Ought to be Obeyed* (Geneva, 1558), pp. 185, 191; Buchanan, op. cit. (1689 edition), pp. 54–8.
20. Richard Strier, 'Faithful Servants: Shakespeare's Praise of Disobedience', in *The Historical Renaissance: New Essays on Tudor and Stuart Literature and Culture* (ed. H. Dubrow and Strier, Chicago U.P., 1988), pp. 108, 111–26.
21. Goodman, op. cit., pp. 145–6; Ponet, *A Shorte Treatise of Politicke Power*, Sig. Dv, Gviii.
22. Davenant, op. cit. (ed. D. F. Gladish, Oxford U.P., 1971), p. 30.

rights.[23] In the Parliament of 1610 defence of their property was clearly a main concern of M.P.s James Whitelocke said, 'We are masters of our own and can have nothing taken from us without our consents; . . . laws cannot be made without our consents, and the edict of a prince is not a law'.[24] 'The King cannot alter the law', said Thomas Hedley, 'the chief subject and object whereof is property in lands and goods'. The law takes even greater care of a man's lands and goods than of the liberty of his person. If the King had absolute power to take subjects' goods, 'then they are . . . little better than the King's bondsmen'. 'It is the laws, liberties and government of this realm' that makes us superior to other countries.[25] Nicholas Fuller added that 'by the laws of England the subjects have such property in their land and goods as that without their consent the King can take no part thereof from them lawfully . . . without act of parliament'. They have an absolute property in their goods. 'The common laws . . . do so measure the King's prerogative as it shall not tend to take away or prejudice the inheritance of the subject'.[26]

But royal facts did not live up to Parliamentarian theory. Henry Parker agreed that laws were important, but complained that 'for these seventeen years last past' laws have not defended the rights of Englishmen. Since he was writing in 1642 the precise reference to the years of Charles I's government was unmistakable. But the theory went on being proclaimed. Samuel Rutherford said that property in one's own goods was antecedent to kings.[27] More succinctly, Adam Baynes in the parliament of 1656 declared that 'all government is built on property, else the poor must rule it'.[28] Another M.P. in the same Parliament declared 'we promised Englishmen freedom, equal freedom. . . . Did we not make the people believe we fought for their liberty? Let us not deceive them of their expectation'.[29]

From the 1640s we have, for the first time, records of general discussions on what the nature of church and state should be. For two decades we may begin to talk about public opinion – or rather various opinions, for there was no unanimity. Henceforth there was no going back to the state

23. Quentin Skinner, op. cit., II, p. 69.
24. Ed. Elizabeth Read Foster, *Proceedings in Parliament, 1610*, II, *The House of Commons*, p. 109.
25. Ibid., pp. 189–96.
26. Ibid., pp. 152, 157–8.
27. Parker, *The Counter-Replicant, his Complaint to His Majestie* (January 1643), pp. 5–6; Rutherford, op. cit., p. 121.
28. Ed. J. T. Rutt, *The Diary of Thomas Burton*, III, pp. 147–8.
29. Burton, *Diary*, I, p. 228.

of affairs before 1640, when political discussion was abnormal and could be suppressed. In 1645 a man reproved by his parish authorities for entertaining young people and apprentices on the Sabbath retorted that 'this was not a time to curb servants or restrain them of their liberties.'[30] Winstanley expressed a general radical conviction when he wrote

> God's shaking nations, trying men,
> And changing times and customs.

'The Lord hath appeared in our days to do great things', declared Edmund Ludlow.[31]

God's direct intervention in human affairs, of which there are many Biblical examples, made possible acceptance of the consequence of resistance to authority even while disapproving of it in theory. A preacher at Otley in the West Riding of Yorkshire, on the very eve of civil war (30 March 1642) used David's revolt against Saul and succession to his throne to make this point: because Saul had failed to carry out God's law, 'God rends his kingship from him and gives it to David, one that will execute all his wills'.[32] The modern equivalent of putting the responsibility on God is to attribute revolutionary change to 'the historic process'.

Among those who saw God directly intervening in English affairs we may list radicals as diverse as Oliver Cromwell, Major-General Harrison, John Cook, prosecutor in the trial of Charles I in 1649, the Presbyterian Philip Henry, the Independent John Owen, the Fifth Monarchists Thomas Venner, John Tillinghast and John Carew, John Reeve, the Baptist Robert Purnell, the Quakers Edward Burrough and Isaac Penington, William Erbery and Joshua Garment.[33] In such a time, traditional institutions lost their traditional respect.

The most thorough-going of the radical critics was John Hare, who in a series of pamphlets published in and after 1647 declared that 'All our great victories and triumphs' in the civil war were useless if the Norman laws remained. If 'our statesmen should . . . persecute the assertors of English liberty as enemies', they must be resisted to the death.[34]

30. Sharpe, *Crime in seventeenth-century England*, p. 54.

31. Sabine, *Winstanley*, p. 336; Ludlow, *A Voice from the Watch Tower* (ed. A. B. Worden, Camden 4th series, vol. 21, 1978), p. 307.

32. William Sheils, 'Provincial Preaching on the eve of the Civil War: some West Riding fast sermons', in *Religion, culture and society in early modern Britain* (ed. Anthony Fletcher and Peter Roberts, Cambridge U.P., 1994), p. 303.

33. My *Experience of Defeat*, pp. 319–21.

34. Hare, *St. Edwards Ghost, or Anti-Normanisme* (1647); *Plaine English* (1647), in *Harleian Miscellany* (1812), IX, p. 91; *Englands Proper and onely way to an Establishment* (1648), pp. 2–6.

Lilburne thought that 'the tedious, unknown, and impossible-to-be-understood common law practices . . . came in by the will of a Tyrant, namely William the Conqueror'. Wildman was briefer: 'Our very laws were made by our conquerors'. Richard Overton said that Magna Carta was 'but a beggarly thing'.[35] Hugh Peter (as reported by Lilburne) declared that the civil war had been fought not for 'the continuity or preservation' of the laws 'but to be freed from them'; we should 'burn all the old Records, . . . the monuments of tyranny'.[36] Peter and Lilburne disagreed hotly over their interpretation of English history, but both rejected the existing common law as Norman. John Warr in *The Corruption and Deficiency of the Lawes of England* (1649) declared that 'many times the very law is the badge of our oppression, its proper intent being to enslave the people. . . . The more fundamental a law is, the more difficult, not the less necessary, to be reformed'.[37]

In December 1649 the Digger poet Robert Coster inquired 'whether particular property was not brought into the room of public community by murder and theft?' He cited Biblical authority for asserting that 'livelihood' is 'the right and property of every man'. 'All men (by the grant of God) should be alike free, and all to enjoy the earth with the fullness thereof alike (Genesis 1:26 and 9:1–15) until they sell their birthright and inheritance for a proud idle life (II Thessalonians 3:6–13).' But, he concluded, 'there is no statute law in the nation that doth hinder the common people from seizing their own land'.[38]

Coster almost certainly got his ideas from Gerrard Winstanley, who looked back to the freedom of Eden before the Fall rather than to Anglo-Saxon freedom before the Norman Conquest. Winstanley wrote 'When mankind began to quarrel about the earth; and some would have all and shut out others, forcing them to be servants: this was man's Fall, it is . . . the cause of all divisions, wars and pluckings up'.[39] Winstanley generalized his critique of the law, asking 'whether any laws since the coming in of kings have been made in the light of the righteous law of our creation,

---

35. Lilburne, *The Just Mans Justification* (1646), pp. 11–13; Woodhouse, *Puritanism and Liberty*, p. 65; *A Remonstrance of Many Thousand Citizens* (1646), in Haller, *Tracts on Liberty*, III, p. 365.
36. R. P. Stearns, *The Strenuous Puritan: Hugh Peter, 1598–1660* (Illinois U.P., 1954), p. 349; Peter, *Good Work for a Good Magistrate* (1651), pp. 32–3.
37. Warr, op. cit., in *Harleian Miscellany* (1745), III, pp. 240–42.
38. Coster, *A Mite Cast into the Common Treasury*, in Sabine, op. cit., pp. 655–7.
39. Sabine, op. cit., p. 424.

respecting all alike, or have not been grounded upon selfish principles . . . to uphold freedom in the gentry and clergy, and to hold the common people in bondage still?'[40] The regicide John Cook said that reform of 'corruptions and oppressions in Courts of Justice' was 'the one great thing that my honoured friends in the Army told me they fought for'.[41] The anonymous *Tyranipocrit Discovered* alleged that 'the rich artificial thieves do rob the poor, and that under a feigned show of justice'.[42]

Thomas Tany ('Theaureaujohn') no doubt took over from Winstanley the argument that 'now our Lands being freed from the Norman subjection' thanks to Parliament's victory in the civil war, 'we may lawfully claim our lands and inheritances in the Common-wealth'.[43] Ireton had objected to the Leveller Agreement of the People because it 'takes away . . . that constitution by which I have any property'.[44] Prynne similarly defended 'fundamental laws and liberties' left to freemen by their forefathers, against Leveller attacks on behalf of the natural rights of all men.[45] Lilburne wanted decentralization of justice by abolishing the 'Norman innovation' of courts at Westminster, and returning to county and hundred courts, as before the Norman Conquest – as he also had done in elevating the jury above the judge.[46]

Quakers, like Levellers before them, insisted that they should be tried by a jury drawn from the neighbourhood, 'or others who shall well know each other'. They would know that some witnesses were persons 'of no credit', and that the Quaker defendants were far too principled to commit the crimes with which they were charged. But in the courts at Westminster juries were composed of anonymous property-owners, selected *because* they had no knowledge of the facts in dispute. The distinction is parallel to Tyndale's elevation of the parish congregation over a national or international church. Both are appealing from the central state power to local community institutions. We may contrast Hyde's

---

40. Ibid., pp. 287–8.
41. Quoted in Ogilvie, *The King's Government and the Common Law*, p. 165.
42. Op. cit. (ed. A. Hopton, n.d.), p. 14; cf. pp. 47–51.
43. *Theaureaujohn High Priest to the Jewes, His Disputive Challenge to the Universities of Oxford and Cambridge* (1651), pp. 1, 8–9; cf. [Anon.], *The Extent of the Sword* (1654), pp. 2–3.
44. Woodhouse, *Puritanism and Liberty*, p. 60.
45. Prynne, *The first and second Part of a Seasonable, Legal and Historical Vindication and Chronological Collection of the Good, Old, Fundamental Liberties* (1653), p. 3.
46. Lilburne, *The Just Mans Justification*, p. 15; cf. W. Schenk, *The Concern for Social Justice in the Puritan Revolution* (1948), pp. 67–8. See also p. 260 below.

encouragement to Charles I to rely on 'the law of the land' against revolutionary aggression from Parliament and populace.[47]

Most Quakers rightly claimed to have supported Parliament 'for our rights and liberties' during the civil war. 'Many precious men ventured their lives' to win liberty 'as men and as Christians', said Howgil. The Long Parliament had been 'the first assertors and contenders for England's . . . long-lost liberty', wrote Edward Burrough; he, like James Nayler, Fox, George Fox the Younger, and many others complained of the 'great and heavy oppressions of the law', including its great fees. 'Whosoever are against the Good Old Cause and perfect freedom', Burrough proclaimed, early in 1660, 'we are against them and will engage our lives against them' – a reminder that Quakers were not pacifists before 1661.[48]

Quakers shared many of the radicals' views on the law; they expected man's laws to be 'agreeable to the just principle of God in every man', and asserted their right to disobey any positive law which contradicted the law of God in their consciences. Since for them the inner light rejected tithes, a state church and outward demonstrations of respect for social superiors, this was to call for revolution. Quakers demanded a more accessible legal system, decentralization of justice, election of judges, no fees, and an end to some harsh legal punishments. What was unique (and totally unacceptable to their betters) was the Quaker assumption that their inner light was self-evident to all.[49]

Defenders of the law made similar points with the opposite intention. *Mercurius Pragmaticus* in November 1648 suggested that the radicals' 'design against property is the reason why they are such enemies against lawyers, there being no further use of *meum* and *tuum*, nor of laws, to lay lime-twigs against liberty of conscience, nor of a king to execute them, nor of lords to assist him.'[50] Albertus Warren in 1653 thought that critics of the law were either 'turbulent spirits pleased with no government', 'vulgar heads of small estates and illiterate', or former tradesmen 'pragmatically petulant against law because it is not loose enough for their illegal

---

47. See my 'Lord Clarendon and the Puritan Revolution', in *Puritanism and Revolution*. For Tyndale see pp. 179–80 above.
48. Nayler, *A Few Words occasioned by a Paper lately printed, Stiled, A Discourse concerning Quakers* (n.d.), p. 23; see my *Experience of Defeat*, pp. 131–3, 144, 150.
49. I have drawn for this paragraph on R. Michael Rogers's useful article, 'Quakerism and the Law in Revolutionary England', in *Canadian Journal of History*, XXII (1987), esp. pp. 152–62.
50. In *Making the News* (ed. Raymond), p. 351.

aims'. Well-bred men educated in liberal studies did not, he was sure, write against the law.[51]

Moses Wall, on the other hand, thought that the standard of living of ordinary people must be raised by 'an improving of our native commodities, as our manufactures, our fishery, our fens, forests and commons, and our trade at sea, etc.', together with abolition of 'that cursed yoke of tithes' and of copyhold. Until then 'the people are not free but straitened in accommodations for life', and their spirits will remain dejected and servile.[52] Cowley hedged prudently by saying that 'the liberty of a people consists in being governed by Laws which they have made themselves, under whatsoever form it be of government'.[53] That was safe either under the Commonwealth or the restored monarchy, provided only that we do not ask 'Who are the people?'[54]

Anxiety to prevent ordinary people having any say in law-making was especially acute in the plantations. In April 1650 Peter Bulkeley feared 'putting too much liberty and power in the hands of the multitude, which they are too weak to manage. . . . The heady or headless multitude' were insolent towards authority.[55] Sir William Berkeley at the time of Bacon's rebellion (1676) referred to 'an insulting rabble, . . . who account the law their manacles, and like swine turn all into disorder.'[56]

51. Warren, quoted by D. Veall, *The Popular Movement for Law Reform*, pp. 123–4.
52. Masson, *Life of Milton*, V, pp. 602–3.
53. Cowley, 'Of Liberty', in *Essays and Plays* (ed. A. R. Waller, Cambridge U.P., 1906), p. 377.
54. See Chapter 20 below.
55. Bulkeley, quoted by P. F. Gura, *A Glimpse of Sion's Glory: Puritan Radicalism in New England, 1620–1660* (Wesleyan U.P., 1984), pp. 82–3.
56. I regret that I have mislaid my reference for this quotation.

20. Liberty and Equality: Who are the People?

Even in Great Britain, where property is better secured than anywhere else in the Universe . . . it is impossible to prevent men of the lower class from plundering their Fellow-Subjects.

Captain Charles Johnson, *A General History of . . . the Most Famous Highwaymen, Murderers, Street-Robbers, etc.* (1736), Sig. B.

Security of property! Behold in a few words the definition of English liberty!

Mary Wollstonecraft, *Works* (ed. M. Butler and J. Todd, 1989), V, pp. 14–15.

I

Historically liberty means privilege. The liberties of London are the special privileges of London: to be free of a City company is to enjoy its privileges. A freeborn man is one who by the good fortune of his birth enjoys rights and privileges which the other three-quarters of the population do not. Sir Walter Ralegh made the point: 'A Monarch Tyrannical is he who without regard to the Law of God or Nature commandeth Freemen as Slaves, and useth their Lands and Goods as his own.'[1] Freedom went with property: a man in receipt of wages was unfree, as stage players were often reminded. Compare the New Model Army's boast, on the eve of taking decisive political action in 1647, to be 'no mere mercenary army'.

For many historians the history of freedom in England is the history of the establishment of security for property, and of the sovereignty of a Parliament representing the propertied ('free') classes. Town charters bestow liberties on the inhabitants (for a price). Magna Carta, the great charter of liberties, bestowed privileges on a small minority of the

1. Ralegh, *The Cabinet-Council*, in *Works* (1751), I, p. 43.

propertied. The words 'liberty' and 'free' are slippery, and change their meaning over time. Henry Neville, looking back to the 1640s from 1681, recalled 'how easily an army of natives is to be deluded with the name of liberty, and brought to pull down anything which their ringleaders tell them tends to enslaving their country'.[2]

Clarendon warily observed, after the revolution, that 'though the name of liberty be pleasant to all kinds of people, yet all men do not understand the same thing by it'.[3] He might almost have been quoting Winstanley: 'All men have stood for freedom ... and now the common enemy is gone you are all like men in a mist, seeking for freedom and know not where nor what it is'. Winstanley added, 'those of the richer sort of you that see it, are ashamed and afraid to own it', because it is liable to be mocked by 'scoffing Ishmael'. The language of the enemies of freedom tells us a good deal about what the word meant – 'the finest compendium of humouring and pleasing all those little fellows that love not, that endure not, to be subject to their betters'.[4] The opponents of liberty made much of the variations in meaning given to the word. 'The name of Liberty hath ever been the watch-word used before rebellion, the idle echo of uncertainty'.[5]

The word 'freeborn' also tells us a good deal. It shared the ambiguity of 'freedom'. For those who claimed to be freeborn themselves, the word implied a certain social status, a certain level of financial stability. One of the oldest of the Robin Hood ballads was addressed to 'gentlemen / That be of freeborn blood'.[6] It was socially subversive when radicals like Winstanley and Coppe claimed that all Englishmen were freeborn. In the play *Sir Thomas More* (?1586–95) one of the rebels asked 'shall we be held under? No: we are freeborn'.[7] Apprentices became 'freeborn' only when they were their own masters.[8] William Browne assures his readers that he did not write for money:

2. Neville, *Plato Redivivus* (1681), in *Two English Republican Tracts* (ed. Caroline Robbins, Cambridge U.P., 1969), pp. 179–80.
3. Quoted by Felix Raab, *The English Face of Machiavelli* (1964), p. 148.
4. Winstanley, *Works*, p. 316; William Nicolson, *An Apology for the Discipline of the Ancient Church* (1659), Sig. A 3v.
5. John Crouch and Marchamont Nedham's *Craftie Cromwell*, a play-pamphlet of 1648 satirizing Oliver, quoted by Nigel Smith, *Literature and Revolution*, p. 78.
6. *A Lytell Geste of Robyn Hoode*, Ritson, op. cit., p. 115.
7. Op. cit., Act II, scene ii.
8. Nigel Smith, *Literature and Revolution*, p. 132.

> My freeborn muse will not . . . be
> Won with base dross to clip with slavery.[9]

George Wither, too, in opposition to 'proud courtiers', trusted to find 'virtue in a freeborn mind', which

> the greatest kings that be
> Cannot give, nor take away from me.[10]

Robert Heath claimed that

> My birth styles me as freeborn too:
> No peasant blood doth stain or chill my veins.[11]

Denham, in *The Sophy* (1642), made one courtier say to another, with heavy irony,

> If the many-headed beast hath broke,
> Or shaken from his neck the royal yoke,
> With popular rage religion doth conspire,
> Flows into that, and swells the torrent higher;
> The power's first pedigree from force derives,
> And calls to mind the old prerogatives
> Of free-born man; and with a saucy eye
> Searches the heart and soul of majesty:
> Then to a strict account and censure brings
> The actions, errors and the end of kings;
> Treads on authority and sacred laws –
> Yet all for God, and his pretended cause.[12]

Milton, seven years later, spoke of 'the liberty and right of freeborn men to be governed as seems to them best', relying on the joint authority of reason and Scripture. 'Not to have in ourselves, though vaunting to be free-born, the power of our own freedom and the public safety, is a degree lower than not to have the property of our own goods. For liberty of person and the right of self-preservation' are 'more worth to all men than the property of their goods and wealth. Yet such power as this did the King . . . challenge to have over us'.[13]

9. Browne, *Britannia's Pastorals*, in *Poems* (ed. G. Goodwin, Muses Library, n.d.), I, p. 317.
10. Wither, *Fair Virtue, The Mistress of Phil'arete* (1622), pp. 184–9.
11. Heath, *Poems and Songs* (Hull, 1905), p. 13. First published 1650.
12. Op. cit., Act IV, scene i, in *Poems and Translations* (7th ed., n.d.), p. 176.
13. Milton, *The Tenure of Kings and Magistrates* (1649), *Complete Prose Works* (Yale

George Fox the Younger held that 'many thousands of men in England have been wronged of their birthright' by Parliament's failure to extend the franchise after victory in the civil war. This failure meant that 'rich, covetous oppressing men' will make all laws.[14] Samuel Butler mocked republicans as 'all free-born in Fairy-Land, but changed in the cradle; and so being not natives here, the air of the government does not agree with them'. A republican 'supposes the right of [government] to be only in those that are incapable of the use of it, that is all men'.[15]

II

The gospel narrative is about carpenters, shepherds and fishermen. Protestant encouragement of discussion of the newly-translated Bible could not but stimulate egalitarian sentiments. In *The Parable of the Wicked Mammon* William Tyndale insisted that 'in Christ we are all of one degree, without respect of persons'. There is 'difference between washing of dishes and preaching the word of God, but as touching to please God, none at all'. In *The Obedience of a Christian Man*, usually cited as elevating the role of the king, Tyndale wrote 'the most despised person in his realm is the King's brother and fellow-member with him, and equal with him in the kingdom of God and of Christ'. All men are equal in prayer – cobbler and cardinal, butchers and bishops, a baker and the Pope. All must have equal rights under the law, even the King.[16]

Human equality is almost a commonplace in Elizabethan and Jacobean literature. In a memorable phrase Ralegh proclaimed 'When every man wears but his own skin, the players are all alike'.[17] 'Shepherds are men, and kings are no more', says the leading character in *Mucedorus* (1598).[18] In *Cymbeline* the exiled princes preach human equality; the loutish Cloten

---

ed.), III, p. 206; *Eikonoklastes* (1649), ibid., III, p. 454: first published 1649. I quote from the second edition, in which this last sentence was added.

14. Fox, *A Few Plain Words* (1659), pp. 2–5.
15. Butler, *Characters and Passages from Notebooks* (ed. A. R. Waller, Cambridge U.P., 1908), p. 26.
16. Tyndale, *Doctrinal Treatises*, pp. 98, 102, 202–4, 256–8.
17. Ralegh, *History of the World* (Edinburgh, 1820), I, p. xl.
18. Act III, scene 1.

thinks to establish his superiority by his clothes (Act IV, scene 2). 'What is the city but the people?' asks the tribune in *Coriolanus* (Act III, scene 1). In Massinger's *The Bondman* Timoleon proclaims

> I have ever loved
> An equal freedom, and proclaim'd all such
> As would usurp on others' liberties
> Rebels to nature.

But this fine principle is limited by socio-economic considerations, for

> Such as have made forfeit of themselves
> By vicious courses, and their birthright lost
> 'Tis not injustice they are marked for slaves (Act I, scene 3).

Whereas Marullo, the Bondman, declares that

> Equal Nature fashioned us
> All of one mould . . .

We are taught by the example of the animals 'to love our liberty' (Act II, scene 3). In Chapman's *Ovid's Banquet of Sense* (1595), Ovid propounds the subversive idea that

> Virtue makes honour, as the soul doth sense,
> And merit far exceeds inheritance.[19]

When in Chapman's *An Humerous dayes mirth* (1599) Count Laberuele tells a Puritan woman that 'there is difference in all estates by religion', she replies flatly 'there is no difference'.[20]

Samuel Rutherford in *Lex Rex* (1644) had no doubt that 'every man by nature is a freeman born. . . . Freedom is natural to all', except as limited by subordination to parents, and only to them. Since all men are born free, 'there is no reason in Nature why one man should be king and lord over another'. 'No man bringeth out of the womb with him a Scepter and a crown on his head'. Winstanley agreed that 'every particular man is but a member and branch of mankind'.[21] In reviewing the different forms of government, Rutherford said interestingly that democracy was 'for liberty, and possibly for riches and gain, best'.[22] But

19. Chapman, *Works* (1875), p. 34.
20. Chapman, *Dramatic Works* (1873), I, p. 58.
21. Winstanley, *Works*, p. 261.
22. Op. cit., pp. 3, 75, 91, 387; cf. p. 157.

his definition of democracy was not ours. Edwards in 1646 saw with horror soldiers exulting in their power over priests, gentlemen and the City.[23]

III

In an essay originally written for a Festschrift for George Rude, belatedly published in 1985, I pointed to many late sixteenth-century and early seventeenth-century writers who did not regard the poor as people in the sense of having any political rights.[24] During the revolutionary decades there was much talk of 'the people' controlling Parliament and thus the law; but there was no agreement on who 'the people' were. Parliaments were elected on a propertied franchise. Even the Levellers were doubtful about whether the whole male population could be trusted with the vote, including servants and paupers: nobody seems to have seriously proposed giving votes to women. James Harrington, the major political theorist of the period, thought that the distinction between freemen and servants was 'natural', existing before the state was set up. For him only those who own property are 'people'. Servants cannot be free, cannot share in the government of a commonwealth. In England the yeomanry are the true people.[25]

For the great Puritan William Perkins 'rogues, beggars and vagabonds' were outside church and commonwealth. William Gouge insisted that only Anabaptists thought that servants were the equals of their masters. The saintly Bishop Lancelot Andrewes distinguished between 'the common sort' and 'true Christians'. Oliver Cromwell equated 'poor men' with 'bad men'; Harrington 'robbers and Levellers'. Servants were excluded from the 'solemn contract' made by 'the people' on the Mayflower.[26] 'The meaner sort of people and servants' were excluded from the English militia. Among others who drew lines of distinction between 'the people' and the majority of the population I cited Elizabeth's Secretary of State, Sir Thomas Smith, General Ireton and Colonel Rich

23. Edwards, *Gangraena*, III, pp. 16, 270–82.
24. 'The Poor and the People', in *People and Ideas in 17th-century England*, pp. 247–73.
25. My *Experience of Defeat*, pp. 194–5; Harrington, *Oceana and other Works* (1737), p. 292; cf. pp. 429–30, 657–60, 840.
26. Andrewes, *XVI Sermons* (2nd ed., 1631), p. 459; my *People and Ideas*, p. 255.

in the Putney Debates, General Monck, William Stoughton, Thomas Edwards, Sir Thomas Aston, Marchamont Nedham, Adam Baynes, Algernon Sidney, James Tyrell and John Locke. I might have added William Perkins, Sir Simonds D'Ewes, Richard Hooker and William Gouge. The double-think existed in theology too. In one sense Christ died for all men, in another sense for the elect only.[27]

Winstanley too had to face the problem of an uneducated populace, though his solutions were rather different. In his *The Law of Freedom* (1652) 'the law was added' against the wild unruly people: suppression of some sort would be necessary as a temporary measure till the abolition of private property was generally accepted. Unlike Milton, Winstanley had had to face unruly Ranters in his colony on Cobham Heath.

Richard Baxter gave reasons for what most others took for granted. He argued that servants, the poor and 'the rabble' are commonly judged incapable of freedom to take part in elections because their necessity makes them dependent on others. 'In most parts the major vote of the vulgar . . . is ruled by money and therefore by their landlords'. Only freeholders and holders of leases for lives have the necessary independence.[28] Milton restricted 'the people' to heads of households: in 1654 he feared that 'the giddy multitude' might demand 'that Charles should be restored to the kingdom'.[29] Henry Stubbe, a defender of the Good Old Cause, in 1659 distinguished between 'the nation' and 'the people'. But he thought that even landless men who had served in Parliament's army should enjoy the rights of 'people'.[30]

IV

The early protestant theology of 'the priesthood of all believers' placed more emphasis on the freedom of individuals and communities than on the law of the state; and many protestants, as we saw, rejected the law of Moses. Tyndale's translation of *ekklesia* as congregation (linguistically correct) contrasted the parish community with the state church. The

27. Ibid., pp. 247–73.
28. Baxter, *A Holy Commonwealth*, pp. 172, 226–31, 236–7, 243, 247–56.
29. Milton, *Complete Prose Works*, IV, p. 635; see my *Milton and the English Revolution* (1977), esp. pp. 160–64.
30. For Stubbe see J. R. Jacob, *Henry Stubbe, Radical Protestantism and the Early Enlightenment* (Cambridge U.P., 1983).

Pilgrim Fathers were committted to congregational autonomy and thought they could establish the liberty of congregations by emigrating to New England, away from 'the wretched and loathsome prisons of London'. In New England congregations elected and ordained their own ministers, rejected the liturgy of the state church, and permitted lay preaching.

I suggested that there is a fairly clear analogy between wanting to liberate individual congregations from the authority of the state church and the demand – shared by Levellers, Fifth Monarchists and Milton – to decentralize justice by returning cases from Westminster to local county and hundred courts. Both emphasize the local community as against the impersonal authorities of a centralized state. New England was fortunate in having no centralized state to contend with, at least in the early days; and even then toleration was denied to Baptist congregations.[31]

The Bible in English led radicals to demand the law in English too. Levellers demanded 'that all Lawes of the Land (lockt up from common capacities in the Latin or French tongues) may be translated into the English tongue'. This should cover all legal proceedings whatsoever, 'that so the meanest English commoner that can but read written hand in his own tongue may fully understand his own proceedings in the law'.[32]

In Massachusetts church membership was restricted to 'visible saints'. The power of congregations appeared to be above that of the state. But 'freedom' in Massachusetts in the early days belonged effectively neither to godly nor to the people but went with land-ownership. 'No one would go to America to have less freedom than in England', Captain John Smith had said in the early 1620s. True liberty, he thought, depended on all heads of families being landowners. This proved a point of conflict. In 1626 Thomas Hooker, and later Robert Williams, left Massachusetts because they were unhappy with congregations controlling access to civil rights and to the franchise. The massive purge of magistrates accused of

---

31. W. R. Parker, *Milton: A Biography* (Oxford U.P., 1968), I, pp. 539, 544–55; Bremer, *Congregational Communion*, pp. 107, 240; cf. pp. 111, 117. Cf. p. 157 above.
32. *An Appeal from the degenerate Representative Body of the Commons . . . To the Body Represented, the free people* (1647), in D. M. Wolfe, *Leveller Manifestoes of the Puritan Revolution*, p. 192. An Act for turning the law into English was passed in November 1650. Cf. pp. 237–41 above, and pp. 259–60 below.

unorthodoxy after the scandal over Mrs Hutchinson led to thirty-eight heads of families leaving the colony.[33]

Milton, who believed in the desirability of discipline and thought that all men ought to join a disciplined congregation, himself appears never to have found a church with which he could happily associate himself. In *Samson Agonistes* the enemy is not a tyrannical individual but the Philistine state itself. Milton rebuked Dr Matthew Griffith as a 'notorious abuser of Scripture' for comparing Charles II to an avenging Samson.[34]

V

The execution of the King raised new problems about the relation of state to people. 'The state at large is King', proclaimed a pamphlet of 1649, possibly written by Hartlib, 'and the King so-called is but its steward or highest officer'.[35] But if there was no king, who was it who controlled that state, and in whose interests?

In the late 1640s there seemed possibilities of the Army using state power for the benefit of the common people. Levellers in the winter of 1648–9 negotiated an Agreement of the People with the generals which the former took more seriously than the latter. William Erbery, who at one point believed that 'the Lord God is coming forth in judgment to turn the earth upside down', soon decided that King and Parliament had been 'the two powers who kept the people of the Lord and the people of the land from their expected and promised freedom. For the Keepers of the Liberties of England were Keepers indeed, and of our liberties from us'. He disliked the version of the Agreement of the People which was under discussion in January 1649 because it 'set up a state religion'. But he believed that 'God appearing in the saints shall punish the kings of the earth upon the earth'. 'The day of God has begun, though the saints have

33. K. O. Kupperman, 'Definitions of Liberty on the Eve of the Civil War: Lord Saye and Sele, Lord Brooke and the American Puritan Colonies', in *Historical Journal*, 32 (1), 1989, pp. 20–25, 32.
34. Milton, *Brief Notes Upon a late Sermon, titl'd, The Fear of God and the King, Preached and since Published by Matthew Griffith, D. D.* (1660), in *Complete Prose Works*, VII, p. 476.
35. S. H., *Rectifying Principle*, quoted by C. V. Wedgwood, *The Trial of Charles I* (1964), pp. 87–8.

been and still are in confusion'.[36] The Army leaders were 'the rod of God' the Ranter Joseph Salmon told them in 1649.[37]

The idea that the saints themselves should take over the government gained strength during and after the Barebones Parliament. As John Tillinghast put it, 'there must be civil and military power in the hands of saints ... before the day of Christ's appearance'. Spittlehouse in 1654 thought a point had been reached at which magistrates should make themselves redundant and allow the state to wither away.[38] Men like Christopher Feake and John Canne committed themselves to support the Rump of the Long Parliament. Only the failure of Parliament to carry out their programme created the Fifth Monarchist movement. For a brief period they placed their hopes in Cromwell. In 1652 Winstanley dedicated his *The Law of Freedom* to Cromwell: 'You have power in your hand . . . . to act for common freedom if you will; I have no power'.[39] 'All the people of God at this day', wrote Tillinghast in 1654, 'look for their redemption to be at hand'.[40] After Cromwell had disappointed their hopes, they were reduced to conspiracy, with little hope of success and little mass support: the desperate revolts of 1657 and 1661 were the consequence.

In 1659–60 hope briefly revived. 'That time is not long', Burrough wrote in May 1659, 'till a good thing may be accomplished by our English Army' – the Army which Margaret Fell had called 'the battle-axe in the hands of the Lord'.[41] Quakers rejoined the Army from which they had been purged, and offered their services to defend the Commonwealth. Feake still hoped in 1659 for 'the breaking forth of the next dispensation', 'an outward visible kingdom' of the saints; but he was in jail at the time of writing, an isolated figure.[42] The outward visible kingdom became Charles II's, and first the Quakers and then other sectaries had to decide that Christ's kingdom was not of this world.

36. Erbery, *Testimony*, pp. 25, 30–35, 40–42, 59, 205, 336.

37. Salmon, *A rout, a rout*, pp. 4–5.

38. *Mr. Tillinghast's Eight Last Sermons* (1655), pp. 60–68; Spittlehouse, *Rome Ruined*, pp. 330–37, 357.

39. Winstanley, op. cit., pp. 275–85, 510.

40. Tillinghast, *The Knowledge of the Times: Or, the resolution of the Question, how long shall it be unto the end of the wonders*, pp. 41–97, 306, 325.

41. M. Fell, *To the General Councill of the Officers of the English Army* (1659).

42. Feake, *A Beam of Light Shining in the Midst of Much Darkness and Confusion* (1659), Sig. A4–8v, a 4v–6v; my *Experience of Defeat*, pp. 57–8, 149–52.

21. *Whose law? and whose liberty?*

===

Liberty and property are as contrary as fire to water.

Sir Robert Filmer, *Observations Upon Aristotle's Politics* (1652), in *Patriarcha and other Political Works* (ed. P. Laslett, Oxford, 1949), p. 223.

The law as it is now constituted serves only to maintain the lawyers and to encourage the rich to oppress the poor.

Cromwell, reported by Edmund Ludlow, *Memoirs*, I, pp. 244–8.

There is one general grievance in the nation: it is the law.

Cromwell, speech to Parliament, 17 September 1656, in *Writings and Speeches*, IV, p. 270.

Property is but the creation of law. Whoever makes the law has the power of appropriating the national wealth. If they did not make the law they would not have the property.

The Poor Man's Guardian, 1835, quoted by E. P. Thompson, *Customs in Common* (1991), p. 176.

The questions asked in the title of this chapter should always be in our minds when we attempt generalizations about seventeenth-century society. Laws were passed by the two houses of Parliament. The House of Lords – far more important than today – was composed of the richest and most powerful landowners in the country. The House of Commons represented 'the people' only in the narrow sense of the word discussed in Chapters 4 and 20: 'people' as opposed to 'the poor'. M.P.s were elected almost exclusively from substantial landed proprietors in their counties, many of them clients of peers. Some M.P.s had more radical ideas about religion and politics than others, but it is impossible to think of them as representing anything other than the landed interest, plus a few wealthy merchants.

The answer to our first question must be that suggested by the fourth epigraph to this chapter: a minority of the upper propertied class makes the law. The answer to the second question is similar: liberty for the ruling class to have secure ownership of its property and guaranteed opportunities for acquiring more. This depends on the effective subordination of the lower classes, by force if necessary, but preferably by convincing them that they have as much freedom as is compatible with the good of society and the will of God. William Penn, both a Quaker and a member of the propertied class, put it succinctly in 1679: 'If we would preserve our government, we must endear it to the people'.[1]

Parliament passed the laws. They were administered by judges and lawyers whose education at the Inns of Court was so expensive as to be beyond the means of any but sons of well-to-do families. Judges had been successful lawyers: their earnings added to their inheritance and made them doubly rich. They were members of the propertied class. Jurors had to own freehold property to the value of £4 *per annum* from 1585 to 1665, when the limit was raised to £20. (The Hales Commission of 1652 had recommended that the property qualification should be raised to 1000 marks, £300 in towns.)[2] So juries were not in general unfavourable to the interests of property. They were drawn from the middling sort of landed freemen, capable of independent views but as anxious as their betters to keep the poor in subjection. They were often excessively lenient towards employers accused of killing their servants: 'a relatively common offence', Sharpe tells us.[3] The names which Bunyan gives to his jurors in *The Pilgrim's Progress* (Mr Blind-man, Mr No-good, Malice, etc.) prepare the reader for the death sentence which is to be passed on Faithful.[4]

Under the Statute of Artificers (1559) one third of all free scholarships to the universities were reserved for gentlemen's sons; others had to pay, as well as for grammar school education.[5] A few fortunate boys might be helped by a patron. 'Benefit of clergy' (see p. 258 below) helped to ensure that there was one law for the rich and another for the poor. In Chapter 26 I discuss some of the problems which affected a poet of genius even in the nineteenth century, who could get his writings published only thanks to the mediation of rich patrons, and who in consequence was not able to write as he wished.

Society was divided into the privileged and the unprivileged. The law

1. Penn, *Address to Protestants*, p. 52.
2. Veall, *The Popular Movement for Law Reform*, pp. 156–9.
3. J. A. Sharpe, *Crime in Seventeenth-century England* (Cambridge U.P., 1983), p. 126.
4. Bunyan, op. cit., pp. 96–7.
5. Tawney, *Tudor Economic Documents*, I, p. 326.

existed to protect property, and to compel the idle lower classes to work. Its penalties were savage – whipping for stealing goods to the value of one penny. Only gentlemen wore swords. Gentlemen might become officers in the army or navy; but no gentleman was conscripted into either force.[6]

Though the law of the state was always the enemy for libertarians, we must distinguish. In the early seventeenth century, with the village community on the way to dissolution, freedom meant escape from the vagabond laws trying to shore up the decaying community.. By the eighteenth century freedom meant getting money, the only way of escaping from the increasing tyranny of wage labour. For this purpose theft, piracy or highway robbery seemed the most promising methods for those without capital, certainly the most exciting and glamorous.

In the sixteenth and seventeenth centuries they made no bones about the class nature of politics. Sir Walter Ralegh had declared that 'the popular state is the government of a state by the choicest sort of people, tending to the public good of all sorts, viz. with due respect to the better, nobler, richer sort'. In England the people (in this sense) 'are no less to be pleased than the peers'. A commonwealth, by contrast, is 'the government of the whole multitude and poorer sort'. He distinguished carefully between 'the middle sort' and the 'base, rascal beggarly sort'.[7] 'Law in a free country', wrote Swift, 'is, or ought to be, the determination of the majority of those who have property in land'.[8] Halfway between Ralegh and Swift the House of Commons in 1640 decisively rejected a suggestion that votes might be given to the poor.[9] In parish elections those who did not pay poor and church rates had no vote. Oliver Cromwell in a speech to Parliament had condemned Fifth Monarchists who 'tell us that liberty and property are not badges of the kingdom of Christ'.[10] Bacon had no doubt that the justices of the peace who administered local justice are 'the body of the gentlemen of England.'[11] Employers and J.P.s – the same

---

6. See pp. 164–8 above.

7. Ralegh, *Works* (1751), I, pp. 3, 5, 9, 125, 206–7; cf. p. 183.

8. Swift, 'Thoughts on Various Subjects', in *Works* (1814), IX, p. 439.

9. My 'The Poor and the People', in *People and Ideas in 17th-century England* (Brighton, 1986), p. 254.

10. Cromwell, *Writings and Speeches* (ed. W. C. Abbott, Harvard U.P., 1937–47), III, pp. 435–40.

11. Bacon to James I, 25 July 1617, in *Works* (1826), p. 474.

thing – effectively controlled wage rates. Those who were licensed to beg had to wear 'some notable badge or token'.[12]

When Parson Haberdyne was ordered by thieves who had just robbed him to preach a sermon in praise of thieves and thieving, he found it easy. 'Thieving is a thing most usual among all men', he declared; and he instanced Jacob and David from the Old Testament, and the vagabond Christ himself from the New Testament. Thieves, he said, were free.[13] George Wither produced an extreme paradox, which by implication said the same thing: his nymph told a rural swain

> Thou art rich in being poor . . .
> He that heaps of wealth collected
>   Should be counted as a slave;
> And the man with few'st things cumb'red
> With the noblest should be numb'red . . .[14]

The law had never been particularly interested in preserving the rights of the poor, beyond their right to live. A statute of 1493 had ordered all beggars unable to work to return forthwith to the hundred where they last lived, 'there to remain and abide'. A statute of 1530 directed against 'the most damnable vice of idleness' ordered all beggars found outside their hundred to be 'sharply beaten and scourged' and then flogged back to their place of settlement. In 1559 the statute of I Edw. VI cap iii, by which idle persons and vagabonds might be made slaves, was revived with additions. These additions included the provision that 'no servant or labourer at the end of his term depart out of the hundred or place where he dwells'.[15] The Statute of Artificers (1563) laid it down that all persons unmarried or under the age of thirty should be liable to forced labour in the craft in which they were trained; every person between the age of twelve and sixty, not being a gentleman born or a university student, should be liable to forced labour in husbandry. Anyone leaving his job without permission should be whipped and treated as a vagabond; anyone employing such a person would be liable to a fine of £5. Forging such a permission was also punished by whipping. The hours of work for day

---

12. Lipson, *Economic History*, III, pp. 255, 262, 457; Beier, *Masterless Men*, pp. 154–5.
13. *A Sermon in Praise of thieves and thievery*, in *Cony-Catchers and Bawdy-Baskets* (ed. G. Salgado, Penguin, 1972), pp. 381–2.
14. Wither, *Fair Virtue, The Mistress of Philarete* (1622), pp. 193–4: 'The nymph's Song'.
15. Tawney and Power, *Tudor Economic Documents* (1953), I, pp. 325–6.

labourers were fixed. The object of course was to keep wages down; any employer paying more than the fixed rate might suffer ten days' imprisonment and a fine of £5, the recipient twenty-one days in prison. Any unmarried woman between the age of seventeen and forty could, at the discretion of any two J.P.s be directed to serve by the year, the week or the day, at such wages as they should allot. There was no poor relief for young women able to work. Vagabonds were branded so that they could be recognized if they offended again – as how could they not? Anyone failing to denounce a beggar was liable to a fine of 10s.[16]

At a time when their social betters were prospering, often flagrantly, the words of the pirate Captain Bellamy must have struck a chord with the less fortunate: he refused 'to be governed by laws which rich men have made for their own security. . . . They rob the poor under cover of law forsooth, and we plunder the rich under the protection of our own courage'.[17]

Marriage for the upper classes was an economic transaction, aimed at increasing the family wealth. It was virtually impossible to marry outside the social class into which you were born. Only a revolutionary like Gerrard Winstanley could contemplate complete freedom of choice in marriage – because he envisaged the abolition of private property.[18] The society was becoming more mobile with the rise of capitalism, but apprenticeship to a trade or profession was restricted to sons of 40/– freeholders, or of gentlemen or merchants. Anyway, it cost money; it was still assumed that children should follow their parents' occupation.[19]

The law indeed was busy abolishing customary liberties. Popular literature reflected the aspirations of the lower classes in this more mobile society: Dick Whittington, Jack of Newbury. Ballads and the popular theatre reflect some of the different values of the unfree. In *Henry VI*, *King Lear* and *Coriolanus* Shakespeare captured the mood of the poor during the hungry years of the 1590s and the following decade. He had an eye for social injustice, though for the benefit of the censor his most forceful passages are given to the mad Lear, speaking for society's outcasts. ('Change places, and handy-dandy, which is the justice, which is the thief?' 'A dog's obeyed in office'. 'Thou rascal beadle, hold thy bloody hand'.) The simple humanity of Lear's 'I am a very foolish, fond old man'

16. Trotter, *Seventeenth-century Life in the Country Parish*, p. 165.
17. *History of the Pyrates*, pp. 585–8.
18. See Chapter 23 below.
19. Tawney and Power, *Tudor Economic Documents*, I, p. 326.

goes oddly with the doctrine of the divine right of kings. Romeo was no doubt besotted with love when he reminded the apothecary that

> The world is not thy friend, nor the world's law;
> The world affords no law to make thee rich.
> Then be not poor, but break it [the law].[20]

He had no doubt that 'the world's law' existed for the benefit of the propertied.

In Massinger's *A New Way to pay old Debts*, printed in 1633:

> When he was rogue Wellborn no man would believe him,
> And then his information could not hurt us;
> But now he is right worshipful again
> Who dares but doubt his testimony? (Act IV, scene 2)

In the same author's *The Duke of Milan* a character is mocked:

> Why, sir, you have been whipt,
> Whipt, signior Graccho; and the whip, I take it,
> Is to a gentleman the greatest trial
> That may be of his patience. (Act III, scene 2)

That John Lilburne, a gentleman's son, was flogged through the streets of London in 1638 for distributing illegal literature was a terrible blow to his pride: henceforth, despite his radicalism, in all his litigation he invariably stressed the fact that he was a gentleman. No murderer described as a gentleman was executed. In 1618 Sir Henry Wotton was shocked to find that the Venetian republic failed to observe class distinctions in imposing punishments.[21] Clarendon made it a point of criticism of the Commonwealth's High Court of Justice that it did away with 'distinction of quality' in capital cases, and made 'the greatest lord and the meanest peasant undergo the same judicatory and forms of trial'.[22] Some might think this was to the credit of the Commonwealth.

Peacham, in his *Complete Gentleman* (1634), had laid it down that 'noble or gentlemen ought to be preferred in fees, honours, offices and other dignities of command and government before the common people ... We ought to give credit to a nobleman or gentleman before any of

20. *Romeo and Juliet*, Act V, scene i.
21. L. P. Smith, *Life and Letters of Sir Henry Wotton* (1907), I, p. 156.
22. Clarendon, *History of the Rebellion*, IV, p. 500.

the inferior sort'. He ought to be tried by others of the same rank as himself, and in case of conviction 'his punishment ought to be more favourable and honourable'. 'His imprisonment ought not to be in base manner, or so strict as others''.[23] In the play *How a man may choose a good wife from a bad* (1602), Young Master Arthur says

> Now, lead me to what prison you think best:
> Yet, use me well, I am a gentleman.[24]

In 1575 three men were sentenced to be hanged for having no means of livelihood.[25] We recall the words which Shakespeare put into the mouths of Kett and his rebels in *Henry VI*, Part II: 'Because they cannot read thou hast hanged them' (Act IV, scene 7). By then this traditional protection for the clergy had become a shield for the propertied. Many of Kett's rebels' arguments suggest that they are irresponsible agitators; but this accusation is a fair statement of the cultural reasons for resentment of class privilege. Anyone who was literate could escape hanging for felony by reading the 'neck-verse' from the Bible. This was in effect a class distinction; cf. 'Let the magistrates be labouring men' (ibid., IV, 2) – a remark which Shakespeare may well have overheard in the starvation- and riot-ridden 1590s. That the Cade scenes are such a curious medley of farcical caricature and truthful observation no doubt tells us something about the censorship and the need for caution.

Burton in his *Anatomy of Melancholy* anticipates *The Beggar's Opera* by telling us that 'a poor sheep-stealer is hanged for stealing of victuals, compelled peradventure by necessity (cold and hunger); but a great man in office may securely rob whole provinces' and be rewarded.[26] Burton rejected the commonly-held view that 'Baseness of birth is a great disparagement to some men, especially if they be wealthy'. He took eight pages to prove the contrary, concluding 'To be base by birth, meanly born, is no such disparagement'.[27] Francis Osborn made a similar point a generation later: 'when a felony or murder is committed, the next poor homes are ordinarily searched.'[28]

23. Op. cit. (1906 reprint, Oxford U.P.), pp. 13–14.
24. Op. cit., Act V, scene 2 (in *Old English Drama*, 1825), I.
25. Osborne, *Justices of the Peace*, p. 24.
26. Burton, op. çit. (Everyman ed.), I, p. 62; cf. p. 51: 'magistrates make laws against thieves and are the veriest thieves themselves'.
27. Ibid., II, pp. 136–44.
28. Osborn, *Essays*, p. 35, in *Works* (1722), I.

In 1649 the anonymous author of *Tyranipocrit Discovered* complained that 'rich, artificial thieves . . . make themselves thieves by Act of Parliament. . . . All that they rob and steal is their own, by so good right as the lion has to the whole hart. They . . . hang a poor man if he do steal, when they have wrongfully taken from him all his maintenance' – by enclosure, presumably.[29] The Quaker James Nayler declared that the law 'as it is now used, is scarce serviceable for any other end but for the envious man who hath much money to revenge himself of his poor neighbours'.[30]

William Tomlinson in 1657 denounced hanging for theft – 'even a pair of shoes, or stockings, or a shirt'. He registered the novelty of such a law by asking 'How will this stink in the nostrils of the ages following?' Remarkably, he suggested that the thief should make restitution by labour: hanging does his victim no good. 'The thief is as dear to [the Lord] as the covetous man who is an idolator'. And he asked 'the high and lofty in the earth' – 'Are you sure . . . the greatness of your family' was not built upon 'tyranny, cruelty, oppression, covetousness, fraud and injury?' 'What do you think are those Mountains and Hills that are to be cast down, and those Valleys that are to be born up?'[31]

Both Samuel Daniel and Fulke Greville argued that the law ought to be in a language comprehensible to countrymen, not in French or Latin; just as church services were now in English. Shakespeare made Jack Cade say that the fact that Lord Saye could speak French was evidence that he was a traitor. The complexity and incomprehensibility of English law was captured by the chorus of Bashas in Fulke Greville's *Mustapha*. Laws are

> As sophistries of every Common-weale;
> Or rather nets, which people do ask leave
> That they, to catch their freedoms in, may weave
> And still add more unto their Sultan's power.[32]

But the play was not published, and dealt with oriental tyranny only.

The substitution of the rule of a Parliament composed of the men of property for the rule of a king did not make much difference to those who had no property. In 1655 Edward Burrough told Oliver Cromwell

---

29. Op. cit., pp. 99, 108.
30. Nayler, *A Few Words* . . . (n.d., quoted in my *Experience of Defeat*), p. 139.
31. W.T., *Seven Particulars*, pp. 11, 17, 20–22.
32. Greville, *Mustapha*, First Chorus of Bashas, in *Poems and Dramas* (Edinburgh, 1938, II, p. 75).

that 'the same laws stand still in force by which tyranny and oppression is
acted. . . . You are not ignorant of the grievous cry of the poor, under the
burden of oppression laid upon them by your laws' – and he spoke of
bribery, of the law being concealed in unknown languages.[33] In the following year a letter from another Quaker to Chief-Justice Glynn began: 'We
are free men of England, free born; our rights and liberties are according
to law and ought to be defended by it'. But they were not. Like Levellers
and other radicals, George Fox called for the law to be in English, and for
'all the law books in the nation' to 'be thrown away . . . that everyone
may know the law in short and plain words'. Legal documents should be
simplified and shortened.[34] A rich man, said Fox, is 'the greatest thief',
since he got his wealth 'by cozening and cheating. . . . And if the thief steal
it . . . then thou hangest thy fellow creatures contrary to the law of
God'.[35] With less sense of outrage, Robert Burton had said 'magistrates
make laws against thieves, and are the veriest thieves themselves'. Wither
agreed that laws 'catch small thieves, and let the great ones go'.[36] At his
trial in 1649 Lilburne told the jury that they were judges of law as well as
of fact. 'You that call yourselves judges of the law are no more but
Norman intruders'. If the jury so decided, he continued, judges were 'no
more but cyphers, to pronounce their verdict'.[37] (Jeremy Bentham's comment is appropriate here. The Saxon system of local courts and juries, he
said, 'was far too favourable to justice to be endured by lawyers', and was
replaced by centralized courts whose business was conducted in a language
unknown to most of the inhabitants. 'In British India', he added sardon-
ically, 'this state of affairs may be conceivable'.[38])

   'The best laws that England hath', wrote Gerrard Winstanley, 'are
yoaks and manicles, tying one sort of people to be slaves to another'.[39]
Levellers opposed all class privileges at law, whether founded on historical
precedent or not. The journalist Marchamont Nedham in his royalist
phase said of the Levellers that 'by placing the supreme power of making
and repealing laws in the people' they 'aim to establish a mere popular

33. Burrough, op. cit., pp. 97–8.
34. My *Experience of Defeat*, pp. 154–6.
35. Fox, *Newes Coming up out of the North* (1654), p. 11. This tract was not reprinted
in Fox's *Gospel-Truth Demonstrated in a Collection of Doctrinal Books* (1706).
36. Burton, *Anatomy of Melancholy*, I, p. 51; cf. pp. 83–5; Wither, *Poems* (reprint of
1622 edition, n.d.), II, p. 174, Emblem 18.
37. *The Tryall of Lt. Col. John Lilburne* (2nd ed., 1710), pp. 18, 98, 106–8, 126.
38. Bentham, *Works* (1842), II, pp. 151–2, V, p. 48.
39. Sabine, op. cit., p. 303.

tyranny . . . to the destruction of our laws and liberties'.[40] The contrast between 'the people' and '*our* laws and liberties' is instructive. But the local view of the reasonableness of the law might on occasion be closer to that of smugglers and poachers than to that of magistrates. Joan Kent suggests that village constables might be 'prevented or deterred from fulfilling their police duties by the defiance which they encountered', not only from offenders but sometimes also from fellow villagers.[41] Juries' opinions of what was right and what wrong might differ from the views of judges, who 'are commonly gentlemen by birth and have had an honourable education'.[42] But from 1495 onwards statutes provided for summary punishment of vagrants without trial by jury, Magna Carta notwithstanding. Village constables and J.P.s could put vagrants in the stocks for three days, or brand them, on their own authority. From 1579 suspect vagabonds in London could be judged summarily in Bridewell.[43]

Juries often were reluctant to convict where a death sentence was involved: stolen goods might be grossly undervalued so as to avoid this.[44] In 1676 Sir Roger North complained that Cumberland juries (mainly yeomen) always seemed to favour 'tenant-right, . . . a customary estate not unlike our copyhold'. The gentry could only change this by serving on the common juries themselves.[45] In 1651 Thomas Hobbes said that 'the definition of INJUSTICE is no other than *the not performance of covenant*'. Justice is the keeping of contracts: no more and no less.[46]

After the seventeenth-century revolution there was a growing consensus among those who mattered in favour of Locke's dictum 'Government has no other end but the preservation of property'.[47] Harrington had made the balance of property the basis of all government. Blackstone lent his great authority to the statement that 'Nothing so

---

40. Nedham, *A Plea for the King and Kingdome* (1648), pp. 24–5.
41. J. R. Kent, *The English Village Constable, 1580–1642* (Oxford U.P., 1986), p. 276. Cf. Chapters 7 and 8 above, for poachers and smugglers.
42. Henry Parker, *A Letter of due censure . . . to Lt. Col. John Lilburne* (1650), quoted by D. Veall, *The Popular Movement for Law Reform, 1640–1660* (Oxford U.P., 1970), pp. 156–90.
43. Beier, *Masterless Men*, pp. 156–8.
44. Keith Wrightson, *English Society, 1580–1680* (1982), pp. 156–8. For an example see Richard Gough, *The History of Myddle* (Firle, Sussex, 1979), p. 78.
45. Quoted by M. Campbell, *The English Yeoman*, p. 153.
46. Hobbes, *Leviathan* (Everyman ed.), p. 185.
47. Locke, *Second Treatise of Governement* (1690), sections 85 and 94.

generally strikes the imagination and engages the affections of mankind as the rights of property'.[48] In defence of private property, offences liable to capital sentence increased from about fifty to two hundred between 1688 and 1820 – one of the bloodiest criminal codes in Europe.[49] In 1769 the death sentence was decreed for food rioters; enclosure rioters were liable to transportation.[50]

'For the gentry', Fletcher sums up, the law after 1660 'became more certainly than ever . . . the means of their purchase upon power and the facilities of social life'. Their control 'was confirmed, through the panoply of the law, on the people'. The *idea* of the rule of law was essential to the reality of gentry hegemony. The game laws were more harshly enforced after 1660; summary convictions for poaching, gleaning, wood-gathering, were more frequent and more severe. Those who continued to glean 'according to the custom in harvest-time', or to collect wood, were liable to meet with physical violence from landlords.[51] As ever more statutes threatened death for offences against property, the severity of the law could be mitigated by pardons. Douglas Hay has shown how the law was manipulated by the 'enormous discretion given to men of big property'. They could decide when an example of severity was needed, and alternatively when gracious clemency might be more effective in preserving respect for the law by preventing it appearing to be a system of naked class rule.[52]

A speech made by the second Duke of Buckingham in the House of Lords in 1675 illustrates the fact that some of England's rulers after the revolutionary 1640s and 1650s appreciated that concessions to men of small property were now necessary. 'There is a thing called Property (whatever some men may think) that the people of England are fondest of'. But property can never be securely protected 'without an indulgence

48. Blackstone, *Commentaries on the Laws of England* (12th ed., 1793–5), II, p. 2. 'Mankind' perhaps begs a few questions.
49. Sir Leon Radzinowicz, *A History of the English Criminal Law and its Administration from 1750* (1948–68), I, p. 4.
50. D. Hay, 'Property, Authority and the Criminal Law', in *Albion's Fatal Tree*, p. 21. See E. P. Thompson, ibid., pp. 255–344, for a sample of letters against the law written by free individuals from the classes usually inarticulate.
51. *Order and Disorder in Early Modern England* (ed. A. Fletcher, Cambridge U.P., 1985), p. 114; cf. D. E. Underdown, 'The Taming of the Scold', ibid., p. 126, and Chapter 7 above.
52. Hay, 'Poaching and the Game Laws on Cannock Chase', in *Albion's Fatal Tree*, pp. 22, 38, 42, 48, 51.

to all protestant dissenters'.[53] Even in this speech the fact that property is the main concern of the law is not forgotten, and 'the people of England' excludes those who are so unfortunate as to have no property.

Gulliver's account of how things were done in the land of the wise Houyhnhnms was only a mild caricature of practice in the England of Swift's day. 'The judge first sends to sound the disposition of those in power; after which he can easily hang or save the criminal, strictly preserving all the forms of law'. There were no terms in the Houyhnhnm language into which the words 'power, government, war, law, punishment' could be translated. 'A decree of the general assembly . . . is expressed' by a word 'which signifies an exhortation; . . . they have no conception how a rational creature can be compelled, but only advised, or exhorted'.[54]

Fielding has some ironical observations about liberty and the law in *Amelia*. Mr Bondman the bailiff, discussing a man who writes about 'liberty and freedom, and about the constitution of England', remarks 'I am all for liberty'. To the retort, 'I thought you had lived by depriving men of their liberty', Mr Bondman replies, 'That's another matter, . . . all according to law and in the way of business'. For him liberty meant the right to have a man arrested for non-payment of lawful debts.[55] Samuel Johnson, writing of the bravery of the English common soldier, asked 'What has the English more than the French soldier? Property they are both commonly without. Liberty is, to the lowest rank of every nation, little more than the choice of working or starving. . . . The English soldier seldom has his head very full of the constitution. . . . They who complain, in peace, of the insolence of the populace, must remember that their insolence in peace is bravery in war'.[56] Chatterton expressed himself more robustly:

> Engage, ye Britons, in the glorious task . . .
> Assert your rights, remonstrate with the throne;
> Insist on liberty, and that alone.
> Break every link of slavery's hateful chain.[57]

53. Quoted by Howard Nenner, *By Colour of Law: Legal Culture and Constitutional Politics in England, 1660–1689* (Chicago U.P., 1977), p. 37.
54. Swift, *Gulliver's Travels*, Part IV, Chapters IV, V and X.
55. Fielding, *Amelia*, Book VIII, Chapter II.
56. Johnson 'The Bravery of the English Common Soldiers', in *Prose and Poetry* (ed. Mona Wilson, 1950), pp. 626–7.
57. Chatterton, *Complete Poetical Works* (ed. H. D. Roberts, Muses' Library, 1906), I, pp. 158 ('Resignation') and 188 ('An Elegy on the . . . death of William Beckford').

Swift's suggestion that the children of the Irish should be served up at the dinner tables of the English gentry was a logical conclusion from the view that Irish natives were not really human. Goldsmith summed up the ballads' view of liberty and law – after the law had won. The lines are familiar, but that perhaps makes a point.

> Even liberty itself is bartered here.
> At gold's superior charms all freedom flies.
> The needy sell it, and the rich man buys. . . .
> Laws grind the poor and rich men make the law. . . .
> That independence Britons prize too high
> Keeps man from man, and breaks the social tie. . . .
> [They] call it freedom when themselves are free.

It is not for us to throw stones: in Great Britain's welfare state racialism is still with us, homeless men and women still have to live rough, and New Age travellers are harried from pillar to post. But since we have lost our empire, pauper children are no longer shipped off to Commonwealth countries, and no one today congratulates travellers or the homeless on their freedom. Progress, I suppose.

22. 'Away with Lawyers!'

That general and inbred hatred which still dwells in our common people against both our Laws and Lawyers.

John Hare, *Plain English* (1647), in *Harleian Miscellany* (1812), IX, p. 91.

Take away the name and power of thine and mine, or make and. maintain an equality of all such of God's creatures as God hath given for the use and benefit of mankind, and then laws and lawyers would be superfluous and needless.

[Anon.], *Tyranipocrit Discovered* (ed. A. Hopton, n.d., ?1991), p. 50. First published 1649.

To the grave and learned writers of Histories my advice is, that they meddle not with any point or secret of any Art or science, especially with the lawes of this realm, before they confer with some learned in that profession.

Sir Edward Coke, *Reports*, III (1619), Sig. D 2.

'"Woe be to you, lawyers", saith Christ (Luke 12:46) ... Ye lade men with burdens which they are not able to bear. Ye have taken away the key of knowledge'. Those words were written by William Tyndale in *The Obedience of a Christian Man*.[1] The unpopularity of lawyers became explicit during the English Revolution. Robert Burton quoted Plato to the effect that to have many lawyers 'is a manifest sign of a distempered melancholy state'. Burton himself thought that lawyers (together with physicians and surgeons) ought to be paid by the state, and not to take fees.[2] Lawyers would have been banned from More's Utopia. An anonymous tract of 1648, written on behalf of 'the plaine-men of England, Against the Rich and Mightie', called lawyers 'manifest perverters of justice, . . . the vilest of men and greatest abusers of mankind', who made

---

1. Tyndale, *Doctrinal Treatises*, p. 245. See p. 180 above.
2. Burton, *Anatomy of Melancholy*, I, p. 103.

it 'vain for any plain honest mean man to expect justice against any sort of . . . rich and wealthy men'.[3] Legal training was so expensive that only sons of the rich could afford it: 'sons of the best or better sort of gentlemen of all the shires of England . . . of three descents at least'.[4] In 1648 John Cook warned his fellow lawyers that 'there is a great storm arising in this kingdom against us'. 'Every man complains of the horrible delays in matters of justice. . . . The remedy is worse than the disease. . . . A man must spend above £10 to recover £5'.[5] 'The price of right is too high for a poor man', John Warr added; 'the law becomes anything or nothing, at the courtesy of great men, and is bended by them like a twig'. It 'entangles the small flies and dismisseth the great'. 'Freedom hath no voice here'.[6]

Quakers joined in this denunciation of lawyers and of the law. 'Away with lawyers', cried Fox with divine simplicity. 'Who are greater liars than the lawyers?' asked Richard Farnworth. Fox, Burrough and many others opposed death sentences for theft, whether of money or cattle.[7] The young John Milton, listening to lawyers 'shouting at each other' in 'a jargon which one might well take for some Red Indian dialect, or even no human speech at all', wondered 'whether men who had neither a human tongue nor human speech could have any human feelings either'. 'Sacred justice . . . cannot speak our language'. Milton quotes Boccalini to the effect that study of the law was not 'a liberal art but . . . a trade and a really mechanical art, brought into the world to harass the human race'.[8] Lodowick Muggleton accepted that 'the poor . . . can have no law at all, though his cause be ever so just, no judge will hear him, nor no lawyer will give him any counsel, except he hath monies in his hand; nor no judge will do the poor any justice, except he go in the way of the law,

---

3. Burton, *Anatomy of Melancholy*, I, pp. 83–5, 103–4; [Anon.], *Englands Troublers Troubled*, pp. 2–3.
4. John Stow, *Annales or a General Chronicle of England* (1631), pp. 1068–73; cf. Tawney and Power, *Tudor Economic Documents*, I, pp. 326–7 on the social and political privileges of the upper classes.
5. Cook, *Unum Necessarium: Or, the Poore Mans Case*, p. 66.
6. Warr, *The Corruption and Deficiency of the Laws of England* (1649), in *Harleian Miscellany* (1745), III, pp. 240–49. Cf. Walter Carey, *The Present State of England* (1627), ibid., pp. 197–204.
7. Fox, *A Warning from the Lord* (1654), p. 24; *Several Papers Given Forth* (1660), pp. 32–3; Farnworth, *The Generall Good of all People* (1653), p. 40. Cf. my *Experience of Defeat*, pp. 153–7.
8. Milton, *Complete Prose Works*, I, pp. 301, 468.

and that the poor cannot do'. 'So that if the birthright of the poor be ever so great or just, it must be lost for want of monies to fee lawyers'. Although 'the government of this world hath brought a necessity of the use of lawyers', none of the saints should enter that profession. Lawyers will be condemned to hell in the last judgement. The 169th Song in *Divine Songs of the Muggletonians* rejoices that lawyers 'are damned without mercy to all eternity' – a sentence which Milton reserved for bishops.[9] Thomas Tomkinson, a very early convert, rejoiced that the prophets Reeve and Muggleton 'have brought us from bondage'; the faithful would 'sing songs of praises for this liberty'. They did. 'Freedom, freedom, freedom's mine', sang George Hermitage. When William Cates saw the writings of Reeve and Muggleton 'Freedom's sword struck me with awe'.[10]

Liberty of publishing in the 1640s let loose a tirade of abuse against the law and lawyers. Lawyers are 'the vilest of men, and greatest abusers of mankind', 'manifest perverters of justice, and corrupters of all places'. 'It is vain for any plain honest mean man to expect any reason, equity or justice against any sort of you rich and wealthy men'.[11]

William Cole in 1659 summed up in an impassioned plea to Parliament to reform the laws before it was too late. 'The major part of the laws made in this nation are founded on principles of tyranny, fallacy and oppression for the benefit of those that made them' – kings and lords of manors and 'other great officers who were the King's creatures' – so that 'not only tenants but other poor that live near them must run, and go, and work and obey them as they shall please to command them'. At present judges are bribed, lawyers obtain vast wealth, all cases have to be tried in London, though 'countrymen, clothiers, weavers etc. are most competent judges . . . of those callings they live on'. There should be local courts, with no appeal beyond the county. 'Monarchy is an absolute antagonist to a free state', and so are all the laws and rules made by monarchs. Parliament must undertake wide-ranging reforms, following the example of the Dutch after establishing their republic. 'From a poor

9. Muggleton, *Acts of the Witnesses of the Spirit*, in *Works of Reeve and Muggleton* (1832), III, pp. 112–13; Milton, *Of Reformation* (1641), in *Complete Prose Works*, I, pp. 116–17.

10. *Divine Songs of the Muggletonians* (1829), III, pp. 441, 82, 346, 366–7, 466–71; Milton, *Of Reformation* (1641), in *Complete Prose Works*, I, pp. 116–17.

11. [Anon.], *Englands Troublers Troubled, Or the just Resolutions of the plaine-men of England Against the Rich and Mightie* (1648), pp. 2–6.

miserable people, a distressed state, they are now become potent, rich and dreadful'. For 'God is pulling down the high and mighty, is discovering the wickedness of men in power, hath, most miraculously slain the glory of princes. . . . I do not altogether despair that before I die I may see the Inns of Court, of dens of thieves, converted into hospitals, which were a rare piece of justice: that so as they formerly have immured those that robbed the poor of houses, so they may, at last, preserve the poor themselves'.[12] The Inns of Court, like the poor, are still with us.

Lawyers were forbidden to practise in Massachusetts in its early days.[13] But in England, alas, 'the real victors of the civil wars were the lawyers' – victorious both over royal absolutism and over radical reformers.[14] Peacham in *The Beggar's Opera* sums up:

> A fox may steal your hens, sir,
> A whore your health and pence, sir,
> Your daughter rob your chest, sir,
> Your wife may steal your rest, sir,
>   A thief your goods and plate.
> But this is all but picking,
> With rest, peace, chest and chicken;
> It ever was decreed, sir,
> If lawyer's hand is fee'd sir,
>   He steals your whole estate.

Jenny Diver agrees:

> The gamesters and lawyers are jugglers alike,
>   If they meddle your all is in danger:
> Like gypsies, if once they can finger a souse,
> Your pockets they pick, and they pilfer your house,
>   And give your estate to a stranger.
> (Act I, scene ix; Act II, scene v)

Samuel Butler, as so often, summed up the cynicism of the radicals for restoration wits in his Character of a Lawyer. He is 'a retailer of justice that uses false lights, false weights and false measures. He measures right and wrong by his retaining fee'.[15] But the last word should go to William

12. Cole, op. cit., in *Harleian Miscellany*, IV, pp. 305–12.
13. Stuart E. Prall, *The Agitation for Law Reform during the Puritan Revolution* (The Hague, 1966), p. 36. They were forbidden in Winstanley's ideal commonwealth too. See p. 290 below.
14. Ogilvie, *The King's Government*, p. 168.
15. In *Character Writings of the Seventeenth Century* (ed. H. Morley, 1891), p. 406.

Manning, a self-educated American farmer writing much later: 'From their professions and interest lawyers are the most dangerous to liberty and the least to be trusted of any profession whatsoever'.[16]

16. *The Key of Liberty: The Life and Democratic Writings of William Manning, 'A Laborer', 1747–1814* (eds. Michael Merrill and Sean Wilentz, Harvard U.P., 1993), p. 141.

VI. Aftermath

23. Gerrard Winstanley:
The Law of Freedom[1]

Liberty cannot be provided for in a general sense if property be preserved.

Commissary-General Ireton in the Putney Debates in the Army Council (29 October 1647), in *Puritanism and Liberty* (ed. A. S. P. Woodhouse, Everyman ed., 1992), p. 73.

There cannot be a universal liberty till this universal community be established.

Winstanley, *The New Law of Righteousness* (January 1648–9), *Works of Gerrard Winstanley* (ed. G. H. Sabine, Cornell U.P., 1941), p. 199.

Freedom is Christ in you and Christ among you.

Winstanley, *A Watchword to the City of London and the Army* (August 1649), ibid., p. 316.

> Freedom is the mark, at which all men should aime
> But what true freedom is, few men doth know by name,
> But now a light is ris, and nere shall fall
> How every man by name, shall freedom call.

Winstanley, *Englands Spirit Unfoulded* (1650) (ed. G. E. Aylmer), in *Past and Present*, 40, 1968.

The Digger movement appeared at the crisis of the English Revolution. The introductory letter to *The New Law of Righteousness*, the tract in which Winstanley announced his communist programme, was dated four

1. For the purposes of this chapter I have concentrated on secular aspects of Winstanley's ideas. Their basis, however, was in contemporary radical theology. I have tried to show this in my 'The Religion of Gerrard Winstanley', in *Religion and Politics in 17th-century England* (Brighton, 1986). Cf. esp. pp. 230–33 for his fusion of the theory of the Norman Yoke and his theory of communism with his theology.

days before the execution of Charles I. A fortnight before the digging started the Act of 17 March 1649 abolished kingship; two months later (19 May) another Act declared England to be a commonwealth and free state. Anything seemed possible, including the Second Coming of Jesus Christ.

Twenty-five years ago Sir Keith Thomas said that 'the whole Digger movement can be plausibly regarded as the culmination of a century of unauthorized encroachment upon the forests and wastes by squatters and local commoners, pushed on by land shortage and the pressure of population.'[2] These are by now familiar to us. But Winstanley himself was no vagabond and the Diggers denied being vagrants. The son of a Lancashire merchant, Winstanley had been apprenticed to a London clothier. 'Thou City of London', he wrote in August 1649, 'I am one of thy sons by freedom'.[3] Ruined by the interruption of trade between Lancashire and the capital during the civil war, Winstanley withdrew to his wife's county of Surrey. Even there, 'by the burden of taxes and much free-quarter' he 'found the burden heavier than I could bear'. Most of the members of his commune seem to have been local householders.[4] Winstanley's stress is always on arrangements for settled communal living.

The word 'freedom' resounds throughout Winstanley's writings. As early as 1648 he had believed that 'liberty is not far'.[5] He headed his address to the City in *A Watchword to the City of London and the Army* (August, 1649) 'Freedom and Peace desired'. He did not use the word 'liberty' in the sense which Ireton and most of the Parliamentarian leaders used it – as equivalent to security for property (see first epigraph to this chapter).

Winstanley shared characteristics which were attributed to those 'brave assertors of liberty', pirates: class-consciousness, anti-clericalism.[6] It may be that his superb prose gave expression to the half-formed ideas of the inarticulate men and women whose outlook I have been fumbling to recapture in this book – those whom Sir Keith Thomas describes. For such men and women 'the law' was opposed to their 'freedom'.

---

2. Thomas, 'Another Digger Broadside', in *Past and Present*, 42 (1969), p. 58.

3. *A Watchword to the City of London*, Sabine, p. 315.

4. Ibid., pp. 348, 434. The same seems to have been true of the Digger colony at Iver, one of the ten or so which sprang up under the influence of Winstanley's Surrey commune (Thomas, op. cit., pp. 60–61).

5. Winstanley, *The Saints Paradise* (1648), pp. 22–3, 62–3.

6. My *Writing and Revolution*, pp. 115–16. See Chapter 9 above.

Winstanley spoke for those that 'hitherto have had no land and have been forced to rob or steal through poverty; hereafter let them quietly enjoy land to work upon, that everyone may enjoy the benefit of his creation, and eat his bread with the sweat of his own brow'. 'Beggary and oppression shall be done away'. Like Bunyan, Winstanley sympathized deeply with the plight of the landless poor. Private property, he complained, 'hath made laws to hang those that did steal: it tempts people to do an evil action, and then kills them for doing of it'.[7] 'If they beg, they whip them by their law for vagrants; if they steal they hang them'. Yet the authorities will not suffer the poor 'to plant the commons for a livelihood' – as the Diggers tried to do on St George's Hill.[8]

Winstanley insisted that he did not get his ideas from books or from other people. He says that an inner voice told him that 'the earth shall be made a common treasury of livelihood to whole mankind, without respect of persons'. We may interpret that to mean that he had reached this conclusion after thinking about the matter deeply; and he realized that he must declare this message 'all abroad', 'for action is the life of all, and if thou dost not act thou dost nothing'.[9] He then discovered that 'divers' others had been thinking along similar lines. Even when soldiers came to destroy the Digger settlement in 1650, most of them, Winstanley tells us, were friendly and sympathetic. One of them passed the Diggers twelve pence to buy a drink.[10]

Winstanley listed four current versions of 'freedom' which were not his concern:

(i) 'Free use of trading', against monopolies – i.e. freedom for merchants.

(ii) Freedom of conscience – religious freedom.

(iii) Freedom from matrimonial regulations – Ranter freedom.

(iv) Absolute freedom of property, with no regard for customary limitations – which big landlords had gained by the abolition of feudal tenures in 1646.[11]

---

7. Sabine, pp. 201, 220; cf. p. 634 (*More Light Shining in Buckinghamshire*, March 1649) and 650 (*A Declaration from Wellingborough*, March, 1650).

8. Sabine, pp. 435, 387.

9. *A Watchword*, Sabine, p. 315; cf. Winstanley's Preface to *Several Pieces Gathered into one volume*, in Winstanley, *The Law of Freedom and other Writings* (Cambridge U.P., 1983), pp. 155–7.

10. *A New Yeers Gift for the Parliament and Armie* (January, 1650), Sabine, pp. 168, 208–9.

11. *The Law of Freedom*, Sabine, p. 519.

Winstanley does not say anything about constitutional liberty, the right to vote, which others in the seventeenth century thought important, as well as historians later. In *The Law of Freedom* he denounces the control of Parliament by landlords and freeholders: 'all inferior people were neither to choose nor to be chosen'.[12] But what was the alternative, given an uneducated population, influenced by their landlords and their clergy? The Levellers, for instance, were democrats in principle: they wanted reforms, greater equality, representative government. But manhood suffrage might well lead to a return of the King. How could the radicals find an electorate which would agree with them? Milton would have liked to see an electorate composed of 'good' members of the middle class; but definition was difficult. Supporters of the Good Old Cause, perhaps? But how are they to be identified? In practice the Army would intervene to prevent the King being brought back; but by the 1650s the Army was no longer a democratic body; it had been purged of revolutionaries and professionalized.

Winstanley came to see the question in terms which James Harrington would elaborate into a political theory. If power went with property, as Harrington argued, then the balance of property had to be changed. Winstanley and Harrington thought that the balance had shifted from big landowners to men of smaller property. But still of *property*. Winstanley could only hope to see a really democratic assembly, elected by manhood suffrage, when property belonged to *all*, not just to a rich minority. This meant a profound social revolution, including the overthrow of the laws of the Norman conquerors.[13] Winstanley's anonymous contemporary, the author of *Tyranipocrit Discovered*, made the point: 'Take away the name and power of thine and mine, or make and maintain an equality of all such of God's creatures as God hath given for the use and benefit of mankind, and then laws and lawyers would be superfluous and needless'.[14]

Freedom is Winstanley's continuing theme. But he expected a different sort of freedom to emerge after the civil war, a freedom based on equality. He recalled St James's Epistle: 'Whoso looketh into the perfect law of liberty and continueth therein, he being not a forgetful hearer but a doer

---

12. Ibid., pp. 585–6.
13. Thompson, *Witness against the Beast*, p. 200.
14. *An Intelligencer to the Reformers*, in *Tyranipocrit Discovered* (ed. A. Hopton), p. 50. The reference to creatures given 'for the use and benefit of mankind' is a thrust against enclosers and enclosing laws' which tried to confine this benefit to the rich.

of the work, this man shall be blessed in his deed. . . . So speak ye, and so do, as they that shall be judged by the law of liberty' (I. 25, II. 12).

Many years ago Russell Smith suggested that Harrington's theories might owe a debt to Winstanley.[15] No one has yet taken this seriously enough. A mysterious character, Richard Goodgroom, who signed one of the Digger manifestoes in April 1649 (*The True Levellers' Standard Advanced*) and was one of several Diggers sued for damages at Kingston Court of Record under the name of Abraham Pennard,[16] is generally taken to be the R.G. who in 1656 published a proto-Harringtonian tract, *A Copy of a Letter* – before Harrington had published anything. Historians have assumed that Goodgroom had seen Harrington's *Oceana* in manuscript, though no one has explained his access to it. It is much more likely that he got his ideas from Winstanley, whom he must have known well. Further confusion has been caused by the fact that the tract, which the author said was written two years before it was published, is dated from Waterford in Ireland. There is no other evidence that Goodgroom was ever in that country. But the object may have been to confuse.

As Tawney long ago demonstrated, Ralegh, Bacon and many others had put forward something like Harrington's historical account half a century earlier. One possibility is that Goodgroom saw the applicability of Winstanley's class analysis to this line of thought, but used it for different social purposes; and that this gave Harrington the basis for *Oceana*, published (according to R.G.) two years after *A Copy of a Letter* had been written. Goodgroom later became a Fifth Monarchist and was engaged in plots in 1656 and after the restoration, when he was often in jail. Pocock is anxious to stress differences between 'R.G.' and Harrington; 'R.G.' appears to be closer to Winstanley than to Harrington in his emphasis on market relations and the power of money.[17] The question is still open.

Winstanley's solutions came to be revolutionary rather than reformist. Looking round at the society in which he lived, he concluded that private property in land and the wage-labour system must be abolished. 'No true freedom can be established for England's peace . . . but such a one as hath respect to the poor as well as the rich'. 'Without exception, all sorts of people in the land are to have freedom', not just 'the gentry and clergy'.

15. H. F. Russell Smith, *James Harrington and his Oceana* (Cambridge U.P., 1914).
16. Sabine, pp. 17–18, 266.
17. *The Political Works of James Harrington* (ed. J. G. A. Pocock, Cambridge U.P., 1977), pp. 58–60.

'Let Israel go free', Winstanley cried; he thought – anticipating Marx – that true freedom was possible only if wage labour was abolished. 'Israel shall neither give hire nor take hire'.[18]

In January 1649, the month in which Charles I was executed, Winstanley declared to 'all labourers or such as are called poor people, that they shall not dare to work for hire for any landlord ... He that works for another, either for wages or to pay him rent, works unrighteously: but they that are resolved to work and eat together, making the earth a common treasury, doth join hands with Christ to lift up the creation from bondage, and restores all things from the curse'.[19]

Existing English law, Winstanley thought, defended the 'murder and theft' by which the Norman invaders, ancestors of the present lords of manors, had stolen the land from the conquered people of England. (The fact that to have 'come over with the Conqueror' was the hallmark of aristocracy makes Winstanley's point). More recently, big landowners had benefited enormously by the abolition of feudal tenures and the Court of Wards in 1646; Parliament persistently refused to give equivalent benefits to small proprietors by abolishing copyhold. The law remained 'the strength, life and marrow of the kingly power, upholding the conquest still, hedging some into the earth, hedging out others, ... which is contrary to the law of righteousness. ... Truly most laws are but to enslave the poor to the rich'.[20]

Anthony Ascham summed up the Digger position, not totally unfairly, as maintaining that 'the law enslaves one sort of people to another. The clergy and gentry have got their freedom, but the common people are still servants to work for the other'.[21] Winstanley believed, or hoped, that 'kingly lordly conquering government is cast out of England by the victory of the Army [over Charles], and by words and acts of Parliament.'[22] The Act of 17 March 1649 'breaks in pieces the kingly yoke and the laws of the Conqueror, and gives a common freedom to every English-

---

18. *A Watchword*, Sabine, p. 316, and *The New Law of Righteousness*, p. 199.
19. Ibid., pp. 194, 199.
20. Sabine, pp. 179, 323–4, 387, 464–6, 470, 505. For the popular legend of the Norman Yoke, to which Winstanley continually returns, see Sabine, pp. 303–4, 311–12, 357–8, 521–2, 587, 618–19 (*Light Shining in Buckinghamshire*), and my 'The Norman Yoke' in *Puritanism and Revolution* (Penguin, 1986), pp. 58–125, as well as Chapter 6 above.
21. Ascham, *Of the Confusions and Revolutions of Governments* (1649), pp. 18–19.
22. *An Humble Request to the Ministers of both Universities and to all Lawyers in every Inns-a-Court* (April 1650), Sabine, pp. 429–30.

man to have a comfortable livelihood in their own land, or else it cannot
be a commonwealth'. This Act and that of 19 May 1649 declaring England
a commonwealth and free state, he thought, together 'take away all lords
of manors'.[23] 'If that [kingly or lordly] power be taken away, then they
[lords of manors] must be equal to other Englishmen their brethren'.[24]

Winstanley's contemporary Thomas Tany ('Theaureaujohn') also
thought that 'our lands being freed from the Norman subjection' by
Parliament's victory in the civil war, 'we may lawfully claim our lands
and inheritance in the Commonwealth, as is due right', since they belong
to us by the law of God and of man. He thought that the poverty of his
parents had been due to 'the tyrannical power reigning in the Norman
Yoke'.[25]

Winstanley came to see that 'kingly power is like a great spread tree.
. . . That top bough is lopped off the tree of tyranny . . . but alas, oppression
is a great tree still, and keeps off the sun of freedom from the poor
commons still'. 'So long as the Sword rules over brethren (mind what I
say), so long the Kingly power of darkness rules. If this Kingly power of
Covetousness . . . did not yet rule: both Parliament, Army and rich people
would cheerfully give consent that those we call Poor should Dig and
freely Plant the Waste and Common Land for a livelihood.'[26] Buying and
selling, lords of manors, lawyers, priests and the state which protects the
rich all form one Antichristian kingly power. If Parliament re-establishes
the old Norman laws and enslaves the common people again to lords of
manors, it will be evident that their aim 'was not to throw down tyranny
but the tyrant' – and they will pull the guilt of the civil war and regicide
on their own heads. The great change must be made not by 'a few, or by
unrighteous men that would pull the tyrannical government out of
other men's hands and keep it in their own'. It is to be done by 'the
universal spreading of the divine power which is Christ in mankind,
making them all to act in one spirit, and in and after one law of reason
and equity'. After explaining that in his utopia theft or living on other
people's labour will be demonstrably irrational, Winstanley declared,

23. Sabine, op. cit., pp. 419–30; Thomas, 'Iver', p. 66. Winstanley's interpretation of
these two acts is his own.
24. G. E. Aylmer, '*England's Spirit Unfoulded, or an Incouragement to take the Engage-
ment:* by Jerrard Winstanley. A newly discovered pamphlet', in *Past and Present*, 40
(1968), p. 11.
25. *Theaureaujohn High Priest to the Jews, His Disputive Challenge to the Universities of
Oxford and Cambridge* (1651), pp. 1, 8.
26. Sabine, op. cit., pp. 353–7, 574; cf. p. 296 below.

slightly optimistically, 'every one shall know the law and every one shall obey the law, for it shall be writ in every man's heart'. Kingly power and 'that beast, . . . kingly covetous property' must be cast out and the crown set upon Christ's head.[27]

The revolution of 1648–9 had not gone far enough. 'The power of lords of manors remains still over their brethren, . . . beating them off from the free use of the common land unless their brethren will pay them rent'. 'The law of justice . . . is but the declarative will of conquerors, how they will have their subjects [to] be ruled. . . . These reign in power, while property rules as king'.[28] To regain Paradise on earth we must do more than remove the Norman Yoke, though that is a necessary first step. For the law was not the product only of the Norman Conquest. The establishment of private property and of buying and selling, the rise of covetousness, the God of the propertied, were 'the curse', the consequences of the original Fall of Man, and of Cain's murder of Abel.[29] All landlords live in breach of the seventh and eighth commandments, Thou shalt not steal nor kill.[30] Anyone who had money could buy land, and 'if once landlords, then they rise to be justices [of the peace], rulers and state governors, as experience shows'. 'Cain is still alive in all great landlords', declared the Diggers of Iver – a sinister threat if we recall Cain's recognition that 'everyone that findeth me shall slay me' (Genesis 4:14). 'Justices and most state officers', the Iver Diggers continued, 'doth more oppress than deliver us from oppression'.[31] What 'is called by some men the state of nature', or the state of war, wrote Winstanley in Hobbist vein, was ended only by people giving up their freedom and setting up kingly power and oppression over themselves. Winstanley can hardly have read Hobbes before 1650, the date of *Fire in the Bush* from which I quote. But Hobbism was in the air.[32]

For Winstanley it was axiomatic that 'everyone without exception . . . ought . . . to have liberty to enjoy the earth for his livelihood and to settle

27. Ibid., pp. 307–8 (*An Appeal to the House of Commons*, July 1649), p. 181, 196–8 (*The New Law of Righteousness*, January 1648–9) and 385–6 (*A New Years Gift*, January 1650).
28. Sabine, op. cit., pp. 464–6.
29. Ibid., pp. 423–7.
30. Sabine, pp. 258, 287–91, 323–4, 491; cf. pp. 187, 248–54, 264–5, 270–72, 297, 332, 336, 354–5, 375, 379, 383–4, 465, 489–90, 493–5, 531–2.
31. Ibid., pp. 188, 258, 491; Thomas, 'Iver', p. 61; cf. Sabine, pp. 159, 179–82, 292.
32. Ibid., pp. 493, 531. For Winstanley and Hobbes see my *The World Turned Upside Down*, pp. 387–94 and *A Nation of Change and Novelty*, pp. 127–8. The great difference is that Winstanley, unlike Hobbes, believed that human nature could be changed.

his dwelling in any part of the commons of England, without buying or renting land of any'. For during the civil war the common people had paid taxes and undergone free quarter, and had 'adventured their lives to recover England out of bondage'. Yet church, crown and royalists' lands and forests, 'everyone's birthright' by equal conquest, had been sold to those who had money to buy them.[33] There is a still continuing battle between 'the law of property' or covetousness on the one hand and community on the other. 'As the sword pulls down kingly power with one hand, the King's old law builds up monarchy again with the other'. One of the two 'greatest sins in the world' is 'for any man or men first to take the earth by the power of the murdering sword from others; and then by the laws of their own making do hang or put to death any who takes the fruits of the earth to supply his necessaries, from places or persons where there is more than can be made use of by that particular family where it is hoarded up'.[34]

'Their law itself says that the commons and waste belong to the poor . . . by the law of our creation', by conquest and by 'the last excellent two acts of Parliament'. The land 'was made for all' as 'their creation-birthright'. Winstanley made out an economic as well as an equitable case for the cultivation of commons by the poor. 'One-third part [of England] lies waste and barren, and her children starve for want, in regard lords of manors will not suffer the poor to manure it.'[35]

If Winstanley's system was introduced, improved cultivation of waste lands would bring down the price of corn as well as uniting the hearts of Englishmen to resist any foreign invader. Whereas now the poor see that even if they fought and defeated an invader they would still be slaves. 'Say they, we can as well live under a foreign enemy working for day wages as under our own brethren with whom we ought to have equal freedom'.[36] 'Particular property . . . is the cause of all wars, bloodshed, theft and enslaving laws that hold the people under misery'. 'The laws of kings have been always made against such actions as the common people

---

33. Sabine, pp. 363–4, 371, 510–13, 524, 557–60, 616; *More Light Shining in Buckinghamshire*, ibid., p. 638. It is interesting that the demand for these lands was first put forward in *Light Shining in Buckinghamshire*, a near-Digger pamphlet of December 1648 which it is unlikely that Winstanley wrote (Sabine, op. cit., p. 616). But he took up the suggestion in *A New Years Gift Sent to the Parliament and Armie* (January 1650), and elaborated on it in *The Law of Freedom*, where he added monastic lands seized at the Reformation and sold to those who then had money.

34. Ibid., pp. 496–7, 505.

35. Ibid., pp. 304, 306, 334, 374.

36. Ibid., pp. 414–15.

were most inclinable to'. They made money for lawyers and clergy, hence they were written in French or Latin which the poor could not understand. 'Their God is covetousness'; yet kingly power is not even consistent in its acceptance of a market economy: for it will destroy buying and selling 'as he [covetousness] pleaseth, . . . by patents, licences or monopolizing'. 'Money must not any longer . . . be the great God that hedges in some and hedges out others'. The poor 'are left still in the straits of beggary, and are shut out of all livelihood but what they shall pick out of sore bondage, by working for others as masters over them'. Locke later agreed with Winstanley, that buying and selling were the source of inequality, though not that they should be abolished.[37]

'We claim our freedom in the commons, that elder and younger brothers may live quietly and in peace, together freed from the straits of poverty and oppression'. 'I speak in the name of all the poor commoners', Winstanley told General Fairfax. The *Declaration from the Poor Oppressed People of England* (June 1649) was signed by forty-five Diggers 'for and in the behalf of all the poor oppressed people of England and the whole world'. Their objective, Winstanley explained, was 'to plant the pleasant fruit trees of freedom in the room of that cursed thornbush, the power of the murdering sword'. 'The poor people by their labours . . . have made the buyers and sellers of land, or rich men, to become tyrants and oppressors over them'. 'Many that have been good house-keepers . . . cannot live but are forced to turn soldiers, and so to fight to uphold the curse, or else live in great straits and beggary'. But 'the poorest man hath as true a title and just right to the land as the richest man. . . . I see the poor must first be picked out and honoured in this work; but the rich generally are enemies to true freedom'. 'Let Israel go free, that the poor may labour the waste land that they starve not', and that 'all the impoverished poor in the land may get a comfortable livelihood by our righteous labours thereupon'. 'This is the bondage the poor complain of, that they are kept poor by their brethren in a land where there is so much plenty for everyone. . . . There is but bondage and freedom, particular interest and common interest'.[38]

Some Levellers had arrived at a rudimentary labour theory of value.[39]

---

37. Ibid., pp. 265, 270, 276, 288, 384, 532, 589. See my *A Nation of Change and Novelty*, pp. 126–7; J. Dunn, *Locke* (Oxford U.P., 1984), pp. 36–44.

38. Ibid., pp. 264–5, 277, 326, 335, 337, 347, 423–4, 558–9.

39. Lilburne, *The Charters of London* (1646), p. 43; *Englands Troublers Troubled* (1648), p. 6; *The mournfull Cryes of many thousand poor Tradesmen* (1648), in Wolfe, *Leveller Manifestoes of the Puritan Revolution* (1944), pp. 275–6. Cf. Penn, *No Cross, No Crown* (1669, written in prison), Chapter 18 for a similar labour theory, which Penn may have taken from Winstanley.

The near-Digger pamphlets *Light Shining in Buckinghamshire* (1648) and
More Light . . . (1649) developed the idea. Winstanley picked it up and
elaborated it in *The Law of Freedom* (1652): 'Rich men receive all they have
from the labourer's hand, and what they give, they give away other
men's labours, not their own'.[40]

The solution is to put an end to wage labour and payment of rent. 'No
man shall have any more land than he can labour himself, or have other
men to labour with him in love'. Let the rich 'labour their own land with
their own hands'. So the transition to a new society could be made peacefully. Once private property and the giving or taking of wages were
illegal, people could organize their own communal production and share
the proceeds. No violence would be necessary. Big landowners would be
encouraged peacefully to throw their lands into the common stock; since
they could hire no one to work for them, their large estates would be
useless to them. At Wellingborough, we are told, 'some of these rich men
amongst us, that have had the greatest profit upon the common, have
freely given us their share of it' when digging began.[41] That was a hopeful
augury; if and when private property came to be abolished most landlords
would, perforce, have to accept the situation and contract in to the new
community, taking their share of what was produced with everybody
else.

It sounds ideally simple: either Christ would rise in sons and daughters,
creating a new consciousness, a new 'inner light' which would recognize
the advantages of a communist society; or Cromwell and the Army
would preside over a transitional phase in which power and land would
pass to the cultivators. In the long run the advantages of communism
would be so obvious that there could be no turning back. As the Ranter
Jacob Bauthumley put it, 'if men were acted and guided by that inward
law of righteousness within, there need be no laws of men to compel or
restrain them'. 'It is not so safe to go to the Bible to see what others have
spoke and writ of the mind of God as to see what God speaks within me,
and to follow the ducture and leading of it in me. . . . The Bible without is
but a shadow of the Bible which is within'.[42]

'So long as we . . . own landlords and tenants, for one to call the land
his, or another to hire it of him, or for one to give hire and for another to
work for hire, . . . we consent still to hold the creation down under that
bondage it groans under. . . . England is not a free people till the poor

40. Sabine, op. cit., pp. 616, 633–4, 511–12, 595; cf. pp. 190–91, 194–6, 262, 423–4.
41. *A Declaration* [from] *Wellingborough* (March 1650), in Sabine, op. cit., p. 650.
42. Bauthumley, *The Light and Dark Sides of God* (1650), p. 76.

that have no land have a free allowance to dig and labour the commons and so live as comfortably as the landlords that live in their enclosures'. Then 'within a short time there will be no beggar nor idle person in England'. '– The name of community and freedom . . . is Christ', 'who doth not enslave but comes to set all free.' 'This new law [of liberty] . . . is to be writ in every man's heart, and acted by every man's hand'.[43] 'Do not all strive to enjoy the land?' Winstanley asked. 'The gentry strive for land, the clergy strive for land, the common people strive for land; and buying and selling is an art whereby people endeavour to cheat one another of the land'.[44]

'If you would find true magistracy indeed, go among the poor despised ones of the earth: for there Christ dwells'. 'These great ones are too stately houses for Christ to dwell in. He takes up his abode in a manger, inn, amongst the poor in spirit and despised ones of the earth'. 'That Scripture which saith "the poor shall inherit the earth" is really and materially to be fulfilled'. 'This poor man is he that saves mankind from utter ruin'.[45] 'Will you be slaves and beggars still, when you may be freemen?' Winstanley asked. Then, said the Iver declaration, we shall enter into 'the glorious liberty of the Sons of God . . . and that is equality, community, fellowship with our own kind; for the first shall be last, and the last shall be first'.[46]

'The great searching of heart in these days', Winstanley wrote, 'is to find out where true freedom lies, that the Commonwealth of England might be established in peace'. 'All men have stood for freedom, . . . and now the common enemy is gone, you are all like men in a mist, seeking for freedom and know not where nor what it is'. 'Freedom is the man that will turn the world upside down', Winstanley promised; but he added 'therefore no wonder he hath enemies'. 'The actors for freedom are oppressed by the talkers and verbal professors of freedom'. 'Without exception, all sorts of people in the land are to have freedom'. Parliament claimed to represent the people of England, but notoriously it represented only the men of property. Winstanley insisted that the whole population should be represented, including 'the common people, being part of the nation, and especially they that bore the greatest heat of the day in casting out the oppressor'.[47]

43. Sabine, pp. 190–91, 195–6, 258–65, 337, 414, 447; cf. Thomas, 'Iver', p. 65.
44. Sabine, pp. 373–4 (*A New-Yeers Gift*).
45. Ibid., pp. 245, 316–17, 337, 389, 427, 473–4.
46. Ibid., p. 408; Thomas, 'Iver', p. 62.
47. Sabine, op. cit., pp. 305, 316–17, 371.

This was a novel principle: from Sir Thomas Smith, Queen Elizabeth's Secretary of State, to George Monck, who became Duke of Albemarle a century later by switching sides to bring about the restoration of Charles II, it had been accepted by those who ruled England that (in Monck's words) 'the poorer and meaner people have no interest in the commonwealth but the use of breath'.[48]

Winstanley's insistence that the two acts of the Parliament of the Commonwealth had established the right of the poor to the commons won no assent: one wonders whether he ever expected it. After the suppression of the Levellers in 1649 his confidence in Parliament must have been shaken. Yet he saw that, nevertheless, further economic and social change was impossible without the survival of the republic. Hence the realism of his recently recovered pamphlet, *Englands Spirit Unfoulded* (?summer 1650), calling for acceptance of the Commonwealth, even though in *Fire in the Bush* (March 1650) he had rejected any government 'that gives liberty to the gentry to have all the earth, and shuts out the poor commoners from enjoying any part'. Such was 'the government of . . . self-seeking Antichrist; and every plant which my heavenly Father hath not planted shall be rooted out'.[49] After the suppression of the Digger colonies in 1650 Winstanley was to show a similarly realistic compromise in dedicating *The Law of Freedom* to Oliver Cromwell in 1652.

In 1650 he had written 'You blame us who are the common people as though we would have no government'. He replied that 'the government we have gives freedom and livelihood to the gentry to have abundance and to lock up the treasures of the earth from the poor'. 'England is a prison. . . . The lawyers are the jailers, and poor men are the prisoners'. To the accusation that his programme 'will destroy all government, and all our ministry and religion', Winstanley replied nonchalantly, 'it is very true': existing government and religion 'is to be thrown down and plucked up, that Christ alone may be exalted in the day of his power'. But not by violence: 'the people shall all fall off from you, and you shall fall on a sudden like a great tree that is undermined at the root'.[50]

The Diggers, like outlaws, wished to contract out of the state legal

---

48. Monck, *Observations Upon Military and Political Affairs* (1671), p. 146; cf. Smith, quoted on p. 67 above.

49. Aylmer, op. cit., pp. 3–15; Sabine, pp. 361, 472. See also K. V. Thomas, 'The Date of Gerrard Winstanley's *Fire in the Bush*', in *Past and Present*, 42 (1969), pp. 160–62.

50. Sabine, op. cit., pp. 361, 390, 471.

system. They were 'not against any that would have magistrates and laws
to govern, as the nations of the world are governed; but . . . we shall need
neither the one nor the other in that nature of government'. Among the
Diggers land, cattle, corn and other products of the earth were not to be
bought and sold, and so there would be no litigation, no need of 'imprisoning, whipping or hanging laws'. 'But if you that are the elder brothers
and that call the enclosures your own land, hedging out others – if you
will have magistrates and laws in this outward manner of the nations, we
are not against it'. They were 'ready to answer all the laws of the land as
defendants but not as plaintiffs'. The Quakers were later to make a similar
attempt to contract out of the English legal system. 'But while we keep
within the bounds of our commons', Winstanley continued, and do not
commit theft outside the community, 'your laws shall not reach to us'.[51]
'The kings' old laws . . . cannot govern a free commonwealth', for they
'have always been made against such actions as the common people were
most inclinable to'. 'Most laws are but to enslave the poor to the rich, and
so they uphold the conquest'[52] – notably in reducing the peasantry to the
position of landless wage labourers. The Diggers' preference would be for
'all laws that are not grounded upon equity and reason, not giving a
universal freedom to all but respecting persons . . . to be cut off with the
King's head'. This means that the class privileges of the gentry would be
abolished in Winstanley's free commonwealth. For 'the King's blood was
not our burden, it was those oppressing Norman laws whereby he
enslaved us that we groaned under'.[53]

Winstanley was no anarchist. 'True government', he wrote in *Fire in
the Bush*, 'is that I long to see, I wait till the power, authority and government of the King of Righteousness rule over all'. Initially he confidently
expected that 'a few years now will let all the world see who is strongest,
love or hatred, freedom or bondage'. In April 1650, the month in which
the colony on Cobham Heath was suppressed, he wrote more cautiously
'Before many years pass, . . . I can set no time'. 'Christ . . . calls to
freedom', but men 'call still for bondage'. 'That government that
gives liberty to the gentry to have all the earth, and shuts out the poor
commoners from enjoying any part', was 'the government of self-seeking

51. Ibid., pp. 282–5, 296.
52. Ibid., pp. 585–9, 388.
53. Ibid., pp. 288 (*A Letter to the Lord Fairfax*, June 1649), and 308 (*An Appeal to the
House of Commons*, July 1649).

Antichrist. And every plant which my heavenly Father hath not planted shall be rooted out'.[54]

He had tried to persuade himself and others that the Commonwealth government would establish the freedom that he called for. In that hope he wrote *Englands Spirit Unfoulded*, which Gerald Aylmer provisionally dates to the early months of 1650. By that time at least ten similar communist communities had established themselves in central and southern England, in contact with Winstanley's colony. It looked as though his ideas were spreading. 'For the voice is gone out, "freedom, freedom, freedom"'. 'The work of digging' is 'freedom or the appearance of Christ in the earth'.[55]

Hitherto the Army had refused to respond to requests from local gentry and clergy to suppress the Diggers. But now the Council of State thought enough was enough. In April 1650 the colony on Cobham Heath was forcibly suppressed; the others soon followed. Winstanley had to rethink his position. He remained a pacifist – as indeed was sensible in view of the powerlessness of his following. 'Victory that is gotten by the sword is a victory that slaves get one over another'. In January 1650 he had declared that 'Jesus Christ . . . is the head Leveller'. A few months later he used a less optimistic and more apocalyptic phrase: Christ is 'the restorer . . . yea and the true and faithful Leveller'.[56] By then – though Winstanley presumably did not know this – some Levellers were actually intriguing with the exiled Charles Stuart against the Commonwealth.

Winstanley could not do that. In 1652 he published his last pamphlet, *The Law of Freedom in a Platform, or True Magistracy Restored*.[57] The title compares interestingly with that of one of the first of Winstanley's pamphlets to advocate communism – *The New Law of Righteousness*. From righteousness to freedom marks a shift from religion to politics, which illuminates the relationship between law and freedom, the subject of this book. Winstanley's title sounds paradoxical, since exisiting law defends unequal property. But in 1652 he no longer set law and freedom in opposition, because he envisaged as a necessary condition of freedom the abolition of private property and the establishment of a changed,

54. Ibid., pp. 297–8, 432, 472–3.
55. Ibid., p. 448, 437; cf. K. V. Thomas, 'Another Digger Broadside', in *Past and Present*, 42 (February 1969), p. 57.
56. Ibid., pp. 378–9, 390, 454.
57. For the background to *The Law of Freedom* see my 'Religion of Gerrard Winstanley' in *Religion and Politics in 17th-century England*, pp. 220–28.

egalitarian, society, a righteous society, in which a *new* law would be necessary to ensure the new freedom.

Freedom for Winstanley was not just negative, not merely 'freedom from'. He had hoped that Christ would rise in sons and daughters (the only Second Coming he expected to see) and would convert them to the necessity of a communist society. But that hope had failed, and the brutal suppression of the Digger communes revealed the impotence of the Diggers alone. Freedom from the law appeared to be impossible here and now, until true magistracy was restored. So Winstanley dedicated *The Law of Freedom* to Oliver Cromwell, because he had power in his hand; 'I have no power'.[58] With our hindsight knowledge it seems an absurd hope; but Oliver had done some surprising things in his time. And what other hope was there? Winstanley wished at least to record his vision of an ideal commonwealth in which the law would incorporate freedom. *The Law of Freedom* is in a sense a dialogue between Winstanley and Oliver Cromwell. 'You must either establish Commonwealth's freedom *in power* [my italics], making provision for everyone's peace, which is righteousness; or else you must set up monarchy again'.[59] Oliver at least did not want that.

In the 1640s Cromwell had often used the rhetoric of freedom against authority. 'The man is an Anabaptist: what of it?' The state is not interested in men's opinions, so long as they serve it loyally. Cromwell preferred a 'russet-coated Captain' who knew what he fought for and loved what he knew to 'what you call a gentleman and is nothing else'. He would shoot the King if he encountered him on the battlefield; later he did in fact cut off his head with the crown on it. He besought Scottish Presbyterians 'in the bowels of Christ, think it possible you may be mistaken'.

Cromwell told the Scottish kirk that 'Your pretended fear lest error should step in' if religious freedom was established 'is like the man that would keep all wine out of the country lest men should be drunk'.[60] He defended all those 'with the root of the matter in them' – a matter of definition. Under him the New Model Army had been a body of dedicated free men. But after victory? In *The Law of Freedom* Winstanley told Cromwell that 'God hath made you a successful instrument to . . .

58. Sabine, op. cit. p. 510.
59. Sabine, p. 527. cf. p. 284–5 above.
60. Cromwell, *Writings and Speeches*, II, pp. 337–9. The striking last phrase had been used by Milton in *Tetrachordon* (1645), *Complete Prose Works*, II, pp. 64–5. It goes back at least to Burton's *Anatomy of Melancholy* of 1621 (Everyman ed.), II, p. 84.

recover our land and liberty again by your victories'.[61] But this was unrealistic. At Putney, when pressed by Levellers, Cromwell came down on Ireton's side, for freedom for property. As Protector he equated 'poor men' with 'bad men'. By that date Levellers, Diggers and Ranters had all been suppressed, but maintenance of control over the lower orders still seemed to Oliver necessary.

In earlier pamphlets Winstanley had rejected the laws of a government which 'may well be called the government of highwaymen, who hath stolen the earth from the younger brethren by force, and holds it from them by force'.[62] But the Diggers' attempt to win freedom by contracting out of the state had proved unsuccessful. There was now, Winstanley may have convinced himself, just a faint possibility that, through the Army, state power might be used to secure his objectives. The Army was the people; Winstanley had retained hopes of it as late as January 1650, and he still thought that in their hearts many of the rank and file were Diggers.[63] The Army had played a revolutionary part in 1647 and the winter of 1648–9; it might do so again. It was a slim chance, but there seemed to be no other hope.

Winstanley now recognized that, short of a divine miracle, 'true Commonwealth's freedom' could be introduced only by a government, and that laws would be necessary, backed up ultimately by coercion. 'It is the work of a Parliament to break the tyrant's bonds'. 'This Commonwealth's government . . . *in time* will be the restorer of long lost freedoms to the creation'.[64] Laws existed, in Winstanley's view, either (1) for common preservation, which was the foundation rule of all government; or (2) for private profit, 'the root of all tyranny . . . and all particular kingly laws found out by covetous policy to enslave one brother to another'.[65] Experience led Winstanley to foresee that laws would be necessary even

---

61. Sabine, op. cit., p. 501.
62. Ibid., p. 529. It is not worth discussing Professor Davis's remarkable allegation that Winstanley was always an authoritarian, who came to conclude that communism could only be imposed in 'a society. . .where slavery replaced imprisonment', and where flogging, judicial violence and torture, and capital punishment, were accepted as essential parts of the machinery of social discipline' ('Winstanley and the Restoration of True Magistracy', *Past and Present*, 70, February 1976, p. 90). There is no evidence whatsoever for such a statement, which appears to confuse the gentle and pacifist Winstanley with Josef Stalin.
63. Sabine, pp. 368, 395–6.
64. Ibid., pp. 558, 534 (my italics). The text's 'Tyrants' could be read either 'tyrant's' or 'tyrants''.
65. Ibid., p. 537. For Commonwealth's laws see Sabine, op. cit., pp. 526–7, 583–600; pp. 586–7 for the king's old laws.

in his new society. But only, he wrote in a significant phrase, against 'the unruly ones, *for whom only the law was added*, . . . that so peace may be preserved among them in the planting of the earth, reaping the fruits, and quiet enjoyment'. 'As Paul writ, "The law was added because of transgression".'[66]

Winstanley insisted on many safeguards. Laws should be 'few, short and often read'. Governments were to be elected by all males over twenty years of age, excluding royalists and land purchasers. Poor men should receive pay if elected to office. State officials should be elected annually, following the example of London, a practice by which 'the peace of London is much preserved'. In general, there was to be arbitration, peace-making, reconciliation between quarrelling citizens: the law was to be a last resort.[67] And no paid lawyers: 'there is no need of them, for there is to be no buying and selling'. The legal system is 'a nursery of idleness, luxury and cheating, the only enemy of Christ the King of Righteousness'. The law pretends justice, 'yet the judges and law officers buy and sell justice for money'. They oppress the poor and let rich offenders go free.[68]

Simultaneously we shall get rid of 'those nurseries of covetousness, the Inns of Court'. 'The law is the fox, poor men are the geese; he pulls off their feathers and feeds upon them'. There would be no standing army: only a militia of all the citizens in arms. 'Tyranny is tyranny', Winstanley observed pointedly, 'in a poor man lifted up by his valour as in a rich man lifted up by his lands'.[69]

Winstanley's religious provisions for his utopia are interestingly indicative of pre-1640 English practice: he speaks of 'kings, bishops *and other state officers*' (my italics). In *The New Law of Righteousness* (January 1649) Winstanley had insisted that 'the declaration of the righteous law shall spring up from the poor, the base and despised ones, and fools of the world; and human learning, and such as love the oppression of exacting tithes, shall not be honoured. . . . For they that stand up to be public teachers are *Judas*. . . . They will hinder Christ from rising and betray him . . . that so the covetous and proud flesh may rule in oppression over their fellow creature quietly – Mat. 23. 16'.[70]

Under the law of freedom (unlike the law of Massachusetts) church

66. Ibid., pp. 533, 536, 539, 552. My italics.
67. Ibid., pp. 541–2, 544, 590, 596.
68. Ibid., pp. 361–2, 512, 590; cf. pp. 182–3, and Chapter 22, above.
69. Ibid., pp. 188, 198, 361, 468, 573.
70. Ibid., pp. 541, 205–6.

membership was not to be necessary to citizenship. 'No man shall be troubled for his judgment or practice in the things of his God, so he live quiet in the land'. '*His* God': does each man choose his own? Kingly government was 'that god, which appointed the people to pay tithes': they are to be abolished, together with the gentry's rent and the impropriated tithes which they had acquired at the dissolution of the monasteries. The clergy in their courts 'most times oppresses the poor and lets the offending rich go free, by laying aside the letter' of Scriptures, as J.P.s and officers of state do in the secular courts.[71]

Winstanley blends secular and religious themes and myths, as do so many of his contemporaries. England has long lain 'under the power of that Beast, kingly power'. Antichrist, the Beast, must be cast out and the crown set upon 'Christ's head, who is the universal love or free community'.[72] The 'university public preachers', on the other hand, are 'Antichrist's ministry'. They are useless and dangerous. 'The old kingly clergy, that are seated in parishes for lucre of tithes, are continually distilling their blind principles into the people' and holding back Christ from rising.[73] They 'tell us of a heaven and hell after death, which neither they nor we know what will be'. Winstanley referred pointedly to '*your* Scriptures' (my italics). People must 'become like unto wise-hearted Thomas, to believe nothing but what they see reason for'. For God is not to be found 'in some particular place of glory beyond the skies'; he is within each one of us.[74] The younger brother's 'eyes are put out, and his reason is blinded . . . for fear of damnation in hell . . . and hopes to get heaven'. In an anticipation of Marx's 'opium of the people', Winstanley wrote 'they see not what is their birthrights, and what is to be done by them here on earth while they are living. . . . And indeed the subtle clergy do know, that if they can but charm the people by this their divining doctrine, to look after riches, heaven and glory when they are dead, that then they shall easily be the inheritors of the earth, and have the deceived people to be their servants. . . . This . . . was not the doctrine of Christ'.[75] The Diggers' song promised 'Glory *here*, Diggers all' (my italics).

In an extraordinary passage in *The Law of Freedom* Winstanley wrote

---

71. Ibid., pp. 290, 504, 532, 543, 591; cf. pp. 637 (*More Light Shining in Buckinghamshire*) and 669 (*The Diggers' Christmass Caroll*).
72. Sabine, pp. 385–6.
73. Ibid., p. 544 (*The Law of Freedom*).
74. Ibid., pp. 188, 290, 474, 523; *The Saints Paradise* (1648), Sig. B, pp. 54–5, 89.
75. Sabine, op. cit., pp. 522–4, 567–70.

'the inward bondages of the mind, as covetousness, pride, hypocrisy, envy, sorrow, fears, desperation and madness, are all occasioned by the outward bondages that one sort of people lay upon another'. The clergy add to this bondage. Winstanley's hostility was not limited to the state church. He went beyond contracting out by religious separatism. To 'run and hide yourself . . . in a congregation . . . and . . . sow the fig-leaves of your own observing forms and customary invented righteousness' – that was not enough. 'All your particular churches', he wrote, 'are like the enclosures of land which hedges in some to be heirs of life, and hedges out others'.[76] The hedge with which Norman freeholders shut the common people out of the common land is analogous to the barriers with which priests try to prevent us from realizing the spiritual equality of all men and women. Christ the true Leveller will cast both down. 'Your Saviour must be a power within you to deliver you from that bondage within,' Winstanley told 'all the Several Societies of People called Churches'. 'The outward Christ, or the outward God, are but men Saviours'.[77] 'The greatest separation that ever was' will 'gather the scattered of Israel together out of all Egyptian bondages and self-seeking oppressive government'.[78]

Hence Winstanley's educational programme – rational, scientific, sceptical of clerical divinity. 'When men are sure of food and raiment, their reason will be ripe, and ready to dive into the secrets of the creation'. Kingly power had 'crushed the spirit of knowledge', but in a free commonwealth it could 'rise up in its beauty and fullness'. 'Fear of want and care to pay rent to task-masters hath hindered many rare inventions'. But now men will be able to 'employ their reason and industry' in making discoveries which will benefit all, not just the inventor.[79] All young men must be brought up to a trade 'and some bodily employment, as well as in learning languages or the histories of former ages', and 'be acquainted with the knowledge of the affairs of the world and of the nature of government'. 'Traditional knowledge, which is attained by reading or by the instruction of others, and not practical but leads to an idle life', is to be avoided.[80] Winstanley seems most modern when he discusses the possibilities of democratically-controlled science, of applying 'reason and under-

76. Sabine, pp. 445–6 (*Fire in the Bush*).
77. Ibid., p. 496.
78. Ibid., pp. 163–4.
79. Ibid., pp. 571, 579–80 (*The Law of Freedom*).
80. Ibid., pp. 576, 579.

standing' to inventions which should benefit society. There will be a free state medical service.[81]

In this ideal commonwealth there would be no wage labour, no private trading. Earlier Winstanley had said that to execute a man for murder was to commit another murder. Now, in his new society, the death penalty would be retained, not only for murder but for buying and selling (which 'killed Christ and hindered his resurrection'), for taking money as a priest or lawyer, and – interestingly – for rape. Civil marriage will replace a church ceremony, and 'every man and woman shall have the free liberty to marry whom they love, if they can obtain the love and liking of that party whom they would marry; and neither birth nor portion shall hinder the match, for we are all of one blood, mankind'. 'For portion', Winstanley added with a touch of realism, 'the common store-houses are every man and maid's portion, as free to one as to another'.[82]

Winstanley's emphasis on freedom of choice in marriage was, I imagine, consciously contrasted with marriage for money and with Ranter libertinism, which disrupts the community and amounts to unfreedom for women. Similarly rape is singled out for the severest punishment because it destroys the basis of love, trust and mutual respect without which a good society cannot exist. Milton sloganizes against Ranters: 'licence they men when they cry liberty'. Winstanley has thought through his opposition to them, as part of his communal ethic. By contrast Milton's moralistic approach: 'for who loves [liberty] must first be wise and good' seems rather remote from reality.[83]

Like the Chartists after him, Winstanley always comes back to access to the land. 'From the thief upon the highway to the King who sits upon the throne, do not every one strive, either by force of arms or secret cheats, to get the possessions of the earth one from another, because they see their freedom lies in plenty, and their bondage lies in poverty?' This is true alike of gentry, clergy and common people. But the land 'was made for all'.[84] 'True freedom lies where a man receives his nourishment and preservation, and that is in the use of the earth'. 'A man had better to have had no body than to have no food for it'. 'Oh you rulers, make the poor

81. Ibid., pp. 565–80, 593, 598; *A Nation of Change and Novelty*, pp. 120–21. For the defects of academic education see Sabine, op. cit., pp. 474–5, 480.
82. Ibid., pp. 193, 580, 595–9.
83. Milton, Sonnet XII – 'I did but prompt the age to quit their clogs'.
84. Sabine, op. cit, pp. 373–4, 519–20.

as free to the earth as yourselves'. The kingly conqueror's laws against riots were imposed 'lest the common people by their often meeting should understand their creation-freedom and so should join together to conquer and cast out him that had conquered them'. The Diggers who 'dig and plant upon the commons' are not vagabonds or rioters. If vagabonds are punished for wandering up and down idly, should not this penalty apply to 'the idle gentry rather than the laborious poor man?'[85]

'True religion and undefiled', Winstanley wrote, is 'to make restitution of the earth, which hath been taken and held from the common people by the power of conquests formerly, and so *set the oppressed free*'. On a later occasion he wrote with fine irony 'true religion and undefiled is to let every one quietly have earth to manure, that they may live in freedom by their labours'. The homely word 'manuring' was no doubt intended to mock the Laudian 'beauty of holiness' and Puritan emphasis on preaching and preaching and preaching. Heaven is 'a comfortable livelihood in the earth', Winstanley continued: it and hell are to be found within men and women.[86]

But arguments drawn from history, religion, or justice were not the only ones Winstanley used. Economic considerations pointed in the same direction. 'The common land hath lain unmanured all the days of his ['the Norman oppressor's'] kingly and lordly power over you, by reason whereof both you and your fathers . . . have been burdened with poverty' and the land has been unfruitful. 'According to the words of the Scripture: "A fruitful land is made barren because of the unrighteousness of the people that ruled therein" . . .' 'If the waste land of England were manured by her children, it would become in a few years the richest, the strongest and [most] flourishing land in the world, and all Englishmen would live in peace and comfort'. But the descendants of the Norman conquerors 'would be free men themselves, but would have all others bondmen and servants, nay slaves to them'.[87]

Winstanley preferred the word 'Reason' to 'God', 'because I have been held under darkness by that word, as I see many people are'.[88] He wanted to construct a righteous because rational society – or perhaps rational because righteous: the two concepts are interchangeable. He had much in

85. Ibid., pp. 387, 431–2, 435, 519–20, 533, 615.
86. Ibid., pp. 216–19, 373, 409, 428; cf. pp. 153, 226–7.
87. Ibid., pp. 408–15, *An Appeale to all Englishmen*, March 1650.
88. Ibid., p. 105. This was in *Truth Lifting Up its Head above Scandals*, the pamphlet in which Winstanley first proclaimed his communism, dated 16 October 1648.

common with antinomian radicals. 'The word of life, Christ the restoring spirit, is to be found within you'.[89] Learning is no help. 'Go read all the books in your university', mocked Winstanley; 'your hearts still shall be a barren wilderness . . . till you read in your own book, your heart (Isaiah 32:9–16).' 'Christ himself . . . fights against you by the sword of Love, patience and truth'.[90] 'To conquer them by love, come in now, come in now' ran the Diggers' song. Blake might have written it.

The fact that Winstanley shared many of his heresies and unorthodox opinions with Milton throws light on both men.[91] It helps us to appreciate the sophistication of Winstanley's ideas, and to understand that Milton was fully involved in the irreverent discussions which took place among the radicals after censorship and ecclesiastical controls had broken down in the 1640s. Nearly all their shared heresies are denounced in Thomas Edwards's *Gangraena.*

So Winstanley, alone among those whom we have been considering, abandoned hope of finding freedom from laws by contracting out of the state, whether in the greenwood, the highways, the common lands, or in a separatist congregation, 'to live out of sight or out of slavery'. He came to recognize that in the modern world freedom could be established only by law, and that this would involve changing the nature of the state by political action. England's battles now are all spiritual – 'Dragon against the Lamb, and the power of love against the power of covetousness'.[92] 'The name of community and freedom . . . is Christ', as Reason is Winstanley's word for God.[93]

Winstanley's original idea, that the Digger community had contracted out of the law of the land, reminds us of Robin Hood and his outlaws, and of Captain Ward who claimed sovereign independence at sea. But outlaws and pirates had weapons: the Diggers had none, and very sensibly proclaimed their pacifism. They relied not on military force, but on Christ rising in sons and daughters. Translated into modern terminology, this is equivalent to reliance on a public opinion which they hoped to create; for 'if thou dost not act, thou dost nothing'. 'Words and writings' are 'all nothing, and must die'.[94]

89. Sabine, pp. 454–5, 460, 475–6, 495–6; cf. Bauthumley, quoted on p. 215 above.
90. Sabine, p. 471.
91. For Milton see my *Milton and the English Revolution*, pp. 298–313.
92. Ibid., pp. 336, 359.
93. Ibid., p. 337.
94. Sabine, op. cit., p. 315.

Stuart Prall drew attention to two pamphlets published in 1652 'in the name of all the commons of England'[95] which echo Winstanley, almost verbatim. 'If so be the kingly authority be set up in your laws again, King Charles hath conquered you and your posterity by policy, and won the field of you, though you seemingly have cut off his head'.[96] 'As the sword pulls down kingly power with one hand, the king's old laws builds up monarchy again with the other. And indeed the main work of reformation lies in this, to reform the clergy, lawyers and law; for all the complaints of the land are wrapped up within these three, not in the person of a king'. The exact verbal echo in the first quotation, and the fact that both tracts were published within approximately a week of *The Law of Freedom*, suggests that Winstanley's relation to them deserves further investigation.[97]

The Diggers were suppressed, easily. But their ideas were not so soon forgotten. In 1659 they recur in pamphlets by William Covell from the old radical centre of Enfield, where in 1650 there had been a Digger colony. In 1649, and again in 1659, there were riots against the enclosure of Enfield Chase. Covell wanted all common and waste lands to be settled on the poor for ever. Cooperative communities were to be established, which differed from those of the Diggers only in that they were – more realistically – to be financed by rich men. Within these communities there was to be no private property, no buying and selling, Covell wanted to abolish an endowed parish clergy: 'if any will have parish ministers, let them that will have them pay them'. Tithes, together with the lands of royalist delinquents – and of the universities – should be confiscated and used to pay public debts. All other laws were to be nul for ever.[98]

95. S. E. Prall, *The Agitation for Law Reform during the Puritan Revolution* (The Hague, 1966), pp. 70–72.

96. [Anon.], *A Declaration of the Commoners of England to the Lord General Cromwell. Concerning the Crown, Government, Liberty and Priviledges of the People* (13 February 1652), p. 8. This repeats word for word Winstanley's *Law of Freedom*: Sabine, op. cit., p. 574.

97. [Anon.], *Articles of High Treason Drawn up in the Name of All the Commoners of England against One Hundred and Fifty Judges* (21 February 1652), pp. 4–5. I owe this reference to the Pisa University thesis of Stefano Villani, 'Il Comunismo degli Illuminati: saggio su Gerrard Winstanley (1609–1676)', of which he very kindly sent me a copy. Chapters I and II of Part IV of this thesis usefully list references to Winstanley in the eighteenth century and later.

98. See my *Experience of Defeat*, pp. 40–42.

Winstanley's writings lead us into the world of modern politics. He aspired to create a much wider public opinion than the Parliamentarian leaders had managed to mobilize in the 1640s. The author of *Tyranipocrit Discovered* had a simpler remedy: 'if you cannot make all the poor rich, yet you may make the rich poorer'.[99] Winstanley's solution was more fundamental. He wanted to change not just one aspect of policy but the whole structure and ethos of his society. 'The power that is in [the Diggers] will take the rule and government from you [lords of manors and Norman gentry] and give it [to] a people that will make better use of it'.[100] The task was beyond the Diggers' strength, and they failed. But succeeding generations took up the task, and Christ has risen, slowly, in an increasing number of sons and daughters. He still has some way to go.

99. Op. cit., p. 51.
100. Winstanley, *A Watch-Word to the City of London and the Armie*, Sabine, op. cit., p. 333.

24. *The Society of Friends and the Law*

I remember I have read that King Charles I, in his sufferings, expressed that he was sensible that there was nothing worse than legal tyranny, that is oppression under pretence of the execution of a law, for you know tyranny is not legal.

Samuel Duncon to the Norwich magistrates, 1671, quoted by Craig W. Horle, *The Quakers and the English Legal System, 1660–1688* (Pennsylvania U.P., 1988), p. 101.

If they did believe that the Quakers did meet to MAKE MARRIAGES or TURN PAN-CAKES, they might find it for the appellant [i.e. not guilty], but if to WORSHIP GOD, they might find it for the king [i.e. guilty].

Pennistone Whalley, J.P., charge to the jury in Nottingham Quarter Sessions, January 1677, quoted by Horle, op. cit., p. 137.

It is convenient the Friends that suffer beyond the limits and severity of the law ... may know in what cases relief may be had, they having their liberty in the Truth to accept thereof or to suffer ... That in all such cases wherein Friends want information in point of law they may send up their questions to Thomas Rudyard or Ellis Hookes to procure and send them a resolve, both as to such cases wherein they may have relief and wherein they may not, that they may not remain in any groundless or uncertain expectation.

Minutes of London Yearly Meeting, October 1675, quoted by Horle, p. 161.

In the 1650s the Quakers had been notorious as a belligerent group, calling on Cromwell to carry anti-Catholic war on to the continent and sack Rome, telling soldiers that they must be *efficient* soldiers. They had been as fierce in their denunciation of the law and lawyers as any radicals. But during the early years of Charles II's reign they transformed themselves into the pacifist, law-abiding and indeed law-utilizing Society of Friends, geared to using the law and lawyers to defend their members from persecution. This is the subject of a recent book, *The Quakers and the English Legal System, 1660–1688*, by Craig W. Horle. It has not yet attracted the attention it deserves from English seventeenth-century historians. As will appear, I have drawn heavily on it in writing this chapter.

In the 1650s Quakers had received some degree of tolerance. But as the restoration approached conservative Parliamentarians raised their heads again. To them Quakers seemed dangerous. In 1659 Edward Byllynge followed Fox in denouncing the 'terrible and lawless lawyers, under whose oppression the whole nation smarts.'[1] Quakers shared with other radicals the demand for 'a legal system more accessible to the majority of the English nation'. They appealed to 'reason and equity' as well as sometimes to the 'fundamental laws of England', including Magna Carta. If their demands had been accepted, Michael Rogers suggests, they would have 'de-professionalized the law and ended or threatened the careers of a host of judges and lawyers'.[2]

So when in the Declaration of Breda the future Charles II promised that 'no man shall be disquieted or called in question for differences of opinion in matters of religion which do not disturb the peace of the kingdom', the last clause might have been interpreted to exclude Quakers. In any case Parliament refused to confirm Charles's Declaration of Indulgence, and the question of religious toleration see-sawed up and down as relations between the two authorities fluctuated. It may have been this uncertainty that led Quakers first to think of using the law to defend themselves.

In 1661, when an attempt was made to have a Quaker marriage declared unlawful because no church ceremony had been performed, the Quakers concerned hired a former judge and a bencher of Lincoln's Inn to defend their case. The trial judge proved sympathetic and declared that it was 'consent of the parties that made a marriage'.[3] But the lawfulness of Quaker marriages – and of their wills – remained uncertain. In the 1660s some juries seem to have been prepared to side with Quakers, arguing back against pressure from some judges. But there were significant periods

1. Fox, *An Instruction to Judges and Lawyers*, pp. 27–8; cf. his *The Law of God and the Rule of Law-makers* (1658), pp. 4, 15–16; Byllynge, *A Word of Reproof and Advice*, p. 20; Horle, op. cit., pp. 62–3, 65.
2. See R. Michael Rogers,'Quakerism and the Law in Revolutionary England', in *Canadian Journal of History*, XXII (1987), pp. 149–74.
3. Horle, op. cit., pp. 235–6.

of persecution in 1661–5 and 1670–71, and again in 1683–6. In 1664–5 mass arrests of Quakers meant that gaols were seriously overcrowded.[4] In 1664 Richard Farnworth published a tract entitled *The Liberty of the Subject by Magna Carta*, in which he attacked the use of Latin and French in law courts. 'If the common law be so hard to be understood', wrote William Penn in the same year, 'its far from being common'. He was supported by another Quaker, Thomas Rudyard, later in the same year. Latin indictments, he said, were intended 'to keep the people ignorant', especially jurors. He made the Leveller point that juries drawn from the neighbourhood would be able to distinguish between witnesses who were persons 'of no credit' on the one hand and Quaker defendants on the other.[5]

Charles's Declaration of Indulgence (15 March 1672) appeared to hold out new prospects of toleration, and although Parliament forced him to rescind it in March 1673 it seems to have led to a turning point in Quaker thinking during the fourteen months' imprisonment of George Fox in 1673–4. Henceforwards Friends, and Fox himself, 'revealed an increasing willingness ... to employ legal counsel, to pay the fees necessary for copies of indictments, mittimuses and writs, and to combat the laws with legal weapons'. Fox's case 'focused Quaker attention dramatically on the need to provide appropriate legal counsel and strategy for those Friends who wished to utilize it, and to create a centralized committee to co-ordinate legal and lobbying efforts ... That committee would be the Meeting for Sufferings, the prototype of a modern legal defence organization'. In April 1675 Fox urged Friends throughout the country to record and send to London full details of their sufferings.[6]

The leadership had to proceed cautiously with this new policy, which seemed to some Friends to conflict with 'Truth' as they had come to accept it. In 1675 the Yearly Meeting found it necessary to stress that although no Friend who wished to seek lawful remedy should be 'discouraged or reflected upon', the intention was not to encourage any Friend 'either to contention nor to take any indirect course at law either to the prejudice of Truth ... or giving advantage to the adversary'. In the following year the Yearly Meeting insisted that no Friend was to 'wrong

4. Ibid., pp. 104–18, 268–70.
5. Penn, *The Peoples Antient and Just Liberties Asserted in the Trial of William Penn* (1670); Rudyard, *The Second Part of the Peoples Antient and Just Liberties Asserted*, p. 60.
6. Horle, op. cit., pp. 82–3, 164, 172–4.

Truth's testimony through seeking of ease to the flesh', and warned against 'entangling themselves in the law because of some *small irregularities in proceeding*'. Action should be taken only if the law was 'materially transgressed and the severity of it exceeded by our persecutors'.[7]

The next step was to advise provincial Friends in May 1676 to lobby the 'most moderate, swaying and considerate men in authority' to check inferior officers who were 'persecuting' Quakers. If any of these 'considerate men' resided at court or in London, their names and addresses should be sent to London Friends, who might also be able to help. There is much evidence for Quaker use of influence to obtain support. But royal favour was very uncertain, blown backwards and forwards by the winds of politics.[8]

The first official Meeting for Sufferings took place in June 1676. Soon 'standing counsel' were appointed, with power to recommend others in difficult cases. In May 1678 the Yearly Meeting recommended that sufferings should first be presented in writing to J.P.s at petty and quarter sessions, and to judges of assize if no remedy was forthcoming: failing that to the King and Privy Council or to Parliament. The Meeting for Sufferings was to appoint 'knowing or capable' Friends to lobby the assize judges about individual cases before they went on circuit. In 1679 provincial Friends were instructed to lobby newly elected M.P.s and to help to pay for it all. This marked a more direct turn towards politics. Quakers played an active part in the elections of 1679 and 1681. The centre repeatedly insisted that reports of sufferings must be discreetly drafted, accurate, impartial, complete, witnessed and 'without any reflections upon the magistrates and persons by whom Friends have suffered or against whom complaint is made'. In 1682 Yearly Meeting declared its intention of establishing a regular system for printing sufferings, to be given to the King, Privy Council and Parliament. Provincial and quarterly meetings were told to provide themselves with copies of the *Statutes at Large* 'to which on all occasions they may have recourse'.[9]

The reaction of rank and file Quakers to the offer of legal advice and support was favourable, no doubt in reaction to the renewed persecution of the 1680s. 'Some of the finest legal minds in England' were employed. Horle lists some forty-four advisers, including Lord Somers and eleven

7. Ibid., pp. 174–5.
8. Ibid., pp. 174–5, 248, 254–6, 263–5.
9. Ibid., pp. 25, 176–9.

men who 'at various times held superior common-law judgeships'. He gives details of different types of tactical and procedural advice. In 1686 James II agreed to a conference of Quakers, informers and royal commissioners, and seems for a time to have given Quakers his support. The Meeting for Sufferings had signalled a further policy shift when in 1682 it advised that 'moderate consideration of clerk's fees was permissible' if necessary in order to avoid imprisonment. Many Bristol Friends, 'being very poor men', rejected this advice.[10]

The 'battery of Lawyers' was particularly useful in producing technical arguments to prevent Quakers being penalized for their refusal to swear oaths: Horle gives a number of examples. The Yearly Meeting left it to Friends' 'liberty and freedom in the Truth' whether or not to appear in court. By 1680 they were having to warn Friends against 'unscrupulous solicitors and attorneys'; 'counsel and advice of some knowing Friends' should be taken before employing solicitors.[11]

Horle has some interesting pages discussing Quaker marriages. If they were not recognized as legal, any children born would be illegitimate, and their inheritance could be challenged. There were instances of non-Quaker members of families taking advantage of this to try to get wills annulled. In 1688 the Meeting for Sufferings pronounced confidently that at common law proof of cohabitation was proof of marriage, though it was not so accepted in the ecclesiastical courts. Friends had to be reassured that they were not 'guilty in the sight of God nor men' if any court or magistrate was satisfied by testimony regarded as 'equivalent with an oath'. The reassurance was needed, and is a sign of the times.[12]

Horle sums up: 'Although the legal advice they received was often self-serving and questionable', Quakers still 'had far greater likelihood of success on legal grounds than most of their opponents'. 'They were able to muster resources far superior to informers or ministers; to prosecute a Quaker became an expensive proposition'. Meanwhile the wealth of some leading Quakers was increasing substantially. Horle leaves unanswered his question 'what impact the paying of fines for some Friends had on those less fortunate Quakers who remained in prison' for lack of means.[13]

Rich Quakers would benefit more than poor in terms of hard cash from having good legal advice at well below the market price; and for

10. Ibid., pp. 187–8, 197–209, 285–91.
11. Ibid., pp. 210, 230–33.
12. Ibid., pp. 234–45, 248.
13. Ibid., pp. 268, 270, 277.

some smaller men shrewd advice on tactics might well make the difference between solvency and bankruptcy. So the new system worked to the advantage of many, and helped to maintain solidarity and friendship among Friends. It was reassuring to be told that the legal tricks and stratagems which advisers recommended were recognized by the Society as not contrary to the Truth, since recent denunciations of the law and lawyers by leading Quakers would be fresh in the memory of Friends.

Horle's pioneering book suggests that Quakers as a group bridged the gap between the rich (who used the law to enrich themselves) and the poor, some of whom Quakers regarded as fellows in the Truth. The Society retained something of the community spirit which had been destroyed in English villages. By using the law the Society of Friends came to perform some of the functions of a friendly society. There was indeed an insurance company in the early eighteenth century called 'The Society of Friends', from which the phrase 'friendly society' is believed to derive. A nineteenth-century definition of trade unions equated them with friendly societies.[14]

Horle's important book suggests further questions which call for future research. First, were the Quakers unique in their systematic use of the law for the benefit of their members? I suspect they were, but that may be only because no one has yet asked for other sects the questions which Horle has posed. The Muggletonians might be worth investigating with such a possibility in mind. Their denunciations of law and lawyers had been even fiercer than those of the Quakers, and they were great survivors who kept good archives. But Muggleton himself put lawyers beyond the pale, and his personal authority was far greater and less challengeable within the sect than that of any leading member of the Society of Friends.

Secondly, when and how exactly did the turn to making use of the law originate? Was it cause or consequence of the sharp turn from bellicosity to pacifism? The introduction of the peace principle caused vast controversies and splits within the Society: many left with John Perrot in the early 1660s, who thought that some of the eminent Quaker leaders might decline and fall. The Wilkinson–Story separation of the late 1670s started from those who objected to the 'tyrannical government' being introduced into the Society, to the 'edicts and canons' which issued from

14. I take these facts from that very useful historical source, the *Oxford English Dictionary*.

the centre. Braithwaite in his *Second Period of Quakerism* describes this as 'Fox's action in strengthening church government', which had 'involved to some extent the subordination of individual guidance to the spiritual leading which came to the meeting'. This spiritual leading was resented by some as giving undue influence to those – like Fox – who saw themselves as spiritual leaders. Something of the original Quaker impulse was lost in establishing the discipline which preserved the Society of Friends.[15]

Thirdly, if the turn to the use of the law and the peace principle were connected, were they both related to what some contemporaries saw as the rise to influence within the society of William Penn (convinced 1666), Margaret Fell and other members of the landed ruling class? Margaret Fell, whom George Fox married in 1669, was born into a family 'of ancient lineage and good estate' (*D.N.B.*). She was the widow of Thomas Fell, lawyer, M.P. and Vice-Chancellor of the Duchy of Lancaster. A necessary concomitant of the use of law, as Horle demonstrates, was to have friends at court. Perhaps the peace principle, the use of legal advisers and the rise to prominence of socially more elevated Quakers were part of a single development?

By 1676, Horle tells us, many of the Quaker leaders 'represented a newer generation of Quakers whose interests were more commercial and less agricultural' – no longer mainly peasants from the North of England. They were 'pragmatists who understood that organization, lobbying and legal tactics were imperatives to any strategy of survival in a hostile political and religious environment'.[16] Penn and other Quakers had a foothold at court.

The new Quaker policy – if we can call it a policy – accepted that Christ's kingdom was not of this world (at any rate in the near future) and aimed to alleviate the very considerable sufferings of persecuted Friends. Whenever possible it tried to utilize royal influence on their behalf, and so became inextricably entangled with the personal politics of Charles II and James II. Charles was not a man of steady political principle, except in his determination not to go on his travels again. But he appears to have disliked the excessive vindictiveness of the persecution of Quakers by returned royalists and newly-royalist Presbyterians. At

15. Braithwaite, *The Second Period of Quakerism* (1919), Chapters XI and XII, esp. p. 324.
16. Op. cit., p. 163.

various times during his reign he played the dissenting card against the Parliamentary majority of those who wished to persecute sectaries. Quaker principles were steadfast, though practice was flexible. The Quaker peace principle had announced a new and controversial policy, and as we have seen reassurances had to be given that the use of legal advice and legal tactics were fully compatible with Quaker 'Truth'.

Anne Boleyn persuaded her future husband to recognize the political advantages to be gained from use of Tyndale's protestantism. Did Margaret Fell persuade her future husband to see the possibilities of utilizing the law and the court in the interests of the people called Quakers? As rich Friends prospered, the Society of Friends also became richer and acted as a trade union or friendly society for its members, collecting money to buy legal advice and help. It scrupulously left to individual Quakers' freedom whether or not to take advantage of the legal advice and to use the legal tactics which were open to all. Socially most Friends were neither oppressed wage slaves, vagabonds or conscripts, nor rich business men. They retained egalitarian principles which led fortunate members to use their wealth to help their poor. They were *Friends* first and foremost. This seems the likely explanation of what appears to be the fact that far fewer Friends, as they prospered, left the Society for the Church of England and county respectability than was the case in other dissenting connections.

25. *Apocalypse and After*

God changes circumstances, assigns kingdoms and takes them away . . . through the agency of men.

Milton, *A Defence of the People of England* (1651), in *Complete Prose Works*, IV, pp. 394–5.

This may be the door to usher in the things that God has promised, which have been prophesied of, which he has set the hearts of his people to wait for and expect. . . . You are at the edge of the promises and prophecies.

Oliver Cromwell, speech to the 'Barebones' Parliament to which he resigned power on 4 July 1653.

When we shall come to give an account to them [the electorate] we shall be able to say, Oh! we have quarrelled for and we contested for the liberty of England.

Cromwell, speech to his first elected Parliament, 12 September 1654; in *Writings and Speeches*, III, p. 461.

When Milton said that the Mosaic law was abolished and 'we are released from the decalogue',[1] he meant that the sins forbidden in the Ten Commandments were not necessarily sins when committed by one of the elect. But most of the sins forbidden in the decalogue were also regarded as crimes by the law of the state. Did Milton (and other antinomians) really mean that God's chosen elect were above the secular law as well as the Law of Moses? In times of revolutionary crisis the answer for some might perhaps be yes, but only then. In normal times it would not have seemed a satisfactory argument against a charge of murder to say that it had been committed in the faith. Rhetorical flourishes aside, there were real problems here, affecting day-to-day conduct. If Robin Hood or Dick Turpin really had robbed the rich in order to give to the poor, would that

1. See Chapter 19 above.

be a sin, a crime or a virtuous action? The consciences of believers might give answers here conflicting with the law of the land. A Milton would differ from a shady character like Clarkson in his attitude towards other people's property. One can understand that those who thought the laws of the land should be obeyed in the interests of peaceful life in society became very impatient with the minority who wanted drastic change here and now. And one can see why antinomianism appealed to the lowest classes in society; still more can one see why the propertied classes expected it to have this appeal.

In the eyes of alarmed conservatives and moderate reformers, 'liberty' had led to regicide – an unprecedented act, in complete breach of the law of the land. ('If they can do this to me', the King shrewdly commented, 'which of you is safe?') 'Liberty' had also led to an anarchy of squabbling religious sects, in place of the single (true) church, which might need reforming but could never be abolished. Some sectaries thought sin had been abolished as well as the state church. Many moderates began to feel, as their successors were to feel during the French Revolution, that crimes were being committed in liberty's name.

William Erbery, whom in 1646 Thomas Edwards had reported as expecting new heavens and a new earth, came to see himself as 'bewildernessed, as a wayfaring man, seeing no way of man on earth, nor beaten path to lead him'. 'A wilderness condition . . . with God is the most comfortable state . . . in that apostacy we now are'.[2]

The daring speculations of the radicals were profoundly shocking to conventional thinkers, as Mrs Hutchinson's view that there had been no magistracy since the Apostles' time, nor could there be, had shocked Governor Winthrop. Milton no doubt believed that the elect, in pursuance of God's purposes, might act in ways that would be sinful for the unregenerate. But how do we know who the elect are? Or indeed what God's purposes are?

Some radicals felt that the situation was so catastrophic, and appreciated by so few, that it must presage the coming of Christ to rule through his saints. Those who used to be condescendingly called 'the lunatic fringe' were those who were sane enough to see that liberty could not be established by the merely human forces available. Divine intervention seemed the only possible solution. They thought that the end of human

2. Edwards, *Gangraena*, I, pp. 77–8; *The Testimony of William Erbery* (1658), pp. 18, 22, 100.

history was at hand; the saints must seize and utilize political power to overthrow the rule of Antichrist and prepare the way for Christ's coming.

Oliver Cromwell illustrates the changes of mind of a radical gentleman who found himself an actor in the drama of the English Revolution. In the Putney Debates of November 1647 he described himself as 'one of those whose heart God hath drawn out to wait for some extraordinary dispensations, according to those promises that he hath held forth of things to be accomplished in the latter time, and I cannot but think that God is beginning of them'.[3] A year later the eccentric Lady Eleanor Davies presented some verses to him inscribed 'Behold the Lord cometh with ten thousand of his saints to execute judgment on all (Jude 14–15)'. Oliver put his spectacles on, smiled – we may imagine a little wryly – and replied 'But we are not all saints'.[4]

But then came Pride's Purge of the elected Parliament, regicide, the republic, the ejection of the Rump of the Long Parliament, and the summoning of the hand-picked Barebones assembly. Cromwell used remarkable words in his speech resigning power to this assembly's hands on 4 July 1653. 'Jesus Christ is owned this day by your call.'[5] And he continued in the no less remarkable words cited as the second epigraph to this chapter.

Whatever were Cromwell's hopes and aspirations in July 1653, the Barebones 'Parliament' brought him back to earth. He came ultimately to see it as 'a story of my own weakness and folly'.[6] But it was no body of religious fanatics. It appointed a committee to consider reformation of the whole legal system and to codify the law, and it voted to abolish the Court of Chancery. Among other very practical reforms discussed were a reduction in the number of offences liable to the death sentence, an end to burning as the death sentence for women and to pressing to death for those refusing to plead: that genuine bankrupts should not be imprisoned and that the goods of fraudulent debtors should be seized and sold. Committees were appointed to make recommendations for the relief of the poor and the victims of enclosure, and for the advancement of learning. Marriage was made a civil ceremony, and the abolition of tithes was

3. Cromwell, *Writings and Speeches*, I, p. 543.
4. T. Spencer, 'The History of an Unfortunate Lady', *Harvard Studies and Notes in Philology and Literature*, XX, p. 56.
5. Cromwell, *Writings and Speeches*, III, pp. 64–5.
6. Ibid., IV, p. 489.

discussed. Such reforms would have established many of the liberties which we have been discussing, but they went too far for many of the propertied members even of that godly assembly. A majority of its members met early one morning to vote their own dissolution, denouncing their colleagues for 'endeavouring to take away their properties by taking away the law, to overthrow the ministry by taking away tithes' – for trying to establish liberty against the law, in fact. Cromwell, a property-owner himself, accepted the vote of self-dissolution. 'Ministry and property were like to be destroyed', he reminded a meeting of his officers in February 1657. 'Who could have said anything was their own if they had gone on?'[7]

The saints having failed to establish Christ's kingdom on earth, Cromwell reverted to rule through a Parliament elected on the old franchise. 'It is some satisfaction', he told his first elected Parliament on 22 January 1654, 'if a Commonwealth . . . must needs suffer' that 'it should suffer rather from rich men than from poor men'.[8] The 'normality' of the rule of property had defeated the godly libertarians. But many must have reflected that property would be more secure under a hereditary monarchy than under the commander of an army which had in the past often made radical interventions into politics. So England returned to suffering under rich men.

Nothing fails like failed apocalypse, as Doomsday Sedgwick learnt when he was foolish enough to give dates in the near future for Christ's Second Coming. The Fifth Monarchist revolts of 1657 and 1661 were courageous and bloody but never had a hope of success. The vision of Christ's kingdom on earth faded into the light of common day when 'normality' returned with Charles II.

Historians have however not meditated sufficiently on the widespread influence of ideas about the imminence of Christ's coming in the 1640s and 1650s – affecting Milton no less than Sedgwick. It is difficult for us to recapture the apocalyptic atmosphere of those years, the spiritual turmoil of vast surging ideas in conflict. Scholars of the present generation, like W. A. Cole and Barry Reay, have rediscovered the pre-pacifist history of the early Quakers, and their conclusions are now accepted, notably by the Society of Friends themselves. In the revolutionary decades some felt – like Milton – that the apostasy of 1,500 years was ending, in which 'not

7. Ibid., IV, pp. 417–18.
8. Ibid., III, p. 584.

Christ but Antichrist' had dominated. Others were appalled by the competing ideas which Milton had welcomed in *Areopagitica*.

So accustomed have we got to this 'normality' that historians have I
think still not sufficiently appreciated the 'rationality' of the belief in
imminent divine intervention as the only way of mending society's ills,
and in consequence have not felt it necessary to explain the sudden eclipse
of apocalyptic ideas after 1660. It is of course possible that this apparent
eclipse is an optical illusion caused by the restoration of the 'normality' of
censorship with monarchy and bishops.

The fact had to be faced that there was to be no last battle between
Christ and Antichrist, no big bang. By the end of the seventeenth century
many had come even to doubt whether Antichrist was ruling at Rome.
Perhaps there was something of Antichrist in *all men*, and the battle
against him was personal, internal.[9] Simultaneously with the decline of
Antichrist came a decline of the Calvinist predestinarian theology; doubts
about the number and visibility of the elect. 'We are all Arminians now'.
Men no longer see two armies facing one another, Christ's elect and the
synagogue of Satan: the holy war is conducted inside each believer. Sober
propertied protestants now had less reason to fear Antichrist in Rome
than they had to fear the indiscipline of the lower classes at home. Even
Gerrard Winstanley came to think that laws would be necessary to
safeguard the abolition of private property against 'the rudeness and
ignorance that may arise in mankind'.[10]

After 1660 ordinary people still felt themselves oppressed by the laws,
but they seem to have come to accept that a society without law is more
rather than less antichristian. Antinomianism survived into the eighteenth
century, but antinomians came to ask only to be left alone, no longer
aspired to rule the world. Or if they had such aspirations they would be
those of the Diggers – 'to conquer them by love'.

9. See my *Antichrist in Seventeenth-century England*, Chapter IV.
10. See Chapter 23 above.

26. John Clare, 1793–1864

O Time how rapid did thy moments flow
That changed these scenes of joy to scenes of woe!

Clare, 'Home', in *Early Poems* (ed. E. Robinson and D. Powell, Oxford U.P., 1989), II, p. 3.

The sad life of John Clare rounds off my story. His early reading was in chapbooks and ballads. His father claimed to be able to sing or recite over a hundred ballads; and Clare's 'Village Minstrel' would joy to hear 'ancient songs' about 'feats of Robin Hood and Little John'. Clare was fond of *The Beggar's Opera*.[1] The destruction of rural freedom by enclosure shattered him. His struggle to write and publish the sort of poetry he wanted to write seems to relate to the story I have tried to tell.

I wrote this chapter at an early stage of compiling this book. After I had completed it, Cambridge University Press published in 1994 *John Clare in Context*, a collection of articles edited by Hugh Haughton, Alan Phillips and Geoffrey Summerfield. Most of the articles in this useful book contain new information and fresh insights. But I did not feel that anything in it conflicted significantly with what I had written, since my object was to place Clare in his historical context. So I have left the chapter as I wrote it, adding (with acknowledgments) some material from these articles which confirmed or elaborated on points which I had tried to make.

Clare felt joy in writing poetry. 'Joys delight [the poet] which he cannot name'. 'All nature brings me joy'.[2] 'Come Hither, Isabel' is a paean to rural peace and solitude. 'I found the poems in the fields', he explains, 'and only wrote them down'. In 'The Progress of Rhyme' he tried to recapture some of his early feelings ('fields were the essence of the song'):

1. Clare, *Autobiographical Writings* (ed. E. Robinson, Oxford U.P., 1986), pp. xii, 2, 5, 56; cf. *Early Poems* (ed. E. Robinson and D. Powell, Oxford U.P., 1989), I, p. xviii, II, pp. 162, 295.
2. *Early Poems*, I, p. 452; *Later Poems* (ed. E. Robinson and D. Powell, Oxford U.P., 1984), I, p. 13.

No matter how the world approved,
'Twas nature listened, I that loved. . . .
Until I even danced for joy,
A happy and a lonely boy.

One of the few things Clare tells us about his parents links them with the themes of this book:

O'er the songs my parents sung
My ear in silent musings hung . . .
They sang, and joy was my reward . . .
I dared not sing aloud for shame.
So all unheeded, lone and free,
I felt it happiness to be
Unknown, obscure and like a tree
In woodland peace and privacy. . . .
A clownish, silent, aguish boy
Who even felt ashamed of joy,
So dirty, ragged and so low,
With naught to recommend or show.[3]

But then 'vile enclosure came', in the form of legislation of 1809. 'Joy' and 'freedom', two key words in Clare's poems, frequently linked, were ended by the actions of a few persons totally unknown to him, sitting at Westminster, who destroyed everything that had given Clare delight. No longer could ordinary people roam where 'the fields themselves seem happy to be free', 'free as air', 'free for all', 'free as the winds that breathe upon my cheek'.[4] That freedom and joy had been destroyed by the greed of the rich.

But who can tell the anguish of his mind
When . . . curst improvement 'gan his fields enclose.
O greens, and fields, and trees, farewell, farewell.
His heart-wrung pains, his unavailing woes
No words can utter and no tongue can tell
When ploughs destroyed the green, when groves of willows fell. . . .

3. *Later Poems*, II, pp. 1021–2, I, p. 19; *The Midsummer Cushion* (ed. A. Tibble, 1978), pp. 227–31; *Poems of John Clare* (ed. J. W. Tibble, 1935), I, p. 436.
4. *Poems* (ed. J. W. Tibble), I, p. 420, II, p. 307; *The Shepherd's Calendar* (ed. E. Robinson and G. Summerfield, Oxford U.P., 1973), p. 101; *The Midsummer Cushion*, pp. 455, 44.

There once was lanes in nature's freedom dropt
There once was paths that every valley wound;
Enclosure came, and every path was stopt,
Each tyrant fixed his signs where paths was found
To hint a trespass now who crossed the ground.
Justice is made to speak as they command . . .
Enclosure thou'rt a curse upon the land. . . .
O England! boasted land of liberty . . .
Thy poor slaves the alteration see . . .
Like emigrating bird thy freedom's flown. . . .
And every village owns its tyrants now
And parish slaves must live as parish kings allow.[5]

Henceforth Clare's ramblings were curtailed, and too often ended in grief at the recollection of 'the joys I used to find'. He now found only 'manhood's withered root of faded joy'.[6] He wanted to 'seek the road again', 'the road where all are free'. In nature there was still freedom everywhere – 'on roars the flood, all restless to be free'; 'a noise like waters that for freedom rush'; 'the wind, . . . pining for freedom like a lovesick nun'; 'the very weeds left free to flower' beside

the very road that wanders out of sight,
Crooked and free.[7]

Clare's emphasis is always on the dire consequences of enclosure for the poor as well as for himself.

I could not bear to see the tearing plough
Root up and steal the forest from the poor.

He looked back to the days

'Ere vile enclosure took away the moor
And farmers built a workhouse for the poor.

Now 'the woodman's axe . . . cuts down every tree'; 'the well-known brook, the favourite tree, . . . that green for ever dear', are all gone. But

The man of science and of taste
Sees wealth far richer in the worthless waste.[8]

5. *Early Poems*, II, pp. 168–9.
6. *The Midsummer Cushion*, pp. 9, 104.
7. *Early Poems*, II, p. 8; *The Midsummer Cushion*, p. 452.
8. *Poems of John Clare*, II, p. 323; I, pp. 394, 407, 466.

Clare's incarceration in an asylum limited even this mobility.

> The spring is come forth, but no spring is for me
> Like the spring of my boyhood on woodland and lea
> When flowers brought me heaven and knew me again
> In the joy of their blooming o'er mountain and plain.
> My thoughts are confined and imprisoned; oh when
> Will freedom find me my own valleys again?
>
> I envy e'en the fly its gleams of joy
> In the green woods.[9]

References to joy, present or past, recur continually. The frequency of the appearance of the word is rivalled only by 'freedom/liberty' which had also been lost. Psalm 137, one of those which Clare chose to imitate, denounced ruin on Babylon which had destroyed the joy of Jerusalem.[10]

The mental disturbance to which Clare finally succumbed must in large part have been due to the sense of tragic loss which enclosure brought. It came to be associated in his mind with his first love, Mary Joyce, with whom he had roamed the fields and woodlands, sharing thoughts which did often lie too deep for tears. In love 'my very bondage, though in snare, is free'.[11] But

> Now this sweet vision of my boyish hours,
> Free as spring clouds and wild as forest flowers,
> Is faded all – a hope that blossomed then
> And hath been once as it no more shall be.
> Enclosure came, and trampled on the grave
> Of labour's rights, and left the poor a slave. . . .
>
> The skybound wastes in mangled garb are left,
> Fence meeting fence in owners' little bounds . . .
> In little parcels little minds to please,
> With men and flocks imprisoned, ill at ease.
> For with the poor scared freedom bade farewell.
>
> Even in prison they [flowers] can solace me,
> For where they bloom God is, and I am free.
>
> In prison o thrall seeing naught but the sky
> Shut out are the green fields and birds i' the bushes

---

9. *Later Poems*, I, p. 394; II, p. 1023.
10. John Clare, *Selected Letters* (ed. M. Storey, Oxford U.P., 1990), pp. 125–6.
11. *Poems of John Clare*, II, p. 390, 'The Exile'.

> In the prison yard nothing builds,
> Blackbirds or thrushes.
>
> I'm a woe-worn prisoner here
>   No more with freedom roaming
>
> Here prisons injure health and me:
> I love sweet freedom and the free.

He still 'kept my spirit with the free'. The song of a skylark could take him back to see again 'old friends with old faces' – violets, primroses and daisies.[12]

Clare found refuge and consolation in writing poetry. But here too problems arose. The peasant poet had to find patrons if he was to publish. Thanks to aristocratic help, Clare did publish, and his poetry gained him a reputation. But this brought its own unfreedom. Enclosure threatened the liberty and joy of thousands of poor peasants. But Clare in his personal life was oppressed not so much by the tyranny of the law as by the conventional polite-society standards of his patrons and admirers. They were apt, often with the best of intentions, to take upon themselves correction not only of his grammar and vocabulary but also of his ideas. Clare was much less free to write as he thought than Winstanley had been.

It has been difficult to assess this matter, because few of Clare's poems were published exactly as he wrote them until very recently. They were 'corrected' for grammatical reasons, or to conform with accepted literary practice, or for political reasons. In a sense all the 'corrections' were political: they were designed to establish conformity with the 'law' of the dominant classes. There is a great deal of peeling off to do still. Clare's roots were with the peasantry who were shut out of the land by enclosure, and denied the vote by the Reform Bill of 1832. Any reader with a sense of history can feel in Clare's poems the passionate hatred of enclosure by the rich against the poor, resentment of Whigs mouthing radical slogans whilst enclosing and evicting. 'Lobin Clout's Satirical Soliloquy on the times' breathes class-consciousness under a veil of irony.[13] In 'The Parish' Clare wrote

> I fearless sing: let truth attend the rhyme –
> Tho now adays truth grows a vile offence,
> And courage tells it at his own expence.[14]

12. *Later Poems*, I, pp. 313, 373, 400; II, 730; *Poems of John Clare*, II, p. 526: 'The Sleep of Spring'.
13. *Early Poems*, I, pp. 137–8; cf. pp. 310 and 365, and *Later Poems*, I, pp. 29, 39.
14. *Early Poems*, II, p. 698.

But in fact only brief and relatively harmless extracts from 'The Parish' were published in obscure periodicals.

Clare fought hard to retain the language which he spoke, against attempts to translate him into standard English. He simmered in helpless rage when the egregious Lord Radstock presumed to excise ten lines from his poem 'Helpstone' because they were too disrespectful to 'accursed wealth'. Clare recognized the need for polishing his vocabulary, but resented attempts to translate what he wrote into City-speak. Yet he could not afford to alienate his patrons. He was isolated against a phalanx of critics more worldly-wise and more confidently successful than himself. Often unconvinced by their arguments, he had to retain their patronage and support. But always 'I felt that I'd a right to song'.[15] For Radstock 'improving' Clare's 'radical slang' meant altering the content as well as changing the words. Where would Clare have been without Lord Radstock – a peer, an admiral, an ardent evangelical and a rich man? When Radstock said, 'Expunge, expunge', he added, 'if he has still a recollection of what I have done and am still doing for him'.

It did not often come to open conflict. Clare must have made many concessions to prevent that happening. He spoke bitterly of the 'false delicacy' of 'meddlers'; but 'I must keep the peace with his lordship' – 'interest urges me'. 'I would much rather avoid than court the notice of my superiors. When I say superiors I mean men of titles, wealth and fashion with nothing or little of impartial feeling towards an inferior'. There is heavy irony in his 'fashion is everything, and it would evidently be considered radicalism to think otherwise'.[16] In 'The Flitting' he remarked

> For books, they follow fashions new
> And throw all old esteems away.[17]

He wrote more openly in 'To the Memory of Bloomfield':

> Some feed on living fame with conscious pride . . .
> The breed of fashion haughtily they ride
> As though her breath were immortality
> Which is but bladder puffs of common air.

15. John and Anne Tibble, *John Clare: His Life and Poetry* (1957), pp. 71–2. For Radstock see also *Selected Letters*, pp. 28, 34–41, 231; *The Midsummer Cushion*, p. 225.
16. *Selected Letters*, pp. 37, 110, 154.
17. *Poems of John Clare*, II, p. 253.

> . . . Many a fame shall lie
> A dead wreck on the shore of dark posterity.

But 'the dazzling fashions of the day' were not for Bloomfield, 'sweet unassuming minstrel'. His 'gentle song' dealt, like Clare's, with 'field and cloud and tree, and quiet brooks far distant from the throng':

> Nature owns thee, let the crowd pass by;
> The tide of fashion is a stream too strong
> For pastoral brooks that gently flow and sing.
> But nature is their source, and earth and sky,

and Bloomfield's poems

> shall murmur on to many a spring
> When their proud streams are summer-burnt and dry.[18]

It is impossible to doubt that Clare was consoling himself here.

So it is not always easy to be sure what Clare really thought. When he wrote in his *Journal*, à propos Hazlitt, 'I hate politics', or when he described Paine as a low blackguard – though without reading him – are we to take such remarks at face value? 'Is politics to rule genius?' he asked, thinking of Keats. If so, liberty will be 'thrown to the dogs'.[19] Are we to disregard Clare's later poems – such as 'Liberty'?

> I've loved thee, as the common air
> And paid thee worship everywhere;
> I've loved thy being from a boy.[20]

In his correspondence Clare is perhaps careful too; but we may note his frequent references to cant and humbug, his desire to tax the rich whilst denying being a 'Leveller', his sense of the nearness of revolution in 1831, his objections to priestcraft.[21] He sentimentalizes social relations prior to enclosure, writing of

> That good old fame the farmers earned of yore
> That made as equals, not as slaves, the poor.

18. *The Midsummer Cushion*, p. 397: 'To the Memory of Bloomfield'.
19. *Prose of John Clare* (ed. J. W. and A. Tibble, 1951), pp. 116, 140; *Selected Letters*, p. 53.
20. *Later Poems*, I, p. 274.
21. *Selected Letters*, pp. 14, 18, 103, 106, 157–8, 168, 171; *Later Poems*, I, pp. 39, 87; II, p. 764.

He praised

> The old freedom that was living then
> When masters made them merry with their men,
> Whose coat was like his neighbour's, russet brown
> And whose rude speech was vulgar as his clown.[22]

Clare sneered at 'the parson' who 'is now stirring up to radicalism (which some years ago he cried down as infidelity) . . . because . . . he wishes to keep his tithes and his immense livings untouched'. That 'tyranny and cruelty appear to be the inseparable companions of Religious Power' was the lesson he learnt from reading Foxe's *Book of Martyrs*.[23]

> Freedom-preaching is but knavery's game
> And old self-interest by a different name.

'Tyrant laws' and 'good church-going godly' knaves combine against the poor.[24]

The middle-class humbug which accompanied destruction and exploitation by agricultural 'improvement' particularly infuriated Clare. He had no sympathy with 'picketers for freedom', or the man

> Who spouts of freedom as the thing he craves
> And treats the poor o'er whom he rules as slaves. . . .
>
> Thou'st heard the knave abusing those in power
> Bawl freedom loud, and then oppress the free. . . .
>
> Then came enclosure – ruin was its guide
> But freedom's clapping hands enjoyed the sight
> Though comfort's cottage soon was thrust aside
> And workhouse prisons raised upon the site.
> With axe at root he felled thee to the ground
> And barked of freedom.
> It grows the cant term of enslaving tools
> To wrong another by the name of right.[25]

In a poem called 'England, 1830', he wrote

---

22. *Early Poems*, II, p. 702; *The Shepherd's Calendar* (ed. E. Robinson and G. Summerfield, Oxford, U.P., 1973), pp. 68–9; cf. *The Midsummer Cushion*, pp. 23–4.
23. *Selected Letters*, p. 157; *Prose of John Clare*, p. 103.
24. *Early Poems*, II, p. 737.
25. *Early Poems*, II, p. 736; *The Midsummer Cushion*, pp. 192–3: 'The Fallen Elm'.

Like to prison-cells her freedoms grow
Becobwebbed with these oft repeated songs
 Of peace and plenty in the midst of woe . . .
Forging new bonds and bidding her be free.

And there are knaves that brawl for better laws
And cant of tyranny in stronger powers,
Who glut their vile unsatiated maws
And freedom's birthright from the weak devours.[26]

It is instructive to compare the peasant Clare with Blake. The latter had
a solid base in the London artisan community, and pride in his craftsman-
ship gave him self-confidence. He had no need for aristocratic patronage.
Blake moreover inherited a continuing Muggletonian antinomian tradition. Clare's timid interest in the Primitive Methodist 'Ranters' was that
of an outsider.

Here we might profitably think of the personae with whom Clare
identified himself in his lucid moments. That he saw himself as a professional pugilist (prize-fighter Jack Randall) speaks for itself: it may tell us a
great deal about his suppressed rage. To be Lord Byron was to be a
radical aristocrat, whose rank permitted him to say things which no
peasant poet would dare to utter. As Clare put it, with one eye upon his
own problems, Byron 'looked upon critics as the countryman does on a
magistrate; he beheld them as a race of petty tyrants that stood in the way
of genius. They were in his eyes more of stumbling blocks than guides.
. . . He was an Oliver Cromwell with the critics: he broke up their long-
standing Parliament and placed his own will in the Speaker's chair, and
his will they humbly accepted'.[27] That nicely encapsulates popular hatred
for magistrates and their law, and Clare's awareness of his own ambiguous
position *vis-à-vis* the literary establishment. Cromwell gives a suitably
violent political thrust to the argument. We may compare Clare's favourable reference to Cromwell in 'The Village Minstrel', and his sonnet
praising Blake, the admiral of the Commonwealth:

Blake though insulted by a king's decree
Thy fame stirs onward like the mighty sea.
Time . . . rusts crowns into baubles, kings to dust.[28]

26. *Poems of John Clare*, II, p. 117; *The Midsummer Cushion*, p. 193.
27. *Prose of John Clare*, pp. 206–10.
28. *Early Poems*, I, pp. 162–3; *The Midsummer Cushion*, p. 446. At the restoration the
royal government ordered Blake's body to be removed from Westminster Abbey and
thrown into a pit with 'scores' of other republicans.

Clare told his publisher John Taylor in 1820 that in his illness 'I get more into the company of the rustics of the village, harmless cottagers recollect, and there I am at home again. . . . This . . . I think will be the only means of getting well till I am accustomed to the ways of the world, her overpowering flattering reception or overwhelming disgust'.[29] Once he came into a public reputation he had to fight for his freedom to sing as he wished, and not as others expected him to.

> The sparrows in the thatch . . .
> Contrive with doubtful faith to build
> Beyond the reach of man.[30]

Clare sought out nests hidden away deep in the woods, built of odds and ends of common materials; there the bird can enjoy his right to sing. Unlike Wordsworth or Keats, Clare did not see the lark or the nightingale as proud singers dominating the sky: they nest where 'they feel no mood of fear' and are safe to sing 'nature's song of freedom', undetected by men. Clare himself never felt sufficiently secure to sing absolutely freely. He marvelled that 'so famed a bird' as the nightingale 'should have no better dress than russet brown'.[31]

Weeds are symbolic too. In Clare's poem 'Spring' 'Every wild weed in perfection glows'. He thought that weeds 'should be reckoned flowers' because they 'made a garden free for all'. The thistle '– could not be / A weed in nature's poesy'. And the thistle is a symbol of Scotland and freedom.[32]

We must read very carefully between the lines even of Clare's letters and autobiographical statements, and take note of cuts made in deference to his wealthy patrons. This curbing of his freedom even after his moment of apparent triumph must have been very hard to bear. Clare is explicit in 'The Return: Northborough, 1841', after his unsuccessful attempt to escape from the prison of his madhouse:

29. *Selected Letters*, p. 17.
30. *The Midsummer Cushion*, pp. 123–4.
31. Ibid., p. 201: 'The Nightingale's Nest'; *Early Poems*, I, p. 54. Cf. Hugh Haughton's 'Progress and Rhyme. "The Nightingale's Nest and Romantic Poetry"', in *John Clare in Context*, pp. 55–6, 62, 79.
32. *Later Poems*, II, p. 987; *The Midsummer Cushion*, pp. 225–6: 'The Progress of Rhyme'.

> Fame blazed upon me like a comet's glare;
>   Fame waned and left me like a fallen star,
> Because I told the evil what they are
>   My life hath been a wreck. . . .[33]

In his published writings Clare pays frequent lip-service to established religion, but in the unpublished 'The Parish' he wrote

> Religion now is little more than cant
> A cloak to hide what godliness we want.[34]

It is in this context that we should see Clare's flirtation with 'Ranters', enthusiastic Primitive Methodists, 'priests that take the street to teach'.[35] Theirs was, in Edward Thompson's words, 'a religion *of* the poor', not '*for* the poor'. Many Primitive Methodists became Chartists.[36] Clare never told the poor that it was their religious duty to be humble and deferential – as his hypocritical Farmer Finch did in 'The Parish' – and as the Rev. George Crabbe did in real life.[37]

Clare and Crabbe both had considerable imaginative sympathy for the problems of the poor, but (as Clare put it) 'Crabbe writes about the peasantry as much like the Magistrate as the Poet'. Crabbe came from a different social class. 'What's he know of the poor, musing over a snug coal fire in his parsonage box?'[38]

Clare found himself more at home in the company of gypsies than of Lord Radstock. From around 1814 he cultivated friendly relations with them, and 'was often tempted to join them'.[39] He saw gypsies as fellow-victims of enclosure, whose lawless freedom and disregard for hedges attracted him:

> You, poor ragged out casts of the land,
> That hug your shifting camps from green to green . . .
>   Your groups did beautify the scene . . .
> Poor wandering souls, to fate's hard want decreed.

---

33. Op. cit., in *Poems of John Clare*, II, p. 394.
34. *Early Poems*, II, p. 715; cf. pp. 736–7, 748–9.
35. Ibid., II, p. 718.
36. See Edward Thompson, *The Making of the English Working Class* (Pelican ed., 1968), p. 41; cf. pp. 325, 426–9, 435–6.
37. *Early Poems*, II, pp. 748–9. For Crabbe see p. 63 below.
38. Ibid., I, p. xix, II, p. 791.
39. *Autobiographical Writings*, pp. 31, 69–72. For Clare and gypsies cf. pp. 135, 141 above.

He defended their reputation against slanders: 'pilfering' was forced upon them by their post-enclosure hardships.[40]

'The Gypsy Song' makes explicit Clare's reasons for respecting them:

> We pay no rent nor tax to none
>   And live untithed and free;
> None cares for us, for none care we
>   And where we list we roam . . .
>
> Bad luck to tyrant magistrates,
>   And the gypsies' dwelling free.

Their songs'

> Echo fills the woods around
> With gypsy liberty . . .
>
>   Our joys are uncontrolled . . .
> Though the wild woods are our house and home
>   'Tis a home of liberty.

So long as they

> Can find a common free
> Around old England's heaths we'll tramp
>   In gipsy liberty.[41]

This liberty included sexual liberty. Gypsy women are 'fond and free'; 'no parson's fetters link us in: our heart's a stronger bond'. I have already quoted 'Not felon-like law-bound, but wedded in desires'. Clare was sceptical of church marriage.[42]

Gypsies were 'lawless, . . . driven from stage to stage', but they were

> A picture to the place
> A quiet, pilfering, unprotected race.

They have

> honest faces, fresh and free
> That breathe of mountain liberty . . .

40. *Early Poems*, II, pp. 171–3, 250.
41. *The Midsummer Cushion*, pp. 325–7: 'The Gipsy Song'. 'Untithed' is of course a hit at the clergy of the Church of England.
42. *The Midsummer Cushion*, pp. 325–7; cf. pp. 35, 104, 114, 123, 173, 459. See p. 202 above.

Right glad of freedom from the prison yard . . .
[In] gypsy camps in some snug sheltered nook . . .
These wild wood roamers dwell
On commons where no farmers' claims appear
Nor tyrant justice rides to interfere . . .[43]

On the common . . .
The gipsies lie basking themselves at their ease
And the gipsy boys shaking their rags to the sun
Are head over ears in their frolic and fun . . .

Those brown tawny lasses . . .
The mole hillocks make . . . soft cushions for love . . .
As blest as the rich who on sofas repose.[44]

   The gipsy he builds in a day
A house without trouble or wealth . . .
O I think though the world has grown old in its care
I should meet with the garden of paradise there.[45]

So Clare lamenting the final triumph of enclosure over the poor, and Clare fighting for freedom to write as he wished, offered a fitting conclusion to the story I have tried to tell of the defeat of freedom by law, property and accepted middle-class standards. As a contributory factor to his madness, Clare cherishing a hopeless passion for Mary Joyce, a girl who was socially too superior for him to be able to marry her, also makes a relevant point. Clare's was not a sentimental romantic nostalgia. It was a practical, personal sense of shared loss. The things he loved, and which inspired him to write, were doomed; but he retained solidarity with the victims of transportation and imprisonment, and with the Swing rioters executed for opposition to the 'vast numbers of newly-made laws that took away rights from the common people'. Although he

43. *Early Poems*, II, p. 157; *Later Poems*, I, pp. 29, 405; *The Shepherd's Calendar*, pp. 75–8, 112–13.
44. *The Midsummer Cushion*, p. 173.
45. Ibid., pp. 356–7. John Goodridge and Kelsey Thornton in their contribution to *John Clare in Context* ('John Clare: the trespasser') are good on his attitude towards gypsies. James McKusick in 'Beyond the Visionary Company: John Clare's resistance to Romanticism' also stresses the 'sense of class solidarity with gypsies, beggars and other social outcasts', which appears especially in Clare's later poems (op. cit., pp. 108–13, 232–5).

often expressed himself cautiously, Clare retained strong social and political feelings.[46]

46. See John Lucas, 'Clare's Politics', in *John Clare in Context*, p. 168 and *passim*. His contribution is an admirable corrective to the often-expressed view of Clare as non-political.

27. *Some Conclusions*

===

Give me the making of the songs of the people; I care not who makes their laws.

R. Chisty, *Proverbs, Maxims and Phrases of All Ages* (1888), I, p. 602.

I

In the process of writing this book I have learnt – and I hope I have convinced some readers – that a great number of seventeenth-century English men and women did not associate liberty exclusively with property or Parliament. We started with outlaws, beggars, the poor, vagabonds, for whom the law was the enemy. Then we looked at godly nonconformists, some of whom rejected the law of Moses, and all of whom felt it to be their religious duty to break the law in some circumstances. Not all of these groups would react in the same way, but we can assume that a very sizeable proportion of the population would be critical of the law. Only the gentry and better-off merchants seem to be relatively satisfied with it – say perhaps 20 per cent of the population? If merchants occasionally stretched the law, they were less likely to be found out than the poor, and so less liable to appear in the historical record as law-breakers.

But Parliament represented this minority, and its assertion of freedom for property through the law has been treated by many historians as though Parliament was representative of the whole population. It was not.

So if our first question is 'Who makes the law?', the second must be, 'Liberty for whom to do what?' Our answer to the first question is factual – a minority of the upper propertied class; the answer to the second is similar: liberty for the ruling class to have secure ownership of property and guaranteed opportunities for acquiring more. This depends on the effective subordination of the lower classes, by force if necessary, but preferably by convincing them that they have as much freedom as is compatible with the good of society and the will of God. William Penn, both a Quaker and a member of the propertied class, put it succinctly in

1679: 'If we would preserve our government, we must endear it to the people'. If the navy is to win battles for us and to extend the empire, it cannot be recruited and disciplined by impressment and the lash alone.[1]

'Liberty' is theory, laws are facts. Or at least, in theory they are facts. Liberty is an abstract concept: laws are intended to be enforced. 'Intended to be': but they were not always enforced, and so remained theory rather than facts. In considering smuggling and poaching we saw that those who were supposed to administer the laws sometimes found it in their interests to break them. Laws against dissenters were unevenly enforced. 'The comfortable doctrine of original sin' could explain such tolerated lapses. Walwyn was told that 'a natural and complete freedom from all sorrows and troubles was fit for man only before he had sinned, and not since; let them look for their portion in this world that believe no other'. 'If Paradise were to be replanted on earth', Walwyn was told, 'God had never expelled man [from] Paradise'.[2]

The proverb says 'give me the making of the songs of the people; I care not who makes their laws'. How true was this, and for how long? The ballads of Robin Hood put liberty before law. The growing efficiency of the state machine in the sixteenth and seventeenth centuries helped to depersonalize 'justice', and ultimately led to the victory of the law over the songs of the people. The proverb ceased to be applicable as local communities lost their coherence, as they were disrupted by what in shorthand I have called 'enclosure'. ('Improvement' was the euphemism employed in the seventeenth and eighteenth centuries, and still by some historians; 'modernization' is preferred by economic historians who shrink from using the word 'capitalism'.) The communities survived for a long time, but in the long run 'enclosure' won. We have in this book been looking at the transitional period. By Clare's day the battle was over.

Taking the relatively recent definition of law as 'arrangements for living together' it is difficult to think of a society without laws. In our market society commodities have to be moved for vast distances, large numbers of workers have to be housed and hired to make the factory

1. Penn, *Address to Protestants*, p. 52; cf. Chapter 13, above.
2. [Anon.], *Walwins Wiles* (1649), in *The Leveller Tracts, 1647–1653* (ed. W. Haller and G. Davies, Columbia U.P., 1944), p. 312. Some of those who originally migrated from Castile to America did so not 'out of necessity' but 'in order to raise our children in free and royal lands', away from the jurisdiction of feudal landlords (ed. I. A. A. Thompson and Bartolomé Yun Casalilla, *The Castilian Crisis of the Seventeenth Century: New Perspectives on the Economic History of Seventeenth-century Spain*, Cambridge U.P., 1994, p. 269).

system work. If 'laws they are not which public approbation hath not made so', then the question becomes not 'law or no law' but 'who makes the law effective?' Who is the 'public'?

It was easier to conceive of a society without law in medieval times. Then the sword could decide what was right and what wrong. The sword in the hands of the aristocracy could prevail over a large crowd: Spanish conquests in America demonstrated that. But gradually, although swords continued to be worn, they became symbols of power rather than means of enforcing it; they showed that it would be dangerous to offend the wearer of the sword. Soon even this use dropped out of existence. Whether men liked it or not, the rule of law had prevailed.

I have tried to suggest some of the many ways in which in the seventeenth century the law might seem inimical to some people's liberty. Robin Hood and his men were outside the law, breaking it daily in order to obtain food: yet tales about them seem to have enjoyed wide popularity. Pirates and highwaymen lived by breaking the law, yet they are commemorated in ballads; Tyburn crowds treated them with sympathy and respect. Smugglers and poachers performed services to some members of the community by their illegal activities, and were accepted by the respectable as well as by others. Gypsies were more marginal.

Separatist congregations thought it their religious duty to break the law in order to worship God as they believed he wished. Some protestant theologians preached freedom from the Mosaic law, and many of the preciser sort believed with Milton that law had been abolished by the gospel. Some rejected church marriage and the fees attached to it, and broke the law by adhering to older, more traditional forms of sexual union.

Taking all together, this adds up to a significant proportion of the population feeling at least sympathy with law-breakers. And why not? The law was made by a small minority of the population. Old French and legal Latin came back with the monarchy, perpetuating the alienation of the lower classes from legal processes.[3] Attempts to extend the Parliamentary franchise made by radicals during the English Revolution were effectively defeated by governments which wanted liberty for men

3. See Stephen Copley, 'Judicial Wigs and the Majesty of the Law: Hogarth's *The Bench* and Representations of English Legal Costume', in *Literature and History*, 3rd series, Vol. 4, no. 1 (Spring 1955), esp. pp. 20–21.

of property. Their liberty was maintained by laws which often appeared to be directed against the classes not represented in Parliament.

This is especially true of the agrarian changes which I have summed up in the word 'enclosure'. For the peasantry, 'freedom' meant custom, security of livelihood at a low economic level. 'The law' in the seventeenth century aimed at turning the mass of the peasantry off the soil and forcing them into wage labour to produce wealth for their employers and their country, though not for themselves. The Scottish School's account offers a key to the mass acceptance of the idea that liberty and law were opposed.[4]

II

We have been looking at two different types of source material. Whether or not I am right in claiming that social justice motifs underlay the attraction of the Robin Hood ballads and the stories of highwaymen and pirates, clearly they did not appeal only to victims of social injustice. They told good stories; and people can be unhappy about social injustice without actually suffering it themselves.

With antinomians and similar religious libertines we are dealing with literature and ideas put forward by articulate individuals and groups with polemical intent. The Ranters were deliberately naughty and provocative, not least in claiming Biblical authority for their heresies. They wanted to provoke argument perhaps even more than to convince. They emerged from a milieu in which the Bible was regarded as a sacred text, but one which had hitherto been interpreted by men of socially secure and conservative background. Ranters were not middle-class intellectuals who could afford to be unconventional in moral behaviour – in the literal sense of 'afford', by being well-to-do. They spoke for humbler people, whose traditional function was to labour for their betters. As Mandeville pointed out, it is dangerous for them to start thinking for themselves. Ranters deliberately aimed to shock the godly, to provoke them into re-thinking their assumptions about religion and society. Coppe's 'recanta-tion' is a masterpiece of double-talk, in which he admitted to sinning but claimed that 'our rulers, our priests, our judges, all have sinned and gone astray'. He suggested that his peccadilloes were at least no worse

4. See p. 232–3 above.

than the sins of pride and self-indulgence to which his persecutors were inclined.[5]

The Ranters would claim to want social justice, but for them a just society necessitated a much freer and less conventional morality. As Crisp put it, 'To be called a libertine is the most glorious title under heaven'.[6] Their more sober contemporaries among the godly relished attacking Ranters on their own intellectual ground, but were also sufficiently alarmed to call on the sanctions of the law to silence these purveyors of subversive ideas who brought religion into discredit. Ranters differed from restoration rakes in that they were not interested only in shocking the godly: they had some sort of vision of a society which need not be hidebound by traditional morality. Infuriatingly, they found much evidence in the Bible to support their heresies. A long-term consequence of their efforts was perhaps to reinforce the taboos of respectability and conventional morality which were to characterize eighteenth- and nineteenth-century dissent, despite the efforts of provocateurs like William Blake.

The Ranters remain as literary curiosities because they could write vivid and convinced prose in defence of paradoxes which had hitherto been monopolized by the likes of the Marlowe circle under Elizabeth and were to be picked up by Rochester and others under the merrie monarch. The fact that they claimed the sanction of religion for their heresies united respectable society against them.

Potential supporters of freedom from the law, or those whose self-interest should have led them to support freedom, were almost certainly a majority of the population. But they were unorganized outside their communities, perhaps unorganizable except in moments of extreme crisis; and they had no conception of politics apart from what had traditionally existed, and myths of a freer past. Levellers during the English Revolution were divided on the property issue: many of their leaders and supporters were yeomen, men of some property. Their profits depended on law, not on custom. Winstanley and the Diggers made a great success of propaganda by example on St George's Hill. So long as they did not seem dangerous, the Army was sympathetic, both rank-and-file troops and General Fairfax. But when the prospect of a rapid extension of the

5. *Copps Return to the wayes of Truth* (1657)* Cf. my 'Abolishing the Ranters', in *A Nation of Change and Novelty*, pp. 175–80. For Mandeville see pp. 64–5, 171 above.
6. *Crisp's Christ Alone Exalted, Being the Complete Works of Tobias Crisp, . . . containing Fifty-Two Sermons* (ed. J. Gill, 1832), p. 122.

movement loomed, the government succumbed to the pressures of local
gentlemen and clergy, and the Army carried out the government's orders
to suppress the colonies. There could be no effective resistance. Hence
Winstanley's desperate appeal to Oliver Cromwell in *The Law of Freedom*.[7]
The Army was the decisive political force. But only posterity heard
Winstanley's message.

Experience of revolution convinced theorists of the dangers of too
much liberty – a lesson which Luther had learnt a century earlier. The
Lutheran pastor Johannes Agricola told a Münzerite rebel, 'You say that
you want to be "free", but you mean free to give nothing to anybody,
for there is no obedience in you; free indeed to fall upon people and take
from them by force what you claim to be your own'. Even before the
German Peasants' Revolt Melanchthon had warned that 'a wild, untamed
people like the Germans should not have as much freedom as they pres-
ently enjoy. . . . Germans are such an undisciplined, wanton, bloodthirsty
people that they should always be harshly governed. . . . As Ecclesiastes 33
teaches, food, discipline and work are the lot of a servant'.[8] It was a
lesson soon learnt elsewhere. As the future bishop John Gauden elegantly
put it, 'There is no jewel which swine delight more to wear in their snouts
than this of liberty'. Servants deserve less freedom than their masters.[9]

Thomas Edwards in *Gangraena* came to the defence of magistrates,
judges, lawyers, mayors, aldermen and other officials, against sectaries
who rejected state authority in religion. They 'have pretended the liberty
of the subject, the public liberties of the kingdom'; but in practice 'for the
advancing of their own opinions' they have 'done the highest acts against
the liberties of the people that ever were'. 'If they should come to have
the upper hand they would make the people of England the greatest
slaves that ever they were in any time'.[10] After John Owen had
experienced these unprecedented liberties in the 1640s and 1650s, he
observed that 'We are like a plantation of men carried into a foreign
country. In a short space they degenerate from the manners of the people
from whence they came, and fall into that of the country whereunto they
are brought'.[11]

7. See Chapter 23 above.
8. Quoted by Steven Ozment, *Protestants: The Birth of a Revolution* (1993), pp. 144,
244.
9. Gauden, *Hieraspites* (1653), p. 437.
10. Edwards, *Gangraena*, III, pp. 270–71, 279–82, 331–43.
11. Owen, *Of Temptation, the Nature and Power of it* (1658), in *Works*, VIII, p. 112.
Owen had been in Ireland.

James Harrington said that 'the liberty of a commonwealth consists in the empire of her laws, the absence whereof would betray her to the lust of tyrants'. William Walwyn, a radical antinomian, was warned by seven Independent and Baptist ministers that 'We cannot upon any rational and Scriptural ground expect a complete, full, absolute and perfect freedom from all kind of pressures and grievances in the land; surely a natural and complete freedom from all sorrows and troubles was fit for man only before he had sinned and not since. Let them look for their portion in this life that know no better, and their kingdom in this world that believe no other: to what end are the graces of faith, patience and self-denial vouchsafed unto us?' Christ was quoted to demonstrate that we should not 'expect perfect freedom here below'.[12]

Enemies of the Quakers accused them and Levellers of being against magistracy. Quakers were 'undoubtedly the most persistent Anglo-American law-breakers in the seventeenth and eighteenth centuries'. They constituted 'an internal enclave'.[13] Fox thought that 'rich, covetous oppressing men' would make all the laws unless there was an extension of the franchise.[14] In 1659 he put before Parliament a sweeping programme for reform of the law. No man should be imprisoned because he could not or would not fee a lawyer. The death sentence for stealing cattle or money should be abolished. Legal documents should be simplified and shortened. 'Away with lawyers' and we shall have 'a free nation, a free people'.[15] Francis Howgil asked the rulers of the Commonwealth plaintively: 'Was it only a form of government . . . that ye pursued? . . . Or was it not . . . freedom itself?'[16] Edward Burrough in 1659 proclaimed that 'the great and heavy oppressions of the law' had 'been long felt and cried out against, the long delays in courts and the great fees of officers, which causeth many to be excessively rich out of the ruins of the poor, which hath brought odium upon the law itself'.[17]

12. Harrington, *Oceana and Other Works* (1737), p. 45; *Walwins Wiles* (1649), in Haller and Davies, *Leveller Tracts*, p. 312. Cf. p. 326 above.
13. Staughton Lynd, *Intellectual Origins of American Radicalism* (1969), pp. 101–4; cf. p. 111.
14. G. Fox, *A Few Plain Words* (1659), pp. 2–5.
15. G. F., *To the Parliament of the Comon-Wealth of England*, pp. 3–5. Cf. *Newes Coming up out of the North* (1654), p. 22 and *An Instruction to Judges and Lawyers* (n.d.), pp. 18–19, 31–40.
16. Howgil, *Works* (1676), pp. 335–8.
17. Burrough, *The Memorable Works of a Son of Thunder and Consolation* (1672), pp. 136–52, 275–324.

The perplexing shifts in political power in the 1640s and 1650s made the association of any one group with 'freedom' difficult to maintain. 'Honest intentions are rotten rags', William Sedgwick told the Army leaders in 1649, 'and too narrow to cover your nakedness'.[18] Cromwell's 'way is in the wilderness', he added in 1656, 'and 'tis crooked'. But 'hath not our course been so from the beginning?' Though 'this Army and people had an absolute freedom . . . to do what they would', they used it to rebuild 'what God had destroyed'. 'We drove Pharaoh and the Egyptians out of Egypt, and kept Egypt for ourselves'. 'While you thought to reform the world you were defeated by it'. We have asked for liberty only for ourselves, but 'the first step into freedom is out of ourselves'. Freedom cannot be won by force of arms.[19] Sedgwick was not a typical Puritan there; but his views help to explain the recognition by post-restoration dissenters that Christ's kingdom was not of this world.[20] Over a century later, to the question, 'Who is to judge whether human or divine laws are in conflict', William Lloyd Garrison replied, 'the individual conscience'. Staughton Lynd comments: it was an answer which 'expressed his Quakerly confidence in the uneducated common man'.[21]

III

This book does not aspire to be definitive, but to raise some questions which call for further investigation into the different interests of different groups in a rapidly changing society. Outlaws were a nuisance in the age of stage coaches; pirates had to be suppressed if Britannia was to rule the waves and protect British commerce. Antinomians flourished during the free-for-all discussions of the English Revolution, but they were suppressed after the realigned propertied classes gained control in 1660. Antinomians contributed to growing secularization and suffered from it. Charles II's legalization of *licensed* sects ended the state church's monopoly, accepted a more pluralist society.

18. Sedgwick, *A Second View of the Army Remonstrance* (1649), pp. 15–18.
19. Sedgwick, *Animadversions upon A Letter and Paper first sent to His Highness by certain Gentlemen and others in Wales* (1656), pp. 21–2, 37–9, 53–9, 74–6, 88–90, 100, 189–92; cf. pp. 65–6.
20. See my *The Experience of Defeat*, pp. 115–17.
21. Staughton Lynd, op. cit., p. 111.

Since the seventeenth century law has been progressively modified to meet a slowly expanding democracy. *Lady Chatterley's Lover* and *Ulysses* are no longer forbidden books, the death penalty has been abolished, prohibition proved unworkable in the U.S.A. Laws they are not which public opinion hath not sustained. However inadequately, 'public opinion' imposes some constraints on governments, witness John Major's government's surrender on the poll tax.

Polonius's 'put money in thy purse' was the right advice to give a young man who would make good in the modern world. The traditional feudal lord did not need money. Everybody knew him, with his vast lands and troops of retainers. But by the seventeenth century – perhaps his lands are mortgaged, his faithful servants' wages unpaid, it would not only be beneath his dignity to bang down on the table a couple of gold sovereigns; it might be beyond his power.

So liberty in the seventeenth century could mean many very different things. The girls in *A Jovial Crew* sought freedom in joining the beggars; women became pirates to enjoy informal marriage and divorce. The ladies who in ballads ran off to gypsies represent a pre-Romantic reaction against the boredom of respectable society where income comes in with no apparent effort, certainly with no excitement or interest. The world of gypsies and vagabonds was *different*, unknown and for some therefore attractive. Gay's 'Council of Horses' gives a robust middle-class view. An old steed upbraids a young hothead who advocates revolt against men by pointing out that horses get very favourable terms when they are pensioned off in old age. He stood for prudence against romantic but risky freedom.[22] Sylvanus Taylor in 1692 said 'it is natural for all men to love property'.[23] Who are men? We saw in Chapter 24 that Quakers, notable in the 1650s for their extreme hostility to the law and lawyers, later learned how to make use of them.

IV

There are no simple generalizing conclusions to be drawn from the untidy assembly of facts and ideas which I have collected. But perhaps a few thoughts may be ventured. The mid-seventeenth-century revolution was a turning point in our story. The radical revolution was defeated, but the

22. Gay, *Poetical Works*, pp. 268–9.
23. S.T., *Common-Good*, p. 5.

abolition of feudal tenures brought about a decisive change in the relationship both between landowners and the crown and between landowners and their tenants. It was a long-cherished aspiration of the landed class, although its importance has been unaccountably neglected by historians. 'Feudal tenures' assume that the important thing for the landowner is to have docile tenants who will fight for him when necessary: landowners in the sixteenth century were coming to think rather of money returns, for which production for the market and long-term agricultural planning were more important. Blackstone thought that the abolition of feudal tenures and wardship was a more momentous event in the history of landed property even than Magna Carta itself.[24]

In 1588 Cardinal Allen had proposed to win popularity when the Spanish Armada had conquered England by offering the bait of the abolition of wardship and feudal tenures. There had been rumours of a deal for their abolition from the last years of Elizabeth's reign. When Parliament met in 1604, the overwhelming majority of M.P.s favoured abolition. Prolonged negotiations in that Parliament for abolition in return for a regular tax broke down, despite Robert Cecil's persuasive words 'you may return into your countries [counties] and tell your neighbours that you have made a pretty hedge about them'.[25] When the Long Parliament met in 1640 a committee was at once set up to consider the question, and as soon as the civil war was won Parliament abolished the hated feudal tenures and the Court of Wards. The abolition was confirmed by Parliament in 1656, when it seemed that a Cromwellian dynasty was about to put an end to the revolution. In 1660, when Charles Stuart from exile announced his intention of returning to England and his throne, Parliament's first action after agreeing to accept him was to appoint a committee to confirm again the abolition of feudal tenures, so important did the issue seem to them. Also confirmed, and not less important, was Parliament's insistence that copyholders should not enjoy the security of tenure which big landowners had voted to themselves.

The abolition of feudal tenures and wardship transformed the relationship between landowners and the crown. Before 1640 the crown was the source of patronage and favour, and a potential source of disaster for any family of tenants-in-chief who suffered the misfortune of a minor succeeding to the family estate. For both these reasons it was essential for a

24. Hurstfield, *The Queen's Wards* (1958), p. 330.
25. Ibid., pp. 330, 319.

landowning family to enjoy the favour of the ruling monarch, either in order to purchase the wardship and the right to marry the heir, or at least to ensure that it did not pass into hostile or merely speculative hands. But after the abolition of feudal tenures and of wardship royal favour was much less important. Tenants-in-chief were no longer dependent on the crown for favours: they were free and independent as they had not been before the revolution – free to undertake long-term planning of estate management, secure in the knowledge that the accident of wardship would not interrupt these plans.

A second factor was the sale during the revolutionary decades of crown lands, bishops and dean and chapter lands, and of the lands of 'delinquent' royalists. Crown, bishops and deans and chapters had been absentee landlords, who notoriously had not exploited their property efficiently. Those who bought their lands sunk large capital sums in the purchase, and were anxious to recover their money as quickly as possible: many may have anticipated that the lands might ultimately be restored to their original owners. Both reasons contributed to what was referred to as 'the racking of rents of ʒ2–3'.[26] A desire to make quick profits transformed what had been a relationship of patronage and clientship into a merely business relationship. The successor landlords were no longer dependent on King or church, but were free economic men standing on their own feet. Their land had become a commodity in an increasingly competitive society. It could be freely bought and sold, mortgaged and bequeathed. Wisdom dictated making the most of their own while they could.

The restoration of monarchy ended a period in which law had been at the mercy of an arbitrary army, whose generals got rich quick and soon forgot the radical principles they had once proclaimed. The restoration restored the former owners of crown and church lands, but it could not bring back the pre-1640 society, did not restore the old relationships. The crown no longer had a Star Chamber or Court of High Commission to coerce the recalcitrant, and the church was aware that royal favour might be diverted to papists or dissenters at the whim of the devious and often financially desperate Charles II. Purchasers of church or crown lands did not always secure the long-term profits they had anticipated, and so had all the greater incentive to make the management of the estates which remained to them as profitable as possible.

A third factor concerned questions of religious toleration. Professor

26. See pp. 35–6, 41 above.

Greaves has shown that after the gentry had welcomed back Charles II, there was still a serious possibility of revolt by religious radicals of the lower classes.[27] Charles II had a difficult game to play in using favour to dissenters as a balance against the pressures of the re-established Church of England, and in toying with using Catholic support to establish royal independence of both the established church and the dissenting interest. The overthrow of the foolish James II shows how wise Charles had been not to play this card too openly. Charles made his granting of independence to dissenting congregations dependent on their being licensed by the crown (and so on not forfeiting royal favour) and on their accepting a sectarian label (which had the long-term effect of keeping dissenters isolated in their separate churches, unable to act as a united interest).[28]

Before 1640 there had been no possibility of organizing mass revolt against a corrupt and tyrannical government among a politically naïve and uneducated population. This point had been reflected in Beaumont and Fletcher's tragedy *Valentinian* (1619 or earlier), where murder of the emperor or suicide were seen as the only ways out of a tragic situation.[29] The victims of enclosure were mostly illiterate. They were not influenced by the Greek and Roman classics to which Hobbes attributed the opposition which led to civil war, but they rioted no less violently for that. Separatist sectaries started from rejection of the state church, which forced them to demand religious freedom. From quite different angles, economic and religious opposition to the laws of the land and of the state church converged.

The years from 1660 to 1688 were transitional, with all parties feeling their way to power and influence. But 1688-9 confirmed that Parliament, not the King, was now the deciding force in the land; and that protestant dissenters could not be used in the hands of a king aspiring to absolutism as a weapon against Parliament, gentry and the state church. The conspicuous absence of lower-class revolt in 1688-9 demonstrated that the empire, the navy and the East India Company were already bringing sufficient prosperity to minimize the danger of social revolt. Dissent had become respectable, dissenters accepting the position of second-class citizens in

27. R. L. Greaves, *Deliver Us from Evil: The Radical Underground in Britain, 1660–1663* (Oxford U.P., 1986); *Enemies under his Feet: Radicals and non-conformists in Britain, 1664–1677* (Stanford U.P., 1990).
28. See pp.186–7 above.
29. Op. cit., Act IV, scene iv.

return for religious toleration. Ranters, Diggers and Anabaptists had disappeared from public view. Quakers too were learning to adapt to a society whose leaders were confident enough to grant them freedom of worship. They learnt to use the law to protect themselves against conviction for their illegal practices.[30] The English discovered their genius for compromise when their society became rich enough to afford it. The 'gloriousness' of the 'Revolution' of 1688 lay in that a king was expelled and property secured without any disturbance from the unpropertied. When the old republican Edmund Ludlow returned from twenty-eight years of exile, thinking his day had at last come, Whigs and Tories dropped their differences to unite in hustling him out of the country. The dedicated radical Robert Ferguson in despair turned Jacobite.

V

For all its incompleteness, the mid-century revolution as adjusted in 1688–9 was a turning point. The 'revolution settlement' to which eighteenth-century rulers looked back complacently was achieved by law, by front bench agreement in Parliament between Whigs and Tories, not by violence. This laid the basis for the ideology of the 'freeborn Englishman', whose freedom was finally guaranteed by the wars which ensured the liberty of the English state from the power of international Catholicism which had threatened English independence, or was held to threaten English independence, for a century and a half.

In the long run, impressment and the lash could not in themselves create and maintain a great navy. The maintenance of discipline on merchant or naval vessels could not rest on arbitrary force alone. There had to be some acceptance of the objectives of the voyages, whether in making trading profits or defending and extending England's commercial empire. Mariners, in the navy as well as in the mercantile marine, could sometimes make profits for themselves out of judicious speculations during fortunate voyages. Market contracts replaced the customary liberties of the producers, and this was acceptable because the market was expanding. As Britannia came to rule the waves, to her great profit, the navy began to offer an interesting career for which some might opt voluntarily. The language of contract supplanted the language of custom

30. See Chapter 24 above.

at sea, and seamen appealed 'to contract to fight . . . unfair payment of wages'.[31]

Edward Thompson surprised some of his readers by praising the rule of law after capitalism's victory in England.[32] The vast expansion of English trade in the late seventeenth and eighteenth centuries demanded a workforce whose wages were guaranteed by contract. Attitudes towards the law in consequence changed. Just as Quakers began to find legal defence of their rights economically useful,[33] so some sections of the newly-mobilized workforce found themselves legally better off than their vagabond forefathers. It was possible to believe in the ideology of the 'freeborn Englishman'. The wage system was no longer seen merely as slavery, because the market now permitted some element of choice: hence the necessity of retaining impressment for the armed forces. Defoe, a confident asserter of the importance of trade, once found himself grumbling about the insubordination of English servants claiming liberty for themselves. They were regrettably less docile than their French equivalents.[34] But then he recalled that the independence and freedom of choice of Englishmen, even of the lower classes, was the consequence of the seventeenth-century Revolution, and was the secret of England's superiority to France. Mutual acceptance of the wage system was satisfactory so long as the goods were delivered. Now that the goods are not being delivered quite so satisfactorily, we have come to recall that the law is as the law does.

After 1688 the new balance of forces was secure. Crucial was the fact that judges – so often agents of would-be 'royal despotism' – passed from royal control to the control of Parliament. Veiled in the decent obscurity of a learned language, judges held their position now '*quamdiu se bene gesserint*', which being translated meant 'so long as they give satisfaction to us' – 'we' being the undefined natural rulers, the Parliament which represented the alliance of the gentry with the commercial interest.

1660 was a defeat for those radicals who had hoped to build a more equal society in England. But the colonies offered a refuge for the most disgruntled among the defeated, and top persons in the 'two nations', Anglican and dissenting, shared in the accumulation of wealth which

31. Rediker, *Between the Devil and the Deep Blue Sea*, p. 150. See pp. 69, 119 above.
32. Thompson, *Whigs and Hunters: The Origin of the Black Act* (1975), pp. 258–69.
33. See Chapter 24 above.
34. Defoe, *The Great Law of Subordination considered; Or, the Insolence and Insufferable Behaviour of Servants in England duly enquired into* (1724), pp. 16–20, 52–62.

derived ultimately from colonial conquest and the slave trade. Not much of this wealth came down to the lowest classes, except to some fortunate individual mariners; but the legend of the 'trickle-down' effect has survived till our own day. We noticed that the popular activities of smugglers helped to bring down the price of tea.[35] But apart from political Jacobitism gentlemen no longer put themselves at the head of rural revolts against the crown. The Black Act of 1723 was passed by a landed Parliament. Trade unions slowly organized themselves to protect sections of the working class, but they had no gentry leadership. The court was the source of more generous pickings for those who frequented it: hence their likeness to beggars in Gay's work.

By the eighteenth century the poor in England's villages were no longer peasants holding land but wage-labourers. This no doubt accounts for the fact that there was never a significant anarchist movement in England – anarchism being elsewhere an organized social protest movement representing preponderantly the peasantry. In England, because of its priority in industrialization, the peasantry was eliminated earlier and more completely than in any other European country.

The religious sects were bought off and tamed by Charles II and their own awareness of their minority status, made manifest in the 1640s and 1650s. 'Indulgence' led to their gradual inclusion in the political nation, confirmed in 1689. Landless former peasants were absorbed into wage labour as England prospered, thanks especially to sea power. The state became stronger and more confident. Its power, and prospects of prosperity through emigration, put an end to organized outlawry. By Clare's time the possibility of an extension of the franchise revived, and with it a share in law-making. But by that time there was no longer an English peasantry. The empire brought prosperity and jobs as well as impressment. There was much collusive connivance at smuggling and poaching, as we have seen. Begging was a negative alternative, still with us; but it had become institutionalized and state-controlled. Laments for a lost peasantry died away with the Romantic poets, who were more horrified by the obscenities, physical and moral, of industrialization than by rural exploitation, poverty and vagabondage. The Chartist 'back to the land' movement was too little and came much too late. Slowly developing trade unions gave some protection to individual workers, but there was no effective lower-class organization which could challenge the law.

35. See pp. 110–12 above.

The Romantic revival siphoned off alienated intellectuals but had no appeal for the lowest classes. Ballads ceased to be a special form of lower-class literature as the peasant communities disappeared. Clare's madness was an individual response: lone protesters like him were isolated and gave up hope. The nineteenth-century popularity of artificially created utopian communities – here and especially in America – from which only the irrational and wicked would wish to contract out; cycling and rambling clubs, hiking, thatched cottages as country residences – all these have some relevance to the ineffectiveness of movements of revolt. The godly proved more law-abiding than most, once their fundamental demand for freedom to worship in their own way had been conceded, however grudgingly. But 'the nonconformist conscience' has remained a factor in politics: dissenters have often taken the lead in agitating for causes which they believe to be good, even if it means opposing the government of the day.

My title contrasted 'law' and 'liberty'. Winstanley hoped by his 'platform' – i.e. programme – to bring them together by abolishing private property. He failed, and history soon forgot him. Religious hopes declined too. Christ and the millennium were no longer expected to appear on earth after the revolutionary 1790s. When trade unions developed sufficiently to permit working-class bargaining, this marked an *acceptance* of wage-labour; contracting out was no longer a viable alternative. Trade union discipline was set against the discipline of wage-labour and of the market. Practices like the observance of St Sunday remained a strong working-class tradition, an assertion of freedom at least one day a week. Well-organized colliers succeed in retaining many of the abolished saints' days as non-working days: from saints' days to holidays.[36] Acceptance of the permanence of capitalism and its state meant that political reform was the only answer to the problems of the poor.

During the two centuries which we have been considering, we noted the beginnings of a recognition that 'the public' might include poor as well as rich. This was still very imperfectly accepted in practice, but law is no longer as blatantly and unashamedly class-slanted as it was during our period. To that extent we have been dealing with history. Clare represents a last whimper of *principled* opposition to some laws, and Clare recognized that he could complain but not change the law, or control it.

36. L. Stone, 'An Elizabethan Coal Mine', in *Economic History Review*, II (1950), pp. 97–106; ed. C. Cippola, *Fontana Economic History of Europe: the 16th and 17th centuries* (1974), p. 110.

When we don't like laws today we organize to try to get them changed. This makes it difficult for us to accept imaginatively that there might be an attitude of contempt for law as such which was not expressed in political action. Most men did not normally reveal this contempt, since that would have been dangerous. But the facts and opinions presented in this book, I suggest, show that if we look for it we can find at least enough evidence for the question to be asked. Historians, unless they are very careful, tend to think that present-day attitudes and prejudices existed in the past if there is not sufficient documentary evidence to demonstrate the contrary.

Above all, democratization has made the law *seem* less alien. Winstanley's vision of law which will protect the abolition of private property still lies ahead. So long as private property survives some may well think the law alien. But the *ideal* of a law which represents the wishes of the community has changed attitudes. This is especially true of dissenters, who have accepted the compromise of 'indulgence' and no longer think it a duty to break the law. For the two centuries with which we have been dealing the law claimed to be above private interests; but only the interested believed it.

The law, like the doors of the Ritz Hotel, has long been open to rich and poor alike: only the poor don't often think of mentioning it publicly because the Ritz Hotel is beyond their reach. Today we glamorize train-robbers rather than pirates. As I write these words London traffic is blocked by crowds observing the semi-state funeral of the gangster Ronnie Kray. Always the streets of our cities are lined with homeless people sleeping rough; but no less a person than our Prime Minister reassures us that there is no justification for anyone to offend the delicate sensibilities of well-housed, well-paid and well-fed citizens by indulging in begging. Beggars may even discourage foreign tourists from visiting London, he moans. In the national interest they must disappear – to somewhere where they will not be visible. Some may see evidence of progress in the fact that we no longer flog the impotent poor out of town.

Index

Index

Berkshire, 18, 24
Bernard, Richard, 196–7
Berry, Anne, pirate, 120
Bible, the, 60, 74, 80, 87–9, 155, 170, 180,
    183, Chapter 7 *passim*, 223, 234, 238,
    249, 283, 308, 329
Black Act, the (1723), 9, 16–18, 101, 339
Black Death, the, 47, 75
Blackstone, Sir William, 85, 261, 339
Blake, William, 29, 173, 219, 221–6, 295,
    319, 329
Bloomfield, Robert, 39, 316–17
Blyth, Walter, 63
Bocking, Essex, 59
Boleyn, Anne, Queen of England, 179–80,
    305
Bolingbroke, Henry St John, Viscount, 18
Borrow, George, 134n.
Bowden, Professor P., 22
Bower, Walter, 73
Bownde, the Rev., 74
Bradshaw, William, 181n.
Braithwaite, William C., 304
Brearley, Roger, 185, 215
Breda, Declaration of, the, 299
Bridewell, 165, 261
Brigden, Susan, 72
Bristol, 169, 302
Brome, Alexander, 8
Brome, Richard, author of *A Jovial Crew*,
    Chapter 1 *passim*, 56, 61n, 161
Brooke, Robert Greville, Lord, 204
Browne, Sir Thomas, 61, 137
Browne, William, 10, 134, 243–4
Brownists, 48
Buchanan, George, 235
Buckingham, George Villiers, second
    Duke of, 94, 136, 230, 262
Buckinghamshire, 193, 196
Bulkeley, Peter, 29
Bullinger, Henry, 210, 220
Bunyan, John, 39–40, 50, 54–5, 61–2, 128,
    138, 186, 204, 211–12, 214–18, 229,
    231, 253, 275
Burford, Oxfordshire, 199
Burghley, William Cecil, Lord, 52
Burke, Peter, 41n.

Burnet, Gilbert, Bishop of Salisbury, 48
Burns, Robert, 63, 111–12
Burrough, Edward, Quaker, 51, 237, 240,
    251, 259–61, 266, 331
Burton, Robert, author of *The Anatomy of
    Melancholy*, 57, 197, 258, 265
Bury St Edmunds, Suffolk, 11
Bush, Douglas, 7
Butler, Martin, 5, 7
Butler, Samuel, 12, 52, 62–3, 129, 245,
    268
Byllynge, Edward, 299
Byron, George Gordon, Lord, 319

Cade, John, 77, 258–9
Caiaphas and Annas, High Priests, 226,
    233
Cain, 32, 165, 280
Caliban, 52, 153–4
Calvin, John, Calvinists, 182, 207–9, 218–
    20, 310
Canada, 108
Canne, John, 251
Cannock Chase, 102
Canny, Nicholas, 196
Canons of 1604, the, 195
Carew, Bampfield-Moore, 140
Carew, John, 237, 239
Carlson, L. H., 189
Cartouche, French robber, Cartoucheans,
    121
Cartwright, Thomas, 181
Cates, William, 262
Catherine of Aragon, Queen of England,
    179
Catholicism, Roman, 74, 80, 184, 337
Cato's Letters, 42
Cecil, Robert, later Earl of Salisbury,
    334
Censorship, 92, 100, 116, 124–5, 137, 183,
    203, 236
Cervantes, Miguel de, 136
Chamberlen, Peter, 99
Chancery, court of, 338
Chapman, George, 246
Charles I, King of England, 29–30, 33, 41,
    80, 83–7, 209, 274, 278, 291, 298